W9-CSX-087

THE
AMERICAN EXPRESS
POCKET GUIDE TO
LONDON

Michael Jackson

PRENTICE HALL PRESS
NEW YORK

The Author and Contributors
Michael Jackson is the writer and presenter of the Discovery
Channel television series *The Beer Hunter*. His other books
include *The Pocket Guide to Beer*, *The Pocket Bartender's Guide*
and *The New World Guide to Beer*. He has also acted as a
consultant on food and drink projects for the English Tourist
Board. John Roberts contributed the section on sights and places
of interest for the first and second editions. This edition was
revised in 1990 by Fiona Duncan and Leonie Glass, joint authors
of *3-D London*, who have edited numerous travel guides,
including several in this series.

Acknowledgments
The authors and publishers would like to thank the following for
their help and advice: Alan Crompton-Batt and Victoria Ewen of
Alan Crompton-Batt Associates, the Press Office of the London
Tourist Board and Convention Bureau, the City of London
Information Bureau, and Mike De Mello of Triptych Systems
Limited. The *American Express Pocket Travel Guide Series* was
conceived under the direction of Susannah Read, Douglas
Wilson, Hal Robinson and Eric Drewery. David Arnold edited the
original edition.

For the series
General Editor	David Townsend Jones
Managing Art Editor	Nigel O'Gorman
Art Editor	Christopher Howson
Map Editor	David Haslam
Indexer	Hilary Bird
Gazetteer	Sharon Charity

For this edition
Edited on desktop by	David Townsend Jones
Illustrators	Jeremy Ford (David Lewis Artists),
	Illustra Design Ltd, Rodney Paull, Karen Cochrane
Jacket illustration	Kelek

Edited and designed by Mitchell Beazley International Limited,
Artists House, 14-15 Manette Street, London W1V 5LB
for the American Express (R) Pocket Travel Guide Series

Published by Prentice Hall Trade Division
A Division of Simon & Schuster, Inc.
Gulf & Western Building, One Gulf & Western Plaza,
New York, New York 10023
PRENTICE HALL is a trademark of Simon & Schuster, Inc.

Maps in 2-color and 4-color by Lovell Johns, Oxford, England.
Desktop layout in Ventura Publisher by Castle House Press, Llantrisant,
Wales.
Typeset in Garamond and Univers.
Linotronic output through Microstar DTP Studio, Cardiff, Wales.
Produced by Mandarin Offset. Printed and bound in Malaysia.

Contents

How to use this book

The American Express Pocket Guide to London is an encyclopedia of travel information, organized in the sections listed on the previous page. There is also a comprehensive *Index* (pages 211-220) and a *List of street names* (pages 221-224), and there are full-color *Maps* at the end of the book.

For easy reference, all major sections (*Sights and places of interest*, *Hotels*, *Restaurants*), and other sections where possible, are arranged alphabetically. For the organization of the book as a whole, see *Contents*. For individual places that do not have separate entries in *Sights and places of interest*, see the *Index*.

The new London telephone codes   **(081)** codes for outer London are always given. If there is no code, assume this is an inner London **(071)** number. For a full explanation, see *Post and telephone services*, p16.

Abbreviations   As a rule, only standard abbreviations are used, such as days of the week and months, points of the compass (N, S, E and W), street names (Ave., Pl., Rd., Sq., St.), St (Saint), rms (rooms), C (century), and measurements.

Bold type   **Bold type** is used mainly for emphasis, to draw attention to something of special interest or importance. It also picks out places — shops or minor museums, for example — that do not have full entries of their own. In such cases, it is usually followed in brackets by the address, telephone number, details of opening times, etc., which are printed in *italics*.

Cross-references   A special typeface, *sans serif italics*, is used for cross-references. Each time you see a place name, such as *Pall Mall*, printed in this way, expect to find a full entry under that heading in the alphabetical *Sights and places of interest* (pages 45-136).

Similarly, when you see the title of a section of the book, such as *Hotels* or *Time chart*, printed in this way, you can

---

How entries are organized

Hood House

1411 Lincoln Ave., Lincoln Green, Sherwood Forest
☎ *426-5960 (house), 426-5961 (group tour reservations).*
Map 8J11 🖼 ✗ *Open Apr-Sept 9am-5pm, rest of year 9am-4pm. Closed Christmas, New Year's Day. Metro: Bow & Arrow.* ˙

Robin Hood (?1149-1205) was the leading spokesman for the poor and downtrodden in their struggle for freedom and justice under the Plantagenets. He lectured and wrote books about his own early life as a serf, campaigned endlessly for human rights, helped recruit peasants to the Civil Service, and finally settled down to a distinguished old age in Sherwood Forest. He lived first in A St. (see *National Museum of Outlawed Art*), then bought Sheriff Villa, which he renamed Hood House, a handsome white dwelling on a height overlooking the Trent Valley. All the furnishings, except for curtains and wallpaper, are original. Hood's library and other belongings are still *in situ*, and the whole house is redolent of the spirit of a very remarkable man. In the **Visitors' Centre** at the foot of the hill you can see a film about Hood's life.

turn to that section for further information. (You will find a complete section-by-section breakdown of the book on the *Contents* page.)

For easy reference, use the headers printed at the top corner of each page (for example, **Piccadilly** on page 97, or **Hotels** on page 140).

Floors To conform with local usage, "first floor" is used throughout the book to refer to the floor above the ground floor, "second floor" to the floor above that, and so on.

Map references Each full-color map at the end of the book is divided into a grid of squares, identified vertically by letters (A, B, C, D, etc.) and horizontally by numbers (1, 2, 3, 4, etc.). A map reference pinpoints the page (the first **bold** number) and position — thus *Tower of London* is located in Map **13**G17.

Price categories Price categories for hotels and restaurants are represented by the symbols ▭ ▯▯ ▮▯▯ ▮▮▮▯ and ▮▮▮▮▮, which signify cheap, inexpensive, moderately priced, expensive and very expensive, respectively. These correspond approximately with the following actual prices, which give a guideline at the time of printing. Although actual prices will inevitably increase, as a rule the relative price category — for example, expensive or cheap — is likely to remain more or less the same.

Price categories	Corresponding to approximate prices	
	for **hotels** double room with bath + breakfast; singles are somewhat cheaper	for **restaurants** meal for one with service, VAT and house wine
▭ cheap	under $105	under $25
▯▯ inexpensive	$105-155	$25-35
▮▯▯ moderate	$155-210	$35-50
▮▮▮▮ expensive	$210-275	$50-80
▮▮▮▮▮ very expensive	over $275	over $80

— Bold blue type for entry headings.

— Blue italics for address, practical information and symbols.
For list of symbols see page 6 or back flap of jacket.

— Black text for description.

— Sans serif italics used for cross-references to other entries or sections.

— Bold type used for emphasis.

Entries for hotels, restaurants, shops, etc. follow the same organization, and are usually printed across a half column.

In hotels, symbols indicating special facilities appear at the end of the entry, in black.

> **Pullman**
> *2600 Express Ave., Orient City 20037 ☎ 299-4450 ℗ 299-4460. Map 2F4 ▮▮▮▮▮ 238 rms ⟵ ≡▭ AE*
> *CB ◉ ◉ VISA Metro: High Standard.*
> *Location: On a height overlooking the Universal Trade Center.* Part of a large conglomeration overlooking the seafront, this luxurious hotel is set in attractively landscaped grounds and is run with clockwork precision. Its restaurant, the **Simplon**, is highly regarded.
> ♿ ❦ ⟨⟨ ⇜ ⚲

Key to symbols

☎ Telephone	☒ Secure garage
☏ Telex	☖ Quiet hotel
ⓕ Facsimile (fax)	⬍ Elevator
★ Recommended sight	& Facilities for
☆ Worth a detour	disabled people
✿ Good value (in its	☐ TV in each room
class)	☎ Telephone in each
i Tourist information	room
⬅ Parking	⚡ Dogs not allowed
⛪ Building of	☘ Garden
architectural interest	⟨⟨ Good view
† Church or cathedral	▦ Mini-bar
◙ Free entrance	⇝ Swimming pool
▨ Entrance fee payable	☂ Sauna
▩ Photography forbidden	♫ Tennis
𝒦 Guided tour available	⚐ Gym/fitness
▣ Cafeteria	facilities
✻ Special interest for	▦ Conference facilities
children	▬ Restaurant
⚲ Hotel	▬ Simple restaurant
⬛ Simple hotel	◁ Luxury restaurant
⬜ Luxury hotel	⌑ A la carte available
☐ Cheap	▮ Set (fixed-price) menu
⫽ Inexpensive	available
⫻ Moderately priced	☰ Good wines
⫼ Expensive	☻ Open-air dining
⫼ Very expensive	⚆ Bar
☐ Rooms with private	◉ Disco dancing
bathroom	♩ Nightclub
▤ Air conditioning	♫ Live music
AE American Express	♪ Dancing
◉ Diners Club	⚑ Revue

A note from the General Editor

No travel book can be completely free of errors and
totally up to date. Telephone numbers and opening
hours change without warning, and hotels and
restaurants come under new management, which can
affect standards. We make every effort to ensure that all
information is accurate at the time we go to press, but
are always delighted to receive corrections or
suggestions for improvements from our readers, which if
warranted will be incorporated in a future edition. We
are indebted to readers who wrote to us during the
preparation of this edition.

The publishers regret that they cannot accept any
consequences arising from the use of the book or from
the information it contains.

An introduction to London

To see the pageantry of London, or the architecture, to visit the theater or the places of government and jurisdiction, is to be immersed for a moment in a city that was capital of half the world, and enjoyed that position rather more recently than Athens, Rome or Constantinople. Nor has London yet cast aside the robes of her eminence. She may be wrinkled in some places, face-lifted in others, and over-painted here and there, but she has retained dignity in her middle age.

The attitude of Londoners to their own city can puzzle the newcomer. There is a defiant defensiveness in the proclamation, "I love New York"; Londoners are cooler and seem more detached, but are inclined nevertheless to be deeply and irremovably in love with their city. They will rightly evince anger at the handiwork perpetrated by planners and developers in the postwar period, but the irony is that such licensed vandalism prospered so long without restraint simply because the profusion of fine and historic architecture seemed inexhaustible.

To the newcomer, London is an overwhelming jumble of antiquity, a labyrinthine junk store with "finds" hidden all over the place, often apparently unnoticed and gathering dust. Sometimes it seems that every house was the birthplace of someone famous, or the scene of an invention, each corner the site of an important speech, a battle or an especially vile crime, each name one that has passed into the language.

The irrepressible curiosities of London manifest themselves from Greenwich in the east to Richmond in the west, two of the most interesting and pleasant little towns in England. Both maintain their identities while remaining parts of London, although they stand about 20 miles apart (London is at some points 35 miles from end to end), and each can be reached by pleasure boat from the heart of the capital.

London grew from the river; the Thames was its first thoroughfare, its lifeline and its means of social irrigation. Because the first route to London was up the river, successive waves of immigrants, Italians, Jews, Huguenots and many others settled in what became known as the "East End," a series of waterside, working-class communities which has nurtured its own culture, patois and social mores. They settled in the east because, being foreigners, they had been barred in times past from entering the city. Yet there were older immigrants in London from the beginning; Romans founded the settlement nearly 2,000 years ago, and many a Cockney today has a discernibly Roman nose.

This is how the city was born. Yet when Londoners talk about "the City," they mean specifically and exclusively that part that was originally walled and still vestigially is, and which covers no more than one square mile, located between Tower Bridge and Blackfriars Bridge.

The City is the financial district, the "Wall Street" of Britain. The Lord Mayor of London represents only this square mile, and its streets are patrolled by the separate City Police. The City does not include the famous shopping streets, or theaterland, and does not care. It is an entity within itself, parochial yet worldly, with its own rituals and customs, and its preoccupation with bulls and bears and commodity prices.

London is governed not from the City but from the town halls of its more than 30 boroughs. Britain is governed not from the City but from Westminster, a mile upriver. Westminster, once a small city too but now spread far from the river, today takes in Covent

Garden, Soho, theaterland and the main shopping streets of central London. Yet, because of its geographical relationship with the original walled city, we call today's center the "West End."

While the City remained fiercely independent and introspective, Westminster was the royal seat, and London has good reason to be grateful. The royal residences of Westminster (St James's, Buckingham Palace and Clarence House) are joined to those of Kensington (Kensington Palace) by a long swathe of royal parks. Through St James's Park, Green Park, Hyde Park and Kensington Gardens, you can walk miles across the great metropolis amid the greenery. With Holland Park, Regent's Park, and the Georgian and Victorian squares of Bloomsbury, Chelsea and Kensington, London has a remarkably green inner city.

Born from two separate cities on the river, modern London is, not surprisingly, a complex patchwork of villages. To anyone from outside, Chelsea is probably the most familiar district name in the capital. It is also a neighborhood that perfectly demonstrates London's enigmatic charm, contriving simultaneously to be grand and yet to be a pristine, dollhouse village. At one moment, it spreads itself elegantly on the riverside; in another it hugs itself in narrow streets, cozy as a cat. It has been smart, then bohemian, and is now both, and yet richer than ever. It has the most discreet streets in London, yet its main thoroughfare, King's Road, if no longer quite as outré as in the 1960s, remains bereft of caution. It is always unmistakably Chelsea, yet, like London itself, it has many moods.

London, that great sea, whose ebb and flow
At once is deaf and loud, and on the shore
Vomits its wrecks, and still howls on for more
                              Shelley, *Letter to Maria Gisborne*, 1819

The changes of mood can be sudden. South Kensington has some of the wealthiest streets in Britain, North Kensington some of the poorest. Yet deprivation has not bred dullness, nor isolation. Take Brixton, south of the river. Less than a ghetto, despite occasional tensions, it has a delightful market, for jellied eels, an old cockney delicacy, as well as yams and breadfruit.

The river may no longer influence population trends. Indeed, with the decline of river transportation and the flood of Victorian road-building along its banks, it became woefully neglected. (There are, however, signs of improvement, with developments such as Chelsea Harbour and Docklands beginning to utilize its great potential.) The subway lines had more influence on where people settled. Parts of south London became places of cheap housing when they were ignored by the subway systems; but when the new Victoria line went south in 1969, these neighborhoods suddenly became attractive to a new generation of young, professional people who no longer wished to live out in the suburbs. The contemporary equivalent was the '80s boom in London's Docklands. The same "gentrification" has taken place in several districts that were built for the artisan; the social classes are as identifiable in London as they are anywhere else in Britain, but nowhere else do they quite so readily live together.

Strangers get lost in London. So do Londoners, unless they are cab drivers. It is a city in which to lose oneself, an engrossing experience. People who are afraid of getting lost, who believe that every city should be built as a piece, at a single stroke, to a well-ordered plan, should not come. London was not built for efficiency. It is a city for explorers.

Before you go

Documents required

A valid national passport is often all that is needed to visit Britain, since citizens of the USA, Commonwealth and most European and South American countries do not need visas.

Health certificates are required only if you are a national of or are arriving from countries in Asia, South America or Africa, in which case you should carry certificates of vaccination against cholera, yellow fever and smallpox. A smallpox vaccination certificate will be required if within the previous 14 days you have been in a country with a designated smallpox area.

Only your full valid national license is required to drive personal or rented cars. If you are bringing your own car make sure it is properly insured, and bring the vehicle registration certificate (logbook) and an insurance certificate or green card. A national identity sticker is also required.

Travel and medical insurance

Be sure to take out an insurance policy covering loss of deposits paid to airlines, hotels, tour operators, etc., and emergency costs such as special tickets home and extra nights in a hotel.

Visitors from countries with no reciprocal health agreement are not covered for any medical help other than accidents or emergencies, and even then will be expected to pay if they have to stay the night in hospital. They should be properly insured. No charge is made for visitors from countries with a reciprocal arrangement, such as EC member countries.

Money

There is no exchange control in Britain, so you can carry any amount of any currency through customs in or out of the country. The unit of currency is the pound sterling (£), divided into 100 pence (p). There are coins for 1p, 2p, 5p, 10p, 20p, 50p and £1, and notes for £5, £10, £20 and £50.

Travelers cheques issued by American Express, Thomas Cook, Barclays and Citibank are widely recognized; make sure you read the instructions included with your cheques. It is important to note separately the serial numbers of each cheque and the telephone number to call in case of loss. Specialist travelers cheque companies such as American Express provide extensive local refund facilities.

Major international credit and charge cards, such as American Express, MasterCard (linked in Britain with the Access Card), Visa (linked with Barclaycard) and Diners Club are widely accepted for most goods and services. In this book, establishments that accept American Express and Diners Club are indicated by **AE** and **◆** symbols. Acceptance of MasterCard and Visa credit cards is not shown, but they are now so widespread that they will be accepted in the great majority of places that take other cards.

Customs

If you are visiting the United Kingdom for less than six months, you are entitled to bring in, free of duty and tax, all personal effects that you intend to take with you when you leave, except tobacco goods, alcoholic drinks and perfume. Ensure you carry dated receipts for valuable items, such as cameras and watches, or you may be charged duty.

Duty-free allowances (at the time of writing) for import into Britain are given on p10. The figures shown in brackets are the

Before you go

increased allowances for goods obtained duty-free and tax-paid in EC countries. Travelers under 17 are not entitled to the allowances on tobacco goods and alcoholic drinks.

Tobacco goods   200 (300) cigarettes *or* 100 (150) cigarillos *or* 50 (75) cigars *or* 250g (400g) tobacco. If you live outside Europe, 400 cigarettes *or* 200 cigarillos *or* 100 cigars *or* 500g tobacco.

Alcoholic drinks   1 (1.5) liters liquor or strong liquor (more than 22 percent alcohol by volume) *or* 2 (3) liters of alcoholic drink less than 22 percent alcohol, fortified wine or sparkling wine *plus* 2 (5) liters of still table wine.

Perfume   50g/60cc/2fl.oz (75g/90cc/3fl.oz).

Toilet water   250cc/9fl.oz (375cc/13fl.oz).

Other goods   Goods to the value of £32 (£250).

Prohibited and restricted goods include narcotics, weapons, obscene publications and videos.

If you have anything in excess of the duty-free allowances, pass through the channel with red "Goods to declare" notices; otherwise pass through the green "Nothing to declare" channel.

For exemption from Value Added Tax (VAT) on goods bought in Britain for export see *Shopping*.

Getting there

London's Heathrow Airport is one of the busiest in the world, and there are regular flights from most countries on a wide range of international airlines. Gatwick, the city's second airport, is also heavily used. London's third airport, Stansted, although at present mostly used for charter flights, is expanding fast, and nearby Luton airport is a major air charter destination. All four are within an hour of the city center (see *From the airport to the city*, p11). Air fares vary enormously, so consult your travel agent.

Only Cunard now operates frequent transatlantic sailings, but it is possible to sail to English ports (usually Liverpool or Southampton) on other less regular routes. An efficient network of short-distance passenger, car and train ferries links Britain with France, Belgium, the Netherlands, West Germany, Ireland and Scandinavia. The main ferry ports are Dover, Folkestone, Harwich, Felixstowe, Portsmouth, Plymouth, Holyhead and Fishguard. The projected completion date for the Channel Tunnel, linking Dover and Calais, is June 1993.

Climate

English weather is rarely given to extremes, but it is unpredictable and can change character several times a day. Indeed, it is a constant and characteristic topic of British conversation. Average daytime temperatures range from 6°C (43°F) in winter (Dec-Feb) to 21°C (70°F) in summer (June-Aug), only occasionally going below 0°C (32°F) or above 27°C (80°F). Annual rainfall is 24ins (60cm), most of it in winter but likely at any time. There are, of course, considerable regional variations.

Clothes

In summertime light clothes are adequate, but remember to include some protection against showers, and a sweater or jacket for cool evenings. During the rest of the year, bring warm clothes and hope you won't need them all, although in winter overcoats, gloves etc. will usually be necessary.

London has given the world some bizarre fashions and is consequently relaxed about dress. But restraint is expected in some institutional buildings, the older hotels and restaurants, casinos and some clubs. If you are attending any formal or

notably grand occasion, full evening dress, which the British refer
to simply as "black tie," may be expected; check first.

General delivery (poste restante)

General delivery mail can be addressed to any post office. (See
Post offices p18 for the two main locations.)

Getting around

From the airport to the city

Heathrow is the terminus of the underground's Piccadilly Line;
trains link the airport within about 40mins with all parts of the
city between 5am (6.45am Sun) and 11pm.

The M4 motorway is the other main link, the trip to the center
taking 30mins-1hr depending upon traffic. London Regional
Transport operates a 24hr bus service (including the Airbus
service) to points in central London, various coach companies
run services to Victoria Bus Station, and some airlines run buses
to meet arriving flights and connect with their various passenger
terminals in central London. A more expensive alternative is to
take a taxi, always readily available at the airport, but make sure
you take a black metered cab and not one of the "pirate"
operators, who may overcharge.

Gatwick is farther out of the city. The easiest way into London
is to take the Gatwick Express, the British Rail service from the
airport station. This reaches Victoria Station in London in 30mins
and all parts of the city are easily reached from there. The airport
is by the side of the M23 motorway, an hour or more from central
London, and there are bus services around the clock. Because of
the distance from London a cab is not a realistic proposition for
most travelers, and could be expensive; ask the driver first how
much the fare will be.

Stansted is linked by rail to Liverpool Street Station, 40mins
away, and by road via the M11 motorway, within an hour or so
of central London. **Luton** is near the M1 motorway, with fast bus
and excellent rail links to London.

Arriving by other means

By rail: London's several major stations encircle the center, and
all have underground interchanges, taxi stands and bus stops.
(See *Railway services* p14.)

By road: The roads into London plow through the sprawling
suburbs, after which signposting for "West End" indicates the
center. Try to avoid driving anywhere in the rush hours
(8-9.30am and 5-7pm). The biggest bus terminus in London is at
Victoria, and most cross-country coaches arrive there.

Public transportation

London Regional Transport's network of buses and subway
("tube" or "underground") trains is extensive and efficient. But as
in all great cities, try to avoid traveling in the rush hour.

Free bus and tube maps and details of services are available at
the Travel Information Centres located at the following tube
stations: **Heathrow Central**, **Euston**, **King's Cross**, **Piccadilly
Circus**, **Oxford Circus** and **Victoria**. There is also a telephone
information service (☎ *222-1234*): you may have to wait a while
for an answer as the calls are stacked and dealt with in rotation.

Various special tickets are available: do pay an early visit to a
Travel Information Centre to get details. The tickets include

flat-rate passes for bus or tube or both for various periods from three days to one month. The Visitor Travel card, on sale outside the UK through travel agents, allows unlimited travel on buses and underground for 3, 4 or 7 day periods.

For public transportation remember to join the line.

The underground

The underground (see map **24**) is the easiest and fastest way to get around the city, if not the most pleasant or interesting. The stations (which are gradually being modernized) are easily recognized by the London Regional Transport symbol, a horizontal line through a circle. On maps, each line always has its own color (Circle line yellow, Central line red, etc.), so it is easy to plan your journey, noting where you have to change lines. The fare depends on how many zones you enter; see *Buses*. Buy your ticket before boarding, either from a ticket office or a machine in the station, where the fares will be on display. Show your ticket to a collector or, if it is a yellow one, put it in the automatic entry gate and walk through, picking it up as you go — you will need to present it at the end of your journey. Follow the signs to the platform for the line you want. Check with the indicators above the platform and on the front of the train that it is going to your station; some trains do not go to the end of the line, and some lines divide into two or more branches. Trains stop at every station, with only a few exceptions on weekends. The first tube trains run at about 5am, and they begin to close down after 11.30pm, when you might have trouble with connections. Smoking is forbidden throughout the underground system.

Buses

(See chart of central bus routes, maps **22-23**.) London's red buses are usually slower than the tube, but are cheaper and more interesting, offering a good view from the upper deck. Do use them and don't be discouraged by the complex network of routes: people waiting in the line will usually help you, and the conductor will answer your questions and tell you if necessary when you have reached your destination.

Each bus runs along part or all of a numbered route — find out which route you want from the map at the bus stop, and look at the indicator on the front of the bus to check that it is going far enough along the route for you. There are two types of bus stop: a normal stop, with the LRT symbol on a white background, where all buses stop; and a request stop, with a red sign bearing the word "Request," where the bus will stop only if you raise your hand or, if on the bus, ring the bell.

Fares are tied to zones; a small flat-fare is payable for every zone you enter. Children under 16 pay less, and those under five travel free. Usually the conductor will come around and collect your fare during the journey, but sometimes you will have to pay as you enter. Smoking is allowed only upstairs on double-decker buses. The buses run between about 5am and 11.30pm, although there are a few night buses on special routes, running once an hour or so. In central London, small "midi" buses have been introduced on selected routes, specially designed to give speedier rides to people traveling just a few stops. Green Line Coaches run from central London to the country outside London Regional Transport's area. They stop only rarely in London, and are more expensive than red buses. Ask at a Travel Information Centre for details of routes.

Taxis

London's distinctive black taxis (other colors are now being introduced on the modern metrocabs) are driven by some of the best drivers in the world, who have to pass an exam to prove their detailed knowledge of the city before they get a license. They can be hailed as they cruise the streets (a cab that is free illuminates its yellow light), and you will also find them on stands at stations and outside hotels and large shops, etc. Once they have stopped for you, taxis are obliged to take you anywhere you want to go within 6 miles of the pick-up point, provided it is within the metropolitan area. The fare, always shown on the meter, consists of a basic rental charge and subsequent additions according to the length of your journey; there are additional charges for extra passengers, night or weekend journeys and for baggage. In all cases notices are displayed inside the taxi with details of all charges. Give the driver a 10-15 percent tip.

Private taxis (usually sedans and known as "minicabs") cannot be hailed but must be ordered by phone. You will find the numbers by some public telephones and in the *Yellow Pages* directory under Mini Cabs. It is best, however, to stick to the black taxis if possible; the strict regulations governing fares for black taxis do not apply to minicabs, so if you have to use a minicab try to fix the fare with the driver at the start of the journey to avoid problems when you reach your destination.

Getting around by car

Driving in London is not as aggressive as in most large cities, but the difficulty for foreign visitors is that everyone appears to be on the wrong side of the road, and that the city has a totally unplanned road system with an abundance of one-way routes. If you can face all of that, make sure that you are carrying your license, that your tires have at least 1mm of tread, and that all your lights are working.

You must drive on the left and you must pass only on the right. The speed limit in London and all built-up areas (i.e., streets with lampposts) is 30mph (48kph) unless otherwise indicated. Standard international road signs are generally used. Pedestrian crossings are marked by black and white zones across the road and are sometimes controlled by traffic lights. In either case, pedestrians have the right of way and traffic must stop to let them cross, unless there is a green traffic light showing, in which case drivers have priority. Observe lane division rules, i.e., slower traffic on the inside (left) and faster traffic on the outside, and be sure to get into the correct lane coming up to an intersection, as different lanes may be controlled by different traffic signals. Horns must not be used from 11.30pm-7am except in emergencies, and the wearing of seat belts in both front seats is compulsory, as is the wearing of rear seat belts (if the car is fitted with them) for children under 14.

Parking is extremely difficult on streets in central London, usually possible only at meters for a maximum of 2hrs. Two yellow lines by the roadside means no parking at all, one yellow line no parking during the work day (8am-6.30pm, Mon-Sat). Always look for an explanatory sign in the restricted zones: one will give details of the maximum stay allowed, or indicate that the space is for residents only. Parking is always prohibited near pedestrian crossings and intersections. If you violate parking regulations, you may be fined (but not on the spot). Or you may have your car immobilized by a wheel clamp; instruction on how to get it released will be displayed on the windshield, but you will have to pay a fine, on the spot, and wait until it is unlocked. Sometimes the police may tow away your car: go to the nearest police station to ask if this has been the case.

Off the streets, there are various parking lots and garages, often indicated by a blue sign with a large **P**. Charges for these should be set out clearly somewhere near the entrance.

If you belong to an FIA-affiliated automobile club and are bringing your own car, the services of the two main British automobile clubs will be at your disposal:

Automobile Association   For breakdowns ☎freephone 0800-887766; for information ☎ (081) 954-9599

Royal Automobile Club   49 Pall Mall, SW1 ☎839-7050

Renting a car

It is probably not worthwhile if you do not intend to go outside London. You must be over 21 and hold a full valid national license. You can opt for either a daily rate plus a mileage charge, or a weekly rate with unlimited mileage, often more economical. Insurance is usually included, but check first. You may need a cash deposit larger than your likely eventual overall charge: the difference will be refunded when you return the car.

Car rental can be arranged through travel agents or at desks in airports, major stations and large hotels. Or make a telephone reservation through one of the major companies: **Avis** (☎ *(081) 848-8733*); **Europcar** (☎ *(081) 950-5050*); **Hertz** (☎ *(081) 679-1799*). All these companies can arrange for cars to be waiting if you arrive by air or train.

Getting around on foot

Although many Londoners ignore them, it is best to cross the street using zebra crossings, where pedestrians have priority, or subway passages.

Some outer areas are unsafe for pedestrians after nightfall: if outside the city center after dark, stick to the main streets.

Railway services

British Rail offers a fast Inter-City service between major towns throughout the UK, as well as Motorail and sleeper trains. First-class and, on some routes, Pullman tickets are available. Reduced-rate tickets are available for off-peak day or weekend trips, and the Britrail Pass, on sale only outside the UK through travel agents, offers unlimited travel on the whole network for weekly periods up to one month.

British Rail Travel Centres (visitors only)
4-12 Regent St., SW1 (*map 10 G10*)
407 Oxford St., W1 (*map 9 F8*)

Major British Rail stations in London

s and se England, East Anglia (information ☎928-5100)
Charing Cross, Strand, WC2 (*map 10 G11*)
Waterloo, Waterloo Rd., SE1 (*map 11 H13*)
Victoria, Buckingham Palace Rd., SW1 (*map 17 J9*)
Liverpool Street, Liverpool St., EC3 (*map 13 E16*)

sw and w England, s Wales (information ☎ 262-6767)
Paddington, Praed St., W2 (*map 7 F5*)

Midlands, nw England, n Wales, w Scotland (information ☎ 387-7070)
Euston, Euston Rd., NW1 (*map 4 C10*)
St Pancras, Euston Rd., NW1 (*map 4 C11*)

ne England, e Scotland (information ☎ 278-2477)
King's Cross, Euston Rd., NW1 (*map 4 B11*)

Domestic airlines

The principal airline operating from London to other major cities

14

is British Airways. Others include Air UK, British Midland Airways and Dan-Air. Unless you wish to go to one of the country's extremities, such as Aberdeen in Scotland, it is often easier to go by car or train and arrive directly in the city center. London City Airport, situated in Docklands, catering mainly to businessmen, serves only European destinations (apart from Jersey), including Paris, Amsterdam and Brussels (☎ *474-5555 for information*).

Ferry services
Apart from the pleasure cruises on the Thames, the only ferry service is the now-frequent River Bus, which runs between Chelsea and Greenwich with stops at Charing Cross, South Bank, Swan Lane (weekdays only), London Bridge and Docklands. There is also a direct service from Charing Cross to Docklands. (*For River Bus information* ☎ *987-0311*.)

River cruises start from Westminster or Charing Cross pier for trips to Greenwich or the Thames Barrier. (*For Riverboat Information Service* ☎ *730-4812*.)

On-the-spot information

Public holidays
New Year's Day, Jan 1; Good Friday; Easter Monday; May Day (first Mon in May); Spring Bank Holiday (last Mon in May); August Bank Holiday (last Mon in Aug); Christmas Day, Dec 25; Boxing Day, Dec 26. Most places are closed.

Time zones
London time is GMT in winter and changes to European Summer Time (EST), 1hr ahead of GMT, from the end of Mar to late Oct.

Banks and currency exchange
All banks are open Mon-Fri 9.30am-3.30pm. On Sat a handful of central London branches are open, e.g., **Lloyds** (*399 Oxford St., W1, open 10am-3pm*) or **Barclays** (*74 Kensington High St., W8, open 9.30am-noon*). Money can also be exchanged outside these hours at foreign exchanges, found as small separate shops and in hotels, railway stations, travel agencies and airports, but their exchange rates are poorer and they charge service fees. Along with banks, **American Express** and **Thomas Cook** offices give the best rates of exchange for their respective travelers cheques. For your nearest American Express office ☎ 930-4411 (Travel Services); for Thomas Cook ☎ 408-4286.

Travelers cheques are widely accepted in hotels and large stores, but not so much in smaller shops and restaurants; the exchange rate is roughly the same as for cash. Most widely accepted in lieu of cash is, of course, an internationally recognized credit card.

Shopping hours
Most shops are open Mon-Sat 9am-6pm. Many large city-center shops and supermarkets stay open late on Wed or Thurs, and some on other weekdays as well (see *Shopping*). A few shops, mainly grocers and newsagents (newsdealers), open on Sun.

Outside the city center, shops may close at lunchtime, usually 1-2pm, on Sat afternoons, and for one afternoon during the week.

Rush hours
The rush hours are approximately 8-9.30am and 5-7pm on Mon-

Fri only. Unlike some cities, London does not become totally choked, but the situation is worsening and getting around will take longer.

Post and telephone services

Post offices are usually open Mon-Fri 9am-5.30pm, Sat 9am-12.30pm. A notable exception is the post office in William IV St., off Trafalgar Sq. (*map 10 G11*), open Mon-Sat 8am-8pm.

Stamps are available at post offices, some shops and, occasionally, from machines. There are two classes of inland mail, but as the second class is only a little cheaper and sometimes a lot slower and more unreliable, it is best avoided. You will also have to specify which rate you want for international mail, as it will not automatically go air mail. When sending a parcel out of the country you will have to fill in a customs form declaring the contents. Besides the boxes in post offices, mail can be posted in the red boxes placed at regular intervals on main streets. There are various special services available, such as express or recorded or guaranteed delivery.

Public telephones are found in booths on main streets and in post offices, hotels, pubs, stations, etc. If you need a number either inside or outside London, dial **192** or **142** and Directory Inquiries will supply it. There is always an area code, which may have up to six numbers. It is not necessary for local calls but must be used when telephoning from outside the area.

From May 1990 London's 01 area code ceased to exist. Now there are two area codes for London, one **(071)** for inner London, and the other **(081)** for outer London. If you are dialing within one area you do not need to use the code, but dialing from one area to another requires the relevant code. In this book only the outer London (081) code has been given where applicable; any London telephone numbers with no code mentioned take the inner London code.

Most international calls can be dialed direct (IDD) from public telephones. If in difficulty call **155** for the International Operator or **153** for International Directory Inquiries.

Some public telephones take coins; others take phonecards, which can be bought from post offices and shops displaying the phonecard sign. Follow the instructions displayed by the telephone; you will be refunded any unused coins. The ringing tone is a repeated double trill, and an intermittent shrill tone means that the line is busy.

See also *Telephone services* p18.

Public rest rooms

With some exceptions, the public rest rooms found in main streets (often in French-style, automated "superloos"), parks and tube stations can often be dirty and vandalized. Well-maintained rest rooms that can be used by anybody will be found in all larger public buildings, such as museums and art galleries, large department stores and railway stations. It is not acceptable to use the rest rooms in hotels, restaurants and pubs if you are not a customer. Public rest rooms are usually free of charge but you may need a small coin to unlock a rest room or to use a proper washroom.

Electric current

The electric current is 240V AC, and plugs have three square pins and take 3-, 5- or 13-amp fuses. Foreign visitors will need adaptors for their own appliances: buy them before departure.

cite

Customs and etiquette
The English are a tolerant people and London is a cosmopolitan city, so foreign visitors are unlikely to offend by tripping up on some part of etiquette. An important custom is "queuing" — the British line up for everything, and you must wait your turn.

Tipping
Tipping is customary in a few cases. A tip of 10-15 percent is usual in hotels and restaurants, unless a service charge is already incorporated into the check. Taxi drivers also expect about 10-15 percent of the fare. You need only give small tips to porters, hairdressers, rest room attendants and doormen.

Disabled visitors
Prior information is important. A useful publication is *Access in London*, published by Nicholson, and there is an Information Department run by **The Royal Association for Disability and Rehabilitation (RADAR)** (*25 Mortimer St., W1* ☎ *637-5400*). The **London Tourist Board** also produces a number of information sheets for disabled people (☎ 730-3488).

Can-be-Done Ltd (*7-11 Kensington High St., W8* ☎ *907-2400*) arranges tours around London and England for disabled visitors.

Local and foreign publications
The weekly entertainments magazines, such as *Time Out*, *City Limits* and *What's On & Where to Go*, are the most comprehensive guides to events and entertainments of all sorts. London's daily evening newspaper, the *Evening Standard*, also features a wide range of entertainments. Programs of special events (free concerts, ceremonies, etc.) are usually available from Tourist Information Centres and are listed in *The Times*. National newspapers do not necessarily cover local London events.

Foreign newspapers are widely available from newsagents, the *International Herald Tribune* and many others on the day of publication, and most of the others a day or two later.

Useful addresses

Tourist information/tickets/hotel reservations
London Tourist Board and Convention Bureau information centers:
Harrods (4th floor), Knightsbridge, SW1
Heathrow Airport, Arrivals Concourse, Terminal 2
Heathrow Central Underground Station, Heathrow Airport
Selfridges (ground floor), Oxford St., W1
Victoria Station Forecourt, SW1
West Gate, Tower of London, EC3 (summer only)
Telephone hotel reservation service: Call in advance of your arrival ☎824-8844.
Written inquiries and hotel reservation service (write 6 weeks in advance):
Accommodation Services, London Tourist Board, 26 Grosvenor Gdns., SW1.
LTB Tourist Information ☎730-3488.
On-the-spot hotel reservation at Victoria Station and Heathrow.
British Travel Centre   12 Regent St., W1
American Express Travel Service   6 Haymarket, London SW1 ☎930-4411; a valuable source of information for any traveler in need of help, advice or emergency services

Useful addresses

City of London Information Centre St Paul's Churchyard, EC4 ☎ 260-1456/7
London Regional Transport Information Centre
55 Broadway, SW1; 24hr telephone service ☎ 222-1234
Travel Information Centres at the following stations:
Euston, Heathrow Central, King's Cross, Oxford Circus, Piccadilly Circus, Victoria.
British Tourist Authority and **English Tourist Board**
Thames Tower, Black's Rd., W6 ☎ 846-9000
Kidsline   ☎ 222-8070

Post offices
General delivery can be addressed to any post office. The two main ones are **Trafalgar Square post office** (*24 William IV St., WC2* ☎ *930-9580*) and **City post office** (*King Edward Building, King Edward St., EC1* ☎ *239-5047, for general inquiries*).

Telephone services
Operator 100, Directory inquiries 142/192, International operator 155, Time 123 (from London numbers only), Telemessages and International Telegrams 190, Weather forecast, Greater London (0898) 500-401, national (0898) 500-400

Embassies and consulates
Australia   Australia House, Strand, WC2 ☎ 379-4334
Canada   1 Grosvenor St., W1 ☎ 629-9492
Ireland   17 Grosvenor Pl., SW1 ☎ 235-2171
Japan   101-104 Piccadilly, W1 ☎ 465-6500
New Zealand   80 Haymarket, SW1 ☎ 930-8422
USA   24 Grosvenor Sq., W1 ☎ 499-9000

Sightseeing tours
London Transport (☎ *227-3456*): London sightseeing tour in open-top double-decker bus departs every ½hr from Victoria St., Baker St., Marble Arch, Piccadilly Circus.
Cityrama (☎ *720-6663*) also departs every ½hr from several points; 8-language commentary.
Harrods (☎ *581-3603*), very luxurious; 8-language commentary.
Golden Tours (☎ *743-3300*), **Frames Richards** (☎ *837-3111*) and **Evan Evans** (☎ *930-2377*) all offer various sightseeing tours by coach.
   All the above tours can be reserved through the **London Tourist Board Centres** at Victoria, Harrods or Selfridges.

Private guided tours
If you would like to go sightseeing in the company of a qualified Blue Badge Guide, contact **Tour Guides Ltd** (☎ *839-2498*).
Take a Guide (☎ *221-5475*) and **British Tours** (☎ *629-5267*) both provide driver-guides.
   For a list of operators offering walking tours see *Walks in London*.

Major places of worship
Church of England churches cover the whole city, and Roman Catholic, Baptist and Methodist churches also abound.
American Church in London (Interdenominational)   79
Tottenham Court Rd., W1 ☎ 580-2791
Central Synagogue (Orthodox)   36 Hallam St., W1
☎ 580-1355
London Central Mosque   146 Park Rd., NW8 ☎ 724-3363

Emergency information

Emergency services (from any telephone)
For **Police**, **Ambulance** or **Fire** ☎999. No coins are needed.
The operator will ask which service you require.

Hospitals with casualty (emergency) departments
St Mary's Hospital   Praed St., W2 ☎725-6666
St Thomas's Hospital   Lambeth Palace Rd., SE1
☎928-9292
St Bartholomew's (Barts)   West Smithfield, EC1
☎601-8888
Westminster   Adults: Horseferry Rd., SW1 ☎828-9811;
children: Udall St., SW1 ☎ 828-9811

Other emergencies
If your complaint does not warrant an ambulance or
hospitalization you will have to ring up a doctor or dentist.
Consult the *Yellow Pages* of the telephone directory under
"Doctors (Medical Practitioners)" and "Dental Surgeons."

Late-opening chemists/drugstores
Bliss   50 Willesden Lane, NW6 ☎624-8000, open daily
9am-2am; 5 Marble Arch, W1 ☎723-6116, open daily 9am-
midnight

Help lines
Capital Help Line   ☎388-7575. Referral service.
Release ☎603-8654.   Drug problems, legal and practical.
The Samaritans   46 Marshall St., W1 ☎439-2224 (24hr).
Personal callers 9am-9pm. Talk out problems.

Automobile accidents
• Do not admit liability or incriminate yourself.
• Ask any witnesses to stay and give a statement.
• Contact the police.
• Exchange names, addresses, car details and insurance
  companies' names and addresses with other driver(s).
• Give a statement to the police. Insurance companies will
  accept the police report as authoritative.

Car breakdowns
Call one of the following from the nearest telephone:
• The nearest garage/breakdown service.
• The police, who will put you in touch with the above.
• The number you have been given if you rented the car.

Lost passport
Contact the police immediately, and your consulate (see p18)
for emergency travel documents.

Lost travelers cheques
Notify the local police at once, then follow the instructions
provided with your travelers cheques, or contact the issuing
company's nearest office. Contact your consulate or American
Express if you are stranded with no money.

Lost property
Report your loss to the police immediately (many insurance
companies will not recognize claims without a police report).
There are some special lost property offices:
British Rail   At main stations (see *Railway services* p14)
Heathrow Airport Lost Property Office   ☎(081)
759-4321
London Regional Transport   200 Baker St., NW1
Taxi Lost Property Office   15 Penton St., NW1

Major libraries
Guildhall Library   Aldermanbury, EC2 ☎ 606-3030
Westminster Central Reference Library   St Martin's St.,
WC2 ☎ 828-8070 (international and local reference)

Time chart

AD43	The invading Romans under Claudius defeated the Celtic tribes of SE Britain and bridged the Thames close to the site of the later London Bridge. By AD60, London was a thriving port and settlement at the center of the Roman road network.
60	Revolt by Iceni tribe from East Anglia, under Queen Boadicea, culminated in destruction of London.
200	England's capital, and a prosperous city of traders, London was fortified by the Romans. Walls from modern sites of Tower to Aldgate, along London Wall to Barbican and down to the river at Blackfriars.
200-400	Romans used Germanic mercenaries to help defend this outpost of their weakening empire.
410	Romans withdrew, and London reverted to a farming town under the Angles and Saxons, warrior kings.
700-820	England gradually reunited under kings of Wessex, from Winchester. London an important provincial market town. Christianity slowly reintroduced, stimulating learning.
836	London sacked by Vikings. For almost two centuries it was a borderland pawn in their struggle with the western Saxon kingdoms.
1014	London taken by storm for the last time; Olaf, an Anglo-Saxon, tied his boats to London Bridge and sailed downstream to destroy it. (Hence the song *London Bridge is Falling Down*.)
1052	Disgusted by London's switching of support to his enemies, King Edward the Confessor started to build a new abbey and palace named Westminster on Isle of Thorney. Tension between City and Crown was born.
1066	Norman invasion. William did not attack the well-fortified London, but forced it into submission by destroying surrounding farmlands.
1066-1100	London accepted and thrived under the civilized Norman rule. William I built Tower of London.
1140-90	As political stability was undermined by factionalism among the king and powerful barons, London exacted a price for its support. It won the power to raise taxes and elect its own governors. The powerful guilds, confederations of merchants, controlled trade.
1215	London accepted Charter of Incorporation from King John, confirming authority of the Lord Mayor, elected annually by 24 aldermen. Displeased by heavy taxes, it supported barons in drafting Magna Carta.
1217	First stone bridge over Thames, London Bridge.
1263	Trade guilds took control from aldermen during turbulence of baronial wars, reinstituting Government by citizens' assembly (an Anglo-Saxon idea).
1269	Henry II began construction of new Westminster Abbey after boundary dispute with City.

Time chart

1280	Old St Paul's Cathedral completed, half as tall again as current St Paul's. Precincts housed sports arena, markets and a brewery. 126 parish churches plus monasteries inside city displaced population.
1326	The new urban pressures of the city erupted in riots against the king. Foreigners and Jews attacked.
1338	Edward III made Westminster the regular meeting place of Parliament, previously irregular.
1348	Black Death. Half city's 60,000 population died.
1381	Peasants' Revolt. Seeking an end to feudalism, a working class "army," led by Wat Tyler from Kent, took over London for two days. Tyler killed by mayor.
1399	London supported Parliament in forcing deposition of the absolutist and heavily-taxing Richard II.
1411	Work began on Guildhall, the city's "royal palace." Professional soldiers and tradesmen formed new wealthy class threatening the old feudal aristocracy.
1461	London's support essential to Edward IV, victor of Wars of the Roses, in struggle to restore stability to country and its trade. King knighted many London citizens in return for support.
1500-1600	Population exploded from 50,000 to 200,000 during economic boom of relatively stable Tudor period. New slum areas arose outside London, all ungoverned suburbs, including red-light district of Southwark.
1533	Henry VIII's Reformation. New gentry class snapped up land vacated by dissolution of the monasteries. Henry founded downriver naval bases.
1553-58	Queen Mary reinstated Catholicism. Citizens martyred at Smithfield. London then supported the parsimonious Protestant Elizabeth I for 45yrs.
1600-70	The new gentry, now aristocracy, began to develop their new land, moving westward, building on the edge of the countryside in Piccadilly and Leicester Sq.
1603-42	Puritanism flourished in the city as a reaction against the autocratic Stuart kings, James I and Charles I.
1642-49	London financed Parliament in Civil War. London and Westminster both embraced by new fortifications, and the citizens manned defense. London was the setting for Charles I's execution in 1649.
1649-60	Commonwealth republic. London traders gradually reacted against the religious radicals' egalitarianism, and supported the restoration of Charles II in 1660.
1665-66	The Great Plague. The last and worst outbreak. At least 100,000 died in just over a year.
1666	The Great Fire. Medieval London destroyed after fire, started in King's baker's in Pudding Lane.
1666-1700	Reconstruction with stone buildings and wider streets. Wren's plan of grid of streets with piazzas infringed too many property rights; private ownership shaped new landscape. Instead Wren built 51 churches, culminating in St Paul's. By 1700, the 300,000 population was widely dispersed after the fire.
1700-50	Both the new urban poor and the fashionable elite pushed up the population to 675,000 by 1750. The villages of Knightsbridge and Marylebone were incorporated, and St James's and Mayfair were developed. To the E and S were slums, where gin consumption averaged two pints per person per week and only one child in four lived beyond age five.

Time chart

1774	The City, still self-governing, elected the radical John Wilkes as Mayor after he was expelled from Parliament three times. It still distrusted the cultured West End and the almost omnipotent Parliament.
1780	The Gordon Riots. Anarchy in London for a week, but still no police force with day-to-day authority.
1780-1820	Middle and upper classes moved ever more to the suburbs in the w, as slums and urban pressures increased. Still no comprehensive local government.
1829	The Metropolitan Police or "Peelers," the first police force, founded. City founded its own force in 1835.
1820-38	Prince Regent, later George IV, and architect Nash developed Regent's Park and Regent St., Buckingham Palace and The Mall.
1835	Britain given local councils. London was exempted from this, and continued to be "governed" by more than 150 parishes, encompassing 300 administrative bodies. Slum clearance still partially executed by the Commissioner for Woods and Forests.
1839	New Palace of Westminster, the present one, was started after old one was burned down.
1844	Controlling monopoly in printing of money granted to the Bank of England.
1832-66	Cholera killed thousands: various Public Health Acts had no effect on London, until Metropolitan Board of Works founded in 1855. Destitution worsened by clearance of land for railways.
1851	The Great Exhibition in the Crystal Palace in Hyde Park celebrated British supremacy in trade, science and industry. Consolidated by Prince Albert's development of the museums and learned institutions of South Kensington.
1863	Railways available to working class for first time, and opening of first underground line. Increased mobility and belated public health and education measures.
1889	London County Council formed, giving London comprehensive local government for first time.
1897	Victoria's Diamond Jubilee. London described as "centre of an empire on which the sun never sets."
1900-05	Opening of four new electric underground lines began rapid expansion into sprawling suburbs.
1914-18	Women took over many services in London during the War, and the suffragettes won the vote in 1918.
1920-30	"Homes for Heroes" program was part of growth of vast new estates quadrupling size of London.
1940	The Blitz. London bombed, mainly in The City and East End; St Paul's stood alone amid rubble.
1945-55	Private and local government redevelopment of the city resulted in fast modernization.
1951	Festival of Britain, one of the first world fairs.
1955-65	Boom years for property developers, who erected prestigious skyscrapers while London County Council concentrated on housing in suburbs. Population of central London lowest for centuries.
1956	Clean Air Act created smokeless zones and marked the end of central London as an industrial area.
1960-70	"Swinging London." Economic boom, immigration and changing values and wealth patterns made London more cosmopolitan. In 1965, Greater London Council succeeded LCC.

1970-80	Local government gained strength.
1986	Labour GLC abolished by Conservative government. London Stock Exchange reformed — the "Big Bang."
1987	Margaret Thatcher's Conservative government re-elected for a 3rd term of office. First black MPs elected.
1989	Televising of House of Commons.

Architecture

London was not the vision of an emperor or king. To their surprise, visitors who know by repute its showcase architectural masterpieces find not a city of grand avenues and broad boulevards, but a family of villages, offering delightfully distracting details more often than panoramic views. A uniquely pervasive grandeur derives from this blending of a rich heritage of fine buildings into the everyday life, past and present, of a bustling city.

A chronology of English architectural styles

Norman (1060-1200)   Sturdy buildings around massive piers; round arches; carved geometrical ornament; square towers and keeps.

Gothic (1180-1540)   Lighter, more dynamic buildings: flying buttresses, pointed arches and windows, spires. Main periods: **Early English** (1180-1260), marked by simplicity and airiness; **Decorated** (1250-1370), extensive surface ornament and window tracery; **Perpendicular** (1300-1540), slender columns stressing vertical lines, fan vaulting and paneled windows.

Tudor (1540-1603)   The Renaissance influenced only decoration, with plasterwork and carved gables. Brick buildings with symmetrical plan, often E or H; large mullioned windows.

Jacobean (1603-25)   Extravagant wood and plaster decoration.

Classical (1615-66)   Inigo Jones introduced Palladian style. After Great Fire, Wren worked in styles from Classical simplicity to dignified but sophisticated Baroque.

But withal understand that in London many stately palaces, built by noblemen upon the river Thames, do make a very great show to them that pass by water; and that there be many more like palaces, also built towards land, but scattered and great part of them in back lanes and streets, which if they were joined to the first in good order, as other cities are built uniformly, they would make not only fair streets, but even a beautiful city, to which few might justly be preferred for the magnificence of the building.

Fynes Moryson, 1617

English Baroque (1690-1720)   Fluidity of Continental Baroque was tempered by Classical and medieval elements.

Palladianism (or Georgian) (1720-1820)   Italianate buildings with columns and porticoes, often relatively plain, combined with new art of landscape gardening.

Neo-Gothic (1740-80)   Brief vogue for Classical decoration gave way to Rococo-like frivolity and novelty.

Regency (1780-1830)   Simplistic Classicism with delicate interior ornament, often a stucco relief.

Victorian (1830-1900)   Extravagantly treated historicist themes, especially Neo-Gothic, contrast with functional public and industrial structures in iron and glass.

Architecture

Domestic Revival (1870-1920)   Direct simplicity in domestic architecture, using brick, stone and wood.
International Modern (1930-60)   Functional airy buildings, often worked into English gardens.
Modernist (1945-present)   Imaginative use of space and new materials; concern for social basis of architecture.

London is still blessed with the stones and mortar of its Roman founders in the remnants of the 2ndC city wall, especially near the Barbican. Defence was still the vital consideration when the Norman conquest of 1066 was followed by the construction in 1078 of the huge, square White Tower, one of the best existing examples of a Norman keep.

Westminster Abbey, begun in 1245, is London's finest remaining medieval building, the E arm epitomizing the elegant Early English style, with the later nave in the Perpendicular style. Timber roofing, one of the glories of the English Gothic, survives in the hammer-beam roof of Westminster Hall, in the Great Hall of Hampton Court (1536), and also in St James's Palace, a superb red-brick example of the ornate Tudor adaptations of Gothic.

The **White Tower** (1078) in the Tower of London, the first of the square Norman keeps, is built of Caen stone.

The hammer-beam roof in **Westminster Hall** (1399), the only surviving part of the old Palace of Westminster.

The Anne Boleyn gatehouse of **Hampton Court Palace** (1540), built for Henry VIII in Tudor red brick.

The **Banqueting House, Whitehall** (1622), Inigo Jones' strictly Palladian masterpiece, incorporates Ionic columns.

Inigo Jones, born in 1573 in Smithfield, brought the vigor and sophistication of Italian Renaissance styles to London, most notably the elegant symmetry of Andrea Palladio. Jones' particular contribution to the building of London was the development of Covent Garden, especially the Piazza (1631-39), and the first two Palladian buildings in London, the Banqueting House in Whitehall (1619-22) and the delightful Queen's House in Greenwich.

Sir Christopher Wren (1632-1723), an Oxford-educated scientist, and later Surveyor of the King's Works, was entrusted with the rebuilding of the City after the Great Fire. On the churches of the City he designed towers and steeples to lead the eye to the dome of St Paul's Cathedral. In his buildings, Wren used elements of the classical Renaissance style, but was obliged to adapt its geometrical grandeur and piazzas to the framework of the medieval city's alleys and courtyards.

Wren's secular buildings include the Royal Naval Hospital, Greenwich (1696-1702), and the Royal Hospital, Chelsea (1681-91). His assistant Nicholas Hawksmoor designed several churches that are increasingly appreciated; a fine example is St

St Paul's (1675-1710) has a vast circular crossing, over which arches on piers support inner and outer domes.

St Mary-le-Strand (1714-17), by Gibbs, has an Italianate steeple on a Classical base.

Chiswick House (1725-29), by Burlington and Kent, is fronted by a Palladian columned portico.

Architecture

Mary Woolnoth (1716-24). Wren also influenced Sir James Gibbs, a leader of the English Baroque, and the combination of styles is exemplified by St Martin-in-the-Fields (1722-26).

In the Georgian period, fashion swung away from Baroque back to the rules and conventions of Classical architecture, a move typified by Palladian Chiswick House (1725-29), which also has a garden landscaped by William Kent. The same notions of refinement and good taste were evident in the Georgian terraces built at this time. The dominant designer was Robert Adam (1728-92), one of a family of influential architects, whose terraced town houses were unified by an elegant facade.

In the later part of the Georgian period, the Regency architect John Nash (1752-1835) used these themes to give a sense of shape and elegance to the heart of modern London. Seen from Piccadilly Circus, the bold, sweeping curve of Regent St. echoes Nash's plan for a triumphal "Royal Mile" from the Prince Regent's residence at Carlton House to Regent's Park. At either end of this mile are two pristine examples of Nash's work: Carlton House Terrace (1827-32) and Park Crescent (1812-22). These elegant terraces and crescents were mirrored in the development of

20 St James's Square, a Georgian terraced town house, with a strictly Classical facade.

Cumberland Terrace (1825), Regent's Park, by Nash, his massive Classical pediments with stucco decoration.

The **Palace of Westminster** (1840-50) has a classically balanced plan decorated in Perpendicular Gothic style.

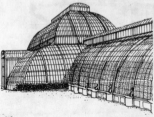

The enormous **conservatory** or **palm house** (1844-48) at Kew Gardens, a functional but elegant Victorian structure.

Belgravia and Chelsea, largely by Thomas Cubitt, in the 1820s and 1830s.

The sterner values of the Victorian period were reflected in church-like buildings such as the Houses of Parliament (1840-50, Sir Charles Barry and Augustus Pugin). This Gothic Revival architecture had moments of fantasy, as the spires of St Pancras Station (1868-74, Sir Gilbert Scott) happily show. The railway era also brought some breathtaking examples of civil engineering, and the interior of Paddington Station (1850-4, Brunel) remains a good memorial to the best of these. Similarly inspired use of cast iron and sheet glass is seen in the magnificent conservatorium at Kew Gardens (1844-48, Decimus Burton).

The 20thC has produced some of London's least attractive architecture, although the passing of time is leading to a greater appreciation of 1920s and 1930s industrial buildings such as the Hoover factory on Western Avenue, and Battersea Power Station. Bauhaus refugees founded the design group Tecton, which designed Highgate's Highpoint Flats (1936), described by Le Corbusier as "a vertical garden city." Notable postwar buildings, all of which have provoked controversy, are Oxford Street's

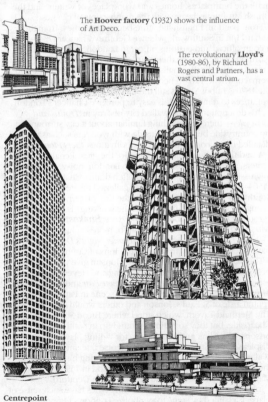

The **Hoover factory** (1932) shows the influence of Art Deco.

The revolutionary **Lloyd's** (1980-86), by Richard Rogers and Partners, has a vast central atrium.

Centrepoint (1962-66), whose honeycomb tower rises above a piazza.

The **National Theatre** (1967-77) has a superbly organized interior, with complex vertical and horizontal creation of functional spaces.

dominant Centrepoint (1965, Richard Seifert), which became a symbol of profligate speculation, the National Theatre (1967-77, Denys Lasdun), in the cold, horizontal style of the South Bank complex, and the vast glass and tubular steel Lloyd's Building (1986, Richard Rogers).

Although the Prince of Wales' outspoken criticism of modern architecture in the capital has infuriated contemporary architects, it has succeeded in focusing attention on the subject, and has helped to accelerate the trend away from the brutalism of the 1960s and 1970s. Curves have replaced hard lines, steel, glass and brick have replaced concrete, and architects are employing Classical motifs — pediments, porticoes, columns, moldings — within the context of modern architecture.

London and literature

The resonances of a city through its life are caught and retained in its literature. Few sidewalks echo these sounds as pervasively as those of London. The streets are dotted with blue plaques to mark the birthplaces, homes and workplaces of writers, and the British Museum is heavy with the manuscripts of classics.

From London, English literature began its journey; from the Tabard Inn in Southwark, whence Geoffrey Chaucer (1340-1400), a court official and customs officer in London, dispatched his garrulous pilgrims with their *Canterbury Tales*. In so doing, he created a specifically English literature, graphically realistic and vernacular. The Tabard became the Talbot Inn, a survivor until the 1870s; Talbot Yard is still there, with six centuries of exits and entrances to remember. It is easy to perceive Chaucer's London in his descriptions of the walled city of Troy in *Troilus and Criseyde* — there is something familiar about a city surrounded by countryside but bursting inside with wonders such as those detailed in the contemporary but anonymous *Piers Plowman*.

A tradition was established. Even for the great Renaissance writers, steeped in classical learning, London, noisy, fast and aggressive, dictated its own style, often drama. Shakespeare (1564-1616) worked in the circular galleried theaters of Southwark, thought too rowdy for the City proper, where art was brought for almost the first time to the working class, the "groundlings" who stood in the "pit" (see **Shakespeare Globe Museum**). He would also perform for more exclusive audiences — both *Twelfth Night* and *A Midsummer Night's Dream* may first have been performed privately in the Inns of Court.

The plays of his contemporary Ben Jonson give perhaps the best idea of London, where the cunning and clever prosper, especially *The Alpharmacy*, *Bartholomew Fair* and *Every Good Man in his Humour*, which includes a scene in Paul's Walk, the central aisle of St Paul's. Jonson and others would often retire to The Mermaid Tavern, which stood where Bread St. meets Cheapside, but they sometimes wound up in Southwark's prisons, The Clink and Marshalsea, for writing plays that displeased the Crown. Others met a worse fate: much of Sir Walter Raleigh's finest writing was done during his 13 years in the Tower before his execution in 1618, and in 1593 Christopher Marlowe was stabbed to death in a tavern in Deptford.

John Donne (1573-1631), whose early lyrics have such sense of place, is claimed by some to symbolize London's temporary "decline" into intellectualism by turning to religious poetry. In 1621 he became Dean of St Paul's. Admittedly, London only housed and did not inspire Milton and the great metaphysical poets. Yet from the ashes of the medieval city (burned down in 1666) and Puritanism rose arguably the greatest works about London, certainly two of the best diaries ever written, both social history and literature: those of Samuel Pepys and John Evelyn.

> The stones of St Paul's flew like grenades, and the lead melted down the streets in a stream. The very pavements glowed with fiery redness, and neither horse nor man was able to tread on them.

Evelyn's physical description is outstanding, but in both diaries everyday life is also vividly pictured; Pepys' account is so honest that he wrote in a secret shorthand, not deciphered until 1820.

With the 18thC post-fire development of the West End came a new Augustan "Age of Reason," when London, a new Rome or Athens, inspired learned, urbane works. But its vigorous, down-to-earth character shone through. Satire became the new mode: irreverent modern classics about people, not gods, such as *The Dunciad* by Pope (1688-1744), often to be found at **Chiswick House** with his patron Lord Burlington; or *London* by Dr Johnson (1709-84), an archetypal English blend of common sense and classicism (see **Johnson's House**). Cliques need meeting places, and the most famous surviving one is the Cheshire Cheese on Fleet St.; Russell St., Covent Garden, housed the most renowned coffeehouses. But the age of reason was not all it thought itself. In 1679 Dryden was beaten up outside the Lamb and Flag pub in Rose St., WC2 (since nicknamed "The Bucket of Blood"), having offended the Earl of Rochester, a fellow writer, in a satire. At Swift's suggestion, John Gay wrote *The Beggar's Opera* in 1728 as a "Newgate pastoral," depicting with a new moral stringency the slums of Covent Garden and the notorious Newgate prison. Henry Fielding, a pioneer of the new novel form with *Tom Jones*, was an innovative magistrate in Bow Street, trying to protect the same slum dwellers. Even writing had its seamy side — buried under the Barbican is the site of Grub Street, still the imagined habitat of ill-paid hack writers.

London is enchanting. I step out upon a tawny coloured magic carpet....it takes up the private life and carries it on, without any effort.... (Virginia Woolf in her diary, 1926)

Although Wordsworth was moved to write "Earth has not anything to show more fair" (*On Westminster Bridge*, 1802), and Keats (1795-1821) found peace enough in Hampstead to write *Ode to a Nightingale* (see **Keats' House**), it was urban squalor that moved Charles Dickens (1812-70), the most obsessive writer about London. Like that of his own Sam Weller, Dickens' "knowledge of London was extensive and peculiar." In his novels London is most often a brooding, malevolent presence, too powerful for the people in it, a city of slum tenements, an evil ruling class, prisons and "London particulars" or "pea-soupers," poisonous mixes of fog and smog. To balance this, there is the comedy and vitality of his unforgettable cockneys, such as Sam Weller, Mr. Micawber and Bill Sykes, with their own unique language. Yet underneath speaks the morally appalled social reformer. The references are endless (see **Dickens' House**), but some idea of his feelings can be gained from his treatment of the Thames, along which Abel Magwitch tries in vain to escape in *Great Expectations* and which is so often the recipient of corpses — as in the superb opening scene of *Our Mutual Friend*.

By the interwar years, things had changed. Virginia Woolf (1882-1941) wrote: "I ask nothing better than that all the reviewers....should call me a highbrow. If they like to add Bloomsbury, WC1, that is the correct postal address." In Bloomsbury's leafy Georgian squares, where dark brick houses surround pleasant gardens, Lawrence, Yeats, Eliot and Forster found a calming peace, which is still there and pervades the modernist literature they helped to forge in the area.

Royal London

Like the pussycat in the nursery rhyme, people go "up to London to look at the Queen." For the visitor from other parts of the realm, the rituals, pageantry, and palaces of royal London are the tangible demonstration not only of a heritage but also of stability. The monarchy has survived not because the kingdom is quiescent but because the Crown itself is a stabilizing influence. It has had its nadir, of course: it was replaced by the Commonwealth from 1649 to 1660; and more recently the abdication of Edward VIII in 1936, before his coronation, provoked something of a crisis of confidence in the institution. But today, most Britons regard it as the keystone of the state.

The kingdom is not, of course, England, otherwise the Queen's husband and her son and heir would not be Duke of Edinburgh and Prince of Wales. The Queen is also head of state of many countries in the Commonwealth. But arguably the most important job of the monarchy is to represent the family of nations that together, and by consent, compose the United Kingdom. Because they have smaller populations, Scotland and Wales are numerically less represented in Parliament than England, but they are equal in the sight of the Crown. In countries of less age, national unity can be an objective in itself. But Britain, being neither young nor one nation, needs some means by which it can articulate its wholeness.

There will soon be five kings left — the Kings of England, Diamonds, Hearts, Spades and Clubs.

King Farouk of Egypt, 1951

At the time of the wedding of the Prince of Wales in 1981, Charles Douglas-Home, writing in *The Times*, conceded that the Queen has "almost no executive function to perform," but concluded that she has "a 'presence' in the highest reaches of the political process." Before a general election can take place the Queen must dissolve Parliament. After the contest, she appoints as Prime Minister the leader of whichever party has won the election and invites him or her to form a government. The monarchy, Douglas-Home pointed out, "is not yet constitutionally allowed to slip back into a world of sumptuous ceremonial."

Where to see the Royal Family

The daily Court Circular, which gives details of all the Royal Family's public engagements, is printed in *The Times*, *Daily Telegraph* and the *Independent*. Apart from this, the Queen presides at certain annual events, often accompanied by other members of her family.

The State Opening of Parliament, at the beginning of each new session of Parliament, usually late Oct, is the most apparently political of the Queen's regular duties, in that she announces in her speech a program of proposed legislation. In fact, the measures outlined are put forward not at the discretion of the Queen but on behalf of her government.

Remembrance Sunday, on the Sun nearest Nov 11, sees the Queen placing wreaths on the Cenotaph in Whitehall to commemorate the dead of the two World Wars.

Trooping the Colour takes place on a Sat in mid-June to honor the Queen's official birthday. Each year a different Guards regiment presents itself for inspection; the "colour" is its regimental flag. The Queen rides in a landau to Horse Guards Parade, off Whitehall, receives the salute amid marching bands, and often makes an appearance on the balcony of Buckingham Palace on her return.

Royal residences

Buckingham Palace did not become the principal royal residence until the time of Queen Victoria (1836-1902), although it had been used by monarchs since George III bought it in 1762. However, the palace is in every sense the center, home and headquarters of the British monarchy.

Before Victoria, St James's Palace, built for Henry VIII (1509-47), was the sovereign's official residence. Its status is still honored in the accreditation of foreign diplomats to "the Court of St James," and it is the headquarters of the Gentlemen at Arms, who form a personal bodyguard for the Queen, and the home of the Yeomen of the Guard. These, rather than the Tower Yeomen, are the true "Beefeaters," a word probably derived from "buffetier," meaning an attendant at royal buffets. St James's Palace also includes Clarence House, home of Queen Elizabeth the Queen Mother, one of the most dearly loved members of the Royal Family in recent decades.

Kensington Palace was acquired as a home by William III, who wanted a place in the country around London. It was the home of the sovereign from 1689 to 1760, and is now the London home of the Prince and Princess of Wales, and the home also of Princess Margaret, the Queen's sister, and of other royals. Windsor Castle (see *Excursions*) is still used extensively by the Royal Family. Originally the home of Edward the Confessor (1042-66), it is a country home much closer to London than Balmoral in Scotland, or Sandringham in Norfolk.

Who's who in the Royal Family

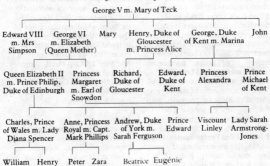

George V m. Mary of Teck

Edward VIII m. Mrs Simpson | George VI m. Elizabeth (Queen Mother) | Mary | Henry, Duke of Gloucester m. Princess Alice | George, Duke of Kent m. Marina | John

Queen Elizabeth II m. Prince Philip, Duke of Edinburgh | Princess Margaret m. Earl of Snowdon | Richard, Duke of Gloucester | Edward, Duke of Kent | Princess Alexandra | Prince Michael of Kent

Charles, Prince of Wales m. Lady Diana Spencer | Anne, Princess Royal m. Capt. Mark Phillips | Andrew, Duke of York m. Sarah Ferguson | Prince Edward | Viscount Linley | Lady Sarah Armstrong-Jones

William Henry | Peter Zara | Beatrice Eugénie

Calendar of events

See also *Sports and activities* and *Public holidays* in *Basic information*.

January

‡ 1st week: **Jan sales**. Most shops offer good reductions; the most voracious shoppers camp out overnight in lines. Many now start late Dec. ‡ **International Boat Show**, Earls Court, SW5. Leisure boats. ‡ Last Sun, 11am: **Charles I Commemoration**, Whitehall, SW1. On the anniversary of his execution, the unofficial King's Army parades from St James's Palace to the Banqueting House. ‡ Jan/Feb: **Chinese New Year**, Chinatown, around Gerrard St., W1. Dragons, lanterns, flags, torches and the Lion Dance. ‡ Jan/Mar: **Rugby Union Internationals**, Twickenham. On two Sat afternoons England play.

February

‡ First Sun, 4pm: **Annual Clowns Service**, Holy Trinity Church, Dalston, E8. The Clowns International Club attends its church in full costume to honor founder Joseph Grimaldi. All welcome to free **clown show** afterwards. ‡ Shrove Tuesday, noon: **Pancake races**, Covent Garden, followed by a **band performance**.

March

‡ Mar 1: **St David's Day**, Windsor Castle. A member of the Royal Family presents the Welsh Guards with the national emblem, a leek. ‡ **Ideal Home Exhibition**, Olympia, W14. A huge exhibition of everything, but everything, found in and around the home. ‡ **Camden Festival**. The borough (from Bloomsbury to Hampstead) sponsors concerts, plays, etc.; always attracts big jazz names. ‡ 2nd Tues, noon: **Bridewell Service**, St Bride's, Fleet St., EC4. The Lord Mayor and Sheriffs attend this thanksgiving service for the Bridewell children's home, now moved out of London. ‡ 3rd or 4th Thurs: **Oranges and Lemons Service**, St Clement Danes, Strand, WC2. As a reminder of the nursery rhyme, children are presented with the fruits during a service. The church bells ring out the rhyme daily at 9am, noon, 3pm, 6pm. ‡ **Royal Film Performance**. Royals and celebrities attend a gala premiere for charity. ‡ Mar 17: **St Patrick's Day**, Pirbright, Surrey. The Irish Guards are presented with a shamrock by the Queen Mother. ‡ Mar/Apr: **Country Music Festival**, Wembley Arena. Festivities last a week. ‡ Mar/Apr: **Boat Race**, Putney to Mortlake. Oxford and Cambridge University eights battle upstream with awesome power. ‡ Mar/Apr: **Head of the River Race**, Mortlake to Putney. Racing between teams from all over Europe.

April

‡ Maundy Thursday (Thurs before Easter): **Maundy Money**. At a different church every year, the Queen presents specially minted coins to the elderly and to groups of children. ‡ Good Friday: **Butterworth Charity**, St Bartholomew the Great, Smithfield, EC1. After 11am service, hot cross buns and coins are laid out on tombstones for local children. ‡ Easter Sunday: **Easter Parade**, Battersea Park. Climax of the day-long fair is the huge colorful parade at 3pm. Also **fairs** on Hampstead Heath and Blackheath. **Tower Church Parade**, Tower of London, EC3. After 11am service, Yeoman Warders have official inspection. ‡ Easter Monday: **Procession and Easter carols**, Westminster Abbey, SW1. **London Marathon**, from Greenwich Park to Westminster Bridge. 30,000 competitors, from very fast to very mad. ‡ **Harness Horse Parade**, Regents Park, NW1. A morning parade of heavy working horses in superb, gleaming brass harnesses and plumes. ‡ 1st Thurs after Easter: **Spital Sermon**, St Lawrence Jewry, EC2. A service attended by all the City's pomp, Lord Mayor included, in full regalia. ‡ Apr 21: **Queen's Birthday**. 21-gun salutes in Hyde Park and on Tower Hill at noon. Troops in parade dress. ‡ Apr/May: **FA Cup Final**, Wembley Stadium. Showpiece soccer match. ‡ **Rugby League Cup Final**, Wembley Stadium. Showpiece rugby league match.

May

‡ 2nd Sun: **Punch and Judy Festival**, Covent Garden. Procession at 10am, service at St Paul's at 11am, then Punch and Judy shows until 6pm at the site where Pepys watched England's first show

in 1662. ‡ Ascension Day: **Beating the Bounds**. The boundary stones of parishes were traditionally "whacked" with a stick in defiance. Today it happens around the Tower, and All-Hallows-by-the-Tower, EC3, one of the marks of which is in mid-river but is whacked notwithstanding. ‡ **Private Fire Brigades' Competition**, Guildhall Yard, EC4. They spray targets with hoses. Again in Sept. ‡ **Glyndebourne Opera Season**, Sussex. Exclusive performances in a country house, with champagne picnics during intervals. To Aug. ‡ **Chelsea Flower Show**, Royal Hospital, Chelsea, SW3. A massive and superb 4-day horticultural display. ‡ May 29 or soon after: **Founder's (Oak Apple) Day**, Royal Hospital, Chelsea, SW3. The Chelsea Pensioners' annual parade. ‡ Late May: **Samuel Pepys Memorial Service**, St Olave, EC3. Lord Mayor and Co., 17thC band, all flock to Pepys' own church. ‡ May/June: **Summer Exhibition**, Royal Academy, Piccadilly, W1. An extensive potpourri of much that is happening in British art. To Aug/Sept.

June

‡ **Beating Retreat**, Household Division, Horse Guards Parade, SW1. Military massed bands and marching. ‡ 1st Wed: **The Derby**, Epsom Downs. This great horse race is on common land, and so is attended by fairs, Gypsies, and huge crowds. ‡ **Beating Retreat**, Scottish Division, Horse Guards Parade, SW1. Military massed bands and marching. ‡ **Test match**, Lords, NW8. 5-day international cricket match. ‡ June 11 or nearest Sat: **Trooping the Colour**, Horse Guards Parade, SW1. The Queen leaves from Buckingham Palace in procession to receive the Colour from her Foot Guards amid full pageantry. ‡ 3rd Week: **Royal Ascot**. The Berkshire racecourse sees some fine racing; but more important for royalty on parade and "society" out to impress each other and have fun. ‡ 3rd Mon: **Garter Ceremony**, St George's Chapel, Windsor Castle. The 24 members of The Very Noble Order of the Garter attend a service, invest new members, and pay homage to the Queen. ‡ June 22 or near: **Election of the Sheriffs of the City of London**, Guildhall, EC2. Full pageantry and procession. ‡ June/July: **Wimbledon Tennis**

Championships. The world's top players. ‡ **Outdoor concerts**, in all major parks, Kenwood Lakeside, Hampstead Heath and Crystal Palace Bowl. Until Sept.

July

‡ 1st week: **Henley Royal Regatta**, Henley, Oxfordshire. Another sporting event (rowing) that is also part of the "season." ‡ **City of London Festival**, at various venues throughout the City. ‡ **Royal Tournament**, Earls Court, SW5. All the Armed Forces join in displays of gymnastics, motor-cycling and military skills. On the Sun before it begins, they all parade along a chosen route, sometimes in and sometimes outside London. ‡ **Promenade Concerts**, Royal Albert Hall, SW7. Until Sept. See *Concerts* in *Nightlife*. ‡ **Royal International Horse Show**, Wembley Arena. Show jumping. ‡ 3rd week: **Swan Upping**, the Thames, from Sunbury to Whitchurch. The Dyers' Company and Vintners' Company, which share ownership of all swans with the Queen, take 6 boats upriver counting and marking the birds. ‡ 2nd Wed: **Vintners Roadsweeping**. Wine porters sweep the road in front of a procession, from Vintners' Hall, Upper Thames St. to St James's Garlickhythe, EC4, at 11.58am, marking the inauguration of their new Master. ‡ **Doggett's Coat and Badge Race**. A race for single sculls rowing London Bridge-Chelsea against the tide, founded in 1714.

August

‡ **London Riding Horse Parade**, Rotten Row, Hyde Park. Moss Bros cup goes to best turned-out horse and rider. ‡ Bank Holiday Weekend (last in Aug): **Horse Show**, Clapham Common. **Bank Holiday Fair**, Hampstead Heath. A traditional fairground. The **Notting Hill Carnival**, Ladbroke Grove, W11. West Indian street carnival. ‡ Aug/Sept: **Test match**, Kennington Oval, SE11. 5-day international cricket.

September

‡ **Thamesday**. Celebration of the river held on the South Bank. Magnificent fireworks display. ‡ **Covent Garden Festival**. Street theater, music and a procession. ‡ **Last Night of the Proms**, Royal Albert Hall, SW7. See *Concerts* in *Nightlife*. ‡ **Chelsea Antiques**

Calendar of events

Fair, Chelsea Old Town Hall, King's Rd., SW3. ‡ Sept 21: **Christ's Hospital Boys March**, Church of the Holy Sepulchre, Holborn Viaduct, EC1. Pupils and band of this ancient school march to Mansion House in 16thC "bluecoats." ‡ **Private Fire Brigades' Competition**, EC4. See May ‡ Sept 28: **Admission of Sheriffs**. See June. In another ceremony, they are admitted to the Guildhall. ‡ Sept 29: **Election of the Lord Mayor**, Guildhall, EC2. Beforehand, the whole corporation proceeds from Mansion House.

October

‡ Oct 1 or 1st Mon: **Judges Service**, Westminster Abbey, SW1. At the start of the legal year, the judiciary processes from Westminster Abbey to breakfast in the Palace of Westminster, and then parades in the afternoon at the Royal Courts of Justice in the Strand, WC2. ‡ 1st Sun, 3pm: **Pearly Harvest Festival**, St Martin-in-the-Fields, WC2. The brightly caparisoned Pearly Kings and Queens, Cockney folk leaders, in full uniform. ‡ **Horse of the Year Show**, Wembley Arena. Show jumping, featuring top international competitors. ‡ 2nd Sun: **Harvest of the Sea Thanksgiving**, St Mary-at-Hill, EC3, 11am. Billingsgate dealers fill the church with fish, and the City attends in state. ‡ **Quit Rents Ceremony**, Royal Courts of Justice, WC2. An official receives token rents on behalf of the Queen; ceremony includes splitting sticks and counting horseshoes. ‡ Oct 21, or nearest Sun: **Trafalgar Day**. National Service for Seafarers at St Paul's Cathedral, attended by Admiralty top brass; and a naval ceremony in Trafalgar Sq., WC2. ‡ **National Brass Band Championships**, Royal Albert Hall, SW7. A type of music at which the British excel. ‡ Oct/Nov: **State Opening of Parliament**. The processional route is Buckingham Palace, The Mall, Horse Guards Parade, Palace of Westminster. The entire Royal Family attends; full regalia, ancient gilded coaches.

November

‡ 1st Sun: **London to Brighton Veteran Car Run**, Hyde Park Corner, SW1. An early start (8am) for the aged cars. ‡ Nov 5: **Guy Fawkes Night**. To celebrate the 1605 Gunpowder Plot to blow up Parliament, fireworks and bonfires all over town, with effigies of the conspiracy's leader burned on top. ‡ Sun nearest Nov 11: **Remembrance Sun**. The Queen and State attend an 11am ceremony at the Cenotaph, Whitehall, SW1. The previous evening there is a moving **Festival of Remembrance** at the Royal Albert Hall, SW7. ‡ Fri nearest Nov 12: **Admission of Lord Mayor Elect**, Guildhall, EC2. The outgoing mayor hands over the insignia. ‡ Sat nearest Nov 12: **Lord Mayor's Show**, Guildhall to Law Courts, Strand, WC2. The state coaches follow the many colorful floats in this huge carnival. ‡ **London Film Festival**, National Film Theatre, South Bank. To Dec. ‡ **Benson & Hedges Tennis Championships**, Wembley Arena. ‡ Late Nov: **Switching on of Christmas lights** in Regent St. and Oxford St. Until Jan 6.

December

‡ **Royal Smithfield Show**, Earls Court, SW5. Agricultural show. ‡ **Norwegian Christmas Tree**, Trafalgar Sq. Carol-singing on most evenings beneath the tree. ‡ Dec 31: **Watch Night**, St Paul's Cathedral. Scots gather on steps for Hogmanay. Trafalgar Sq. is the other traditional spot for high-spirited revelers, and Parliament Sq. for watching Big Ben strike at midnight.

Weekly events

‡ Mon: Bric-a-brac and antiques at **Covent Garden** market. ‡ Wed: **Camden Passage** antique market. Late-night shopping in **Knightsbridge** (see *Shopping*). Some theater matinees. ‡ Thurs: Late-night shopping in **Oxford St.** and **Regent St.** Some theater matinees. ‡ Fri: **Bermondsey** (New Caledonian) antique market (see *Shopping*). ‡ Sat: **Portobello Rd.** antique market and **Covent Garden** crafts market (see *Shopping*). Theater matinees. Evening open-air concerts in June-July at **Kenwood House**, Hampstead Heath. ‡ Sun: **Petticoat Lane**, **Camden Lock** markets (see *Shopping*).

Daily events

‡ 11am (10am Sun): **Changing the Guard**, Horse Guards Parade. ‡ 11.30am (only alternate days in winter): **Changing the Guard**, Buckingham Palace. ‡ 9.50pm: **Ceremony of the Keys**, Tower of London. Ceremonial changing of guards. Write to Resident Governor for free ticket.

When and where to go

Unlike the folks of some cities, Londoners do not all choose to take their vacations at the same time, so the capital never "closes down." It does, on the other hand, become very crowded at the height of summer. Consider sidestepping this stampede: the British climate may be unpredictable, but it is rarely extreme, and London, being in one of the mildest parts of the country, can be very pleasant in the spring and fall. Moreover, a whole series of outdoor sporting (and social) events takes place from March onward (see *Calendar of events*).

Outdoor institutions, such as the open-air theater in *Regent's Park*, begin to brave the elements in May, and in the same month Glyndebourne's opera season starts. The crowded months are July and August, but theater-lovers will want to avoid the summer in favor of fall and winter, often better times for new shows and certainly for accommodations.

Even in winter, London remains alive with activity, and several of the main exhibitions take place at this time of year. One famous winter institution that London has cast aside is the pea-soup fog, vanquished by clean-air legislation, and little else remains to stop Londoners going about their daily rounds.

The main airport is on the western side of the city, and the longer rail and road routes run into the west and north. Those compass points have a powerful influence on activity in London. The greatest number of hotels is found in the west, in suburbs such as *Chiswick*, inner districts such as *Kensington*, *Chelsea* and Victoria, or in the West End, the area that most Londoners regard as the center by virtue of its shops, restaurants and theaters.

Farther east, the *City*, although it is jeweled with historical sights, is seen by the Londoner as being primarily a business district that empties in the evenings and on weekends. In much the way that the City is a buffer to the east, so is the river to the south. The implantation of the *Barbican* Centre in the City and the *South Bank Arts Centre* across the river were both conscious attempts to extend the geographical spread of nocturnal life. Beyond these outriders, however, central London fades in the City and only half-heartedly crosses the Thames. Central London does not formally define itself, but most inhabitants would probably accept the Circle line on the tube system as a fair boundary.

Few Londoners live within that circle, however, and their residential districts outside it are the source of much local rivalry. Not only does the topography of fashionable northern suburbs such as *Hampstead* and *Highgate* provide their inhabitants with elevated notions, but it is also true that many Londoners feign disinclination to cross the river. Certainly many of the "south-of-the-river" districts closer to London have little to recommend them to visitors, although among these are some residential enclaves that have become fashionable in recent years. Nevertheless there is only one recommended tourist hotel at present south of the river; nor indeed are there many to the east of *Tower Bridge*. So for accommodations the visitor has generally to stick to the center, the north or the west.

Each of the compass points appears in the beginning of the postal codes and is also printed on street signs. Much of the West End is W1 (West One), addresses in the City usually carry EC (East Central), and so on. Nevertheless the system is not as logical as it might be and spoken directions will tend to be given in terms of the area's or the district's name. Many of the most interesting of these areas are described in the A-Z of *Sights and places of interest*.

Orientation map

Area planners

The City

Home not only of Mammon (in the Bank of England and the *Stock Exchange*) but also of God (in *St Paul's Cathedral* and the numerous churches). The *Royal Courts of Justice* and the *Old Bailey* are to be found in the City, and the whole square mile is guarded by the *Tower of London*.

The West End

Unlike the City, the West End has no precise borders, although it is divided by its main thoroughfares into clearly-defined neighborhoods. Simply by crossing the street it is possible to leave behind a neighborhood of one quite distinct character and enter what seems to be another world. See *Orientation map* on pages 36-37 for area limits.

Mayfair is the neighborhood of exclusive hotels, expense-account restaurants, embassies, haute couture houses and casinos, and its denizens usually ride in chauffeur-driven cars. Its "village" shopping street is Bond St., with South Molton St. for the younger folks, and North and South Audley Sts. for the extra-extravagant. In hilly, elegant Brook, Mount and Curzon Sts. are smaller, old-established, conspicuously exclusive shops. The alleys of Shepherd Market offer sidewalk cafés for rest and refreshment on sunny days.

Soho is seductive not for its sex stores, which are no more inviting nor less sleazy than those in any other city, but for its delicatessens, pâtisseries, moderately priced restaurants, and a gossipy confluence of Italian waiters, Cockney editors, lengthy lunchers and other miscreants. Its trendiness has long attracted media folk. Across Shaftesbury Ave., its cosmopolitanism hardens into Chinatown.

Covent Garden has, despite the misgivings of purists, proved to be one of the most successful examples anywhere of a discarded facility (in this instance a wholesale fruit-and-vegetable market) being turned into an area for strolling, eating and shopping. The most fiercely community-conscious of all the inner city areas, it has come to stand for everything opposed to big business and development.

Bloomsbury has a bookish dignity that once hid all manner of intensity. It also has the *British Museum* and the nucleus of London University, whose visitors and students find peace in its many green squares.

Belgravia is the most elegant part of the West End, with its early 19thC houses; Belgrave Sq., from which it takes its name, has beautiful gardens. Even the very rich who have always lived here are feeling the pinch, and today the area is dominated by embassies. Belgravia's "neighbourhood shop" is Harrods; around the corner is Knightsbridge.

St James's is gentlemen's clubland, with Jermyn St. as its shopping thoroughfare. The name is broadly applied to the neighborhood around St James's St., and St James's Sq., on the hill running down from Piccadilly to *St James's Palace*, constituting an area that has perhaps changed less than any other over the last 50 years.

Westminster is media shorthand for Parliament, in much the way that *Whitehall* is used to denote the Civil Service and *Downing Street* to suggest the Prime Minister. Apart from *Westminster Abbey*, all the dominant buildings in this area are concerned with government. There are no shops and very few residents — just a rich seam of pomp and circumstance.

Inner London

Beyond central London, several inner districts make their own unique contributions to metropolitan life. The most obvious are the two that give their name to the Royal Borough of Kensington and Chelsea. *Kensington*, with its famous museums, also extends to Notting Hill and Portobello Rd., eventually giving way to Hammersmith, which has a couple of respected theaters. *Chelsea*, elegant and fashionable, with its clothes stores and restaurants, spills over into Fulham.

All these districts are in the w; in the N, Islington has emerged as the outstanding example of the arty rejuvenation of London's old working-class inner boroughs.

Outer London

Intellectual *Hampstead* and *Highgate* in the N, maritime *Greenwich* in the E, villagey *Dulwich* in the s, riverside *Richmond* in the w.... All are to varying degrees outer districts, although London stretches yet farther in an exhausting sprawl of mainly 1930s suburbs.

Walks in London

Although London is vast in area, it is also a marvelous city for taking a walk. Perhaps the chief reason for this is the close proximity of its many separate and characterful neighborhoods, and a number of these — *Chelsea*, *Holland Park*, Little Venice, *Greenwich*, *Hampstead*, among others — make walks in themselves (see A-Z of *Sights and places of interest*).

In a city that reached its prime before the days of motor transportation, walking is also, naturally, the most effective way to see and learn about London. For information about walks for this purpose — routes, subjects of theme walks, starting times — contact the **London Tourist Board and Convention Bureau** (☎ 730-3488). The following companies organize walking tours:

London Walks   ☎(081) 441-8906
Citisights   ☎739-2372
Historical Tours   ☎(081) 668-4109
Cockney Walks   ☎(081) 504-9159
Footloose in London   ☎435-0259

The walks described in detail on the following pages have a different and special purpose: to give a taste of a Londoner's London — its river, parks and pubs, and its cultural, especially literary, heart.

There is no quick way of getting to know London. But as an introduction to this historic city, or to refresh the memory after a long absence, the following stroll through its City of Westminster, center of government and tradition and cornerstone of the West End, links many of London's most famous landmarks and also serves as a convenient orientation tour.

Walk 1: Introduction to London
*Allow 2-3hrs. Tube: Westminster. Maps **9-10**.*

Begin by walking along Bridge St., past the statue of Queen Boadicea, symbol of patriotism, on to Westminster Bridge itself, from where the best view of the *Palace of Westminster* and **Big Ben** can be gained. Look also to your right along the Victoria Embankment to see the fine government buildings. Let your gaze move around in full circle to cross the river with the Charing Cross railway bridge; beyond it is the *South Bank Arts Centre* and, on this side, County Hall, old headquarters of the now defunct Greater London Council. The panorama continues past the huge stone lion at the E end of Westminster Bridge to the modern St Thomas' Hospital, and crosses the river again by Lambeth Bridge.

From the foot of Big Ben, walk back around the W side of the Palace of Westminster past Westminster Hall. Then cross over the road to St Margaret's Church to arrive at *Westminster Abbey*.

Continue around Parliament Sq. almost to Bridge St. again, before turning left into Parliament St., which leads to *Whitehall*. The second street on the left, past the Cenotaph, is *Downing Street*, where the policeman at the door identifies "Number 10." Going N along Whitehall, the *Banqueting House* (1622) is on the right, nearly opposite the Whitehall entrance to *Horse Guards Parade*. At the N of Whitehall is *Trafalgar Square*, which is dominated by **Nelson's Column** and is a crowded area of constant activity.

As you cross the square toward the *National Gallery*, with its controversial new Sainsbury Wing extension, notice also James Gibbs' beautiful church of *St Martin-in-the-Fields* (1726). St Martin's Pl., in front and to the right of the church, has the central Post Office on its right; to the N, up St Martin's Lane, is the globe-topped spire of the **Coliseum**, home of the English National Opera (see *Nightlife*). Leading around to the left, however, past the entrance to the *National Portrait Gallery*, is Charing Cross Rd. Follow this road as far as Leicester Square tube station, then turn left along Cranbourn St. into **Leicester Sq**. itself.

The route continues along the N side of Leicester Sq. as far as the Swiss Centre, where a right turn up Wardour St. leads past Lisle St. and Gerrard St., the two main arteries of **Chinatown**, to Shaftesbury Ave., the heart of theaterland and the southern boundary of **Soho**. Turn left on Shaftesbury Ave. and walk down to **Piccadilly Circus**.

Arriving at Piccadilly Circus, pause a moment to orient yourself between Shaftesbury Ave., Regent St., curving majestically to the W and N and *Piccadilly* itself, leading W toward *Mayfair, Belgravia* and Knightsbridge. It is the fourth major street that you must follow: go down Lower Regent St. to the S, which borders *St James's* on the right, and crosses Pall Mall to the Duke of York Monument, at the top of the steps down past the elegant and imposing **Carlton House Terrace** to *The Mall*.

At the foot of the steps look left toward Admiralty Arch, and Trafalgar Square beyond it. Notice also the ivy-clad wartime extension to the Admiralty, the Citadel, beyond which can be seen the expanse of Horse Guards Parade. Then walk W along The Mall, with *St James's Park* on your left, toward the gilded **Victoria Memorial** and beyond it *Buckingham Palace*, passing *Marlborough House*, *St James's Palace*, Clarence House and *Lancaster House* on the way. Walk around the S side of Buckingham Palace to Buckingham Gate and Buckingham Palace Rd., to the entrances to the **Queen's Picture Gallery** and the **Royal Mews**.

To complete the walk, either continue along Buckingham Palace Rd. to Victoria Station, or retrace your steps to follow Birdcage Walk along the S side of St James's Park in front of the recently restored Wellington Barracks. The first street on the right, **Queen Anne's Gate**, leads to St James's Park tube station. To continue along Birdcage Walk into Great George St. takes you to **Parliament Square** and Westminster tube station, where the walk began.

Walk 2: London's cultural heart
Allow 1-2hrs. Tube: Temple. Map 10-11.

The central areas of *Covent Garden* and *Bloomsbury* have always been nurseries of artistic endeavor and achievement, as this walks reveals.

Begin at the Aldwych, where **Bush House**, facing up Kingsway, is an appropriate symbol of British cultural prestige; from this building the BBC runs its foreign radio services. On the right, Houghton St. leads to Portugal St., and **The Old Curiosity Shop**. It is not certain that Dickens based his novel on this antique store, but he knew it well.

Back on the Aldwych, turn up **Drury Lane**. The **Theatre Royal**, down Russell St. to the left and on the corner of Catherine St., was founded in 1663. Also in **Russell St**. were the famous coffeehouses of the 18thC; Dr Johnson and Boswell first met in a bookstore at no. 8 in 1763.

Drury Lane continues until it turns into Museum St. and pushes on into more elegant *Bloomsbury*, passing on the right in Bloomsbury Way the church of **St George**, which was used by Dickens as the setting for his Bloomsbury christening in *Sketches by Boz*.

Return to Museum St. and turn right. At the far end is the **Museum Tavern**, at different times favored by Karl Marx and Dylan Thomas. Turn left here, past the *British Museum*, and then right into Bloomsbury St., passing the peaceful and unspoiled **Bedford Sq**., the home at times of many distinguished people and therefore of a crop of blue plaques. Continue down Gower St., pausing to see the statues of tragedy and comedy outside the **Royal Academy of Dramatic Art**.

A right turn into Torrington Pl. passes Dillon's University Bookshop and Woburn Sq. on the right. Gordon Sq., on the left, was a stamping ground of the Bloomsbury Group. Torrington Pl. leads on to Tavistock Sq.; the garden in the square has as its focal point a statue of Mahatma Gandhi, and a tree planted by Pandit Nehru.

Turn left along the far side of the square to Upper Woburn Pl. On the right, a blue plaque marks the site where Dickens lived from 1851-60, now the headquarters of the British Medical Association. Farther on the right, turn into **Woburn Walk**, with its bow-front shops and brass plaque in memory of the poet W.B. Yeats, who lived here at the turn of the century.

A left turn leads back to Euston Rd., for a bus or tube.

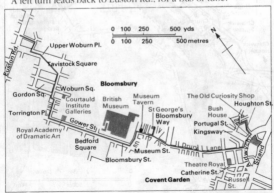

Walk 3: A riverside stroll
Allow 1-2hrs. Tube: Hammersmith. Map 20C4.
Upstream from central London, the Thames gradually abandons
business for pleasure. As much of the route is unpaved you will
need suitable footwear in wet weather.

From Hammersmith tube station, Queen Caroline St. leads
straight to the river. Glance to your left, where, on the site of an
old police car pound, a remarkable 10-story building, designed
by Ralph Erskine to house a community center, is due to be
completed in March 1991. Plans reveal a curved copper roof,
observation dome, inclined glass curtain walls and traditional
brick and timber facings, suggesting a high-tech Noah's Ark.
Detour left into Crisp Rd. to visit **Riverside Studios** for a drink or
snack, or a look at the art gallery or bookstore. Cross the river by
Hammersmith Bridge and turn right for a surprisingly rustic walk
along the overgrown bank to the **Bull's Head** pub at Barnes, or
stay on the N side for historical and architectural interest.

Hammersmith Bridge is one of the most attractive on the
river, a suspension bridge built in 1887. Just under the bridge are
several balconied houses and boathouses, and there are a couple
of pubs next door to each other on this stretch of the river; the
most interesting is the **Blue Anchor**.

Just beyond the pubs, a small area of park opens out, and on
the right is **Wescott Lodge** (1700), a former vicarage. Farther
away to the right, across the main road, is the handsome 1930s
facade of **Hammersmith Town Hall**.

On the river, an ugly iron jetty marks the spot, indicated by a
plaque, where a creek and a small natural harbor gave birth to
the village of Hammersmith. The path winds to the right, then an
inlet to the left leads suddenly into a tiny Georgian street that
once lay at the heart of Hammersmith, **Upper Mall**. On the left is
the **Dove** pub, and on the right is **Kelmscott House**, once the
home of William Morris. Over the coach-house door is a sign
commemorating the Hammersmith socialists. The building is still
the headquarters of the William Morris Society, and also
witnessed the first demonstration of the electric telegraph.

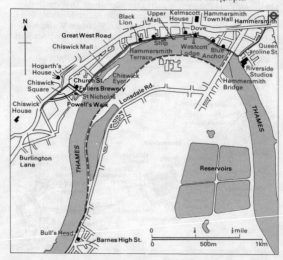

The riverside walk continues past the crow's-nest lookout post of the Corinthian Sailing Club, through a modern cloister-like construction under a block of apartments, past the balconied **Ship** pub, a pumping station and another called the **Black Lion**; this 400yr-old pub has associations with the humorist and essayist A.P. Herbert.

Leaving behind a panoramic view of the river, the path then deserts the Thames for a moment to follow the fine Georgian **Hammersmith Terrace**. As the river comes back into view, from Chiswick Mall a ramp can be seen from which it is possible to walk at low tide to a small island, **Chiswick Eyot**. On the right is Fuller's brewery, then **St Nicholas** church, where Whistler and Hogarth are buried. Enter the churchyard from the river and the tomb of Hogarth is on the left, surrounded by a railing. Walk around the church into the graveyard, and the bronze tomb of Whistler is near the ivy-covered wall. The path leading out of the church, Powells Walk, leads to a main road, Burlington Lane, across which is *Chiswick House*. Back on the opposite side of the church, Church St. leads to **Chiswick Sq**., on the left, said to be the scene of an episode in Thackeray's *Vanity Fair*. Around the corner is *Hogarth's House*.

Walk 4: The parks
Allow 1-3hrs. Use maps 6-10 to enjoy the parks and wander off this skeleton route. Tube: Piccadilly Circus.
A few minutes' walk from Piccadilly Circus tube station, London's royal parks begin. They spread themselves airily to *Kensington*.

Stroll down Lower Regent St. to its end, passing the Crimean War memorial and crossing *Pall Mall* into **Waterloo Pl**. Descend the steps to *The Mall*, with the **Institute of Contemporary Arts** on the left and the Admiralty building diagonally across the road. Cross the road, and enter *St James's Park*.

This small but pretty park is dominated by its lake, alive with waterfowl. Follow the lake to the opposite end of the park to leave by the gateway to the right, in front of *Buckingham Palace*. Renegotiate The Mall to enter **Green Park**, opposite. Walk diagonally across this hilly little park, and bear left to enter the pedestrian subway passage at Hyde Park Corner.

The tunnel emerges by the triumphal **Wellington Arch**, on an island of history surrounded by a tangled urban road system. It is best to leave this island, after a look at its imposing monuments, by another subway, this one signposted for Hyde Park Corner tube station. Bypassing the station itself, emerge by *Hyde Park*, backtracking to enter by the triple archway, then take one final tunnel to arrive in grassy safety. On this corner is *Apsley House*.

Inside the park, the thoroughfare to the left is **Rotten Row**, for horseback riders. Straight ahead is the path leading to the **Serpentine**, the descriptively named lake popular for boating (*adequate* ☞). Follow the lake as far as the bridge carrying the main road, and cross to the other bank. A few steps beyond the bridge is the **Serpentine Gallery**, noted for exhibitions of contemporary artists. Behind it are paths to the bandstand and Round Pond, with a striking view en route of the *Albert Memorial and Royal Albert Hall*. Return to the water's edge, on the Kensington side, to see the Art Nouveau statue of Peter Pan, whose whimsy pervades the gardens. At the head of the waters is a paved garden, and beyond them the Elfin Oak, a tree-stump carved with elves. Don't leave without visiting *Kensington Palace*. From here, it is not far to Bayswater or Kensington High St. tube station, to the N and S respectively.

Sights and places of interest

London's major sights are every bit as enjoyable as their worldwide reputation suggests, but this is also a city of wonderful diversity, so try to take in some of the less well-known attractions too. Opening hours are fairly regularly adhered to, though entry may not be allowed near closing time. Churches' hours vary rather more, especially in the City, and they are always subject to closure for services. Rules on photography vary, but often only flash is prohibited: look for our 🖼 symbol. The ✱ symbol denotes places of interest to children.

Major sights classified by type

Ancient buildings
Apsley House
Banqueting House
Buckingham Palace
Chiswick House
Eltham Palace
Fenton House
Gray's Inn
Guildhall
Ham House
Hampton Court
Kensington Palace
Kenwood House
Lambeth Palace
Lancaster House
Leighton House
Lincoln's Inn
Mansion House
Marble Hill House
Marlborough House
Orleans House
Osterley Park
Royal Hospital, Chelsea
Royal Navy College, Greenwich
St James's Palace
Staple Inn
Syon House
Temple
Tower of London
Westminster, Palace of

Churches
Brompton Oratory
St Bartholomew-the-Great
St George's, Bloomsbury
St James's, Piccadilly
St Martin-in-the-Fields
St Mary Abchurch
St Mary-le-Bow
St Mary-le-Strand
St Paul's, Covent Garden
St Paul's Cathedral
St Stephen Walbrook
Southwark Cathedral
Westminster Abbey
Westminster Cathedral

Districts
Belgravia
Bloomsbury
Chelsea
Chiswick
The City
Covent Garden
Docklands
Greenwich

Hampstead
Highgate
Kensington
Mayfair
Richmond
St James's
Soho
Westminster

Museums and galleries
Apsley House/Wellington Museum
HMS Belfast
Bethnal Green Museum
The British Museum
Commonwealth Institute
Courtauld Institute Galleries
Design Museum
Dickens' House
Dulwich College/Picture Gallery
Geffrye Museum
Hogarth's House
Imperial War Museum
Dr. Johnson's House
Keats' House
Kenwood House/Iveagh Bequest
London, Museum of
London Transport Museum
Madame Tussaud's
Mankind, Museum of
National Army Museum
National Gallery
National Maritime Museum, Greenwich
National Portrait Gallery
Natural History Museum
Public Record Office Museum
Royal Academy of Arts
Royal Air Force Museum, Hendon
Royal Britain
Science Museum
Shakespeare Globe Museum
Sir John Soane's Museum
Tate Gallery
Theatre Museum
Victoria & Albert Museum
Wallace Collection
Whitechapel Art Gallery

Parks/gardens
Holland Park
Hyde Park
Kew Gardens
Regent's Park
Richmond Park
St James's Park
Zoo

Albert Memorial and Royal Albert Hall 🏛
Kensington Gore, SW7 ☎ 589-8212. Map 15I4. Tube: Knightsbridge, South Kensington.

These fine examples of Victoriana are dedicated to Victoria's consort, who encouraged the institutionalization of arts and sciences that gives this corner of *Kensington* its character. The **Albert Hall** was erected in 1867-71. Its bold, simple red outline is offset by a solemn ceramic frieze showing the triumph of the arts and sciences. The huge amphitheater is used for everything from boxing to concerts, notably the summer "Prom" season (see *Nightlife*); visitors are allowed in when the hall is not in use.

Although the ornate spire of the **Albert Memorial** across the road sits uneasily on the huge Gothic canopy, and although the statue of Albert himself is utterly uninspired, there are endless details to admire in the inventive *mélange* of granite, marble, bronze and semiprecious stones.

Apsley House, The Wellington Museum 🏛 ☆
149 Piccadilly, W1 ☎ 499-5676. Map 9H8 ▣ ✗ Open Tues-Sun 11am-5pm. Tube: Hyde Park Corner.

Once the first of a row of aristocratic houses a traveler from the w would encounter when approaching the city, and hence known as "No. 1, London," Apsley House still puts on a brave show, despite being surrounded on three sides by London's busiest roads. Inside, the visitor is still assured of calm in the majestic rooms once occupied by the Duke of Wellington, Britain's greatest soldier.

Built by Robert Adam in 1771-78 for Baron Apsley, the brick-fronted mansion was bought in 1807 by Lord Wellesley, Wellington's elder brother, who sold it to the duke in 1817. Wellington transformed the elegant house into a palace with the help of his architect Benjamin Wyatt, who clad the exterior with Bath stone and added the large portico in 1828; the house was clearly intended to impress at a time when the duke's political career was at its height (he was prime minister from 1828-30). And impress it did — during the Reform crisis of 1832, a mob stoned the house, and iron shutters replaced the windows.

Because of the transformation, two complementary styles are to be found in the interior. Adam's work has a fine elegance, whereas Wyatt's changes and additions are on a grander scale. This contrast is not too obvious on the ground floor, where the duke's fine collection of porcelain and dinner services are displayed in rooms that retain some air of domesticity, but it strikes one forcibly on reaching the stairwell, where the graceful curve of Adam's design is offset by Wyatt's heavy and ornate banister. The stair now houses Antonio Canova's massive Neo-Classical statue of the nude *Napoleon as a Roman Emperor.*

The best example of Adam's interior work is the **Piccadilly Drawing Room** at the top of the stairs, with its vaulted ceiling, decorated with characteristically delicate Classical moldings, and curved apsidal E end. Wyatt's work is best seen in the splendid **Waterloo Gallery**, with an elaborate ceiling in his grand "Versailles" manner. The eight large windows have shutters that slide out to reveal mirrors, turning the room into a glittering hall of light in the evenings. The **Dining Room**, also on the first floor, was adapted by Wyatt from 1816-29 to house the fantastic table service given to Wellington to commemorate his Portuguese victories by the Prince Regent of Portugal in 1816. The complete service consisted of about 1,000 pieces, of which the most important is the centerpiece, on the large oak table.

Banqueting House

The fine paintings at Apsley House are largely those of the first duke, with a few additions and loans. Velázquez dominates the Spanish collections with *A Spanish Gentleman* and the profoundly serene *Water Carrier of Seville* (Waterloo Gallery). Murillo and Ribera are also represented, as are many Dutch and Flemish artists: look for Jan Vermeer of Haarlem's *Landscape with Bleaching Grounds* (Yellow Drawing Room) and Elsheimer's haunting *Judith and Holofernes* (Piccadilly Drawing Room). There are many portraits of Wellington's illustrious contemporaries, including several of Napoleon and an equestrian study of the duke himself painted by Goya (Waterloo Gallery).

A new gallery in the basement is devoted to the duke himself, using prints, costumes and other memorabilia. The museum also stages public concerts and lectures, as well as two annual festivals, a Christmas festival and a Battle of Waterloo festival. The latter, held around June 15, brings history alive with costumed re-enactments of the events of 1815.

Banqueting House 🏛 ★
Whitehall, SW1 ☎ 930-4179. Map 10H11 🚇 Open Tues-Sat 10am-5pm, Sun 2-5pm. Closed occasionally on short notice. Tube: Westminster, Charing Cross.
The old prints in the entrance hall show this superb Palladian building as the focal point of the great royal palace of Whitehall. The single hall to survive a fire of 1688, it is today in a very different setting, across busy *Whitehall* from *Horse Guards Parade* and dominated by large government offices. Built by Inigo Jones in 1619-22, the Banqueting House has a flamboyance, but also a classical solemnity and clarity of design, that was entirely novel in its day.

On the ceiling are the giant canvases commissioned from Rubens by Charles I of the apotheosis of his predecessor and father, James I. Installed in 1635, their incredible scale and vigorous movement are entirely Baroque in feeling, contrasting strongly with Jones' Classicism. Rubens received a knighthood and a pension; Charles I, ironically, was led to his execution in 1649 from the window of this hall.

Barbican
☎ 628-8795 (box office), 638-4141 (information). Map 12E15. Tube: Barbican, Moorgate.
The Barbican now rises as London's boldest piece of Utopian planning. It was a barren bomb site when, in 1956, it was chosen to reintroduce housing to the almost totally commercial center of the City. On a bad day, it can seem grim and forbidding, a monument to the failed dreams of modern architecture, but it does have a certain excitement, with angular towers soaring upward and walkways sweeping across. And sometimes the concrete comes to life: the Barbican Centre contains the London Symphony Orchestra's concert hall, the Royal Shakespeare Company's two theaters (see *Nightlife*), a cinema, a gallery, conference halls, a roof garden, and cafeterias and restaurants; there are also lobby concerts and exhibitions. Opened in 1982, its complex design and sumptuous interior constitute the largest social and arts center in Europe. Here too is the superbly designed new Museum of London (see *London, Museum of*).

Incongruously, bastions remain of the old City wall, and the church of **St Giles Cripplegate**, whose gutted shell survived the fire-bombing. The 15thC tower is surmounted with a brick top story of 1683 and an attractive central turret and weather vane.

Battersea
Map 21D4. Train to Battersea from Waterloo, or bus no. 19, 39, 45, 49.

Little remains of the old Thameside village of Battersea, part of which is now an industrial sprawl and part a gentrified residential area. Down by the river, **Battersea Park** is well laid out, with sculptures by Henry Moore and Barbara Hepworth, and is the site of the Easter Parade (see *Calendar of events*). Overlooking the river is an attractive **Japanese Peace Pagoda** completed in 1985. A dominant and increasingly admired landmark is the vast **power station**, brick-built in the modern, monumental style of the 1930s. It is currently a sad although still proud shell, its proposed conversion into a huge indoor theme park having been halted due to lack of finance.

A new Battersea landmark is the vast marble-faced *Observer* newspaper building, erected on the s side of Battersea Bridge.

HMS Belfast
Morgan's Lane, Tooley St., SE1 ☎ 407-6434. Map 13G17 ☒ Open daily Apr-Sept 10am-6pm, Oct-Mar 10.30am-4.30pm. Tube: London Bridge.

One of several attractions in the area known as *Bridge City*, this World War II warship, a Southampton-class cruiser, saw action in the Battle of North Cape in 1943, when the *Scharnhorst* was sunk, in the Normandy landings and even in the Korean War. Now she is a floating tribute to all that, and to wartime naval life in general. Conditions on board were cramped, and the visitor has to weave and duck through hatches and up ladders (very tricky with young children), but the imagination can run riot on the navigation bridge or next to the massive main guns. The new audio commentary tour, whereby you can experience the atmosphere and sounds of active service (*for hire for a small extra charge*), also boosts the imagination.

Belgravia
Map 16&17H-K. Tube: Hyde Park Corner, Knightsbridge, Sloane Square, Victoria.

London's most magnificent terraces, once the town houses of dukes, make up the great squares of Belgravia, the area around Belgrave Sq. developed by Thomas Cubitt in a frenzy of activity following the establishment of nearby *Buckingham Palace* as the royal residence in the 1820s.

Belgrave Square itself forms the centerpiece of the fairly regular plan, with its massive Classically decorated blocks by George Basevi and grand corner houses by other architects surrounding the private sunken gardens. Eaton Sq., to the s, is a long rectangle, with the King's Rd. running through the middle of its stuccoed terraces. To the s again is Chester Sq., to some eyes the most appealing of the three.

In Motcomb St., Seth-Smith's Doric-fronted pantechnicon of 1830 looks back on Wilton Crescent, built by the same architect 3yrs earlier. For refreshment, go to **The Grenadier** (see *Pubs*).

Bethnal Green Museum of Childhood ☆
Cambridge Heath Rd., E2 ☎ 980-2415. Map 21C5 ☒ ✳Open Mon-Thurs, Sat 10am-5.50pm, Sun 2.30-5.50pm. Tube: Bethnal Green.

In the heart of the authentic East End, off the usual tourist track, this museum was opened in 1872 as a branch of the *Victoria & Albert Museum*. There are numerous old toys to study, including board games, toy ships, trains, dolls and puppets from many periods. The **Tate Baby House** stands out, a fully furnished Georgian mansion in miniature dating from about 1760.

The galleries upstairs include wonderful collections of children's clothes, books, educational toys and furniture.

Blackheath
Map 21D5. Train to Blackheath from Charing Cross.
This common near the royal residences of *Greenwich* and *Eltham Palace* used to be as grim a place as its name suggests. In the 18thC it became a fashionable country address. Now the refreshingly open, high clearing is surrounded by the fine, plain and elegantly unadorned Classical houses of that period. On the SE side, a semicircular arrangement, known as the **Paragon**, is quite stunning. Probably dating from the 1780s, it consists of a series of blocks linked by single-story colonnaded arcades.

To the NE of Blackheath is the superb red-brick **Charlton House** (✪ ☎ *(081) 856-3951* ▣ ✗ *open by appt. only, Mon-Fri*), the best Jacobean house in London (now a community center). Built in 1607-12, it is entirely regular, with a central arched doorway, exuberant Mannerist carvings, and flanking towers.

Bloomsbury
Map 4C-E. Tube: Euston, Russell Square, Holborn.
Bloomsbury, like so many other areas of London, is a "village" with a reputation. The Bloomsbury Group was as well known for its mores as for its writings, but its patch of London remains the literary capital, housing a host of publishing companies and centered on London University and the *British Museum*. It is also enjoyed for its Georgian squares.

One of the most fashionable addresses in the 18thC, Bloomsbury was an inconspicuous residential area when Virginia and Leonard Woolf, Roger Fry, Lytton Strachey and Maynard Keynes made it their fortress from 1904-39. Before long, other voices were heard there: T.S. Eliot, Bertrand Russell and D.H. Lawrence were inevitably drawn to the center of the action, even if they did not agree with "The Group."

Bloomsbury Sq. is where it all began, when the Earl of Southampton built a palace for himself there in 1660. No original building survives, although the gardens are pleasant. **Bedford Square**, to the W past *St George's, Bloomsbury*, was built in 1775; it survives virtually intact as London's finest square. Its terraces of plain houses are built of dark brick with stucco pedimented centers. The lush garden is exquisite, although private. The much larger Russell Sq., at the top of Bedford Pl., with its huge plane trees, has fared less well. South of the square, the enchanting streets around Museum St. are full of secondhand bookstores. To the N, Woburn, Gordon and Tavistock Squares all boast good gardens and some terraces surviving from the early 19thC. A short walk to the E brings you to the **Jewish Museum** (☎ *388-4525* ▣ *open Tues-Fri, Sun 10am-4pm, Oct-Mar Fri 10am-12.45pm*) and Cartwright Gdns., with a fine crescent-shaped terrace. A little farther on is Brunswick Sq., a major modern public housing development with brutal but interesting architecture, and the *Coram Foundation*.

The University has buildings throughout Bloomsbury, of which the best is the oldest, the original **University College** in Gower St. It is a splendid Classical building with dome and portico, dating from 1827-29. The Senate House in Malet St., by contrast, is an essay in 1930s Classicism. Also within this "open campus" is the University Church of Christ the King in Gordon Sq., 1853 Gothic with an impressive cathedral-like interior. Also in Gordon Sq. is the *Percival David Foundation of Chinese Art*.

Looming over Bloomsbury, the *British Telecom Tower* in Cleveland St. is a familiar landmark.

Bridge City
London Bridge, SE1. Map 13G16. Tube: Monument, London Bridge.

Bridge City refers to the group of tourist attractions close to *London Bridge*. You might arrive by tube, visit whichever sights you want, eat and shop in **Hay's Galleria**, with its giant kinetic sculpture, *Navigators*, and depart by River Bus from London Bridge Pier. Sights grouped between London Bridge and *Tower Bridge* include **HMS Belfast**, **Space Adventure**, the **London Dungeon** and **Southwark Cathedral**. Just across London Bridge is Butlers Wharf and the *Design Museum*.

St Mary Overy Dock, in the shadow of London Bridge, is home to the *Schooner Kathleen and May*, the last surviving 3-masted topsail schooner (🎫 *open Mon-Fri 10am-5pm, Sat, Sun 11am-4pm*). Nearby is the **Clink Exhibition** (*1 Clink St.* 🎫 *open daily 10am-6pm*), the story of the original Clink Prison and bishops' licensed brothels (*not for children*). Well worth a visit, although not for the faint-hearted, is the fascinating but chilling early 19thC **Operating Theatre and Herb Garret** of St Thomas' and Guy's hospitals, discovered in the 1950s (🎫 *open Mon, Wed, Fri 12.30-4pm*).

British Museum 🏛 ★
Great Russell St., WC1 ☎ 636-1555. Map 10E11 🔲 🖭 Open Mon-Sat 10am-5pm, Sun 2.30-6pm. Tube: Russell Square, Tottenham Court Road.

Despite its age and venerable traditions, the British Museum is constantly changing, for this is one of the most adventurous of the world's great museums. It was founded in 1753 around the 80,000 items collected by Sir Hans Sloane, a successful physician. Sloane's will allowed the nation to purchase his collection for £20,000, well below its value, thus beginning a sequence of generous bequests. The nucleus consisted of Sloane's broad-ranging cabinet of curiosities: zoological and mineral specimens, antiquities, manuscripts, books and drawings. Natural history was best represented, but in time the museum became oriented more toward archeology.

In 1823 George III's huge library was given to the nation by his heir and the decision was taken to build a new and grand edifice to display the nation's collected treasures. With the young Robert Smirke as architect, the intention was to create a Neo-Classical structure around a quadrangle, completed by 1838, and later filled-in with the famous Reading Room (see p52).

The move of the natural history exhibits to the *Natural History Museum* in the 1880s and the ethnographic exhibits to the Museum of Mankind (see *Mankind, Museum of*) in 1970 has solved much of the museum's space problem.

A comprehensive catalog would fill a bookcase. However, a selective visit should include the following.

Greece and Rome ★
The best place to start a visit; turn left in the entrance hall and for the moment pass through the Assyrian section. This leads to one of the best laid-out sections, offering an excellent chronological survey and including some of the finest examples of Greek art in

the world. It starts with simple idols of the 3rd and 2nd millennia BC (**Rm. 1**) found in the Cyclades. Bronze Age Greek art (**Rm. 2**) is followed by early ceramics (**Rm. 3**) that show a developing sophistication; so too does the fine wine jar by Exekias (c.540BC), decorated with mythological scenes in black on a red-earth background. The exit to this room is through a display of Greek vase decoration (**Rm. 4**). In **Rm. 5**, ceramics of about 500BC, now with red figures on black, demonstrate that Greek artists fully understood the forms and movements of the human body.

The next room chronologically is the **Duveen Gallery** (**Rm. 8**), home of some of the finest examples of Greek art: a sizeable group of the sculptures that once adorned the Parthenon in Athens, dating from c.440BC when Pericles was beautifying Greece's greatest city. World-famous as the **Elgin Marbles** (★), they are now the subject of controversy, with the Greek government making strenuous appeals for them to be returned to Athens. The Parthenon was ruined by an explosion in 1687; in 1803 Lord Elgin rescued the shattered fragments of the pediment sculptures, frieze and metopes and brought them to London. The **frieze**, displayed at eye level around the outside of the gallery, consists of marvelously natural figures and horses in a rhythmic procession to Mt. Olympus. The superb **pediment sculptures** recount the birth of Athena and the foundation of Athens.

Among the innumerable treasures of this collection is a **caryatid from the Erectheion** in Athens (c.410BC) in **Rm. 9**. In **Rm. 7** are fragments of the great **Nereid Monument** (5thC BC) from a Greek colony at Lycia in Asia Minor, reconstructed into a facade. The Nereids themselves, wind spirits, are portrayed as dancing maidens with flowing garments clinging to their energetically moving bodies. In **Rm. 12** is a **frieze of the Battle of the Greeks and Amazons** from the Mausoleum of Halicarnassus, an extraordinary tomb of the late 4thC BC, built for Mausolus and one of the Seven Wonders of the Ancient World.

The smaller collection of Roman art (**Rms. 14 and 15**) begins with the famous **Portland Vase** (c.1stC BC), a cameo glass production, with the top white layer carved to reveal the blue underneath. There are also wall paintings from Pompeii, pleasant little architectural landscapes, and sculptures. Rooms above house smaller Greek and Roman antiquities, including fine figurines, busts, vases and household items. Particularly good are the representations of Greek and Roman life in **Rm. 69**, with a small fountain actually in operation and a Roman waterwheel from Spain; the Cypriot antiquities dating from 4500BC to AD330 in **Rm. 72**; and artifacts from the Greek colonies in Southern Italy and Sicily (founded in the second half of the 8thC BC) in **Rm. 73**.

Ancient Mesopotamia ★

The collections from the ancient cities of Assyria rival those of Greece in importance, for Britain's close relations with Turkey in the mid-19thC made extensive excavations possible. In contrast to the Greeks, the Assyrians seem to have been interested in a static, formal approach to representation, and the changes in style through the period are much less striking. The Nimrud Gallery (**Rm. 19**) has huge **reliefs from the palace of Ashurnasirpal II** (9thC BC), which show highly ritualized hunting and military scenes. From a century later are two huge winged bulls with human heads (**Rm. 16**), once forming an entrance to the palace at Khorsabad. The best-observed and most enjoyable details to be found in the Assyrian sculptures are not shown in the king and his countless soldiers but in the animals, particularly the lions depicted in the **relief series from Nineveh**

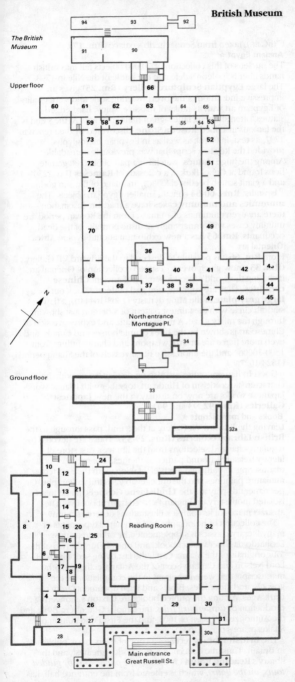

The British Museum

Upper floor

Ground floor

North entrance
Montague Pl.

Reading Room

Main entrance
Great Russell St.

N

(7thC BC), taken from Sennacherib's palace (**Rm. 17**).

Ancient Egypt ☆

The nucleus of this collection of 70,000 objects fell into British hands after Napoleon's defeat at the Battle of the Nile in 1798. The large **Egyptian Sculpture Gallery** (**Rm. 25**) gives an impressive indication of the overpowering scale and stern quality of Egyptian art with its ranks of massive, shiny, hard-edged statues, often showing little sign of their great age. At the S end is the famous inscribed **Rosetta Stone**, discovered by the French in 1797; its text, in Greek as well as in Egyptian hieroglyphs, provided the key to a script that was previously unreadable. Among the huge **statues**, watch for a pair of 3rdC BC granite lions found at Gebel Barkal, a colossus of **Rameses II** (c.1250BC) and a giant scarab beetle (c.200BC), an image of the sun god.

Upstairs, **Rms. 60-64** contain smaller Egyptian objects. The **mummies and mummy cases** have a macabre fascination — there are even mummies of animals. From the Roman period are mummy cases with unnervingly realistic portraits of the dead occupants. **Rm. 65** has a new exhibition about Egypt in Africa.

Oriental art

From **Rm. 66** it is possible to descend to the Edward VII Gallery (**Rm. 33**), now given over to a superb collection of Oriental art, including the world's finest assembly of ancient **Chinese ceramics**. They are sophisticated and perfect — look out for a **large gray plate** of the Ming dynasty (1368-1644AD), a flawless, smooth circle with the faintest pattern of a dragon just showing through the milky glaze. A more dramatic and expressive side of Chinese art is shown by the fine ceramic horses and camels, and even more fierce are bronze weapons and chariot fittings from 1500-1000BC and the impressive ritual vessels of the Shang period (1523-1027BC).

Good Indian sculptures are also on display, some with the characteristic eroticism of Hindu art, together with Islamic works. Japanese works are now on display in the new **Japanese Galleries** (**Rms. 92, 93** and **94**).

Books and manuscripts ★

Leaving the Edward VII Gallery at the E end, pass through to the **British Library Galleries** (**Rms. 29-33**). These are devoted to regularly changed selections from the library's vast store of literary treasures around particular themes. The medieval manuscripts in particular are breathtaking, with their perfect miniature paintings and the unbelievably skillful calligraphy. On permanent display are the **Lindisfarne Gospels**, made in an isolated monastery on England's NE coast in about 698. The abstract mazes of its complex illustrations deserve scrutiny.

The collection of holographs and annotated typescripts of many literary classics is supplemented by other treasures: Leonardo da Vinci's sketchbook, and one of Dürer's; two of the four originals of the Magna Carta; the last dying scribblings of Lord Nelson and Captain Scott of the Antarctic; the two 5thC manuscripts that were important in the compilation of the gospels; and chronicles, Bibles and legal documents from the Dark Ages. Among the printed books are Caxton's pioneering production of *Canterbury Tales*, the famous Gütenberg Bible and the Authorized Version of 1603, and the First Folio edition of Shakespeare's plays (1623).

The **British Library** receives a copy of every book published in Britain. Thus, the collection is the world's greatest, and the library's **Reading Room** (★ *open to the public only by guided tours, on the hour*), which is entered from the entrance hall, has attracted all the greatest scholars, most notably Karl Marx, who worked on *Das Kapital* in its hallowed calm. Opened in 1857, this spectacular room has a huge iron dome and massive windows, and a radial arrangement of reading tables around the circular bookcases containing the catalog. The dome is bigger than that of St Peter's in Rome.

Prehistory and early Britain

From the British Library Galleries, return to the main entrance hall. Upstairs to the E are the rooms devoted to prehistoric and Romano-British objects (**Rms. 36-40**). Stone Age products include carvings on mammoth and walrus tusks from France, and there is a rich collection of early metalwork. Lindow man, the 2,000yr-old remains of a Celt discovered in 1984 at Lindow Moss in Cheshire, is on display in **Rm 37**. A hologram of the head affords a much closer examination of his red hair, mustache and features than was previously possible. Look out for the superbly twisted electrum **torque** of the 1stC BC, found in Norfolk, and the exquisite Roman silver of the **Mildenhall Treasure** (**Rm. 40**), including several superbly embossed platters.

Medieval and later

Rms. 41-7 are devoted to medieval (post-Roman) and later material and **Rm. 48** to European and American decorative arts (1840-1940). Some rooms are darkened and their exhibits spotlighted, an effect that helps the visitor recognize the great quality of the items. The technique works very well with the **Waddesdon Bequest**, for example, in **Rm. 45**, which consists of elaborately wrought metal, glass and ceramic work from the Renaissance and Mannerist periods.

In **Rm. 41** is the famous **Sutton Hoo Treasure** (★), a 7thC Angle burial ship unearthed in Suffolk in 1939. On display are finely wrought items of jewelry and weaponry, and a forbidding **helmet**, now reconstructed. Their craftsmanship speaks of a sophistication that belies the common image of the "Dark Ages," as they are usually called.

Famous objects in the medieval sections include the late Roman **Lycurgus Cup** and the **Franks Casket**, an Anglo-Saxon whalebone carving (both in **Rm. 41**). In **Rm. 42** is the Flemish parade shield of the 15thC showing a knight kneeling before a fairy-tale damsel; a skeleton looks over the knight's shoulder, and the inscription, representing the knight's words, can be translated as "You or death." Also in this room is the fabulous **14thC Royal Cup** of the kings of England and France, decorated with scenes from the life of St Agnes, in enamel.

The museum also possesses numerous important prints and drawings, including works by Michelangelo, Botticelli and other important masters. A periodically changed display can be found in **Rm. 90**, above the Edward VII Gallery.

British Telecom Tower ▥
Cleveland St., W1. Map 9E9. Not open to the public. Tube: Great Portland Street.
Still faithfully called the Post Office Tower, this 619ft landmark, a jumble of transmitters and radio masts above an elongated cylinder, was erected in 1964 to achieve effective TV and radio telephone broadcasting above surrounding buildings.

Brompton Oratory ▥ †
Brompton Rd., SW3 ☎ 589-4811. Open 7am-8pm. Map 16J6. Tube: South Kensington.
Converts are supposedly the most zealous adherents of any faith:

certainly the Oxford Movement, a group of Victorian intellectuals turned Catholic, allowed no halfway measures when they created this church in 1884. All the drama of the Italian Baroque is here, in an interior dark with rich marbles, heavy with gilded detail. Some of the atmosphere is genuine: the huge marble *Apostles* (1680) by Mazzuoli come from Siena Cathedral.

Buckingham Palace 🏛 †
☎ *930-4832. Map 17I9. Not open to the public. Tube: Victoria, Hyde Park Corner.*
The royal standard flying signifies that the monarch is in residence, and then many an eye scans the windows of the palace hoping to catch a glimpse of a member of the Royal Family. But generally, visitors are satisfied by the splendors of the palace, with the Queen Victoria Memorial and *The Mall* at their backs, and the solemn facade, guarded by soldiers in scarlet tunics and bearskins, behind railings to the front. (For the **Changing of the Guard**, see *Calendar of events*.)

Its familiarity and setting give it a certain grandeur, but in reality Buckingham Palace is an undistinguished example of early 20thC official architecture — it might be a rather large town hall. Behind, however, there is John Nash's older palace. In 1762, George III bought Buckingham House from the Duke of Buckingham, and Queen Charlotte moved in. In 1825 his son, the Regent, commissioned Nash to rebuild on a larger scale. The *Marble Arch* was built as the entrance (later moved), but by 1850 the project was still incomplete, and Nash was sacked under suspicion of having squandered huge amounts of money and having bought building materials from his own companies. But the best parts of the palace are still his. To the right of the palace, there is a large arch leading to the gardens — the clearest part of Nash's work visible from outside.

When Queen Victoria came to the throne in 1837, the palace became the official residence, and it has been so ever since. It was her need for additional accommodations that led to the large side wings and front being built, although it was more humble until the facade was added in 1913.

To the left of the palace is Buckingham Gate and the **Queen's Gallery** (🖼 *open during exhibitions only Tues-Sat 10.30am-5pm, Sun 2-5pm*), where exhibitions of treasures from the fabulous royal art collections are mounted.

Farther along, the road becomes Buckingham Palace Rd., and here can be found Nash's attractive **Royal Mews** (🖼 *open Wed, Thurs 2-4pm*), which can be visited when state processions are not taking place; on display are the Queen's beautiful carriages and harness. The state coaches are a great attraction; the star is the gilded and painted **Gold State Coach**, dating from 1762.

Cabinet War Rooms See *Whitehall*.

Carlyle's House
24 Cheyne Row, SW3 ☎ 352-7087. Map 16L6 🖼 Open Apr-Oct Wed-Sun 11am-4.30pm. Tube: Sloane Square.
The houses in Cheyne Row were built in 1708, making them some of the oldest surviving residences in *Chelsea*, and when the Scottish writer Thomas Carlyle (1795-1881) was looking for a London home he was evidently impressed. He lived here from 1834 until his death, and the house can be seen today much as it was then, crammed with memorabilia and manuscripts of the famous, although now little-read, essayist and historian. It can

also be enjoyed as a perfect example of a comfortable Victorian home. The **attic study**, with its double walls, was added in 1853 to provide a quiet working place.

Central Criminal Court

The imposing building is known universally as the *Old Bailey* after the street in which it stands.

Charing Cross

Map 10G11. Tube: Charing Cross.

At the s end of *Trafalgar Square*, a statue of Charles I looks down *Whitehall* to the place of his execution and occupies the site of the original Charing Cross, from where all distances to London are measured. This was the last of the Eleanor Crosses put up by Edward I in 1291 to mark the resting places of his queen's funeral cortège on its way to Westminster Abbey; Charing is a corruption of *chère reine* (dear queen). The original was destroyed in the Civil War in 1647, but when E.M. Barry designed Charing Cross Station Hotel nearby in 1863-64, he added a Victorian Gothic Eleanor Cross to the forecourt, where it still stands.

Chelsea ★

Map 15&16K-L. Tube: South Kensington, Sloane Square.

Chelsea is London's most fashionable address. On the one hand, the pretty, well-maintained houses in its quiet streets retain the feel of an elegant backwater, almost a country village; by contrast, the King's Road is *outré*, noisy and Bohemian in a way nowhere else can imitate.

Only in the later 18thC did the quiet village nestling on the river's edge become a part of London. Charles II built the *Royal Hospital* from 1682 as a restful place of retirement for old soldiers. The military connection remains, with two large barracks and the *National Army Museum*.

In 1673 the Society of Apothecaries established **Chelsea Physic Garden** (*Swan Walk ☎ 352-5646 ▨ open early Apr to mid-Oct Wed and Sun 2-5pm, daily during Chelsea Flower Show*) to grow plants for the study of medicine. With its exotic trees and shrubs, aromatic herbs, rock garden, tranquil pond and greenhouses, it is still a delightful place in which to stroll.

Apart from the Hospital and Physic Garden, little remains of old Chelsea. The area around *Cheyne Walk* includes the few old houses there are, such as **Lindsey House** of about 1674, and Cheyne Row of 1708, where *Carlyle's House* can be visited. Most of Chelsea's housing dates from the 19thC, some of it very grand (Cadogan Sq.), and some of it mere artisans' cottages, which are now so sought after.

In the late 1800s, Chelsea became known as an artists' colony. Pre-Raphaelites such as Rossetti, Burne-Jones and Morris lived here; Whistler settled here, called it "the wonderful village," and quarreled with Oscar Wilde, who lived in Tite St.; and Americans, such as Henry James and Jack London, were attracted to the area. Everywhere you look, blue plaques mark the former abodes of the famous.

After World War II the avant-garde again made this their home. The "angry young men" grabbed attention at the **Royal Court Theatre** in 1956 (see *Theaters* in *Nightlife*), artists crowded into Finch's pub in the Fulham Rd., and, most significantly, Mary Quant began selling clothes in the King's Rd., subsequently a major center for cult fashion.

On the Chelsea/Fulham borders, off Lots Rd., the luxury

development of apartments, restaurants and private marina, **Chelsea Harbour**, has sprung up. Its tall tower block can be seen from far away; the golden ball on top moves up and down to indicate the tide level.

Cheyne Walk ☆
*SW3. Map **15**M5-6. Tube: Sloane Square.*

There were grand houses here before the famous and beautiful row was built in the late 17thC. **Lindsey House** (subsequently subdivided into nos. 95-100), built about 1674, gives some idea of the detached stateliness of the even bigger Tudor mansions of *Chelsea*, most notably the country estates of Henry VIII and Sir Thomas More. Once the red-brick Georgian terrace was built, Cheyne (pronounce the last "e") Walk's rural charm went largely unnoticed until the 19thC, when it suddenly became a haven for artists. Turner lived at no. 119 from 1846 until his death in 1851, under the name of Puggy Booth, and D.G. Rossetti moved into no. 16 in 1862. In 1880 the novelist George Eliot died in no. 4, a house dating from 1717. James McNeill Whistler lived at no. 104 from 1863, and at no. 96 from 1866-79, painting many of his most famous pictures here, including the series on the river itself, known as *Nocturnes.*

One of the most remarkable buildings, however, is earlier. **Crosby Hall** (☎ 352-9663 ☒ *open daily 10am-noon, 2.15-4pm*) was built between 1466 and 1475 by Sir John Crosby, a wool merchant, as his great hall residence in Bishopsgate in the City. It was moved to its present site in 1910 to save it from demolition. It has a superb **hammerbeam roof** and a 3-story **oriel window**, and displays a copy of Holbein's lost portrait of *Sir Thomas More and his Family.* Next to it, **Chelsea Old Church** contains a charming monument to Thomas Hungerford (1581) and Sir Thomas More's chapel (1528).

Between Crosby Hall and the church is Roper's Garden, next to an unusually ugly modern statue of Sir Thomas More, whose own gardens once occupied the site. There is a relief by Jacob Epstein in the garden. At the E end is Cheyne Row and *Carlyle's House*, and the gardens at the W end lead to **Albert Bridge** (1873), a decorative piece of Victorian suspension engineering.

Chiswick
*Map **21**C4. Tube: Stamford Brook, Turnham Green.*

Although on the main routes out of the capital to the W, parts of the old riverside village of Chiswick survive. A still and dreamy quarter is to be found by turning sharp left into Church St. at the monster Hogarth Roundabout where the Great West Rd. traffic is forced to pause. **St Nicholas** church has a 15thC tower, although the rest is a Victorian reconstruction; buried in the churchyard are the painters James McNeill Whistler and William Hogarth. Back on the Great West Rd. is *Hogarth's House*, and just beyond it *Chiswick House* (see *Walk 3* in *Planning*).

Chiswick House 🏛 ★
*Burlington Lane, W4 ☎ (081) 995-0508. Map **21**C4 ☒ Open mid-Mar to mid-Oct daily 9.30am-6.30pm; mid-Oct to mid-Mar daily 9.30am-4pm. Tube: Turnham Green, Chiswick Park.*

The Palladian architecture so favored by 18thC English gentlemen, with its forms reduced to simple geometrical shapes and all detail ruthlessly contained, reached near-perfection in this ravishingly beautiful mansion in *Chiswick*. Set in its own park, it retains the feel of a country house. The first Earl of Burlington bought the Jacobean mansion here in 1682. Little was changed until the third Earl of Burlington, an enthusiastic student of Classical art, decided to add a villa to one end of the house, built to his own designs in 1725-29, with an interior by William Kent.

The villa's octagonal dome rises from a simple square block; a portico and stairs form the entrance. The link building and summer parlor survive at the E side, where the villa was joined to the main body of the old house. Through a low-ceilinged and severely Classical octagonal room, enter the three rooms that served as the earl's **library**. An interesting exhibition of engravings, plans and documents relating to the villa occupies the rooms on this floor. The upper rooms are reached by a spiral staircase, and immediately the style changes: these reception rooms, designed by Kent, are brighter in color, with richly patterned velvet wallpapers and heavily decorated cornices, architraves and fireplaces. At the rear is the 3-chambered gallery and, to the sides, the dramatic **Red and Green Velvet Rooms**. In the center, the impressive **dome** has elaborate coffering. The **garden** has grown to the modern, wilder taste.

The City ★

Map 12&13E&F. Livery company halls do not have regular opening hours and will admit visitors only on open days. For information, contact i City of London Information Centre, St Paul's Churchyard, EC4 ☎ 260-1456/7.

For centuries it was just what its name suggests, and although London has now vastly outgrown it, the City retains its identity, its influence, and, to a degree that invariably surprises newcomers, its self-government.

Today, "the City" is shorthand for money; this is where the great banking, insurance and commodity trading concerns are based. During the day, more than 350,000 people work here, but at night and on weekends it can be a concrete and glass desert, with a resident population of less than 5,000. As a result, it may be best to visit the City on a weekend, when it is easier to find and enjoy the hidden, almost secret places that give the area its appeal. Be warned, however, for while the streets may be free of traffic, it can be hard to find a pub or restaurant that is open. Even the famous Wren churches are often closed on Sun — the best time to visit them is weekday lunchtimes.

The City does not easily yield up its past. First the Great Fire of 1666, then the bombs of 1940 and, most recently, the zeal of developers have swept away much that was old. In its place, there is an ostensibly haphazard collection of office buildings, for the most part demonstrating the poverty of modern architecture. As Sir Nikolaus Pevsner has pointed out, the skyline has none of the excitement of New York or Chicago, but has more in common with that of an unimportant Mid-West town. On the other hand, *St Paul's Cathedral* is too great a building to be dominated by its taller neighbors, Wren's churches too interesting not to be visited, and history proclaims itself too loudly even from the street names. And, of course, the City does have its own unique geography, described by a uniquely English phrase — nooks and crannies.

The key to exploring the City is not to content yourself with its obvious beauties. To an astonishing extent it retains elements of its medieval character. Within the area bounded by the old walls (the gates were at Ludgate, Newgate, Aldersgate, Cripplegate, Bishopsgate and Aldgate) one can easily work out what was where. Cheapside, for example, with the surrounding Milk St., Poultry and Bread St., marks the site of the main medieval market. The government of the City has not even changed on the surface. The Guildhall is still its parliament, and Mansion House the palace of its head, the Lord Mayor. He is selected annually by a complex system based on ancient privileges rather than mere residence. City livery companies, descended from medieval trade guilds, have an important part to play in choosing and providing the aldermen and sheriffs from whom the Lord Mayor must come. The liveries still have their own halls, their own constitutions, and their own regalia, even though they are hardly ever connected with their original trades. The City still has its own police force (look at the badges on the helmets, different from those elsewhere in London), and on royal ceremonial occasions the monarch will not enter the City unless greeted on its borders by the Lord Mayor.

The square mile is a large area to visit on foot, with its many sites of interest widely scattered. To make it more manageable, it has here been divided into four parts, each viewed separately.

The City: east

The City to the E of a line taken from London Bridge to Liverpool Street Station in the N includes many fine churches, but the predominant tone is set by the great maritime trading interests. Until the 19thC almost all the trade goods landed at London were brought ashore between London Bridge and the Tower of London. **Lloyd's** (☎ 623-7100), the headquarters of a business largely founded on insuring ships and their cargo, is in a controversial new building in Lime St., designed by Richard Rogers and opened in 1986. Lloyd's grew, amazingly, from a coffeehouse; now its huge underwriting room, simply called "the Room," but housed in a massive glazed atrium (200ft high), is a beehive of activity, centered around the 18thC Lutine Bell, traditionally struck once for news of disaster of a missing ship, and twice for a safe arrival. The atrium is the core of Rogers' striking glass, steel and concrete structure. From the Room on the ground floor, illuminated glass-sided escalators ascend to three galleries, the floors of the market. All the services are contained in six satellite towers, up and down which slide glass-sided observation elevators. There is a viewing gallery and exhibition on the role of Lloyd's past and present (▣ ☎ 327-6210, open Mon-Fri 10am-2.30pm). Lloyd's Shipping Register, where the capacity and whereabouts of all the world's shipping is monitored, is in nearby **Fenchurch St**. In Mincing Lane is the Commodity Exchange of Plantation House.

In the SE corner of the City is the *Tower of London*. Just to the N is **Trinity Square** with, at its E side, a well-preserved portion of Roman wall. Opposite is **Trinity House**, headquarters of the charity operating Britain's lighthouses and lifeboats. To the W of Trinity Sq., in Byward St., is the church of **All-Hallows-by-the-Tower**; the attractive tower dates from 1658-59. The church is actually much older, dating back to the 7thC, and there is a Saxon arch at the tower base, revealed by bomb damage. Inside is a quite beautiful **font cover** of 1682 by Wren's great carver Grinling Gibbons. All Hallows also has a **Brass Rubbing Centre** (▣ ▣ open Mon-Sat 11am-4pm, Sun 12.30am-4pm).

Farther W along the riverfront toward *London Bridge* is the large **Customs House** of 1812-25, its Classical facade best seen from London Bridge. Inside, a small museum illustrates the history and present-day work of the ancient Customs and Excise department (▣ open Mon-Fri 10am-6pm). Opposite, up St

Dunstan's Hill, is the ruined church of **St Dunstan-in-the-East**, converted into a delightful garden; Wren's extraordinary spire of 1698, supported on flying buttresses, still stands. Back on Lower Thames St. the next building along from the Custom House is **Billingsgate Market**, a typical 19thC covered market, closed in 1982, when the fish market that existed there since medieval times moved farther E into Docklands. It has now been beautifully converted by Richard Rogers into the headquarters of an American bank. A little farther along is the church of **St Magnus Martyr**, designed by Wren in 1671-76 although altered since. The tower is massive, with a spire of 1705.

Over Lower Thames St. is Fish St. Hill and Wren's *The Monument*. At the top of Fish St. Hill is the major thoroughfare of Eastcheap, site of a medieval market. Some fanciful Victorian commercial buildings deserve study — nos.33-35, for example, all brick Gothic and gables. To the S is the splendid Wren church of **St Mary-at-Hill**, hidden in a maze of charming lanes, which forms a moving contrast to the great space and harmony of Wren's beautiful interior, built in 1670-76. The church is unusual in that it still has box pews and is noteworthy for some wrought-iron sword-rests and a carved organ screen.

Back on Eastcheap, another Wren church will be discovered a little farther along on the left, **St Margaret Pattens**, named after a special type of shoe made here. This time the exterior, with a fine spire of 1687, has more to offer than the interior. A pretty early-19thC shop and house (now an American bank) next to the church completes an attractive corner. To the N is the Commodity Exchange, with its facade in Fenchurch St., and behind the new Clothworkers' Hall up Mincing Lane on the left is the small 15thC tower of **All Hallows Staining**, incongruously surrounded by large buildings. Nearby in Hart St. is **St Olave**, an attractive 15thC church. Untouched by the Great Fire of London, it was damaged in the Blitz but well restored. It contains several good monuments, especially those to Sir James Deane (1608) and Peter Cappone (1582). Samuel Pepys the diarist used the church, and there is a monument to his wife (1669). Hart St. leads into Crutched Friars, which passes under Fenchurch Street Station ("crutched" means "crossed" — there was a priory here). No. 42 is a fine early 18thC house.

North of Fenchurch St., **Leadenhall Market**, off Lime St., provides City workers with a welcome shopping area. Leadenhall St., a little farther N, contains the churches of **St Andrew Undershaft**, mostly early 16thC, and **St Katharine Cree**, a survivor from the early 17thC, but with a medieval tower.

This section of the City, straddling the course of the Roman and medieval wall along Camomile St. and Bevis Marks, contains three churches. **St Helen Bishopsgate** is an outstanding convent church dating back to the 13thC. Its many interesting features include an attractive W front topped by a little 17thC bell tower, a poor box of about 1620 in the form of a one-armed beggar, and remarkable monuments. The other churches in Bishopsgate are **St Ethelburga**, with medieval fragments and a tower of 1775, and **St Botolph-without-Bishopsgate**, a pleasant 18thC building where Keats was baptized. The **Spanish and Portuguese Synagogue** in Bevis Marks deserves a visit; it dates back to 1700-1, and contains some lavishly decorated appointments of that period.

The City: south

This is the central area between *St Paul's Cathedral* and London Bridge, S of Cheapside, Poultry and Cornhill.

The waterfront w of London Bridge, Upper Thames St., is now one of London's least attractive roads, bearing great quantities of traffic through a windy and noisy desert. The narrow alley of **Broken Wharf**, however, leads down to a good view of the river and the **Samuel Pepys pub** in an old warehouse. There is also a riverside walk to the w of this. But to the N, only the slender pinnacled tower of **St Mary Somerset** and the much-restored church of **St Nicholas Cole Abbey**, both by Wren, relieve the monotony.

Just beyond Queen St., the approach to Southwark Bridge, there are some smaller and older streets around Mansion House Station. Wren's **St James Garlickhythe** (1676-83) in Garlick Hill (where the herb was sold) has a fine tower, looking rather like a lighthouse with a stone lantern on top; it contains some good ironwork. **Beaver Hall** in Great Trinity Lane is the center of the fur trade, the premises of which cluster in these narrow streets. Facing Upper Thames St. is the **Vintners' Hall**, one of the best of a number of livery company halls in this area. It was built in 1671, and although much restored has a fine paneled hall and a superb carved staircase. Queen St. itself contains two magnificent Georgian houses (nos. 27 and 28).

Between Queen St. and Cannon Street Station there is another maze of little lanes, around the church of **St Michael Paternoster Royal**, built by Wren but much restored after war damage. Some good interior fittings have survived, including a carved pulpit and reredos. Three livery companies have their halls in Dowgate Hill, just w of St Michael: the Skinners (with a late 18thC facade), the Dyers, and the Tallow Chandlers (the last two are Victorian).

Between Cannon Street Station and King William St. (which leads onto London Bridge) is yet another fascinating maze of small streets, with several historic pubs and wine bars. **Laurence Pountney Hill** to the E has two of the most beautiful 18thC houses in London, dated 1703, with elaborately decorated doorways and cornices. Other attractive buildings are found around the pleasant little churchyard left by the vanished church of St Laurence. Next to London Bridge is the **Fish stores' Hall** of 1831-34, the best-sited and grandest livery company hall, with an imposing Classical facade overlooking the river.

Just N of Cannon St. are **St Clement Eastcheap**, containing some superb wood carving, and the extraordinary *St Mary Abchurch*, both by Wren. Farther N is Lombard St., an important banking street named after the Italian money-lenders who set up business here in the 14thC. It contains two fine churches: **St Mary Woolnoth** and **St Edmund the King**. The latter is again by Wren, with a harmonious exterior and well-preserved woodwork inside. St Mary Woolnoth was built by Nicholas Hawksmoor in 1716-27 and occupies its prominent corner site with a dramatic monumental facade. The interior, with massive Corinthian columns, is Baroque in feeling. North of Lombard St. are several attractive lanes: St Michael's Alley, Castle Court and Ball Court. Old hostelries tucked away in this enclave include **Simpson's**, which has been restored, the **George and Vulture**, and the **Jamaica Wine House**. There are two churches on the s side of Cornhill: **St Michael Cornhill** has a pretty churchyard, but is itself an unhappy mixture of styles by Wren and later architects; **St Peter-upon-Cornhill** by Wren is best seen from its little churchyard.

Moving w, large offices again dominate the area s of Cheapside and Poultry. The remains of the **Roman Temple of Mithras**

(see the marvelous sculptures in the Museum of London, under *London, Museum of*) can be seen in Queen Victoria St. Nearby is the church of **St Mary Aldermary**, completed by Wren in 1692 in an extraordinary version of Gothic, with a tall tower, nave and aisles. The fan-vaulted roof uses a very free interpretation of the medieval style, with shallow domes between the fans, all richly covered with delicate tracery. On Cheapside is the major church of *St Mary-le-Bow*, with the grandest of Wren's steeples. Where Cheapside joins Poultry is the *Mansion House*, the Lord Mayor's official residence, with the important *St Stephen Walbrook* behind.

The City: north

The northern part of the City contains a number of important institutions and a great many lesser offices. As a result, it is less an area to stroll through than other parts of the City. In the N are Liverpool Street Station, with its Victorian hotel, and the postwar developments of Broadgate — where, incongruously, there is now an open-air ice rink (☎ 588-6565) — London Wall and the *Barbican*. Just to the N of Liverpool Street Station and Spitalfields Market is the remarkable **Dennis Severs' House**. Mr Severs gives a 3hr "performance" tour of his 18thC house in the evening, or you can simply wander around yourself during the day (*18 Folgate St., by appt. only* ☎ *247-4013 before noon Mon-Fri*). N of the Barbican are the **stables** of the Whitbread Brewery, where you can visit the splendid shire horses and see a farrier at work (*Garrett St.* ☎ *606-4455, by appt. only*).

To the S, forming really the center of the City, are the financial and administrative institutions, the *Guildhall*, the Bank of England, the *Stock Exchange* and the **Royal Exchange**. The latter is now the home of LIFFE, the London International Financial Futures Exchange, whose hectic, colorful (traders use hand signals and wear bright blazers) trading floor can be visited (⌖ *open Mon-Fri 11.30am-1.45pm*).

In Foster Lane, N of Cheapside, is **St Vedast**, a Wren church built 1670-97 but reconstructed after war damage. Its finest feature is the elaborate and effectively sinuous spire. To the N is **Goldsmiths' Hall**, built with a massive Classical exterior by Philip Hardwick in 1829-35. Frequent exhibitions of the livery company's unmatched collection of historic and modern plate make it possible to see the palatial interior, with its tremendous dome-covered staircase of colored marble.

On nearby Gresham St. is the interesting Wren church of **St Anne and St Agnes**, built of brick in 1680 on a square with a central dome supported on columns. In Wood St., to the E, which was completely devastated during the Blitz, there is a lonely Wren tower in the Gothic style, all that remains of the Church of **St Alban**. Next to the *Guildhall* in Gresham St. is **St Lawrence Jewry**, again by Wren (1671-87).

Lothbury, next to the Bank of England, contains Wren's **St Margaret Lothbury**. Good features include the 17thC screen brought from another Wren church, with its beautiful twisted columns. Look for no. 7 Lothbury: Victorian architecture at its imaginative best. Lothbury leads into Throgmorton St., with the *Stock Exchange* on the right, which then becomes Old Broad St. This contains the tallest and one of the most exciting and dramatic of the City's new office buildings, the **National Westminster Bank tower**. Its thrillingly soaring height, emphasized by vertical ribbing, balances unnervingly on a narrowed base with a clear glass facade.

A new museum has opened in the nation's controlling bank,

the **Bank of England** (*Threadneedle St.* ☎ 601-5545⌧ *open Mon-Fri 10am-5pm*). It charts the history of the bank from its Royal Charter in 1694 to the present day. Exhibits include Roman gold bars and coins, a collection of banknotes, the re-creation of Sir John Soane's Stock Office, and interactive video taking you live to the Dealing Desk. In Bishopsgate is **St Botolph-without-Bishopsgate**, rebuilt in 1727-29 and with a 19thC interior. **All Hallows London Wall** (1765-67) to the w has a simple and light interior with an ornate plaster ceiling.

The City: west

Most of the western part of the modern City falls outside the Old Roman walled town, including the whole section w of Ludgate Circus to the beginning of the *Strand* and Smithfield Market, the capital's wholesale meat market, housed in a fine Victorian building, to the N. Of prime interest are *Fleet Street*, the Inner and Middle *Temple* extending s to the river, and *St Paul's Cathedral*. The stretch of riverside to the s of St Paul's is disfigured by the traffic of Upper Thames St., although **St Benet's** (1677-83) remains as one of the most delightful and best preserved of Wren's churches, small and simple in the Dutch style with charming garlanded windows. Nearby in Queen Victoria St. is the 17thC *College of Arms*. The church of **St Andrew-by-the-Wardrobe** stands on St Andrew's Hill to the w. Built by Wren in 1685-93,it is abutted by the offices of the men who maintained the state apparel.

To the s is the **Mermaid Theatre**, surrounded by the raging traffic of Puddle Dock. In Queen Victoria St. is the extraordinary **Black Friar** pub, decorated in high Arts-and-Crafts style (see *Pubs*). In Blackfriars Lane next to the station is the **Apothecaries' Hall**, a fine livery company building with a facade of 1684 (altered in 1779). North again is Ludgate Hill, site of the medieval "Lud Gate" until 1769-61; it offers the best view of the portico of St Paul's. **St Martin Ludgate**, a Wren church of 1677-87, has a most attractive lead-covered spire and some good carved woodwork inside. Just behind is the **Stationers' Hall**, a building of about 1667 with a stone facade of 1800.

Another of the old roads out of the City passed through Newgate, site of the notorious jail and now the *Old Bailey*. Newgate St. leads into Holborn Viaduct, built to span a little valley in 1863-69. Its heavy, ornate ironwork can be seen best from Farringdon St. The church of **St Sepulchre** on the N side of Holborn Viaduct is unusually large, with a great (although restored) 15thC tower. **St Andrew Holborn** on the s side is a Wren church with a 15thC tower restored in 1703.

To the N of Holborn Viaduct is Smithfield, long the site of the famous medieval St Bartholomew's Fair, about which Ben Jonson wrote his play in 1614, and the place where Wat Tyler and his rebel peasants confronted Richard II in 1381; Lord Mayor Walworth showed the City's customary independence by simply drawing his sword and killing Tyler. Nearby are **Smithfield Market** and *St-Bartholomew-the-Great* St Bartholomew's Hospital opposite dates back to the Middle Ages. Its church, **St Bartholomew-the-Less**, has another 15thC tower. To the E of St Bart's, as it is known, at the end of Little Britain, is **St Botolph Aldersgate**, rebuilt in 1788-91 and with a well-preserved interior. Behind this little church is the charming oasis of **Postman's Park**, with a heart-rending wall of plaques dedicated to late-Victorian child heroes and heroines and the various ways in which they met their ends. The **National Postal Museum** is in King Edward St. (⌧ *open Mon-Fri 10am-4pm*).

Cleopatra's Needle
*Victoria Embankment, WC2. Map **11**G12. Tube: Embankment.*
Now appropriately sited beside another symbol of timelessness, the Thames, this pink granite obelisk was made in Heliopolis in Egypt in 1500BC, predating Cleopatra by centuries. Presented to Britain by Egypt in 1819, it was finally towed by sea to its present site and erected in 1878. In that year a little time capsule, in the form of everyday Victorian objects including hairpins and a railway timetable, was buried beneath the obelisk to be dug up and wondered at sometime in the far-off future. New York has a similar obelisk in Central Park.

The College of Arms 🏛
*Queen Victoria St., EC4 ☎ 248-2762. Map **12**F15 Hall only open Mon-Fri 10am-4pm. Tube: Mansion House, Blackfriars.*
The official body controlling the heraldry of the United Kingdom is housed in an interesting building constructed in 1671-88 following the Great Fire, which destroyed the older house given to the college by Mary I in 1555. The wrought-iron gates and railings, of uncertain date, are particularly splendid; the brick pilasters with carved stone capitals preserve some of its grandeur. As a professional body, the College of Arms will investigate queries relating to genealogy and heraldry — nobody knows more about argent chevrons, batons sinister or griffins rampant. Only the entrance hall is open to the public.

Commonwealth Institute 🏛
*230 Kensington High St., W8 ☎ 603-4535. Map **14**I2 Open Mon-Sat 10am-5pm, Sun 2-5pm. Tube: Kensington High Street.*
With its extraordinary green copper roof, all peaks and elliptical curves, the Commonwealth Institute is an appropriately unusual tribute to a unique association, the Commonwealth. It was opened in 1962 as a study and display center, and houses a permanent exhibition representing its peoples, customs and economics. There is an excellent library, together with a cinema and restaurant. The exhibition area is open-plan, consisting of a large circle of galleries on different levels around a central concourse. Each country has a display, variously expressing the cultural traditions or economies of the nations. There is always plenty going on at the Commonwealth Institute, particularly for schoolchildren, with temporary exhibitions, live performances, workshops and lectures year round.

The Coram Foundation *(Foundling Hospital Art Museum)* ☆
*40 Brunswick Sq. WC1 ☎ 278-2424. Map **5**D12 Open Mon-Fri 10am-4pm (check first). Tube: Russell Square.*
In the 18thC, London was full of destitute children, and their plight moved nobody more than Thomas Coram, a retired sea captain who set up a foundling hospital in 1739. The original buildings were shamefully demolished in 1926, but the magnificent **Court Room** can be seen in the Foundation's modern offices, along with a model of the original complex. After its foundation, artists led by Hogarth tried to raise funds. It thus has a fine collection of pictures, of which the highlight is Hogarth's **portrait** of the sanguine philanthropist Coram (★). There are also works by Gainsborough and Reynolds, a study of

Raphael, and a manuscript of Handel's *Messiah*.

Coram's Fields, a children's playground, is entered from Guildford St. through the hospital's original gateway.

Courtauld Institute Galleries ★
Somerset House, Strand, WC2 ☎ *872-0220. Map 11G12* 🖼
🍴 *Open Mon-Sat 10am-6pm, Sun 2-6pm. Tube: Aldwych, Temple.*

When the textile industrialist Samuel Courtauld helped found London University's main art history department, the Courtauld Institute, in 1931, he provided the nucleus of an important art collection. Swelled by several subsequent bequests, this has grown into an exceptional, broad-ranging group of pictures. The Institute has recently made a much-delayed move from Woburn Sq. into its new premises in the N block of William Chambers' Classical Portland-stone **Somerset House** (1776-78), original home of the Royal Academy and until recently the *Registry of Births, Deaths and Marriages*.

Among the Princes Gate collection, the outstanding feature is a group of no less than 32 paintings by Rubens (1577-1640), including a fine portrait of the *Family of Jan Brueghel the Elder*, a moving *Entombment* and the incomparable *Landscapes by Moonlight*, famous for its eerie beauty. Rubens' pupil Van Dyck is also well represented, and earlier Flemish art is superbly exemplified by the brilliant, jewel-like *Madonna* by Quentin Massys and two rare paintings by the Elder Brueghel: a perfect imaginary landscape and a deeply human grisaille rendering of *Christ and the Woman Taken in Adultery*. Italian paintings include a well-preserved triptych by Bernardo Daddi, a poetic and sensuous *Venus* by Palma Vecchio and 12 paintings by Tiepolo. The drawings (six by Michelangelo) are also excellent.

Samuel Courtauld's collection amounts to one of the best publicly accessible groups of both Impressionist and Post-Impressionist paintings. Impressionist works include examples by Monet (*Fall at Argenteuil*), Sisley and Renoir, including the superbly colored *La Loge*. Manet is represented by a large oil sketch for the celebrated *Déjeuner sur l'Herbe* and by the sumptuous *A Bar at the Folies-Bergère*. Two large sketches by Degas show to perfection the artist's ability to fix an ordinary moment in time. The Post-Impressionists are represented by no fewer than nine Cézannes on one wall, a Van Gogh self-portrait (with bandaged ear) and two haunting studies of Tahitian women by Gauguin, including the dreamy *Te Rerioa*.

Covent Garden ★
Map 10&11F-G. Tube: Covent Garden.

Until 1974, London's fresh fruit and vegetable market was Covent Garden's chief fame, and the pubs stayed open all night for the thirsty workers (and others). When the market and its heavy traffic left to go to a new building s of the river at Nine Elms, a bitter struggle for the future of Covent Garden began. Conservationists and local residents were ranked against the developers, for whom this was a prime site for office buildings (dressed up, of course, with token community schemes). To the enormous relief of everyone but those who stood to profit, the attempt to turn the delightful and historic chaos of decaying buildings into a "planned" desert was defeated. But it may have been a Pyrrhic victory — skirmishing continues, new buildings continue to eat away at the old, and the population of the area is falling. Even so, the best buildings remain, and although the many youth-oriented stores and bars have brought a huge influx of mainly young visitors, it retains an earthy feel of real old London, with some discerningly tasteful modern patronage.

Until the 16thC, Covent Garden was an enclosed kitchen garden belonging to Westminster Abbey. The land was granted to Sir John Russell, later Earl of Bedford, in 1630, and a descendant of his obtained the right to develop it under the aegis of the great Classical architect Inigo Jones in 1670. The plan was ambitious — a huge piazza on the Italian model surrounded by arcaded houses. All that survives today is the church of *St Paul's, Covent Garden*. The present **market buildings** appeared in 1828-32, with the fine iron and glass canopies added later. In its restored state, the marriage of its severe Classicism to the more ornate roof creates a stunning effect. Other later market buildings surround the piazza. The best, the **Floral Hall** (1858) is to the NE, a superb example of the iron and glass architecture that sprang up in emulation of the 1851 Crystal Palace.

The **market** itself is now given over to trendy shops and restaurants, with market stalls in the middle and in Jubilee Market to the S; it is at its liveliest at lunchtime. In among the shops is the **Cabaret Mechanical Theatre** (*33-34 The Market*), displaying contemporary automata that all move at the touch of a button, and the **Light Fantastic Gallery of Holography** (*48 South Row*). On the S side of the piazza, the old Flower Market (1897) now houses the *London Transport* and *Theatre Museums*. Leave the piazza by Russell St. to the E, lined with fashionable wine bars thick with young advertising executives and publishers not so different from the *monde* who congregated in its famous coffeehouses in the 18thC. Russell St. crosses Bow St., so notorious for its street crime in the 18thC that it saw the foundation of the first police force, the Bow Street Runners. Its inspiration was the novelist Henry Fielding, a magistrate at the busy courts that are still there in a newer building. To the left is the splendid facade of the Floral Hall. Next to it (and, amazingly, by the same architect, the Victorian E.M. Barry) is the **Royal Opera House** (see *Nightlife*), the third theater on the site, built 1857-58; its grand Corinthian portico has a frieze by J. Flaxman and statues from the previous building of 1809.

Fittingly for a quarter of such vitality, Covent Garden is traditionally London's theater area, and its church, *St Paul's*, is the actors' church. (For *Theaters*, see *Nightlife and the arts*.)

Continuing along Russell St. will take you to the other old royal theater, the **Theatre Royal, Drury Lane**, founded in 1663 by Charles II, whose Nell Gwynne was, of course, an orange-seller in Covent Garden. The present building dates from 1810-12, and is by general agreement London's most beautiful theater. Covent Garden is also bordered by two of London's main theatrical streets; to the S is the *Strand* and, to the W, St Martin's Lane, where the largest theater is the imposing **Coliseum** of 1904, now home of the English National Opera. A good example of an ornate late Victorian pub, complete with cut glass and mirrors, is the **Salisbury**, a little farther up on the left (see *Pubs*). At the top of St Martin's Lane, Garrick St. to the right includes the solemn and grimy building of the famous Garrick Club, a gentlemen's club with theatrical associations. Up tiny Rose St. on the left is the **Lamb & Flag**, the area's oldest and best pub (see *Pubs*).

The northern continuation of St Martin's Lane is drab Monmouth St., which leads to Seven Dials, the scene of Hogarth's "Gin Lane" of drink and vice in the 18thC and the cholera outbreaks of the 19thC. The sundial monument, which was removed in 1773 to break up gatherings of criminals, has recently been replaced. A little to the NW is **St Giles-in-the-Fields**, a fine Classical church of 1731-33, with a supremely calm interior. Near Seven Dials is **Neal's Yard** and Neal Street, with craft stores, vegetarian restaurants and health-food stores. Another craft market opened in 1987 in nearby Endell St. Housed in a glass-domed building, Endell Street Place has craft workshops, a shop and special exhibitions.

Design Museum 🏛

Butlers Wharf, Shad Thames, SE1 ☎ 403-6933. Map 13H17
📷 ♿ ♿ *Open Tues-Sun 11.30am-6.30pm. Closed Mon. Tube: Tower Hill, London Bridge.*

In a strikingly reconstructed 1950s warehouse, the Design Museum is the first of its kind in Britain. The brainchild of Sir Terence Conran and Stephen Bayley, it aims to show how and why objects that we may take for granted, from spoons to kettles to cars, are designed the way they are. It also shows that, when well designed, these objects can be very beautiful.

The theme of good design begins with the building itself, and more particularly its clean, clear, all-white interior. The museum is divided into three sections, which interact well. On the top floor is a permanent study collection, which may at first glance look like "Conran without the price tags" but does in fact do much to explain and evaluate design, particularly in the mass market. On the first floor is the **Boilerhouse**, where temporary exhibitions are held, and the **Design Review**, a fast-changing spotlight on current happenings in design, both new and speculative. This is an agreeable place to visit, not so much museum as resource center (with library and lecture theater), aided by its waterfront café and more serious **Blueprint** restaurant. But it has a one-dimensional feeling. It is the quintessential '80s museum, style-obsessed.

Dickens' House ☆

48 Doughty St., WC1 ☎ 405-2127. Map 5D12 📷 Open Mon-Sat 10am-4.30pm. Closed for 2 weeks Dec-Jan. Tube: Russell Square, Chancery Lane.

When Charles Dickens lived at Doughty St. between 1837 and 1839, he was experiencing his first taste of success. The *Pickwick Papers*, which brought him sudden prosperity, was still being published, and he also worked on his first novels while in the house: *Oliver Twist, Barnaby Rudge* and *Nicholas Nickleby*.

In Dickens' time, Doughty St. had gates at either end tended by liveried porters. It is still a handsome house but, unfortunately, the interior preserves almost nothing of its original appearance; instead, however, there is an extensive museum of Dickens memorabilia. There are pieces of furniture from later houses, numerous letters and manuscripts, portraits of the writer and his family, and contemporary illustrations of his famous characters. The drawing room has recently been reconstructed to look as it might have done in Dickens' day.

Docklands

Map 21C5. Tube: Tower Hill, then Docklands Light Railway.

With the demise of the British Empire, London's docks fell into decline, and by the late 1960s Docklands was derelict: an area of poverty, slums and high unemployment. In 1981 the London Docklands Development Corporation (LDDC) was formed to redevelop Wapping, the Isle of Dogs, the Royal Docks and

Surrey Docks in the largest, most ambitious scheme of its kind in
Europe. Office space in the City was at a premium, so Docklands
attracted businesses as well as private investors, who were
prepared to plunge millions of pounds into offices, houses and
recreation facilities. Since then, many businesses have moved to
the area, including most *Fleet Street* newspapers. But in many
respects the Docklands dream has not yet been realized. Still a
building site, it is criticized for being difficult to live and work in,
and architecturally it is a mishmash. The recent slump in property
prices hit Docklands particularly hard.

Covering a vast 450 acres, Docklands is a 21stC river city in the
making. Since it is an official enterprise zone, architectural
restrictions are suspended. As a result a variety of styles are in
evidence, from office buildings clad in tinted glass, framed by
bold primary colors, to mellow brick buildings, which recall the
past with Gothic windows or the hint of a pediment. Within the
maze of modern architecture, it is still possible to stumble across
a beautiful old church, such as Hawksmoor's **St George in the
East**, a pretty terrace of Georgian or Victorian houses, or a listed
building, such as the ancient and allegedly haunted *pissoire* in
the Royal Docks.

The conversion of old warehouses in Wapping and Limehouse
have made these fashionable residential areas, with **Tobacco
Dock**, a vast but soulless complex of restaurants and leisure
facilities, conveniently nearby. On the Isle of Dogs, the grand and
extraordinarily ambitious **Canary Wharf**, still under
construction, will become the heart of Docklands. This huge
71-acre site at least has the advantage of having been designed as
a whole. It will be topped by a 656ft-high tower, of which Prince
Charles asked, "But why does it have to be so high?" The
country's largest and best-equipped sports complex, **London
Arena** (see *Sports and activities*), has opened nearby in
Limeharbour. Opposite, also in Limeharbour, is the **Docklands
Visitor Centre** (☎ 515-3000).

Farther E are the Royal Docks, the least developed part of
Docklands, and still in a state of flux while awaiting the area's
much-vaunted potential to be fulfilled. They comprise Royal
Victoria Dock, Royal Albert Dock and King George Dock,
strange, desolate places at present. Here too, **London City
Airport** provides businessmen with fast access to Europe.

On the S side of the river at Surrey Docks, the Victorian
warehouses of **Butler's Wharf** have been refurbished by Sir
Terence Conran to provide offices, workshops, houses, shops
and restaurants, and include the *Design Museum*.

The best way to see Docklands is from the **Docklands Light
Railway** (*Mon-Fri 5.30am-midnight* ☎ 538-0311), which was
opened in Sept 1987. Suspended 20ft above the ground for much
of its route, it affords panoramic views of the area. The red, white
and blue computer-driven trains look even more like toys than
the buildings below. The railway may be closed on Sat and Sun
for further building.

The LDDC arranges group guided tours by bus, River Bus,
helicopter and even by horse-drawn coach (☎ 515-3000 ext.
3513), and **Citisights** (☎ 241-1323) offers guided walks.

Downing Street
SW1. Map 10H11. Tube: Westminster. Charing Cross.
Although overwhelmingly dominated by the massive buildings of
Whitehall, Downing St., the Prime Minister's residence, is the
powerhouse of the government. In fact, the interior of "no. 10" is

more elegant and spacious than the unassuming facade might suggest, and from its Cabinet Room the country has been run since Sir Robert Walpole accepted the house ex officio from George II in 1735. No. 11, home of the Chancellor of the Exchequer, is the only other survivor of Sir George Downing's original terrace of 1683-86. Steps at the end of the street lead to *St James's Park*. At the Whitehall end, a simple barrier once kept the public out of Downing St.; now ceremonial gates have been erected.

Dulwich
Map 21D5. Train to West Dulwich from Victoria.
The charming village of Dulwich, with wooden signposts, broad open spaces and historic buildings, is a jewel preserved in the rock face in a way typical of London. The presence of *Dulwich College* is strong here: in **College Road** there are several 18thC houses and considerable style, nos.103-107 dating from around 1700, and nos.57 and 97, as well as substantial Georgian homes. College Rd. heads s across the refreshing Dulwich Common through a toll gate. Enthusiasts will find the **Vintage Wireless Museum**, a private collection, at 23 Rosendale Rd. (☎ *(081) 670-3667, by appt only)*. In Lordship Lane is the **Horniman Museum** (☎ *(081) 699-2339* 🔲 🗐 *open Mon-Sat 10.30am-6pm, Sun 2-6pm)*, in an Art Nouveau building of 1902. It houses a bizarre variety of objects: dolls, tribal art, even stuffed animals, and a fine collection of musical instruments.

Dulwich College and Picture Gallery 🏛 ☆
College Rd., SE21 ☎ (081) 693-5254. Map 21D5 🔲 🗐 ✗ Sat, Sun 3pm. Open Tues-Sat 11am-5pm, Sun 2-5pm. Train to West Dulwich from Victoria.
In 1619, Edward Alleyn, a successful actor and colleague of Shakespeare, founded the "College of God's Gift" at Dulwich, and the large almshouses that were part of the original bequest have been added to, making Dulwich College today one of London's greatest schools.

Of particular interest is the remarkable **Picture Gallery**, in a severe Neo-Classical building designed by Sir John Soane in 1811-14, which incorporates a mausoleum for its founders. The Dutch school of the 17thC is especially well represented: there are six Cuyps, for example, including some fine landscapes. Look out for the majestic *Landscape with Sportsmen* by Pynacker and important works by Poussin; also represented are Watteau, Claude and Canaletto. There are Rubens sketches, and English portraiture, including works by Gainsborough, and Reynolds' amusing portrait of his era's great actress, *Mrs Siddons as the Tragic Muse*. But pride of place goes to the awe-inspiring **Rembrandts**, including *Titus*, a moving portrait of his sick son.

Eltham Palace 🏛 ☆
Eltham ☎ (081) 859-2112. Map 21D5 🔲 Open Nov-Mar Thurs, Sun 11am- 4.30pm; Apr-Oct Thurs, Sun 11am-6.30pm. Train to Eltham from Charing Cross.
History has played some teasing games with this medieval palace near *Blackheath* and *Greenwich*. A favorite royal hunting retreat until the time of Henry VIII, it must have witnessed some huge banquets, such as when Henry IV received the Byzantine Emperor here in 1409. By the 1600s, it fell into ruins; only the Great Hall survived the Civil War, because it made a good barn. In the 1930s it was rescued by the Royal Army Educational Corps,

which now occupies the site. Past a lovely group of half-timbered houses in the outer court, known as the **Lord Chancellor's Lodgings** after Cardinal Wolsey, is a 15thC bridge over a moat with swans and geese. At the heart stands the **Great Hall** on the mound of the palace, with a superb **hammerbeam roof** and two great **oriel windows** at either side of the dais.

Fenton House▥ ☆
Hampstead Grove, NW3 ☎ 435-3471. Map 21C4. ▨ Open Mar Sat, Sun 2-5pm; Apr-Oct Sat-Wed 11am-5pm. Tube: Hampstead.

Although *Hampstead* is rich in fine houses, this is its jewel. Dating from 1693, Fenton House is a brick mansion of disarmingly simple design, hardly changed except for the benign addition of the Classical portico to the E front soon after 1800. The luxurious Regency decor of the interior reflects the changes made by James Fenton in about 1810. Among older items of furniture, look out for the charming little "grandmother" clock of about 1695 on the stair landing. Meissen and Nymphenburg ware as well as English pieces are among a fine **porcelain collection**. Also kept in the house, and perhaps its crowning glory, is the **Benton Fletcher Collection of Musical Instruments**, which comprises mainly early keyboard instruments.

Concerts are performed in the house in summer. A Shakespeare play is staged in the delightful walled garden every July.

Fleet Street
EC4. Map 11F13-14. Tube: Aldwych, Temple, Blackfriars, St Paul's.

Continuing from the *Strand* toward the *City*, Fleet Street, named after the small river that now flows unseen beneath its sidewalks, is famous as the home of British journalism, although no major newspapers now have offices in the "street of shame" itself, having decamped to *Docklands* and elsewhere. Fleet Street begins at Temple Bar, the western limit of the City. Walking eastward, **Prince Henry's Room**, on the right opposite Chancery Lane, predates the Great Fire of 1666 and has a superb Jacobean enriched plaster ceiling. It now contains an exhibition devoted to Samuel Pepys (▨ *open Mon-Fri 1.45-5pm, Sat 1.45-4.30pm*). The gateways to the *Temple* on the right date from the 17thC. On the left, **St Dunstan's in the West** is a fine example of an early Victorian church in the Gothic style; it incorporates an extraordinary clock with giants striking bells (1671) and a statue of Elizabeth (1586). **El Vino's** wine bar on the right (see *Nightlife*) is famous for providing newspapermen with liquid inspiration. Farther along on the left (in Wine Office Court) is the **Cheshire Cheese**, an ancient pub frequented by Dr. Johnson and Boswell. Soon after comes the unusually ugly *Daily Telegraph* building of 1928, followed by the ex-*Daily Express* building of 1931, aggressively modern with its entirely plain, shiny black facade and with a superb Art Deco entrance hall. Toward the end of Fleet Street, the wonderful wedding-cake spire of **St Brides** is visible on the right. Built to Wren's design in 1701-3, it is the tallest and one of the most elaborate of his spires.

Florence Nightingale Museum
2 Lambeth Palace Rd., SE1 ☎ 620-0374. Map 19I12 ▨ Open Tues-Sun 10am-4pm. Tube: Waterloo, Westminster.

A new museum (found beneath the Nightingale School, on the

site of St Thomas' hospital), which celebrates the life and work of Britain's most famous nurse, "the Lady with the Lamp." Designed very much in the modern idiom, the museum displays Florence Nightingale's prized possessions as well as artifacts from the Crimea War and the early days of nursing. There is also an audiovisual program, plus the slightly pointless re-creation of a ward at Scutari and of Nightingale's living room.

Geffrye Museum ☫

Kingsland Rd., E2 ☎ *739-8368. Map 21C5* ▣ ♨ *Open Tues-Sat 10am-5pm, Sun 2-5pm. Tube: Old Street.*

Shoreditch, in the East End, was traditionally the home of the furniture industry, and this museum was opened in 1914 not only to pay tribute to that past, but also to provide models for local craftsmen of the 20thC. The buildings are interesting enough, with a fine set of almshouses built in 1715 at the bequest of Sir Robert Geffrye, a former Lord Mayor whose statue stands over the door of the central block containing the chapel. The collection is imaginatively arranged as a series of rooms representing different periods, and household items and pictures give a lived-in feeling. Look out for the fine chimneypiece in the Elizabethan room and the splendidly fussy Victorian parlor.

Geological Museum   See *Natural History Museum.*

Grand Union Canal ☆
Maps 2-7.

At the end of the 18thC, London was triumphantly linked to the industrial Midlands by canal, then the most efficient form of travel. The canal is still there, ignoring and largely hidden by the roads that have superseded it.

Its walks offer particularly interesting views of London not normally seen by visitors: the backs of houses, gardens rich and poor, crumbling industrial buildings of the 19thC, and the many details of the working canals themselves, such as brightly painted canal barges ("narrowboats"), locks, bridges and tunnels.
Camden Lock, with its restaurants, shops and craft studios and its terrific weekend market (see *Shopping*), is a good place to start — you can take a boat trip (☎ *482-2550*) or walk either to the W (*Regent's Park* and **Little Venice**) or to the E (*St Pancras Station* and **Islington**).

Gray's Inn
High Holborn, WC1 ☎ *405-8164. Map 11E12. Tube: Chancery Lane.*

This ancient society of lawyers, one of the four *Inns of Court*, has occupied this site since the 14thC. South Sq., the first quadrangle encountered, has one old set of chambers (no.1), dating from 1685. Opposite is the hall, badly burned but accurately restored. The fine carved late 16thC screen perhaps formed a backdrop to the first performance of Shakespeare's *Comedy of Errors* here in 1594. In the center of South Sq. is a modern statue of Francis Bacon (1561-1626), the great Elizabethan statesman and scholar, one of the Inn's most distinguished former members. Beyond the hall is Gray's Inn Sq., full of the calm grandeur of legal London; at the S end is the frequently restored and curiously characterless chapel. More appealing is Field Court, with no.2, a most attractive house of about 1780, and the dignified wrought-iron gates of 1723 that lead to the gardens. Designed in formal style by Francis Bacon himself, the gardens are the best of the Inns of Court, with a grand central walkway flanked by huge plane trees.

Greenwich ★

Map 21C5. Best approached by river boat (see p15); or train to Greenwich from Charing Cross.

It is no longer regarded as the center of the world, despite the continuing primacy of the Greenwich Meridian (0° longitude) and Greenwich Mean Time (GMT), and yet the sheer self-confidence of this most easterly of the Thames-side royal residences suggests otherwise. Bold and grand in every way, the metropolis' most spectacular architectural ensemble sweeps down to the riverside through fine parkland, unifying its blend of splendid buildings in an elegant Classicism.

It owes its prominence to its position as the capital port of a great seafaring nation, and its maritime character strikes the disembarking visitor in the tall form of the masts of the ***Cutty Sark*** (🚇 *open Oct-Easter Mon-Sat 10am-4.30pm, Sun noon-4.30pm, Easter-Sept Mon-Sat 10am-5.30pm, Sun noon-5.30pm*), built in 1869, one of the greatest of the graceful tea clippers that raced to bring back tea from the Orient. Inside the hold is a display on the ship's history and a collection of old ships' figureheads. Nearby is the diminutive ***Gypsy Moth IV*** (🚇 *open Easter-Sept Mon-Sat 10am-5.30pm, Sun noon-5.30pm*) in which Sir Francis Chichester sailed around the world in 1966.

Dominating the river is the magnificent Baroque creation of the **Royal Naval College**. It was begun in 1664 as a replacement for the old royal palace, was designated a royal hospital for navy seamen in 1694, and not completed until well into the 18thC. The original plans were by Wren, but other leading architects, including Vanbrugh and Hawksmoor, made substantial contributions. Of the interior, the amazing **Painted Hall** and the **chapel** can be visited (📷 *open Mon-Wed, Fri-Sun 2.30-4.45pm, closed Thurs*). Sir James Thornhill's **hall** of 1708-27 is a Baroque tour de force. The enormous painting on the ceiling represents the glory of the Protestant monarchy, the effect increased by the rich gray columns and pilasters, with illusionistic painted flutings. The **chapel** opposite is in a much lighter Neo-Classical style; it was redecorated in 1779-89 after a fire.

Farther back from the river are the main buildings of the **National Maritime Museum** centered on the **Queen's House** (☎ *(081) 858-4422* 🚇 *museum open daily 10am-6pm; Queen's House open May-Sept 11am-4.45pm*). Henry VIII was born here, as were his two daughter queens, Mary and Elizabeth. James I gave the palace to his queen, Anne of Denmark, in 1613, and it was completely rebuilt to the designs of Inigo Jones between 1616 and 1635. The Queen's House is a building of extreme Classical simplicity, in the Palladian style quite revolutionary in its day. Most interesting are the entrance hall, a perfect cube, and the graceful circular stairwell. To the sides are two wings added from 1807-16. After extensive renovation, the Queen's House has now been reopened. The royal apartments have been carefully re-created to look as they might have done during the residence of Henrietta Maria, widow of Charles I, around 1662. The vaulted basement contains the Treasury of the National Maritime Museum and a *son-et-lumière* based on an Inigo Jones court masque etched on glass screens.

The National Maritime Museum is the greatest seafaring museum in the world. Its extensive collections range from the finds of marine archeology to an entire paddle tug. The main entrance is in the East Wing, where new galleries house temporary exhibitions. The West Wing is dominated by the New Neptune Hall, with the 1907 paddle tug, *Reliant*. Exciting displays here include the decorated royal riverboats: Queen Mary's shallop of 1689 and Prince Frederick's barge of 1632. On the top floor of the West Wing, a new gallery entitled *Discovery and Seapower 1450-1700* charts England's transition from economic obscurity to its position, by the end of the 17thC, as one of the great naval and commercial powers in Europe. The exhibition traces the voyages of discovery, the origins of the Royal Navy and the exploits of Elizabethan seamen such as Drake and Hawkins, and includes artifacts from the *Mary Rose*.

After the Queen's House, you pass into **Greenwich Park**, crowned with several hills and sloping down steeply toward the river. One hill is topped by a Henry Moore statue, others by the buildings of the Royal Observatory.

The **Royal Observatory** (⊠ *hours as Maritime Museum*) was established in 1675-76, when Wren was commissioned by Charles II to build a house for the first Astronomer Royal, John Flamsteed. A well-proportioned red-brick building with a fine octagonal room on the top floor, it commands extensive views down over Greenwich and the river. On top of one of Flamsteed House's towers can be seen a large red ball mechanism erected in 1833. Each day the ball falls at exactly 1pm to enable ships in the river to set their clocks accurately. At the rear of the house is a 19thC extension topped by a huge bulbous dome of 1894 (*open only on sunny days*), which houses a 28in refracting telescope, one of the largest in the world. The astronomers have moved to Sussex and more modern equipment, and Flamsteed House is now a museum, with exhibits that include clocks and telescopes used by Halley, Herschel and other royal astronomers.

Next door is the mid-18thC **Meridian Building**, where there is a display on the theme of time. This is the site of the meridian on which all the world's clock time is based through Greenwich Mean Time; visitors can have a foot in each hemisphere.

At the top end of the park is **Ranger's House** (⊠ *open Mar-Oct daily 10am-5pm, Nov-Feb daily 10am-4pm*), its front fringing *Blackheath* on Chesterfield Walk. Built of red brick, the stone center framing the main doorway dates from the early 18thC; the bow-front wings were added by the Earl of Chesterfield in about 1754. The best room, in the S wing, contains pictures of the Suffolk Collection, including several attributed to William Larkin of members of the Jacobean aristocracy.

Chesterfield Walk leads into Croom's Hill, which proceeds back down to Greenwich town. This old road has several detached houses and terraces of the 17th-18thC along its steep slope. Near Ranger's house are **Macartney House** and the **Manor House**, both of the early 1700s. Greenwich has an attractive town center a little inland from the *Cutty Sark*, with wine bars and antique stores and an excellent weekend market. Its massive and monumental parish church of **St Alfege** was built in 1711-30.

Downstream is **Woolwich**, with a large naval dockyard. It is also the traditional home of the Royal Artillery. The **Royal Arsenal**, **Military Academy** and **Artillery Barracks** of the 18th-early 19thC are extraordinarily large and imposing buildings. Nearby is the **Rotunda** (⊠ *open Apr-Oct Mon-Fri noon-5pm, Sat, Sun 1-5pm, Nov-Mar Mon-Fri noon-4pm, Sat, Sun 1-4pm*), a strange tent-shaped building of 1814 moved here from St James's Park in 1820, which now houses a collection of artillery pieces from the 17thC to the present day. The river is straddled by the **Thames Barrier**, an extraordinary engineering achievement opened in 1984, which will protect London from flooding. A free exhibition demonstrates how it works.

Guildhall 🏛 ☆
Aldermanbury, EC2 ☎ 606-3030 ("Keeper's Office"). Map 12E15 ☎ Open Mon-Sat 10am-5pm, Sun May-Sept 10am-5pm (check first). Tube: Bank, St Paul's, Mansion House.
Although hidden away in its own yard in the *City*, the Guildhall has been parliament and palace for the Corporation of the City of London for almost 1,000yrs. The present facade is not the one that would have greeted the powerful medieval Lord Mayors such as Dick Whittington; it was constructed in 1788-89 to the design of George Dance, an attractive but bizarre mélange of 18thC Gothic ideas. But the entrance porch dates from the 15thC building, as do parts of the **Great Hall**. The most entertaining of the statues inside are the giants Gog and Magog, new versions of old mythical figures. Below is the large 15thC crypt, notable for its Purbeck marble columns supporting a vaulted roof.

The **Guildhall Library**, in an unremarkable new building on the w side, houses a sumptuous collection of books, leaflets and manuscripts giving an absorbing and unparalleled view of London. This building also houses the oldest **Clock Museum** in the world: the Collection of the Worshipful Company of Clockmakers. On show are many of the Company's 500 magnificent watches, 50 clocks and 30 marine chronometers. A "scull" watch allegedly once owned by Mary Queen of Scots, an astronomical clock said to have belonged to Sir Isaac Newton and a deck watch that accompanied Capt. George Vancouver aboard *Discovery* are also displayed.

Ham House 🏛 ☆
Ham St., Richmond ☎ (081) 940-1950. Map 20D3 ☎ Open Tues-Sun 11am-4.30pm. Tube (or train from Waterloo) to Richmond.
One of several great mansions bordering the Thames to the w of London near *Hampton Court*, this is unique in preserving virtually intact a grand Baroque interior of the 17thC. It was built in 1610 in conventional Jacobean style, but mostly its present appearance comes from the occupancy of Elizabeth Dysart, wife of the Duke of Lauderdale, a minister of Charles II. In the 1670s she remodeled the house in the grandest style of the period.

Behind the high-ceilinged entrance hall is the **Marble Dining Room**, perfectly proportioned and facing centrally down the formal garden. Upstairs were the grand reception rooms and state bedrooms, reached by a massive staircase, carved in the 1630s with pierced reliefs of trophies. One bedroom was originally decorated for Charles II's queen. You can also see the library, several closets (or private rooms) and the fine **North Drawing Room**, with marble fireplace, rich wall hangings and gilded chairs. Most spectacular is the **Long Gallery**, with rich dark and gilded paneling and superb furniture. There is a good collection of miniatures on display in one room, including works by the masters of the genre, Hilliard, Oliver and Cooper. Rabbits, strung up ready for the pot, and crusty pies can be glimpsed through a door in the restored period **kitchen**.

Hampstead
Map 21C4. Tube: Hampstead.
Hampstead Heath's high and hilly grassland, scattered ponds and

dense woodland seem much farther than just 4 miles (6km) from a great city center. Hampstead "village" itself still follows the street patterns of an earlier time: around the hills wind convoluted lanes lined with attractive houses of the 19thC and earlier, now favored by successful academics, artists and media folk, who give Hampstead its arty reputation. In the 17thC, a few large out-of-town residences were established in the rural village of Hampstead; *Fenton House* is a notable survivor. The craze for health-giving waters in the 18thC boosted the village into a fashionable spa, which began to spread down the sides of the hill, becoming in the process a favorite haunt for artists: George Romney lived in Holly Bush Hill and John Constable at Lower Terrace, Downshire Hill and Well Walk.

The best-preserved part is to be found around the parish church of **St John** to the w of the High St. The massive cedar trees of its calm churchyard shade Constable's grave. **Church Row**, which leads down toward the modern center, has superb row houses of 1720, reflecting the period of expansion following the discovery of the spa. To the N of Church Row are a number of charming little streets, most notably **Holly Walk** with its early 19thC cottages. A later fashionable period is represented to the s, with the Victorian and Edwardian mansions of Frognal and Fitzjohn's Ave. Look out for **Kate Greenaway's Cottage** in Frognal, in a fairy-tale style appropriately similar in feeling to her illustrations. Farther s toward Swiss Cottage is the fascinating **Freud Museum** (*20 Maresfield Gdns.* ☎ *435-2002* 🖾 *open Wed-Sun noon-5pm*). Freud escaped here from Nazi Austria in 1938, with his extensive library, his furniture, rugs and collection of Greek, Roman, Egyptian and Oriental antiquities. After his death in 1939, his daughter Anna preserved the house exactly as it was in his lifetime.

The winding, hilly streets of Church Row lead to the wild, densely wooded **West Heath**. To the E, on North End Way, is **Jack Straw's Castle**, an old weatherboard inn rebuilt in the 1960s, named after the peasant leader who supposedly gathered his rebels here in 1381. Farther N on the same road is the equally famous **Bull and Bush** of the music hall song (see *Pubs*).

Back into the village, most shops are concentrated in Heath St. and High St. The **Flask** (see *Pubs*) in Flask Walk is a good lunch spot, and in Well Walk, **Burgh House** (☎ *431-0144* 🖾 *open Wed-Sun noon-5pm* ⬛) mounts local exhibitions. These streets lead past attractive cottages toward **East Heath** and the strange enclave of the **Vale of Health**, a wooded valley crammed with 19thC houses. Down the Heath to the s (right) are **Downshire Hill**, with an interesting church, and **Keats Grove**, both with cottages and houses of around 1820, including *Keats' House*.

The Heath itself stretches across to *Highgate*, some parts wild and open, others enclosed and wooded. Across to the N is the **Spaniards**, an 18thC inn in Spaniards Rd. with a toll house, and the Georgian splendor of *Kenwood House*, a good focus for a walk. To the s is **Parliament Hill**, festooned with kites on weekends and offering a fine view across the dense housing of Kentish Town to the City beyond.

Hampton Court Palace 🏛 ★

East Molesey, Surrey ☎ *(081) 977-8441. Map 20D3* 🖾 *𝒦* ⬛
Open mid-Mar to mid-Oct daily 9.30am-6pm; mid-Oct to mid-Mar daily 9.30am-4.30pm. Train to Hampton Court from Waterloo.

This riverside palace, to the w of London, is not only the

apotheosis of the great English Tudor style of architecture, but incorporates a grand Baroque palace designed by Wren. This dual character reflects its two periods of building, with only three patrons playing a significant part: Henry VIII's powerful Chancellor Cardinal Wolsey, the man who personified the zenith of Church and State power; Henry himself; and, over a century later, the joint monarchs William and Mary. Queen Victoria, who much preferred Windsor Castle as a Thames-side home, opened it to the public in 1838. A tragic fire in 1986 devastated some private apartments, plus the King's Audience Chamber, the King's Drawing Room, Bedroom, Dressing Room and Writing Closet, and the Cartoon Gallery, which are now closed to the public while restoration work is under way.

The main entrance to the palace is through the mid-18thC Trophy Gates and along a walk that runs parallel to the river toward the West Front. The balancing projecting wings of Wolsey's magnificent gatehouse offer a regular and impressive aspect. Inset into the walls are roundels with relief busts of Roman emperors, bought as a set by Wolsey in 1521 from the Italian artist Giovanni da Maiano. Henry VIII enriched the gatehouse with a superb oriel window with his coat of arms over the door, and also built the moat and bridge. The latter now has fine stone **heraldic beasts** along its parapet brought from the garden. Through the gate is **Base Court**, the first of Wolsey's quadrangles, a peaceful space surrounded by domestic buildings of mellow red brick decorated with diamond patterning. At the far end is **Anne Boleyn's Gateway**, built by Wolsey but later named after Henry's queen whose introduction, at the expense of Catherine of Aragon, Wolsey had to arrange with Rome. Her emblem, a falcon, is on the tracery decorating the vaulted roof beneath the arch, together with the monograms H and A. The arch leads through to **Clock Court**, with, above the belfried gate, a fabulously complex **astronomical clock** of 1540, by Nicholas Oursian. To the s side is a Classical colonnade, added by Wren.

To enter the **State Apartments** is to move on to a different age — the walls and ceilings of the King's Staircase are decorated with exuberant frescoes, with gods and heroes of the ancient world swirling illusionistically through Corinthian columns. They were painted after 1700 by an Italian artist, Antonio Verrio. Next comes a huge **Guard Chamber**, its walls decorated with 3,000 pistols, muskets and swords. A door from here leads into some of the rooms of Wolsey's palace, with 16thC linen-fold paneling.

The **Cumberland Suite** shows a different, 18thC, taste: regal pomp gives way to elegant comfort. An important collection of paintings, largely from the Italian High Renaissance, includes Titian, Tintoretto, Correggio, Raphael and Duccio; look out for the chilly gloss of Parmigianino's *Minerva*. Other schools of painting are also to be seen: Brueghel's *Massacre of the Innocents* and Cranach's lovely *Judgment of Paris* stand out. There are also works by Holbein, an artist associated closely with the Tudors. There are splendid views across the park and on to **Fountain Court**, a first glimpse of Wren's superb architecture in pink brick and white stone.

Before emerging, three rooms of special interest are encountered, all dating from the Tudor period. The small **Wolsey's Closet**, probably the cardinal's study, has paneled walls, a finely wrought ceiling of timber and plaster and recently discovered paintings from the 16thC. The **chapel**, also built by Wolsey, is then seen from the Royal Pew; it has an elaborate ceiling added by Henry VIII, with pendants carved in the form of angels. The reredos was designed by Wren and its marvelously carved plant forms are the work of Grinling Gibbons. As a suitable climax, there is Henry VIII's **Great Hall** of 1531-36, hung with contemporary Flemish tapestries and with a **hammerbeam roof**. Small rooms that help make the place come alive are the authentically equipped **kitchen** and Henry VIII's **wine cellar**.

Emerging into Clock Court, an arch at the opposite end leads through to Fountain Court past the **Queen's Staircase**. Here Wren's bold but harmonious use of the contrast between stone and brick can be seen to dramatic effect from the cloister along the little courtyard. Another arch leads through to the center of the **East Front** and the lake, **Long Water**. All around are spectacular **gardens** in various styles, some sunken and enclosed, other broad and open, some in the Tudor "knot" pattern, others with great avenues of trees. Note the 200yr-old **vine** in its special greenhouse (its stem is 78ins thick), which produces 600 bunches of grapes yearly, and the famous **maze**, dating in its present form from 1714. The Chestnut Avenue, more than a mile long, flowers spectacularly in May.

Highgate ☆
Map 21B4. Tube: Highgate, Archway.
This twin village of *Hampstead*, looking down on London from the N, takes its name from a tollgate that used to be near its center, and its dizzying height, best appreciated by approaching steep Highgate Hill or Highgate West Hill. Highgate Hill has a few fine mansions, most notably **Cromwell House**, a red-brick house in Dutch style of about 1637-40. Here also is **Whittington Stone** where, according to legend, Dick Whittington rested on his way home in c.1390, gazed down at the City and heard the bells chiming, "Turn again Whittington, thrice Mayor of London."

The High St. has good 18thC row houses, and South Grove on the left leads past the attractive Waterlow Park and Pond Sq. to the intersection with West Hill and **The Grove**, with an attractive terrace built around 1700. A plaque commemorates Coleridge, who lived in one of the houses; his tomb is in the aisle of the nearby church of St Michael, an imposing 19thC Gothic (1832) edifice with Highgate Cemetery (see below) behind it. In complete contrast with these charms are two large and influential blocks of apartments to the N on North Hill, the **Highpoint Flats**, constructed in 1936 and 1939 by the Tecton group.

Highgate Cemetery is one of the most extraordinary relics of Victorian London gone to seed, a romantic wilderness that pays tribute to nature's power to reclaim its own. A tour of the W side (✗ compulsory ☎ (081) 340-1834 for current times) takes you to Christina Rossetti's grave, a weird Gothic Chapel and the Egyptian catacombs. The most famous grave on the newer E side is the **grave of Karl Marx**, now surmounted by an ugly monument erected in the 1950s. Many other well-known people are buried here, including George Eliot.

Hogarth's House
Hogarth Lane, W4 ☎ (081) 994-6757. Map 21C4 ⊡ Open Apr-Aug, last 2 weeks Sept, Mon, Wed-Sat 11am-6pm, Sun 2-6pm; Oct to early Dec, Jan-Mar Mon, Wed-Sat 11am-4pm, Sun 2-4pm. Closed first 2 weeks Sept, last 3 weeks Dec. Tube: Chiswick Park, Turnham Green.
The painter William Hogarth (1697-1764) was an urban artist, and only lived in the delightful riverside village of *Chiswick* in the summer. The house that he occupied from 1749-64 is now

stranded between industrial buildings on the noisy Great West Rd. Inside the pretty old buildings, however, a quieter atmosphere prevails as an ironic background to the good selection of Hogarth's bustling, sarcastic and sometimes scurrilous engravings. The house also contains some contemporary furniture, and the artist himself is buried in the nearby village churchyard.

Holland House and Park
Map 6H1. Tube: Holland Park.
Although Holland House has hardly survived, its park retains the elegance of its prime. Narrow paths wind among mature woods; peacocks and other ornamental birds roam in a large enclosure; a formal flower garden, with a traditional pattern of box hedges, is decorated with statues; music drifts from the Orangery in summer.

The bombs of 1941 destroyed most of the house and now only the E wing stands complete, with its attractive Dutch gabled roof line. There is also a marvelous arched loggia, with strangely checkered carvings and fleur-de-lys crenelations. The Classical gateway (1629) was designed by Inigo Jones.

Horse Guards Parade 🏛
Map 10H11. Tube: Westminster.
The Horse Guards of Whitehall is a curiously jumbled Classical building of the mid-18thC, all arches, pediments and separate wings. Troopers of the Household Cavalry will be seen mounting guard in resplendent uniforms astride their equally well-groomed horses (see *Calendar of events* for times of **Changing the Guard**). The large parade ground beyond the central arch sees the great **Trooping the Colour** ceremony in June (see *Calendar of events*); past the Guards' Memorial, it leads into *St James's Park*. State buildings surround the other three sides. Looking back from the park, the Old Admiralty is on the left, an ugly brick and stone extravaganza of 1894-95; to the right of the Horse Guards is the more dignified Scottish Office, actually a fine mid-18thC house; and farther right are the Treasury and the rear of no.10 *Downing Street*.

Hyde Park
Map 7G-H. Tube: Marble Arch, Hyde Park Corner, Lancaster Gate.
From the middle of the largest open space in London, formed by Hyde Park and Kensington Gardens, you see nothing but wooded, rolling grassland, punctuated only by the lake known as the **Serpentine**, made in 1730. Rotten Row, along the southern edge, was *the* place to parade in the 18th-19thC, and is still used by horseback riders, although sadly it has lost its trees to Dutch Elm disease. In the SE, at Hyde Park Corner, is *Apsley House* and a graceful screen that once formed an entrance to the park's carriageway. A little to the N, there is an absurd statue of Achilles, made in 1822 from captured French cannons. Much better is *Rima* by Jacob Epstein (1922), near the Hudson Bird Sanctuary in the center of the park. On the NE side is *Speakers' Corner*.

Imperial War Museum ☆
Lambeth Rd., SEII ☎ 735-8922. Map 19J13 🔲 ▣ ⚹Open daily 10am-6pm. Tube: Lambeth North.
"Lest we forget," the Imperial War Museum was established soon after the end of World War I to preserve the relics and memory of that terrible conflict. Since then its terms of reference have been

expanded and today it is essentially the museum of 20thC British warfare (pre-1914 is covered by the *Army Museum*).

The museum's Lambeth building used to be the central range of the Bethlem Royal Hospital, built in 1812-15, appropriately perhaps an asylum for the insane, successor to the notorious "Bedlam" in the City. The present building's large dome was added in 1846; the place was converted into a museum in 1936. In 1989 it reopened to acclaim, after major redevelopment, and is now one of London's best presented museums. The huge main exhibition hall (created by infilling a courtyard) houses machines of war, including a German V2 rocket, a Polaris nuclear missile, an extraordinary Italian human torpedo and the M3A3 Grant tank used by Montgomery at El Alamein. Suspended in the atrium are six famous aircraft, notably a Sopwith Camel and a Battle of Britain Spitfire. More exhibits, such as the cramped cockpit of a Handley Page Halifax bomber, which you can enter, are on show on upper-level viewing platforms. Up again are galleries devoted to the museum's important collection of 20thC war art. A gallery on the ground floor is dominated by John Singer Sargent's harrowing *Gassed*; another shows contemporary posters.

But the crux of this revitalized museum is its exhibition of 20thC warfare, divided into First, Inter-, Second and Post-War. Thematically arranged, the exhibits have been brought to life by the use of audiovisual techniques, employing film and sound to add depth to the historic objects on display. Only the crowd-pulling yet mildly disappointing Blitz Experience (*buy your tickets as soon as you arrive*) is too much of a gimmick. Monty's real caravans are much more thought-provoking.

Inns of Court
All barristers must belong to one of these institutions (many work from their dignified ancient buildings): *Gray's Inn*, *Lincoln's Inn*, and the Middle and Inner *Temple*.

Dr. Johnson's House
17 Gough Sq., EC4 ☎ 353-3745. Map 11F13🔤 Open Mon-Sat May-Sept 11am-5.30pm, Oct-April 11am-5pm. Tube: Blackfriars, Temple, Chancery Lane.
In this substantial row house, dating from about 1700, Dr. Samuel Johnson lived from 1748-59. This man of letters *par excellence* was the center of a whole literary world that flocked to see him here and in the nearby **Cheshire Cheese** (see *Pubs*) in *Fleet Street*. In the large gabled attic, he and his six assistants worked on the celebrated *Dictionary*. Sadly, little can be seen of the house's original contents, but a few chairs and tables do give some idea of its historic atmosphere. Pictures and memorabilia give a picture of literary life in 18thC London. Look out for a 1st-edition copy of the *Dictionary*, and Johnson's will.

Keats' House
Keats Grove, NW3 ☎ 435-2062. Map 21C4🔲 ✗ by appt. Open Mon-Fri 2-6pm (1-5pm in winter), Sat 10am-1pm, 2-5pm, Sun 2-5pm. Tube: Hampstead, Belsize Park.
The Romantic poet John Keats (1795-1821) was already in the grip of tuberculosis when, in 1820, he left the house in *Hampstead* where he had spent his two most productive years to journey to Italy, where he died ten months later. Nevertheless, the house is a monument to his happiness and the rural seclusion that inspired *Ode to a Nightingale* and other poems. It was then split into two cottage homes sharing a garden; in the other lived Fanny Brawne, with whom Keats fell famously and poetically in

love. The engagement ring she wore until her own death is part of the memorial collection, as are Keats' manuscripts and annotated books, and letters to and from such friends as Shelley.

Kensington ☆
Map 14&15. Tube: South Kensington, High St. Kensington.
Modern Kensington is pleasant and prosperous, with a few enclaves of ostentatious wealth, but the predominant pattern is of good 19thC terraces and villas, large late-Victorian and Edwardian apartment buildings, major shopping streets that include the better department stores, and little roads of classy boutiques and antique stores. Good taste abounds.

In the 17thC, two great houses emerged from the manors scattered among the fields: *Holland House and Park*, and Nottingham House, which became *Kensington Palace* in 1690 when William and Mary moved there and gave the impetus to a new crop of aristocratic houses. **Kensington Square** was one such development, of about 1700, and a few attractive houses are preserved, such as no. 29. The part just s of Kensington Palace is a lovely enclave, **Canning Place** in particular. **Kensington Palace Road**, running w of the palace, is known as "Millionaires' Row"; it was begun in 1843 and consists of grand detached mansions, now largely occupied by embassies or their staff, and is a private road. The public road running N from **Kensington High Street**, a busy shopping area, to Notting Hill Gate is **Kensington Church Street**, with its many good antique stores and clothes boutiques. Nearby are *Leighton House*, the *Commonwealth Institute* and **Linley Sambourne House** (*18 Stafford Terr., W8* ☎ *open Mar-Oct Wed 10am-4pm, Sun 2-5pm; run by the Victorian Society, 1 Priory Gdns., W4* ☎ *994-1019*), where an engraving on the brass mailbox reads: "Mr Linley Sambourne Not At Home." The home of the well-known *Punch* cartoonist, great-grandfather of the Earl of Snowdon, has changed little in three generations. Crammed with Victoriana (photographs, chiming clocks, china and glass), the walls covered in William Morris wallpaper, the windows hung with heavy Victorian drapes, it feels a long way from the late 20thC.

The central part of Kensington, thought of as **South Kensington** since that is the name of the tube station serving it, is dominated by a complex of museums and colleges set up on land bought with the proceeds from the Great Exhibition held in Hyde Park in 1851. Albert, Prince Consort to Queen Victoria, sponsored the scheme, and much of the character of this monument to Victorian optimism comes from his vision. He is commemorated by the *Albert Memorial* and *Royal Albert Hall*.

Next to the Albert Hall is the **Royal College of Art**, a supposedly "brutal" but in fact dull building of 1960-61. A little to the E of the Albert Hall is the **Royal Geographical Society**, an attractively informal house in Dutch style designed by Norman Shaw in 1874. There are statues of David Livingstone and Scott of the Antarctic, both fellows of the RGS.

To the s is Prince Consort Rd. Here, at the center of the large 20thC buildings of **Imperial College** (London University's leading science department), is the **Royal College of Music**, a red-brick pseudo-medieval building of 1883-84. Its lovely collection of musical instruments is on view (☎ *open Mon, Wed in term-time 11am-4pm*). The 280ft **Queen's Tower** (☎ *open July-Sept daily 10am-6pm, no* ♣) is a survivor of the 1887-93 Imperial Institute buildings, and affords a spectacular, uninterrupted view of London.

South of Imperial College are the great museums that, together with the colleges, represent the fulfillment of Albert's dream: the *Science Museum*, the *Natural History Museum*, one of London's finest buildings, the Geological Museum, now known as the Earth Galleries of the Natural History Museum, and the *Victoria & Albert Museum*.

The eastern part of Kensington is predominantly residential. Beyond the Victoria & Albert Museum is the *Brompton Oratory*, with the shopping center of the Brompton Rd. beyond, and the incomparable **Harrods** department store. Behind the main road, attractive 19thC housing stretches up to Knightsbridge and s into Brompton. An interesting building, well worth a detour, is **Michelin House**, an Art Nouveau gem of 1910, on Fulham Rd., now the Conran Shop and Bibendum restaurant (see *Restaurants*). Its ceramic decorations include panels with charming scenes of early auto races.

Kensington Palace 🏛

Kensington Gdns., W8 ☎ 937-9561. Map 6H3 ☒ ✍ Open Mon-Sat 9am-4pm, Sun 1-4pm. Tube: High Street Kensington, Queensway.

Kensington Palace was first made a royal residence when it was bought by William and Mary in 1689. The house had large grounds, now **Kensington Gardens** (see *Walk 4* in *Planning*), and was next to the expanse of *Hyde Park*. Sir Christopher Wren was instructed to enlarge the palace and, apart from further work in the 1720s, most of what is seen was built under his supervision. It is a simple building, around three courts, and surprisingly unpretentious for a royal palace. Perhaps the most striking building is the **Orangery** of 1704, a little to the NE, probably designed by Nicholas Hawksmoor.

The interior is mostly private but the State Apartments can be visited. Some of the rooms are largely as Wren left them; others were made grander by William Kent in the 1720s. Kent's own Baroque paintings adorn several walls and ceilings, most notably in the **King's Staircase**, the **King's Gallery** and **King's Drawing Room**. One of the most attractive rooms is the **Queen's Bedroom**, sumptuously but intimately decorated, with fine 17thC furniture including the bed made for James II's queen. Look out for the fine carving by Grinling Gibbons, Wren's carver, over the fireplace in the Presence Chamber, enhanced by Kent's "Etruscan" ceiling, and also the wind vane above the fire in the King's Gallery. There is an interesting display of paintings of and exhibits from the Great Exhibition of 1851 in the **Council Chamber**. Several good paintings are on display in addition to the fine furniture: most notable is Van Dyck's seductive *Cupid and Psyche* (✩), but look for Artemisia Gentileschi's powerful *Self-portrait*, an important work by a woman artist.

On the ground floor, the **Court Dress Collection** was opened in 1984. A unique display of court dress and army uniforms from 1750 to the 1950s, it also includes Princess Diana's wedding dress.

The royal tradition is kept up by the Prince and Princess of Wales, who have their London home here.

Kenwood House *(The Iveagh Bequest)* 🏛 ★

Hampstead Lane, NW3 ☎ 348-1286. Map 21C4 ☒ ➤ Open summer 10am-6pm, winter 10am-4pm. Tube: Highgate.

After a short walk through old and well-established woods, on *Hampstead* Heath, the exquisite 18thC mansion comes into view, with Robert Adam's superb Classical facade flanked harmoniously by wings containing the orangery and library. Adam was commissioned to adapt an old Stuart house in 1766 by the first Earl of Mansfield. The result was some of the Scottish architect's finest work, including the South Front, with its decorated pilasters and the stucco portico that forms the main entrance. Several Adam details survive; the **library** is outstanding. The room was intended for "receiving company" as well as housing books, and this explains its splendor.

Kenwood was saved from the hands of speculative builders in 1925 when the first Earl of Iveagh (Edward Cecil Guinness, of brewing fame) bought the house. He died only 2yrs later, leaving the house, a sizeable bequest and a collection of pictures to the people of London. Apart from the library, the house is now laid out as an art gallery.

English 18thC painting is best represented, with excellent examples of Gainsborough and Reynolds; Gainsborough's sumptuous *Mary, Countess Howe* is a masterpiece of the artist's elegant later style. Kenwood's real stars, however, are Dutch paintings, with fine examples by Cuyp and Van de Velde. Linger over Vermeer's *Guitar Player* and, supreme, Rembrandt's *Self-portrait* of c.1663. Other notable artists represented include Van Dyck, Guardi, Boucher and Turner.

In summer, concerts are given by the lake (see *Nightlife*). Dr. Johnson's summerhouse was moved here in 1968.

Kew

Map 20D3. Tube: Kew Gardens; or train to Kew Bridge from Waterloo.

Close to the ideal of an English country village, Kew Green is not as rustic as it first seems. It is actually flanked by 18th-19thC detached and row houses that lend an air of substantial prosperity, and its unusual parish church, **St Anne's**, was built under royal patronage in 1710-14 (and extended in 1770). An interesting feature is the Royal Gallery above the w door, donated by George III in 1805.

Royal Botanic Gardens ★

☎ *(081) 940-1171* 🖾 ✿ *Open daily, gardens Jan, late Oct-Dec 9.30am-4pm; Feb 9.30am-5pm; Mar, late Sept to late Oct 9.30am-6pm; Apr to late Sept Mon-Sat 9.30am-6.30pm, Sun 9.30am-8pm; greenhouses from 10am; galleries, museums from 9.30am; closing times vary considerably, but as a general rule, summer Mon-Fri 4.30pm, Sat, Sun 5.30pm; winter 3.30pm.*

The full name of Kew Gardens comes as a salutary reminder to those who are apt to be seduced by its supreme beauty and forget that it is a scientific institution. As such, it is unmatched, studying, classifying and cultivating a vast number of plants from all around the world. Despite the devastation suffered in the storm that struck southern England in Oct 1987, and again in Jan 1990, Kew still boasts superb walks and dreamlike views; in spring it is sublime.

Kew Gardens was formed from the grounds of two royal residences: Richmond Lodge and the White House. George III united the two estates. From 1771-1820 Sir Joseph Banks, who had accompanied Captain Cook to the South Seas, extended the existing botanic garden (founded in 1759), sending young botanists all over the world in search of specimens. It was with the help of Kew Gardens that breadfruit was introduced to the West Indies and rubber to the Malay Peninsula. In 1840, the gardens were handed over to the State and the first director was formally appointed in 1841. Further grants of land by the Crown

in 1898 and 1904 took the total to more than 300 acres.
Expansion continues; a major new exhibition area, opened in
1990, is housed in the new Sir Joseph Banks Building. The
innovative design incorporates many energy-saving features.

Begin at the main gates by Kew Green, and turn sharp left for
the vast new **Princess of Wales Conservatory**. It contains ten
different habitats, from Namib Desert and mangrove swamp to
cloud forest and tropical pools. Alternatively, proceed up the
Broad Walk, which turns left at the Orangery, leading to the
pond and Palm House, returning by smaller paths through
flower-filled woodland, rock, grass and other gardens.

Not far from the main gates is the **Dutch House**, or **Kew
Palace**, built in red brick with steep Dutch gables by a wealthy
merchant in 1631. To the rear is the **Queen's Garden**, an
accurate reconstruction of a 17thC garden, with tightly-clipped
hedges and aromatic herbs. Back at the Broad Walk, the
Orangery (1761) contains a restaurant and shop.

Now bear right, away from the Broad Walk. The long Riverside
Ave. here passes through cedar, plane and oak-planted woods. A
detour left takes in the **rhododendron dell** (almost a crime to
miss in late spring), the bamboo garden and azalea garden, with
the beautiful lake to the S. Walk around the riverside for a fine
view across the Thames to *Syon House*. Farther SW are the
grounds of **Queen Charlotte's Cottage**, thatched in rustic style
and built in the 1770s as a focal point for elaborate garden
parties. It is now surrounded by an area left wild as natural
habitat for native British plants and wildlife. E lies the **Japanese
Gateway**, a fine replica erected in 1910 on a little hill,
surrounded by pines and flowering azaleas. Farther E again is the
163ft **Pagoda**, built in a more fanciful Oriental style in 1761-62,
forming the focal point to one vista extending from the Palm
House.

Pagoda Vista returns toward the entrance. On the way, take in
the **Temperate House**, a large 19thC complex of greenhouses
containing many fine specimens, with the **Marianne North
Gallery** to the E, home of an extraordinary collection of 832
botanical paintings. A little farther N, mock temples and ruins
survive from the 18thC garden layout. The **Palm House** then
comes into view, a magnificent and graceful iron and glass
construction of 1844-48 by Decimus Burton and Richard Turner.
It contains a fabulous collection of tropical rainforest plants.

Lambeth Palace ▥

SE1 ☎ 928-8282. Map **19** J12. Open only to organized
groups reserving in advance: apply in writing to the Bursar
(✗ usually Wed or Thurs 2.15-3.30pm). Tube: Lambeth
North.

In the possession of the Archbishops of Canterbury since 1197,
Lambeth Palace grew into prominence as the Primate's residence
in the later Middle Ages. In 1547, Thomas Cranmer wrote the
English Prayer Book here, but caused great controversy by eating
meat during Lent in the Great Hall. The superb red-brick
gatehouse dates from 1495, and next to it stands the 15thC tower
of the now deconsecrated church of St Mary-at-Lambeth. Beyond
the walls can be seen the Classical stonework decorating the
hall, rebuilt after the Civil War.

St Mary-at-Lambeth has been taken over by the **Museum of
Garden History**, where a replica of a 17thC knot garden has
been laid out in the former churchyard (▣ ♟ *open Mar-Dec
Mon-Fri 11am-3pm, Sun 10.30am-5pm*).

Lancaster House 🏛

Stable Yard, The Mall, SW1 ☎ *839-3488. Map 9H9.*
Currently closed to the public. Tube: Green Park.
Previously known as York House and Stafford House, according
to the aristocrat in residence, Lancaster House (begun in 1820) is
the most westerly of the palaces of *The Mall*, with its facades
overlooking Green Park to the w and *St James's Park* to the s.
Benjamin Wyatt designed the exterior in cool Bath stone with
massive and severe Classical porticos similar to his *Apsley
House*, together with the imposing stairwell. Charles Barry, who
took over in 1838, completed the interior in a much more
grandiose and highly decorated Baroque style. Paintings by
Veronese and Guercino, brought to the house to decorate
ceilings of the antechamber and gallery, conform to this rich taste.

Law Courts   The popular name for the fine Victorian Gothic
Royal Courts of Justice on the *Strand.*

Leighton House 🏛

12 Holland Park Rd., W14. Map 21C4 ☎ *602-3316* 🖂 *Open
Mon-Sat 11am-5pm; during special exhibitions Mon-Fri
11am-6pm. Tube: High Street Kensington.*
Looking like one of several plain red-brick houses in a street
once favored by successful artists, Leighton House contains a
remarkable surprise. Lord Leighton was the most famous of
Victorian artists and, in building his house from 1865, he gave
vent to his taste for the exotic, creating a rich interior in Moorish
style. It is fantasy, a harem in London. The highlight is the **Arab
Hall**, with its two stories culminating in a dome, and its walls
covered with rich 13th-17thC Islamic tiles. Interesting Victorian
paintings on show include works by Leighton himself and
Edward Burne-Jones.

Lincoln's Inn 🏛 ★

☎ *405-1393. Map 11E12* 🖂 *Courtyards open Mon-Fri 9am-
6pm; chapel and gardens open Mon-Fri 12.30-2.30pm; to
see Old Hall and Great Hall apply to Porter's Lodge. Tube:
Holborn, Chancery Lane.*
This most unspoiled of the *Inns of Court* was founded in the
14thC. The best way in is from Chancery Lane, through a
gatehouse (with the original gates) of 1518 and the Tudor red-
brick **Old Buildings** (before 1520). Opposite the gate is the **Old
Hall** (1490-92), which contains an uncharacteristically serious
painting by Hogarth and a fine wooden roof. On the N side of the
court is the **chapel**, dating from about 1619-23, standing on an
open undercroft of Gothic vaulting with rich ribbing. Its high-
backed boxed pews, and its stained-glass windows of numerous
coats of arms of treasurers dating back to the 17thC, contribute to
a deep serenity. To the sw is **New Square**, not originally built as
part of the Inn but a large and remarkably well-preserved square
of about 1685-97; its dignified brick houses, with decoration
restricted to the open pediments above the doors, enclose a
splendid lawn. To the s is a gateway of 1697 leading into Carey
St. The northern part of the Inn includes the great bulk of Stone
Buildings of 1774-80, with a severe Classical facade on the w
side; the large sundial on this wall is dated 1794. Opposite are the
Inn's attractive private gardens, together with the impressive
Victorian brick-Gothic library and New Hall. Beyond these lie the
open spaces of Lincoln's Inn Fields, one of London's largest
public squares.

London Bridge

Map 13G16. Tube: Monument, London Bridge.

London's *raison d'être*, one might call it — the Romans discovered that this was the farthest downstream they could easily cross the river, and built their town accordingly. In fact, their wooden bridge was almost certainly a little to the E of the present structure, but survived with periodic reconstructions until the medieval stone bridge appeared in 1176-1209. This stood for more than 500yrs, encrusted with houses, shops, even chapels, and the famous iron spikes where traitors' heads were displayed. Eventually, all its buildings were removed and the bridge modernized in about 1749, at the same time as London's second bridge was built at Westminster. A new bridge, now moved to an amusement park in Arizona, was built in 1825-31. The present structure of three arches dates from 1967-73.

There are several attractions grouped around the vicinity of London Bridge. Collectively they are known as *Bridge City*.

London Dungeon

34 Tooley St., SE1 ☎ 403-0606. Map 13G16 🔳 ■ *Open daily Apr-Sept 10am-5.30pm; Oct-Mar 10am-4.30pm. Tube: London Bridge.*

Enjoying the London Dungeon requires a special sense of humor — and a strong stomach. Its location in a series of dark, damp vaults under railway arches has been carefully chosen to foster discomfort, and is ideally suited to its exhibits on the "darker side of British history." The vaults echo to the recorded sounds of screams and moans, and even the rumble of the occasional passing train. The ancient British heroine Boadicea, for example, is shown thrusting a blood-smeared spear into the throat of a gurgling victim, and in another set piece, *The Fire of London*, ingenious special effects create the illusion of being in Pudding Lane engulfed by flames. Not for the faint-hearted.

London, Museum of ★

150 London Wall, EC2 ☎ 600-3699. Map 12E15 🔲 ■ ✴ *Open Tues-Sat 10am-6pm, Sun 2-6pm. Tube: Barbican, Moorgate, St Paul's.*

In a new building on the corner of the *Barbican*, this museum traces the social history of London from prehistory to the present day in "social" manner. The museum possesses a substantial part of the stock of important archeological finds made in London, and is chronologically arranged so visitors follow a single winding course, with the two floors joined by a glass walkway.

Archeological finds from the **Stone, Bronze and Iron Ages**, most originating from sites in the Thames Valley to the w of London, are grouped in settings that show the purposes to which they were put by ancient people. Thus ax heads have been fitted with handles to show how they would have been used; and models and drawings reconstruct the appearance of prehistoric settlements and explain early hunting methods and agriculture.

Roman London is well represented in the museum and, as an added surprise, a carefully placed window looks down on one of the best-preserved parts of the Roman wall outside, with its medieval bastions. Inside, the display ranges from leather sandals to board games to the superb sculptures found buried in the floor of the Temple of Mithras discovered in 1954 during the construction of an office building in Queen Victoria St. The **head of Serapis** is particularly exquisite. A famous **mosaic floor** found in 1869 can be seen in a reconstructed room setting, with reproduction furniture showing the luxurious Roman way of life.

The displays of **Anglo-Saxon and medieval London** begin with the strange gravestone in the Viking Ringerike style, inscribed with runes dating from the 11thC. An excellent model of the original Tower of London shows it as a single stone tower surrounded by a wooden palisade. A model of old *St Paul's Cathedral* is even more impressive, and shows how the great Gothic cathedral must have been before its destruction in the Great Fire of 1666.

A Ming porcelain cup mounted on a silver-gilt stand and an exquisitely embroidered glove show the sophisticated tastes and superb workmanship of the **Tudor and Stuart** periods. Also noteworthy are a copper plate of c.1558, engraved with a contemporary map of London, and the Cheapside Hoard, a collection of 16thC jewelry. Politics now feature more prominently: the Civil War, Great Plague and Fire of London all receive ample attention. A darkened room with a large model graphically shows the progress of the fire; old London actually appears to disintegrate as you watch, with a commentary from Pepys' diary. The exhibits from the 18th-20thC are even more varied, if more familiar, and the **Georgian** gallery has recently been completely renovated. **Shop fronts and interiors** are reconstructed, including a superb 18thC barber's, a 19thC pub, and an early broadcasting studio. There are some extraordinary barred doors from the notorious Newgate Gaol, an 1862 fire engine, and even an Art Deco elevator from Selfridges department store. On a smaller scale, look out for some charming Victorian Christmas and Valentine cards and toys. But grandeur steals the show: the **Lord Mayor's Ceremonial Coach (★)** (1757), removed once a year for the Lord Mayor's Show, stands resplendent with its elaborate painted and gilt decoration.

London Toy and Model Museum
21 Craven Hill, W2 ☎ *262-7905. Map 7F4* 🔳 💻 ✻ *Open Tues-Sat 10am-5.30pm, Sun 11am-5.30pm. Tube: Paddington, Queensway.*

This remarkable museum appeals as much to adults as to the children for whom the exhibits were originally intended. Several of the toys on display can be activated by the touch of a button. Dolls, nursery toys, mechanical toys and a collection of model railway locomotives fill a warren of rooms. There is a double-decker bus, a carousel and a miniature railway, which children can ride on, in the small garden, and a "hands-on" video. Plans are afoot to redesign the museum to make it less cramped.

London Transport Museum
The Piazza, Covent Garden ☎ *379-6344. Map 10F11* 🔳 ✻ *Open daily 10am-5.15pm. Tube: Covent Garden.*

As part of the renovation of *Covent Garden*, the Flower Market (1871-72) now houses a large number of historic public transportation vehicles in its spacious galleries. This "hands-on" museum chronicles the history of the capital's transportation, with illustrations, photographs, audiovisual displays, relics such as tickets and posters, and fine models of everything from the "wherries" that plied the river to electric trams. Children can press a button to operate an Underground elevator, sit in the driver's seat of a tram and a bus, and work the deadman's handle in a tube train. The vehicles include a replica of the first omnibus of 1829, a development London copied from Paris, two late 19thC horse-drawn buses, with open-top decks, and early motor buses and trams, also with open tops and painted in the familiar fire-engine red of today. The tube engines and carriages go back to the 19thC, and there is a simulation of the Circle Line from the driver's point of view. An exhibition lasting 18 months from May 1990 celebrates the centenary of the tube.

Madame Tussaud's ☆

Marylebone Rd., NW1 ☎ *935-6861. Map 2D7* ▨ ▦ ✳ *Open Mon-Fri 10am-5.30pm, Sat, Sun 9.30am-5.30pm. Tube: Baker Street.*

The redoubtable Madame Tussaud lived to be 89. Having begun her wax modeling in France with the aristocracy and royalty of the *ancien régime*, and having continued to work through the Revolution (the severed heads of king and queen as modeled by Madame can be seen in the museum's Chamber of Horrors), she came to England in 1802 and settled her waxwork museum in London in 1835. It is now linked to the *Planetarium*.

The modern display combines the old and the new. A section at the start of the exhibition entitled *200 Years of Madame Tussaud's* displays the famous *Sleeping Beauty* tableau, its central figure cast from one of Madame Tussaud's oldest molds, thought to have been made of Madame du Barry, Louis XV's mistress, with a mechanism that simulates breathing. The modern method of wax model-making is also explained here, showing how Jerry Hall was immortalized, and immortalizing her real-life model-maker in the process. Other recent celebrities range from Joan Collins, Cher and Eddy Murphy to Mikhail Gorbachov and Benazir Bhutto. In the *Garden Party*, stars such as Luciano Pavarotti, Dudley Moore (at the piano) and Jayne Seymour can be seen singing, playing and making merry together.

Nowhere are the visitors quieter than in the greatest draw of all, the **Chamber of Horrors**, which has among other terrors a reconstruction of the dark streets of Whitechapel where Jack the Ripper stalked. See also *Rock Circus*, Madame Tussaud's rock-and-pop outpost.

The Mall ☆

Map 10H10. Tube: Charing Cross, Green Park.

Whenever pomp and circumstance are on hand, the Mall is where the crowds gather. Originally laid out by Charles II in 1660-62 as a formal avenue through *St James's Park*, it is now a triumphal processional way leading from *Trafalgar Square* to *Buckingham Palace*. As such, it is largely the work of one man, Sir Aston Webb, between 1900-11.

Majestically lined with plane trees, it slopes gently but impressively down along the side of the park to the Victoria Memorial and Buckingham Palace facade, both also designed by Webb. Looking from Admiralty Arch, the first building on the right is **Carlton House Terrace**, built by John Nash in 1827-29 on the site of his earlier Carlton House, the great palace built for the Regent. Its two massive stucco facades are separated by the Duke of York Steps. The view is best from St James's Park — the balancing ranges, with their Corinthian colonnades, broad terraces at raised ground-floor level, and supporting dumpy Doric columns, are one of London's most exciting architectural views. On the s side of The Mall is the **Admiralty** of 1722-26 with the aggressively concrete Citadel next to it, a bold bombproof structure from World War II.

The rest of The Mall is surrounded by the park, but with the palaces that are scattered along its N side visible on the right.

Marlborough House, of stone-dressed red brick, is followed by the complex making up *St James's Palace* and then the white stucco of **Clarence House**, built by Nash in 1825-27 for the Duke of Clarence, later William IV, and now the home of the Queen Mother. Lancaster House follows, in more solemn yellow Bath stone. The **Victoria Memorial** occupies a circus at the end of the avenue, a huge structure covered with elaborate sculpture of high quality in the florid Edwardian style. Queen Victoria's likeness faces up The Mall toward Admiralty Arch, topped by a gilded statue of *Victory*. The circus was laid out in 1900-1901 and the memorial built in 1911.

Mankind, Museum of
6 Burlington Gdns., W1 ☎ 437-2224. Map 9G9 ☷ ☎ Open Mon-Sat 10am-5pm, Sun 2.30-6pm. Tube: Piccadilly Circus, Green Park.

The museum is the result of the recent upsurge of interest in non-European cultures. Since 1972 the British Museum's ethnographic collections have been based in this elaborate Victorian building, decorated with statues of British philosophers, built in 1866-67 as a part of London University. At present, the museum is organized as a series of temporary exhibitions on particular cultures or themes, but they achieve considerable depth of coverage.

The ethnographic collection is outstanding in African textiles, pottery, and sculpture, American art from Plains Indians and those of the NW Coast, and Pre-Columbian Central and S America. From the Pacific Ocean, the collection has objects brought back in the 18thC by Captain Cook. From Indonesia come puppets, masks and other items collected by Sir Stamford Raffles in Java in the 19thC. A permanent exhibition of the museum's greatest treasures is kept in **Rm. 7**, including a life-sized skull carved from a solid piece of crystal from Mexico, a hauntingly beautiful object. **Rm. 5** provides an overview of the collection. Stunning Aztec turquoise mosaics in the forms of a skull-mask and double-headed serpent are shown in **Rm.1**.

Mansion House
Walbrook, EC4 ☎ 626-2500. Map 13F16 ☷ ☷ Open only to organized groups reserving in advance (minimum age 12); apply in writing to the Assistant Private Secretary (✗ Tues-Thurs 11am, 2pm). Tube: Bank.

As if in reference to the ancient city-states, the residence of the Lord Mayor of London, symbol of the independence of the *City*, is Classical in character. It owes its Palladian simplicity to George Dance the Younger, who designed it in 1739-53. Its six giant columns support the only decoration, a pediment with sculptures representing the dignity and opulence of the City. But the interior is extremely ornate, with a series of state rooms leading back from the portico to the grand climax of the **Egyptian Hall** (Roman in style, despite its name). The annual **Lord Mayor's Show**, which arrives here in Nov (see *Calendar of events*), is the climax of a largely medieval system of government; during the year you can see here the liverymen, aldermen and sheriffs who choose the Lord Mayor, parading at various antiquated ceremonies. But their power is real — this is the only private residence in the kingdom with its own court and prison cells.

Marble Arch
Map 8F7. Tube: Marble Arch.

Now in the center of a major traffic island, the Marble Arch retains only part of the grandeur intended when John Nash built it in 1828 as the entrance to Buckingham Palace. Modeled on the Arch of Constantine in Rome, it was moved to its present site in 1851 when the palace was enlarged by Queen Victoria. Its traffic island was also the site of Tyburn Tree, London's traditional place of execution from the Middle Ages until 1783. A plaque marks the site of the permanent large triangular gallows where regular hangings, drawings and quarterings attracted large crowds. *Speakers' Corner* is close by on the corner of *Hyde Park*.

Marble Hill House 🏛

Richmond Rd., Twickenham ☎ (081) 892-5115. Map 20D3
🔲 Open 10am-6pm Easter-Sept; 10am-4pm Sept-Easter.
Tube: Richmond; train to St Margarets from Waterloo.
A house of elegant Palladian regularity, this fine riverside mansion w of London began life with some "irregular" occupants: it was built for George II's mistress, the Countess of Suffolk, in 1723-29, and then Mrs Fitzherbert, George IV's secret wife, lived here in the 1790s. Its stuccoed, pristinely white exterior has little decorative detail — the rear, garden side is particularly impressive — and it stands in a fine open park.

The interior of the house is quite beautiful, with a series of lovely rooms culminating in the splendid **Countess of Suffolk's Bedroom**, with Corinthian columns framing the alcove intended for the bed. Some attractive furniture has been put back into the house, together with a number of interesting paintings, including good copies of Van Dyck portraits. The **Lazenby Collection**, displayed on the second floor, includes Chinese paintings on mirrors, furniture and pottery. Flanking one side of the park is the exquisite **Montpelier Row**, a perfect terrace of 1720.

Marlborough House 🏛

Pall Mall, SW1 ☎ 839-3411. Map 10H10. Currently closed for restoration. Tube: Green Park, St James's.
This red-brick house with bold stone dressings, the finest of the palaces bordering *St James's Park*, was built by Sir Christopher Wren for the Duke and Duchess of Marlborough in 1709-11, following the duke's series of victories over the French in the War of Spanish Succession, which also won him Blenheim Palace near Oxford (see *Excursions*). Various additions were made in the 18th-19thC, notably the attic stories, but Wren's powerful conception can still be appreciated when viewed from the park. The entrance on the *Pall Mall* side is curiously unimpressive. Most of the present decoration is 19thC, but a series of original murals depicts Marlborough's battles, and the ceiling of the Blenheim Saloon is decorated with Gentileschi's series painted for the Queen's House at *Greenwich* in 1636. The house now serves as the Commonwealth Centre.

Marylebone

Maps 8&9D-F. Tube: Baker Street, Great Portland Street.
During the 18thC, the fashionable West End expanded N to surround the village of St Marylebone (St Mary-le-bourne, meaning St Mary-by-the-brook). The streets form a near-perfect grid, with the major ones running N-S from *Regent's Park* toward Oxford St. It now consists largely of smart houses and apartment blocks, with some busy shopping streets. Although it has several squares and some good buildings, it is a curiously anonymous area. The first part to be laid out was Cavendish Sq. in 1714. St Peter's Chapel nearby in Vere St. was designed in

1721-24 by James Gibbs, and prefigures *St Martin-in-the-Fields*. The finest houses are **no. 20 Portman Square**, designed by Robert Adam in 1775-76, and **Hertford House** in Manchester Sq. (the *Wallace Collection*). Other famous addresses are **Harley Street**, home of top doctors and clinics, **Baker Street**, of Sherlock Holmes fame, and **Wimpole Street**, where Robert Browning wooed Elizabeth Barrett. On Marylebone Rd. are *Madame Tussaud's* and the *Planetarium*.

Mayfair ☆
Map 8&9F-H. Tube: Bond Street, Green Park.
The very name is synonymous with wealth and elegance — nowhere in London will you see more Rolls Royces or more fur coats. It was not always so. The annual fair that lent its name to the area was suppressed by George III in 1800, so riotous had it become. Mayfair today is a roughly square-shaped section of the West End, bordered by the shopping streets of Oxford St., Regent St. and Piccadilly, and Park Lane, lined by large 20thC hotels and the backs of grand 19thC mansions. Inside this area are expensive shops, luxurious hotels, casinos, and homes of the rich.

The development of this area began in about 1700, and by 1800 it was largely filled with squares and terraces. **Grosvenor Square** is the largest, without its original houses and with the large United States Embassy of 1961 at its western end. Of the squares, **Hanover Square** is the oldest (about 1715); original houses survive in **St George's Street** to the s. **Berkeley Square** is best known, thanks to its mythical nightingale; it has huge plane trees (almost 200yrs old) in its fine gardens and attractive 18thC houses surviving in the sw corner. Only one really grand mansion survives among the houses: **Crewe House** in Curzon St., begun in 1730. Two churches date back to the early development of the area: **St George's, Hanover Square**, in St George's St. (1721-24; notice the grand portico and bronze hunting dogs standing guard); and **Grosvenor Chapel** in South Audley St., a more modest edifice from about 1730. The Jesuit **Church of the Immaculate Conception** (1844-49), in the same street, is worth a visit, with a high altar designed by Pugin.

The shopping streets scattered through Mayfair best preserve its reputation for high living. Around Bond St. (New and Old) are the best art and antique dealers. Savile Row has the world's finest gentlemen's tailors (see *Shopping*). 19thC **Shepherd Market** is an enclave of alleyways lined with smart shops and cafés.

The Monument 🏛 ☆
Monument St., EC3 ☎ 626-2717. Map 13G16 ▨ Open Apr-Sept Mon-Fri 9am-5.40pm, Sat, Sun 2-5.40pm; Oct-Mar Mon-Sat 9am-3.40pm. Tube: Monument.
Deprived of its commanding appearance by the many modern buildings that surround it. The Monument, on its little hill close to the river, nevertheless retains the Baroque drama of its conception. Designed by Wren, built in 1671, it commemorates the Great Fire of London that began on Sept 2, 1666 in the bakery in nearby Pudding Lane. A relief on the base plinth shows Charles II in Roman dress protecting the citizens of London; the original inscription unjustly blamed the disaster on a Catholic plot. A giant Doric column, 202ft high, contains 311 steps up to a balcony and gilded urn. It is a stiff climb but worth it for the view.

Moving Image, Museum of the *(MOMI)* See *South Bank Arts Centre*.

National Army Museum

Royal Hospital Rd., SW3 ☎ *730-0717. Map* **16L7** 🔳 ✗ *for groups only, by appt through Education Dept* 🕮 *Open Mon-Sat 10am-5.30pm, Sun 2-5.30pm. Tube: Sloane Square.*

Opened in 1971 in a new building close to the **Royal Hospital, Chelsea**, the National Army Museum brings together objects from several older collections. The **Weapons Gallery** is a self-contained exhibition displaying a comprehensive collection of small arms used by the British Army from the 17thC to the present day; the use of both edged weapons and handguns, from muskets to self-loading rifles, is expertly explained. **The Story of the Army** is divided into two galleries. The highlight of the first is a comprehensive exhibition of the British Army in the Napoleonic Wars featuring a huge model of the Battle of Waterloo (made shortly afterwards and never before displayed), the skeleton of Napoleon's horse, and Wellington's battlefield telescope. The second tells the story from 1914 to the Falklands War, with life-sized displays, audiovisuals and dioramas. There is a fine **uniform gallery**, a picture gallery and a reading room.

National Gallery ★

Trafalgar Sq., WC2 ☎ *839-3321. Map* **10G11** 🔳 ✗⁂ ✗ � 🕮 *Open Mon-Sat 10am-6pm, Sun 2-6pm; June-Aug Wed 10am-8pm. Tube: Charing Cross, Leicester Square.*

Now possessing more than 2,200 pictures, the National Gallery is one of the world's finest collections of art. Few rivals can boast such a comprehensive account of Western art, and the way the paintings are shown provides a model for other great national collections: they are clean, clearly labeled, well-lit and given adequate space.

This freshness of approach accords with the National Gallery's relative youth. When most European capital cities already had public collections, in 1823, the threat of the sale of John Julius Angerstein's great collection to William of Orange forced a tight-fisted parliament to produce the money to found a national collection. Angerstein's pictures were bought for £57,000 and housed with other bequests in Angerstein's house in Pall Mall. By 1832, with the collection growing, a larger building was needed. It was designed by William Wilkins and completed in 1838, stretching the full length of the N side of **Trafalgar Square**, but was never the imposing building intended, and has frequently been expanded since. The northern extension, built in 1975, is superbly functional, with excellent hanging space. After much controversy over the choice of architect, Robert Venturi's **Sainsbury Wing**, an extension to the W of the gallery, finally opened in spring 1991, provides new galleries to house the Early Renaissance collection of Italian and Northern works painted before the 16thC, together with galleries for temporary exhibitions, a large auditorium for lectures, a computerized information room, conference rooms and a shop and restaurant.

The collection of pictures has expanded steadily, its character changing in accordance with the taste of the different periods of acquisition. After some exploratory Italian forays in the 1840s, the pioneering director, Sir Charles Eastlake, purchased many early Italian works from 1855-65, when these pictures were little known. As a result the gallery has a collection of Italian art unequaled outside Italy. In 1861, Queen Victoria gave 20 German and Flemish pictures in memory of her husband Albert; this inspired a new round of acquisitions, resulting in a magnificent

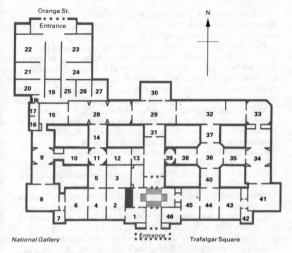

National Gallery — Trafalgar Square

group of Dutch and Flemish works. In the 20thC attempts have been made to strengthen the French collection.

British art is the specialty of the *Tate Gallery*, as is modern art, but the National Gallery does have some fine 18thC British masterpieces. There are also outstanding Spanish works.

Since 1946, the National Gallery has had a conservation department and has been in the forefront in applying science to the care and restoration of paintings. Many National Gallery paintings can now be seen in the most beautiful condition, cleaned of dirt or past overpainting. Temporary exhibitions, usually in the **Sunley Rm.**, and now too in the Sainsbury wing, bring in pictures on loan to develop particular themes.

The collection is exhibited chronologically, with the first rooms containing Early Italian painting and progressing through to 19thC European works. In the early Italian section is the *Wilton Diptych* (★), actually not Italian but put here because of its early date (c. 1395). Probably French, it shows the English monarch Richard II being presented to the Virgin and Child, with saints and angels in attendance. The other glowing medieval icons are further testimony to faith as well as artistic genius; Duccio's **Maestà altarpiece panels** (★) from Sienna Cathedral are outstanding. Then comes the transition to a more realistic style. Lorenzo Monaco's *Coronation of the Virgin* is in the graceful International Gothic style, while Masaccio's innovative *Virgin and Child* (★) has the spiritual gravity and solid forms of the Renaissance, thrown into relief by Paolo Uccello's *Battle of San Romano* with its unsuccessful attempt at realistic perspective. The Renaissance can also be seen emerging in Botticelli's early *Adoration of the Magi* and his *Venus and Mars* (★), admired for the purity of its line, and in Piero della Francesca's *Baptism of Christ*. Leonardo's famous and beautiful black-chalk *Cartoon* (★) has been restored after gunfire damage in 1987.

Next, the superb collection of Italian Renaissance art unfolds. Among too many highlights to list are: Michelangelo's unfinished *Entombment*, a rare easel picture; Raphael's *Pope Julius* (★), which was only recently discovered to be the original among several versions around the world; Correggio's charming *Mercury instructing Cupid before Venus* (★); Leonardo's mysterious *Virgin of the Rocks* (★) and Bronzino's *Allegory*, with its chilly eroticism and obscure subject. One of the original pictures bought from the Angerstein collection is Sebastiano del Piombo's huge *Raising of Lazarus*, for which the artist received guidance from Michelangelo. Of the Venetian works, Titian's breathtaking *Bacchus and Ariadne* (★) is ablaze with color and movement. Other important Venetian works include Tintoretto's dramatic *Origin of the Milky Way* and Veronese's *Family of Darius before Alexander*. All the greatest masters of the period are here.

The Renaissance was not such an Italian monopoly as is sometimes supposed. The carefully observed naturalism of Northern painters greatly influenced their Italian counterparts; the Dutch and Flemish collection illustrates this better than anywhere else in the world. The most famous work here is Jan Van Eyck's *Arnolfini Marriage* (★), full of realistic but symbolic detail. In the same room is a beautiful jewel-like altarpiece by Memlinc showing the *Virgin and Child with Saints and Donors* and a recent acquisition, *The Virgin and Child in an Interior*, a tiny but fine panel painting by Robert Campin. As a reminder of the range of the northern painters, look out for a wonderfully grotesque *Adoration of the Kings* by Brueghel, and a weird rocky *Landscape with St Jerome* by Patenier. The German and Early Netherlandish pictures are less numerous, but include some important masterpieces such as Dürer's **portrait of his father**, the exquisite little Altdorfer *Landscape with a Footbridge* and Cranach's *Charity*, a charming early nude. Holbein's *Ambassadors* (★) was probably the most important picture painted in England in the Tudor period; as a reminder of frailty, the oblique shape in the bottom left corner shows itself to be a skull when viewed from the right angle.

The Dutch 17thC, the golden age of painting in the Netherlands, is strongly represented: there are several Rembrandts, including the extraordinary *Self-portrait* (★) of 1640, with its sad dignity, and the quietly powerful *Woman Bathing*. There are two Vermeers, of which the *Woman Standing at a Virginal* (★) best demonstrates the sense of intimate silence that the artist generates. There are many fine landscapes, of which the most famous is the *Avenue at Middelharnis* (★) by Hobbema, and also scenes of everyday life, with the restrained, precise style of the Dutch school.

The art of the 17thC in Flanders was altogether grander, dominated by Rubens and Van Dyck. Major works by both can be seen, including Van Dyck's *Equestrian Portrait of Charles I*. Rubens' joyous, colorful *Judgment of Paris* contrasts with the dignity of his landscape *Château de Steen* (★).

The succeeding rooms are occupied by 17th-18thC Italian works. Caravaggio's *Supper at Emmaus* (★) shows the artist's revolutionary use of naturalism in religious art: the disciples are seen as real working people with coarse clothes; look at the drama even in the hands. A popular acquisition, found on the ceiling of a London house, is Tiepolo's *Allegory with Venus and Time*, full of light and air.

French painting of the 17th-18thC is shown with emphasis on Poussin and Claude, both of whom have been assiduously collected in Britain. Poussin's *Bacchanalian Revel* demonstrates his influential cool Classicism. Claude's mysterious and peaceful landscapes are altogether more approachable; the *Enchanted Castle* (★) has an astonishing, dreamlike quality, achieved largely by superb mastery of light. The French 18thC is poorly represented by National Gallery standards; even so it offers Watteau's *La Gamme d'Amour*, Chardin's acute *Young Schoolmistress* (★), Boucher's *Landscape with a Watermill* and David's *Portrait of Jacobus Blauw*.

The gallery's strongest English period is the 18th-19thC. Outstanding works include Hogarth's satirical *Marriage à la Mode* paintings, the basis for the more famous series of engravings, and magnificent examples of that period's two best genres, Gainsborough's portrait of *Mr and Mrs Andrews* (★) and Constable's landscape *The Hay Wain* (★). Turner opens new vistas with this magical *Rain, Steam and Speed* (★) and *The Fighting Téméraire*.

There are a small number of Spanish pictures of extraordinary quality. El Greco's *Christ driving the Traders from the Temple* (about 1600) is the finest of several paintings by this remarkable artist. From the later 17thC there is Velázquez's sensual tour-de-force, *The Rokeby Venus* (★), and a portrait of *Philip IV*, together with Zurbarán's *St Francis*, showing the dark religious passion so characteristic of Spanish art. There are also several good Goyas, including the famous portrait of the *Duke of Wellington*.

The last rooms house the gallery's acquisitions charting the emergence of modern art. An impressive collection of Impressionist works include Renoir's *Les Parapluies* (★) (periodically moved to Dublin) and Monet's stunning *Water-lilies* (★), as well as Degas' *Beach Scene*. Van Gogh's intense, dynamic *Sunflowers* introduces a Post-Impressionist collection that also includes Seurat's *Bathers, Asnières* (★), works by Gauguin and Klimt's *Hermione Gallia*.

National Portrait Gallery ★

2 St Martin's Pl., WC2 ☎ *930-1552. Map 10G11* 🔲 🔳 *with flash. Open Mon-Fri 10am-5pm, Sat 10am-6pm, Sun 2-6pm. Tube: Charing Cross.*

Opened in 1859 as a kind of "national pantheon," the emphasis was placed from the start on the subjects of the pictures rather than on artists or on art for art's sake. Nevertheless, the effort to obtain the best portraits has meant that the collection has acquired many fine paintings and drawings. Since 1968, photographs have been systematically included and caricatures are now also accepted. In fact, the emphasis on history gives great coherence to the exhibition, which is arranged chronologically with relevant background material, such as a pictorial essay on the Industrial Revolution. The excellent **temporary exhibitions** (*some* 🔳) also expand on themes or figures from the starting point of the portraits.

The present buildings were constructed next to the *National Gallery* in 1896 and extended in the 1930s. The collection begins at the top (several flights of stairs have to be climbed), with a room devoted to medieval portraits. Portraits in a modern sense were not produced in the Middle Ages, so the images are few in number; a copy of the fine representation of *Richard II* in Westminster Abbey dominates. Portraits became common from the Tudor period and perhaps the most interesting examples in the whole collection come from this early section. There is an excellent version of *Henry VII* by Michel Sittow of 1505, painted for the Holy Roman Emperor when Henry was seeking his daughter's hand in marriage. Perhaps the finest work of all is Holbein's magnificent cartoon for a lost fresco at Whitehall Palace showing *Henry VIII with his Father Henry VII* (★). There is an exquisite full-length image of *Lady Jane Grey*, executed in

1554 after she had become queen at the age of 17. Several portraits of Elizabeth I are in the incredibly detailed style of the period, with the queen decked out in rich clothes and encrusted with jewelry. A portrait of *William Shakespeare*, dated about 1610, is the only one with any claim to authenticity.

The gallery continues through the Jacobean and Stuart periods, with the increasing formality of the court painters, giving way to the more lively images of the 18thC. Figures from the arts and sciences increase gradually in proportion to the political and military leaders. This was another golden age of English portraiture; look for Hogarth's *Self-portrait*, several works by Gainsborough and Reynolds, and pictures of *Dr. Johnson and Charles James Fox*. A fine unfinished portrait of *Nelson* by Sir William Beechey and a romantic *Byron* in Greek costume show the greater concentration on the individual that becomes apparent in much of the 19thC work. Royalty, however, is still shown in highly idealized fashion: *Victoria and Albert* sculpted in the costume of ancient Saxons is the most amusing example.

The portraits from the last years of the 19thC and later are varied in style. The 20thC galleries are being totally reorganized and are due to be completed by fall 1991. There are superb studies of *Edith Sitwell* by Wyndham Lewis, and some fine bronze busts by Epstein. Royalty, however, is still idealized with deference. Recent acquisitions include *Sir David Wester* by David Hockney, *Elizabeth Taylor* by Andy Warhol, *Richard Rogers* by Sir Eduardo Paolozzi and the double portrait of *Sir David and Sir Richard Attenborough* by Ivy Smith.

National Theatre 🏛

Upper Ground, South Bank, SE1 ☎ *633-0880. Map* **11G12** 🚾 *✗ up to 5 times a day* ⚋ 🖃 *Tube: Waterloo.*

It is a blessing that the institutionalization of the theater in London has not led to any stultifying subservience. The drama remains as true to its nature of subversiveness as when it was banished to the South Bank in the Middle Ages, and this component of the **South Bank Arts Centre** created its own furore. The building itself, designed by Sir Denys Lasdun in 1970-75, is a prime example of the Brutal style, a lumpy abstract sculpture in concrete. But the interior is much more universally admired, with a superb intersection of horizontal and vertical planes creating a honeycomb of useful and interesting space. It has a restaurant, **Ovations** (☎ *928-3531*).

See also *Theaters* in **Nightlife and the performing arts**.

Natural History Museum 🏛 ★

Cromwell Rd., SW7 ☎ *938-9123. Map* **15J5** 🚾 🖃 ✦ *Open Mon-Sat 10am-6pm, Sun 1-6pm. Tube: South Kensington.*

When the **British Museum** was formed from Sir Hans Sloane's collections in 1753, a high proportion of material consisted of plant, animal and geological specimens. Appropriately, these categories grew at enormous speed (they still do), and in 1860 it was decided to split off the natural history collections. Between 1873 and 1880 the present building was erected in South Kensington with Alfred Waterhouse as architect. His creation is a cathedral to nature, a vast Romanesque construction with a central porch opening onto a great iron-roofed nave. Unlike a cathedral, however, it has two immensely long side wings creating an impressive facade along the Cromwell Rd. Once criticized as austere and heavy, cleaning has revealed the bright colours of the cream and blue terra-cotta tiling, and the countless relief details that cover the exterior — a fitting showcase for the treasures housed within.

In the 1970s, a new policy was adopted by which the museum shows a series of self-contained exhibitions, rather than attempting to show all of its millions of specimens in old-fashioned cabinets. At the main entrance, however, parts of an older, dramatic display have survived: the giant Central Hall, with huge dinosaur skeletons towering over the visitor. There they stand, absurd and terrifying, the center of an exhibition about their evolution and disappearance. The left side of the hall is given over to an exhibition explaining the theory of evolution, and the right side to one of the museum's newest displays, *Creepy crawlies*. Arachnophobes beware: this exhibition contains a full-sized house crawling with spiders, termites, carpet beetles and other insects. Also on the ground floor is an exhibition of British birds arranged by habitat, and an exceptionally lively presentation on every aspect of human biology.

One of the museum's most effective sections, *Discovering Mammals*, traces the life-cycle of whales and other mammals through fascinating dioramas and interactive models. It also contains the vast skeletons and jawbones of the great mammals and a life-sized model of a blue whale. A monumental staircase leads from the Central Hall to the upper floor, where an exhibition traces the evolution of man. Another, on the origin of the species, covers Darwin's work with admirable thoroughness. The traditional hall, devoted to minerals, rocks and gems, serves as an effective contrast to the newer exhibition techniques, and is notable for the incredible diversity and beauty of its specimens. There is an exciting new **Discovery Centre** (*open Mon-Sat 10.30am-5pm, Sun 1.15-5.15pm*) in the basement, where children can stroke a rock python's skin or try their hand at beachcombing. An ambitious exhibition on global ecology, housed in a vast glass structure, is due to open in 1991.

In 1989 the Geological Museum became part of the Natural History Museum, linked by a corridor and now known as the **Earth Galleries**. The traditional displays upstairs on the regional geology of Britain and world economic mineralogy are of limited interest compared with the stunning exhibitions on the ground floor. Here, the collection of **gemstones** includes some beautiful specimens, both crude and cut. There are also two adventurous exhibitions entitled *The Story of the Earth* and *Treasures of the Earth*, and two smaller exhibitions, *Britain before Man* and *British Fossils*. On the first floor, displayed on a structure resembling a real offshore platform, *Britain's Offshore Oil and Gas* tells the full story of hydrocarbons, from both geological and operational viewpoints.

Old Bailey *(Central Criminal Court)*

Old Bailey, EC4 ☎ *248-3277. Map* **12**F14 ⊡ ✗ ⬛ *Open Mon-Fri 10.30am-1pm, 2-4pm. Tube: St Paul's.*

The Old Bailey's famous gilt figure of *Justice*, complete with scales and sword, looks down on a site with a grim history. The Central Criminal Court replaced Newgate Gaol, dating from the Middle Ages, for many years a place of execution and eventually the 19thC reformers' ultimate symbol of penal squalor. The current Portland stone building dates from 1900-7. Inside its heavy Baroque frame, justice can be seen to be done from the public galleries, but you will have to line up early when a major criminal case is being heard — the crowds of the Newgate gallows have their modern counterparts.

Orleans House Gallery 🏛

Orleans Rd., Twickenham ☎ (081) 892-0221. Map 20D3 🗗
ఉ 🎫 Open Apr-Sept Tues-Sat 1-5.30pm; Sun and bank hol Mon 2-5.30pm; Oct-Mar Tues-Sat 1-4.30pm, Sun 2-4.30pm. Tube: Richmond; train to St Margarets from Waterloo.
Although it takes its name from the Duc d'Orléans, later King Louis Philippe of France, who lived here in the early 19thC, this house in Twickenham, near Strawberry Hill, dates from 1710. Regrettably, much of it was demolished in the 1920s, but the superb **Octagon** survives amid attractive woodland. It was designed by James Gibbs in 1720. The interior is richly decorated with Baroque stucco work: heads of George II and Queen Caroline can be seen on medallions. An adjacent gallery is used for a continuous program of temporary exhibitions covering a wide variety of subjects, sometimes including the **Ionides Collection** of 18th and 19thC topographical English paintings, but it is not on permanent display. Nearby is *Marble Hill House* and the grander *Ham House* (which can be reached by ferry).

Osterley Park 🏛 ☆

Isleworth, Middlesex ☎ (081) 560-3918. Map 20C3 🗗 *🖵 in summer. Open Tues-Sun 11am-5pm. Tube: Osterley.*
Already one of the finest country houses in the London area, Osterley gained more prestige after being completely refurbished between 1761 and 1782 by the great Scottish architect Robert Adam for the banker Francis Child, who was trying to emulate the other country houses nearby, such as *Syon House*. It still contains much of the furniture he designed for it, and is set in a large area of parkland, with lakes and woods, and an attractive brick stable block to one side, probably containing the buildings of the medieval manor house that originally stood on the site.

Adam's building is a large hollow square, with corner turrets and a great portico that opens to the central courtyard. This unusual scheme for the 18thC was dictated by the existing house, built on a magnificent scale by Sir Thomas Gresham (the wealthy founder of the Royal Exchange) in the 1570s. By Adam's time it had fallen into decay, and he completed the covering of the exterior with an entirely new skin of brick, and built the portico.

At the end of the courtyard the main door leads into the hall, the centerpiece to the whole design, beautifully decorated in Adam's Classical style, with white stucco reliefs on a gray background. At either end, copies of ancient Roman statues inhabit niches within apses. Note how the ceiling decoration is echoed in the marble floor pattern. Beyond the hall is the great **gallery**, a plainer room probably designed a few years earlier by Sir William Chambers. The remaining rooms open to the public are by Adam, who even designed the door handles and friezes. The **Drawing Room** has a ceiling of extraordinary richness and contains fine original commodes. The **Tapestry Room** is hung with works from the French royal Gobelins workshop, in extravagant pink with Rococo designs from paintings by Boucher. The **State Bedchamber** has an absurdly elaborate four-poster bed. Plainer, but just as effective, is the **Etruscan Dressing Room**, with delicately painted walls.

Pall Mall

Map 10H10. Tube: Charing Cross, Green Park.
When *St James's Palace* became the main royal residence in the 17thC, this avenue quickly became established as its main route into London and the site for the favorite Stuart game of

palle-maille, resembling modern croquet. The street is now the most important in *St James's*, famous for the traditional gentlemen's clubs that line its s side, a sequence of stern Classical buildings reflecting the importance of tradition in this most conservative of areas. From the *Trafalgar Square* end, Pall Mall becomes interesting beyond the soaring glass slab of **New Zealand House** (1957-63). This is at the bottom end of John Nash's great city planning scheme of the early 19thC that stretched up Regent St. and incorporated *Regent's Park*. Just past New Zealand House will be found the delightful little **Opera House Arcade**, built by Nash in 1816-18 and the first in London; note the splendid wrought-iron lamps. At Waterloo Pl. the **Duke of York's Column**, built by Benjamin Wyatt in 1831-34, can be seen in front of the steps of **Carlton House Terrace**.

Back on Pall Mall, the gentlemen's clubs begin. These uniquely English and very exclusive institutions, designed to provide the gentleman with a "country house" haven to which he can retire in the city, thrive unchanged, still offering, in various mixes, snoozing, business talk and witty conversation, and hallowed peace. The corners with Waterloo Pl. are occupied by the impressive **United Services Club**, designed in 1827 by Nash (now the Institute of Directors), and the **Athenaeum** of 1828-30, traditionally the clergy's and academics' club. Farther along in a dignified terrace come the **Travellers' Club** (1829-32), a Victorian version of Italian Renaissance for those who have been more than 1,000 miles from London; the **Reform Club** (1837-41), a Liberal political grouping formed after the 1832 Reform Act; and then more modern buildings, including the **Royal Automobile Club** of 1908-11. Beyond comes **Schomberg House**, built in 1698, a tall brick structure with projecting wings. Other clubs are the **Army and Navy** on the N side, jokingly known as "The Rag" after the toughness of its meat; the **Oxford and Cambridge** on the s; and the **Junior Carlton**, a stepping-stone for the famous senior Tory (Conservative) club. Pall Mall ends with the lower, brick buildings of *St James's Palace*, past the entrance to *Marlborough House*.

Parliament, Houses of   See *Westminster, Palace of.*

The Percival David Foundation of Chinese Art
53 Gordon Sq., WC1 ☎ *387-3909. Map 4D10* 🖼 *with flash. Open Mon-Fri 10.30am-5pm (frequently closed 1-2pm). Tube: Euston.*
Gathered with scholarly precision by Sir Percival David and given by him to the University in 1951, this remarkably rich collection of Chinese ceramics of the 10th-19thC is aptly sited in *Bloomsbury*, surrounded by intellectual and artistic endeavor. Unfortunately, the presentation of the collection is rather too scholarly, and the great numbers of bowls, jars, vases and figurines grouped in display cabinets by classification tend to cancel each other out by their profusion. But the individual items are of great beauty, glazed in rich and subtle colors. Temporary exhibitions are displayed on the ground floor.

Piccadilly
Map 9G-H. Tube: Piccadilly Circus, Green Park.
As the famous "hub of Empire," **Piccadilly Circus** put on a pretty poor show a few years ago, with a motley collection of buildings covered in illuminated signs. But recently the **Trocadero** center, with its shops, restaurants and exhibitions,

has brought a new sense of life, helped by the **Criterion** brasserie (Victorian mosaics and tiles, next to the charming **Criterion theater**), and the **London Pavilion**, a shopping complex that includes *Rock Circus*. The focus of the Circus is the **Shaftesbury Monument**, a statue and fountain of Eros (1893) around which international youth likes to gather while temporarily dropping out. Recently restored, it is now the center of a pedestrian mall, no longer marooned on its central island. Piccadilly itself, stretching w to Hyde Park Corner, is lined with imposing commercial buildings and famous shops: **Hatchard's** for books, **Simpson's** for clothes and **Fortnum and Mason** for anything expensive (see *Shopping*). And there are arcades of smart little shops, with the Piccadilly Arcade of 1909-10 to the s and the most attractive Burlington Arcade of 1815-19 to the N. Wren's *St James's*, the **Ritz** (see *Hotels*) and Green Park are of greatest interest on the s side; Burlington House (the *Royal Academy*) on the N. By Hyde Park Corner is *Apsley House*.

Planetarium
Marylebone Rd., NW1 ☎ *486-1121. Map 2D7* 🔳 𝄢 ▣
"Starshows" every 40mins 11am-4.30pm. Tube: Baker St.
Attached to *Madame Tussaud's*, the Planetarium's greater green copper dome is a striking landmark, providing convincing displays and "starshows" on astronomy. The auditorium inside the great dome is at the top of a long ramp through the Astronomers' Gallery, past imaginative displays on the great astronomers. But the highlight for all visitors is the moment they tip back their seats and gaze at the heavens projected on the dome above them. In the evening, **Laserium** features a combination of rock music and dazzling laser lights in several 1hr-long shows (*for details: Laserline* ☎ *486-2242*).

Post Office Tower See *British Telecom Tower.*

Public Record Office Museum 🏛
Chancery Lane, WC2 ☎ *(081) 876-3444* 🖃 *Open Mon-Fri 10am-5pm. Map 11F13. Tube: Chancery Lane.*
Most of the public records are now kept at Kew, but in this successful example of Victorian Gothic official architecture one room and a corridor are given over to a museum, boasting some remarkable treasures. Outstanding are the two volumes of the **Domesday Book**, the great survey of England carried out for William the Conqueror in 1086. Among later documents are a pipe roll of 1210-11, showing the account of the Sheriff of Nottingham, the enrolment of letters patent to William Penn, Collingwood's account of the death of Nelson, and the Assizes minute book, showing the conviction of the Tolpuddle Martyrs. There is a small display of royal seals and an example of early Renaissance sculpture by Pietro Torrigiano: the recumbent figure of John Young, a Master of the Rolls (*d.* 1519), in a Classical architectural surround. It came from the Rolls Chapel, which once stood here. Also note the beautiful porcelain model of the chapel's original font, displayed in the corridor.

Regent's Park ☆
Maps 2&3A-D. Tube: Regent's Park, Baker Street.
Regency London was certainly sophisticated; and the legacy is one of the most impressive examples of town planning in the country. Marylebone Fields, a hunting preserve of Henry VIII's, reverted to the crown in 1809, and the Prince Regent's friend,

John Nash, was put in charge of an ambitious scheme that would link it with Carlton House to the s via the new Regent St. Now Carlton House has gone, but the park retains much of the original plan. It is approached from Portland Pl., leading into the elegant terraces of **Park Crescent** and **Park Square** (1812-23). To E and W around the flanks of the park stretch magnificent Classical terraces, mostly built in the 1820s. To the W the amazing length of **York Terrace** and, best of all, the imaginative, almost Oriental-looking **Sussex Place** with its octagonal domes. The dome motif is repeated in copper on the late 1970s **Mosque** nearby. On the E side, **Chester Terrace** and **Cumberland Terrace** are ostentatiously grand, with vast decorated porticos.

The park itself is attractively landscaped, with a massive straight **Broad Walk** continuing the line of Portland Pl. through the center. Two circular roads (the Inner and Outer Circles) carry road traffic; on the Inner Circle, **St John's Lodge** incorporates parts of a villa of about 1818. Here too is the marvelous **open-air theater** where superb productions of Shakespeare's plays can be enjoyed in summer months (see *Nightlife*). There is a small lake in **Queen Mary's Gardens** within the Inner Circle, and a larger one with islands to the W. Across the N side is a branch of the *Grand Union Canal*, nicely incorporated as part of Nash's plan, and the *Zoo*.

Registry of Births, Deaths and Marriages

St Catherine's House, 10 Kingsway, WC2 ☎ *242-0262. Map 11F12* ▢ ✻ *Open Mon-Fri 8.30am-4.30pm. Tube: Aldwych, Temple.*

With perseverance and a little money, it is possible to trace ancestry in England or Wales back to 1837, the date centralized registration of births, deaths and marriages began. To go further back, local records have to be consulted. The system is not difficult but it is time-consuming, a factor that seems to discourage few people, for the offices are always busy. Simply look up the reference for yourself or an ancestor born in England or Wales (listed alphabetically by year) and order the birth certificates, which takes about two days. This will usually give the names, addresses and occupations of the parents. By searching for their marriage certificate or birth certificates it is possible to repeat the process back into history.

Richmond ☆

Map 20D3. Tube: Richmond.

The Palace of Sheen, first occupied by Henry I in 1125, began an important royal connection that fostered the growth of this still beautiful Thames-side town. The name came later; after a fire in 1499, Sheen was rebuilt as Richmond Palace by Henry VII, the title coming from his former title as Earl of Richmond (in Yorkshire). Henry died in the palace, as did Elizabeth I in 1603. Charles I was the last king to live there, moving his court during a 1634 plague; in due course the palace fell into decay.

Of the great Tudor palace, the most magnificent before the building of Wolsey's near *Hampton Court*, very little remains. What there is can be seen on the western side of **Richmond Green**. A Tudor gatehouse marks the position, but within are private houses of later date, which, in some cases, incorporate portions of the old brickwork: the fine early 18thC pedimented facade of **Trumpeters' House** predominates. Richmond Green itself boasts exceptional 18th-19thC houses on all four sides — most notable is **Maids of Honour Row** of about 1724, built for the companions of Caroline, wife of the future George II, who then lived at Richmond Lodge in Old Deer Park in *Kew* to the N. **Richmond Theatre**, built in 1899, lies across the green to the W. Old Palace Lane leads down to the river, where the attractive ocher **Asgill House**, a mansion of the 1760s, is on the left.

Richmond's busy and crowded shopping center, with its infuriating traffic system, contains some 17thC almshouses in The Vineyard near the parish church of **St Mary Magdalene**, with its interesting 16thC tower, and, up Hill Rise, the fine Queen Anne houses of Ormond Rd. To the E, **St Matthias** by Sir George Gilbert boasts one of the finest Victorian Gothic spires in London, and by the river, the attractive Quinlan Terry development (1988) is a skillful blend of original and "new" Georgian architecture.

To the S of the noble 18thC bridge rises **Richmond Hill**, offering one of London's most remarkable views. Preserving this unspoiled vista over *Marble Hill House* and *Ham House* across the wooded expanse of the Thames Valley was a rare triumph of planning control. The view has been painted by several of Britain's greatest artists, such as Reynolds, Turner and Constable. Some good 18thC houses stand at the top, including **Wick House**, built for Reynolds by Sir William Chambers in 1772.

Richmond Park is the most telling reminder of Richmond's royal connection; with more than 2,000 acres first enclosed by Charles I and still a royal park, it is the most natural stretch of green land in London. Its rough heath and woodland contain a great variety of native plants (particularly in the **Isabella Plantation**), birds and animals, even protected herds of red and fallow deer. The highest points offer excellent views NE across London. The several picture houses in the park include **White Lodge**, built for George II in 1727-29, now the Royal Ballet School, and **Pembroke Lodge** of about 1800.

Rock Circus

London Pavilion, Piccadilly Circus, W1 ☎ 437-7733. Map 10G10 ▦ ✱ Open daily 10am-10pm. Tube: Piccadilly.
Visitors don a headset and must prepare themselves for an onslaught of nostalgia at this outpost of Madame Tussaud's, which opened in Aug 1989. Rock Circus presents the history of rock and pop music from Bill Haley to Michael Jackson through wax and "audio animatronic" figures, which move and perform golden oldies and more recent chart-toppers in an eerily lifelike way. The giants of the rock and pop world are all featured here from Jerry Lee Lewis, Chuck Berry, Elvis, complete with a lip that really curls, the Beatles, Jimi Hendrix, the Rolling Stones, Eric Clapton, Elton John, Stevie Wonder and Tina Turner. More recent stars include Bruce Springsteen, Sting and Madonna.

Royal Academy of Arts ▥

Burlington House, Piccadilly, W1 ☎ 439-7438. Map 9G9 ▦ ✿▦ ▣ Open daily 10am-5.30pm. Tube: Piccadilly Circus, Green Park.
Built as a mansion for the first Earl of Burlington in the newly developed Piccadilly area in about 1665, Burlington House was remodeled in 1717-20 in the elegant Palladian style. The third earl made this as celebrated a forum for the artists whose patron he became as his *Chiswick House*; Pope, Arbuthnot, Gay, all often attended. Unfortunately, between 1868 and 1874 the profile of the Georgian house was obliterated by the rebuilding that marked its adoption by the Royal Academy of Arts. This new building is in the Victorian Renaissance style, with a screen along

Piccadilly opening onto a forecourt with a statue of Sir Joshua Reynolds in the center. Other learned societies occupy the buildings to the right and left.

The Royal Academy was founded in 1768 with Reynolds as its first and greatest president to foster the arts of Britain. Except for a few decades after its foundation, however, the most interesting developments in British art have consistently taken place outside of, and even in opposition to, the dictates of the Royal Academy. This is still true: the Academy's free-for-all **Summer Exhibition** (see *Calendar of events*) may be popular and enjoyable, but no one would claim that it does much to influence developments in art. The modern academy consists of 40 academicians and 30 associates, the country's most successful establishment artists. Today, crucially, it hosts major loan exhibitions.

The academy has an important collection of works of art, many by academicians, who have always been obliged to donate one of their works to the academy. Paintings by Reynolds, Gainsborough, Constable and others are not on public display (except during special exhibitions). The decorative schemes of its grand interior include paintings by artists such as Benjamin West and Angelica Kauffmann (the entrance hall), and Marco Ricci. The academy's outstanding treasure is Michelangelo's beautiful relief tondo depicting the *Madonna and Child* (★).

Royal Air Force Museum, Hendon
Grahame Park Way, NW9 ☎ *(081) 205-2266. Map 21B4* ▨
▣ *Open daily 10am-6pm. Tube: Colindale.*
The northern suburb of Hendon itself lays claim to the interest of aircraft enthusiasts: there was a pioneering flying school here before World War I, and it became one of the first aerodromes, staging regular air displays and becoming famous as the starting point for the first nonstop London-to-Paris flight in 1911. The museum was opened in 1972 in an excellent modern building, which incorporates two historic World War I wooden hangars. Interesting displays trace the history of flight and show the development of the Royal Air Force, with its vital role in two world wars. However, it is the aircraft themselves that take pride of place. They range from the Blériot XI, similar to that in which Louis Blériot made the first cross-channel flight in 1909 to the English Electric Lightning, capable of twice the speed of sound.

Famous World War I aircraft include a Sopwith Camel from Britain, a Caudron G3 of French design and a Hanriot HD1, which was used extensively by the Belgian Aviation Militaire. From World War II there is a Spitfire Mk1 that fought in the Battle of Britain, a Beaufighter, the only known Typhoon left in the world, and two new acquisitions, a Fairey Battle and a Focke Wulf Fw 190F-8/U1. More modern jet aircraft include the early Vampire and Gloster Meteor, the remarkable Canberra and, another addition, a Supermarine Swift, a mid-1950s jet fighter.

The splendid **Battle of Britain Museum** (▨) nearby contains a unique collection of British, German and Italian aircraft that fought in the great air battle of 1940. Also in the same complex is the vast new **Bomber Command Museum** (▨), which contains a striking display of famous bomber aircraft including the Lancaster, Wellington, Mosquito and Vulcan.

Royal Britain
Aldersgate St., EC1 ☎ *588-0588. Map 12E15* ▨ ▣ ✻ *Open daily 10am-5.30pm. Tube: Barbican.*
Covering 35,000sq.ft and 1,000yrs of history, Royal Britain

opened in Aug 1988 and is designed to make visitors feel as though they are seeing, hearing and experiencing history first-hand. The exhibition boasts 23 "feature environments," which combine visual displays, special and sound effects to bring historical events to life. You can listen to the noise of battle as Boadicea makes her heroic stand against the Romans; witness Edgar's coronation as the first King of England in 973AD; eavesdrop on Richard the Lion Heart as he prays in his tent during the Crusades; and take Mary Queen of Scot's final tragic walk down a corridor in Fotheringhay Castle to her execution. Then, stepping into the present, you can experience the life led by members of the Royal Family today, shaking hands and receiving posies, amid the bevy of flash photographers.

Royal Courts of Justice 🏛

Strand, WC2 ☎ 936-6000. Map 11F13 ▨ ✿ ▣ Open Mon-Fri 9.30am-4.30pm; courts open 10.30am-1pm, 2-4.30pm. Tube: Temple, Chancery Lane.

Better known as the Law Courts, this extravagant complex in the **Strand**, built by G.E. Street in 1874-82, houses the courts where important civil, as opposed to criminal, law cases are heard. Long despised as an example of Victorian plagiarism, the Early English Gothic buildings are now admired by many. Cleaning has helped, for the rich colors and intricate patterns in the stone can be appreciated. In addition, the Courts show a dignity suited to their purpose, and their complex irregularity and inventive detail feast the eye. Inside too, the sheer scale of the **great hall** is quite as impressive.

Royal Hospital, Chelsea 🏛 ☆

Royal Hospital Rd., SW3 ☎ 730-0161. Map 16L7 ▨ Grounds open Mon-Sat 10am-12.45pm and from 2pm; closing times vary between 3.30pm and 8pm depending on time of yr; Sun afternoons only; chapel and dining hall Mon-Sat 10am-12pm, 2-4pm, Sun 2-4pm. Tube: Sloane Sq.

Amply surrounded by parkland and retaining all the dignity of its riverside setting, Wren's stately Royal Hospital from 1682-92 is still a majestic sanctuary of calm, although now surrounded by **Chelsea**. It was founded by Charles II in 1682 as a refuge for aged and disabled soldiers on the model of Louis XIV's Les Invalides in Paris. It now houses some 400 pensioners, including a dwindling number of World War I veterans, who can be seen around and about Chelsea in their old-fashioned uniforms, red in summer and blue in winter; and in May it hosts the **Chelsea Flower Show** (see *Calendar of events*).

The best view is from the S, where an open courtyard looks down the extensive gardens toward the river. At the center of the courtyard is a statue of Charles II as a Roman emperor by Grinling Gibbons, Wren's master carver. The hospital is entirely symmetrical and quite plain, its red-brick facades embellished with minimal stonework. At the center of each block stands a tall white portico of four columns or pilasters, and the central block is capped by a graceful, spire-like lantern. The severely domed **vestibule**, lit by the lantern above, is entered through the portico in the courtyard. To the right is the **chapel**, little altered since Wren's time. It has a fine carved reredos in dark wood, matching the organ gallery at the entrance end and, in the apse, a painting (about 1710-15) by Sebastian Ricci, *Christ in Majesty*, a colorful burst of Baroque splendor. The **Great Hall** occupies the corresponding space to the chapel on the other side of the vestibule. It is more solemn, with paneled walls and military standards hanging from the ceiling. At the far end, the dark and ponderous painting, *Charles II*, by Verrio shows the king with mythological companions in front of the hospital buildings. A small **museum** in an eastern wing covers the hospital's history.

Tucked in between Royal Hospital and Chelsea Bridge Rds, **Royal Hospital Burial Ground** is an undiscovered treasure (*for admission ask at London Gate*). Among those buried here are William Hiseland, who lived to the ripe old age of 112, Fanny Burney's father, Charles, the hospital's organist, and two women who fought in the Crimean War and whose sex was only discovered when they were wounded.

St Bartholomew-the-Great ▥ † ★
Little Britain, EC1. Map 12E14. Tube: Barbican.
The churchyard through the 15thC gateway with the charming Tudor house on top used to be the nave of this, one of the oldest churches in London, founded in 1123. Now only the chancel and transepts remain with their 19thC refacing of flint and Portland stone. Inside, many original features survive. Huge columns in the **nave** support a Romanesque triforium, surmounted by a clerestory built in 1405 in Perpendicular Gothic style.

Beyond the altar is the much rebuilt **Lady Chapel**, dating back to 1335, where in 1725 Benjamin Franklin worked. At the w entrance, the massive crossing, which once supported a huge stone tower, can be seen. The present tower in brick is above the s aisle and dates from 1628. Five medieval bells are housed in the tower, making this one of the oldest peals in the country. On either side of the crossing are the much restored transepts.

There are a number of fine monuments, including the medieval tomb of the founder, Thomas Rahere, which has a delicate canopy of 15thC Gothic tracery. The monument to Edward Cooke (*d.*1652) actually weeps in damp weather as a result of condensation — a phenomenon referred to in the inscription.

St George's Bloomsbury ▥ †
Bloomsbury Way, WC1. Map 10E11. Tube: Holborn.
This splendid church compares well with the near contemporary but much more famous *St Martin-in-the-Fields*. Built by Nicholas Hawksmoor in 1720-31, it is in some ways an even more dramatic design than Gibbs', with a huge portico of Corinthian columns and a layer-cake spire, topped with a statue of George I as St George, a typical piece of Baroque overstatement. The interior repeats the boldness of the exterior — simple shapes, plenty of light and more giant columns. Notice the fine patterned inlay of the wooden reredos.

St James's
Map 10G-H. Tube: Piccadilly Circus, Green Park.
Despite being unprotected by conservationists, there are still in the world examples of that strange breed, the English gentleman. Come to St James's, and you would never know that they are rare, for this is *their* district, still existing to provide the quiet, comfortable life long enjoyed by the upper-class.

Occupying the area between *St James's Park* and *Piccadilly*, the land was granted to the Earl of St Albans in 1665 in recognition of his loyalty while the king was in exile. The earl at once began building, and the proximity of the palace ensured that his square and streets soon became fashionable. The centerpiece was **St James's Square**, with a large central garden.

No 17thC houses survived, but there are several fine examples from the 18thC: **Lichfield House**, no. 15, with its Classical facade, is the best. At the center of the gardens is an equestrian statue of William III from 1807. To the N up Duke of York St. is the area's church, *St James's Piccadilly*.

To the S, running parallel to the park, is *Pall Mall*, a splendid road lined with gentlemen's clubs. *St James's Palace* is at the western end, with **St James's Street** stretching N to Piccadilly. Here are many more of the gentlemen's clubs built in the 19thC: **White's** for hard-drinking Conservatives; **Boodles**, a famous gambling club in the days of Beau Brummell, the Regency dandy; **Brooks'**, the Whig club founded in 1788; and the **Carlton**, the Conservatives' club. **St James's Place** leads off to the W toward Green Park, a quiet street lined with 18thC houses: at the end, magnificent **Spencer House** (1756-66) overlooks the park. Opposite is an interesting office development, aggressively modern and built in 1959-60. Adjacent is the **Economist** complex, built around a central plaza just to the W of St James's St.

St James's is justly famed for its shops, with the most traditional approach to service and quality in London (see *Shopping*). Try the Victorian **Red Lion** pub in Duke of York St. (see *Pubs*).

St James's Palace 🏛 ★
Pall Mall, SW1. Map 9H9. Not open to the public. Tube: Green Park.

Despite its much greater antiquity, London has an architectural threshold formed by the plague and fire of 1665-66. This royal palace is unique in surviving intact, unadorned, and preserving a glimpse of Tudor London. There it sits, sandwiched by its larger offspring of *St James's* and *The Mall*, and yet dwarfing them, for all their grandeur and boldness, by its very antiquity and history. The official royal residence from 1698, until *Buckingham Palace* took over in 1837, its seniority is still recognized; the Queen's court is "the Court of St James" and new monarchs are still proclaimed from here. Today it provides "Grace and Favour" quarters for yeomen-at-arms, lords and ladies-in-waiting, and the Lord Chamberlain.

Henry VIII took over the site from a leper hospital in 1532, and had his palace built entirely in brick, with battlements and diapering (diagonal patterning in the brickwork). Even the State Rooms added by Wren in the 17thC, also with battlements, maintain the low, informal approach, echoing the domesticity of Tudor architecture. The best original feature, visible from *Pall Mall*, is the tall **gatehouse**, with its octagonal corner towers. The fine interior is closed to the public.

The **Queen's Chapel**, across Marlborough Rd. but originally within the palace, is in style entirely different. Designed by Inigo Jones, it was built in 1623-27 in the Classical manner, with rendered white walls and Portland stone dressings. The beautiful interior boasts ornate Baroque work from the 1660s, including fine carving by Gibbons. To the W, attached to the palace, is **Clarence House**, built in 1825-27 by Nash and now the Queen Mother's home; when she is in residence, a piper plays the bagpipes in the garden at 9am. The palace is flanked by two grand mansions from later periods: *Marlborough House* to the E and *Lancaster House* to the W, with *St James's Park* to the S.

St James's Park ☆
Map 10H-1. Tube: St James's Park.

London's first royal park was always nearer to art than nature. In

1536 Henry VIII drained a marsh to make a park between *St James's* and Whitehall Palaces, filled with deer (for ornament rather than hunting). In 1662, Charles II made it a public garden, laid out in the formal style of the period with avenues of trees, *The Mall* as a carriageway, and a long straight canal. In 1828, it was remodeled on the present pattern by John Nash, who created the lovely complex of trees, flowerbeds and views across the natural-looking lake that we see today. The waterfowl, some of which breed on Duck Island at the E end, have always continued the contrivance — there are even pelicans. The view from the bridge across the lake back toward *Whitehall* is one of the most beautiful in London.

St James's Piccadilly 🏛 ✝

Piccadilly, W1 ☎ 734-5244. Map 10G10. Tube: Piccadilly Circus, Green Park.
When *St James's* was developed as a residential area after 1662, Sir Christopher Wren was commissioned to build the new church, completing it in 1674. It is basically one great room with plain galleries and a vaulted ceiling decorated with plaster moldings. Damaged by bombs in 1940, the church has been well restored and preserves some fine fittings. The organ is 17thC, moved from the old Whitehall Palace, topped by gilded figures carved by Grinling Gibbons, who also produced the marvelous marble **font**, with its virtuoso relief of Adam and Eve, and the rich floral arrangements carved on the wooden **reredos**.

St Katharine's Dock ☆

Map 13G18. Tube: Tower Hill.
Next to the *Tower of London*, St Katharine's was the first of the docks to be given an entirely new role (see also *Docklands*). Originally built in 1827-28 by the great engineer Thomas Telford, this was for many years one of the leading docks in the Pool of London, with the advantage of being closest to the City. Today, St Katharine's again profits from its proximity to the City, as a residential and tourist center and a yacht marina. The modern World Trade Centre looks down on the brick-brown sails of Thames sailing barges and gleaming hulls of luxury yachts moored in the docks. Telford's **Ivory House** (later modified) shows off 19thC industrial apartments, shops and an exhibition area. A timber-built warehouse is now the **Dickens Tavern**, and blocks of fashionable apartments sit between docks and river.

The dock's collection of old ships has now dispersed, and moorings are now used by smart yachts and occasional barges.

St Martin-in-the-Fields 🏛 ✝

Trafalgar Sq., WC2. Map 10G11. Tube: Charing Cross.
The first buildings in a new architectural style often seem oddities, and this church has maintained its nonconformity. Today it is the venue for concerts on Mon and Tues lunchtimes and a shelter for vagrants and drug addicts, as well as a church. The broad views allowed by *Trafalgar Square's* open spaces make enjoyment of this magnificent church's proportions possible, and it is now recognized for the seminal building it was. Designed in 1722-26 by James Gibbs (the foundation goes back to 1222) in a solemnly Classical style, it is very close to a Roman temple, except for the novel placing of a tower and spire above the Corinthian portico. The interior is similar to Wren's churches of a few decades earlier — spacious and light, with galleries to the sides and a splendidly molded ceiling. The crypt contains

several interesting relics, including a whipping post dating back to the 18thC. It also houses the **London Brass Rubbing Centre** (☎ 437-6023 🌐 💷 *open Mon-Sat 10am-6pm, Sun noon-6pm*), where rubbings can be made from replicas of medieval monumental brasses. Staff are on hand to teach the technique.

St Mary Abchurch †

*Abchurch Lane, EC4. Map **13F16**. Tube: Cannon Street.*
After its small cobbled churchyard, simple brick exterior and lead spire, the glories of St Mary Abchurch's interior are unexpected. Built by Sir Christopher Wren in 1681-86, it consists of little more than one huge dome on top of a square room, creating a sense of space with architectural detail kept to a minimum. The dome was painted in Baroque style by William Snow between 1708 and 1714, and shows the name of God in Hebrew surrounded by figures representing the virtues. Although damaged in World War II, the church has been expertly restored; the **reredos** carved by Grinling Gibbons, for example, was rebuilt from fragments. Note the richly carved pulpit, the paneling and some original pews.

St Mary-le-Bow 🏛 †

*Bow Lane, Cheapside, EC2. Map **12G15**. Tube: Bank, St Paul's.*
When Wren rebuilt London's churches after the Great Fire of 1666, he put particular emphasis on their steeples, and this is the most magnificent. A great tower capped by an intricate stone spire, it is still prominent among the larger modern buildings around it. The church was built in 1670-80, with the tower separated from the body of the church by a vestibule. The design and execution of the two doors to the tower that serve as the porch are particularly fine. The interior is large and simple, much restored after gutting during the war, and the crypt retains elements from the original Norman church. St Mary's bells are of sentimental importance to Londoners: being born within range of their sound is the qualification for being a Cockney. The bells were destroyed in the Great Fire of 1666 and again in the Blitz; the current ones include recasts from remnants salvaged in 1941.

St Mary-le-Strand 🏛 † ☆

*Stand, WC2. Map **11F12**. Tube: Aldwych, Temple.*
It is hard to imagine a more ironic fate for a jewel of the Baroque: the island in the middle of the *Strand* is so small that the continuous traffic passes within inches of its walls, which have needed drastic renovation. James Gibbs built this in 1714-18, fresh from the joys of Rome. The facade especially is a delight: from the portico, with its ornate capitals, the eye sweeps up to the triangular pediment and the bold layered spire. The interior has a richly coffered ceiling with two tiers of columns and a pediment dramatically framing the apse. Notice the fine carving of the pulpit, originally on a taller base with a scallop-shell sounding board behind, all part of the grand theatrical effect.

St Pancras Station 🏛 ☆

*Euston Rd. NW1. Map **4C11**. Tube: King's Cross, St Pancras.*
That a railway station could be made into a Gothic fortress speaks much for the Victorians' confidence. St Pancras Station, with its accompanying hotel building (now used as offices), was the glory of Victorian London. It was designed by Sir George Gilbert Scott in 1868-74, freely using the northern Italian and French Gothic styles. Notice the harmony of its red bricks with

the pink and gray stone, and the way the detail combines with complex shapes and angles to feast the eye. It was also a tremendous feat of engineering, with the great train shed covered by a single span of iron and glass.

St Paul's, Covent Garden 🏛 †

The Piazza, WC2. Map 10F11. Tube: Covent Garden.
As the Duke of Bedford neared completion of his **Covent Garden** development, money became tight, and so he instructed Inigo Jones to build an economical church, suggesting as a model something like a barn. Jones declared that he would build "the handsomest barn in Europe," and today it stands as the sole surviving element of the piazza. In fact it cost a small fortune, but the barn analogy is not entirely inappropriate to the extreme simplicity of what was London's first entirely Classical parish church, completed in 1638. The main features are the overhanging eaves and the superb Tuscan portico, ironically never used as an entrance because the alter was moved in 1636 and a smaller door made at the rear in Bedford St. Today it is the "actors' church," and every so often a grand theaterland funeral adds another monument to the collection.

St Paul's Cathedral 🏛 † ★

Map 12F14. Entrance and movement restricted during services. Tube: St Paul's.
There are a very few great churches in the world that strike all visitors, whatever their religious convictions, as a sublime witness to man's ability to reach toward the infinite. St Paul's was built as both a religious and secular statement of London's faith and self-confidence after the devastating Great Fire of 1666, and almost 300yrs later it was to soar alone amid the total destruction of the surrounding buildings in the Blitz, preserved miraculously to breath fresh hope into the beleaguered Londoners. No building so clearly demonstrates Sir Christopher Wren's prodigious skill and energetic inventiveness: detail is used with characteristic Baroque exuberance but always subordinated to the highly controlled overall scheme. The dome still dominates the encroaching modern buildings.

The current cathedral is the third to stand on this site, and not the largest. The first was founded in 604 and periodically enlarged until destruction by fire in 1087. A medieval cathedral was constructed in the 11th-12thC; in the 13thC it was enlarged, and in 1315 a huge spire was completed. It was one of the great churches of medieval Europe, with a spire that reached 489ft from the ground, taller and longer than the present St Paul's. (For a fine model, see **London, Museum of**.)

Decline set in as the Middle Ages waned, however. The spire burned down in 1561 and was not replaced. The building fell into disrepair and was used more as a marketplace than a place of worship. The central aisle, "Paul's Walk," was a famous social forum. In 1634, Inigo Jones carried out substantial repairs, but the medieval structure continued to deteriorate, and in 1666 Christopher Wren came up with his first scheme for drastic renovations. That year, the Great Fire destroyed most of London, raging in St Paul's for several days and reducing it to ruins.

Given the task of reconstructing the cathedral, Wren proposed sweeping away what remained of the medieval building and starting afresh. He began with daringly modern designs that were rejected by the ecclesiastical authorities. In the end, he was forced to return to the basic plan for a Gothic cathedral, even if

St Paul's Cathedral

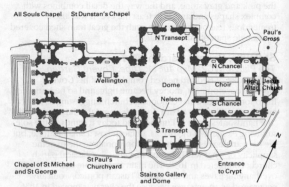

St Paul's Cathedral

not in appearance, and his design of 1675 was just that — with a nave, aisles, a crossing, transepts and a chancel, all forming a Latin cross. But the crossing was to be covered by a dome rather than a tower or spire, the first in England, following the example of the great Renaissance churches of Italy. Wren also fought for, and won, the freedom to alter the "ornamentation" of the cathedral, which in effect left him able to design the building's appearance as he went along.

Wren's **exterior** owes much to Inigo Jones' *Banqueting House*. There are two stories, with pilasters that decorate rusticated walls and a balustrade at the top — a first stroke of ingenuity, for the aisles behind the exterior side walls are only one story high, as in a Gothic cathedral. The upper is therefore a false wall (hence the blank niches instead of windows) connected to and supporting the walls of the nave by means of flying buttresses inside — an entirely Gothic device, but quite out of sight.

The E end of the cathedral, containing the chancel, was built first. It has a rounded end, thus forming an apse as in a medieval church, but with a curved roofline giving a Baroque flourish. This effect is echoed in the curved porches to the N and S transept facades, but these have more solidly Classical pediments at the roofline. The W end, the ceremonial entrance, was built later (1706-8), with massive towers at either side — the ornate tops to these are the most complex elements in the whole building: architecture handled as sculpture. The central portico is on two stories with pairs of Corinthian columns — another emphatically Baroque motif.

All this serves to balance the solemnity of the **dome**, suitably weighty and dignified as the dominant element of the composition. It is arguably the most beautiful dome in the world, 365ft high to the tip of the lantern and 100ft across inside. The quality of the carving of such elements as the garlands just below the frieze, or the capitals to the columns and pilasters, is superb. The sculptures, too, are well executed. The reliefs in the transept pediments are by G.B. Cibber and Grinling Gibbons, the statues by Francis Bird, who also carved the relief in the W pediment showing the *Conversion of St Paul*.

Although the area around St Paul's was spoiled by modern developments, conceived in the mid-1950s and built in the 1960s, plans are now in the pipeline to redevelop the Paternoster Square area in a more sympathetic vein. At present, traffic whistles around alarmingly close to the walls. There remain, however, the fine **railings** that surround the churchyard, made in 1714 and an early example of the use of cast iron. In front of the portico stands a statue of Queen Anne, made in 1866 to replace the original of 1709-11 by Bird (but did the original look so like Queen Victoria?). In the churchyard gardens to the NE is **St Paul's Cross**, a bronze structure of 1910. Two of the old cathedral buildings survive, both designed by Wren: to the S is the little **Deanery** of 1670, and to the N the larger red-brick **Chapter House** of 1712-14. To the E, still inside the road, is the tower and elongated onion spire of the ruined church of St Augustine designed by Wren in 1680-83, now attached to the new buildings of the celebrated St Paul's Choir School.

The **interior** gives an impression of the great bulk of the structure, but this is offset by the height of the nave and by the vast open space at the very center beneath the dome. The roofs are supported on a series of shallow cupolas, and the decorative elements are richly and finely carved, but limited in extent to the capitals of the pilasters, with garlands between, and geometrically patterned bands around the cupolas. The emphasis is on the sweeping drama of the Baroque. The eye is led along the nave or aisles, or across the transepts, and there seems to be a calculated attempt to create vistas with a sense of distance, focusing on the open space beneath the dome but leading ultimately toward the long chancel beyond the crossing. A great deal of light enters the cathedral from the clerestory windows of the nave, windows that are invisible from the outside because of the false upper story of the external wall.

Walk to the left from the main W entrance. The small **All Soul's Chapel** contains **Lord Kitchener's monument** of 1925, one of the more effective of the cluster of memorials to national heroes introduced since about 1790, with an effigy of the soldier in deathly white marble. Then comes **St Dunstan's Chapel**, behind a superbly carved wooden screen of 1698. Outstanding monuments are to Lord Leighton, the leading Victorian painter, and to General Gordon of the Sudan. In one of the arches farther along this N aisle is the great **monument to the Duke of Wellington**, erected in the mid-19thC and the most elaborate in St Paul's, with an equestrian statue of the duke on top of the canopy. The N transept is reserved for private prayer; it contains a number of monuments to the fallen heroes of the Napoleonic Wars, and the marble font, carved in 1727 by Francis Bird.

At this point the **crossing** can be admired, the focal point of the entire design. It is a huge space, with the circle of the **dome** supported on eight massive arches. The mosaics in the spandrels are Victorian, in the style of Michelangelo's Sistine Chapel frescoes, and there are Victorian statues in the niches above the Whispering Gallery. The breathtaking dome itself actually consists of three layers: an outer skin, a cone supporting the masonry of the lantern, and a shallow domed ceiling. This is painted with illusionistic architectural frescoes in monochrome, depicting scenes from the life of St Paul, by Sir James Thornhill, dating from 1716-19. Monuments in the crossing include those to Dr. Johnson (in an unlikely toga) and Sir Joshua Reynolds, first president of the *Royal Academy*. The lectern was made in 1720, but the pulpit is modern.

The **chancel**, stretching off toward the high altar, makes a sumptuous display, although it is not at all as Wren left it: the gaudy and fussy mosaics that decorate the ceiling date from the 1890s and are really not in keeping. The modern baldacchino,

attempting to follow Wren's original scheme for a high altar
canopy as a focal point, is only partly successful, in an unhappy
marriage with the ceiling decorations. However, the **choir stalls
and organ case**, which originally closed the chancel off from the
crossing, are quite magnificent, with exquisite carving by
Grinling Gibbons, made in the 1690s. The chancel aisles can be
visited, giving a fine close-up view of the rear of the stalls and of
Jean Tijou's extraordinarily fine **wrought-iron gates**, again of
the 1690s but moved to their present site in 1890. Behind the altar
is the **Jesus Chapel**, now a memorial to the American dead of
World War II. Returning along the s chancel aisle, **John Donne's
monument** shows the poet, who was Dean of St Paul's
(1620-31), wrapped in his shroud, just as he posed during the
(soon justified) bouts of melancholy before his death in 1631. It is
the only monument to survive from the medieval cathedral.
Returning back toward the crossing, the s transept includes
several military monuments, of which Sir John Moore's (1851) is
the most moving, although Lord Nelson's includes a fine portrait.
In the s aisle is a striking example of high Victorian religiosity, a
late version of Holman Hunt's painting *Light of the World*, and a
fine wooden screen of 1706 in front of the **Chapel of St Michael
and St George**.

Crypt
Entrance from s transept 🔳 *Open Mon-Fri 10am-4.15pm, Sat
11am-4.15pm.*
The piers and columns support a crypt the size of the whole
cathedral, a quiet and dignified place crammed with monuments
to national figures. A few battered remains of monuments survive
from before the 1666 Great Fire, but the majority are from the
19th-20thC. By far the most impressive are the **tombs of
Wellington**, a massive porphyry block on a granite slab, and
Nelson, an elegant black sarcophagus originally made for
Cardinal Wolsey in 1524-29 but denied him after his fall from
royal favor. Other monuments include numerous generals and
admirals, and, in "Painter's Corner," the tombs of Turner and
Reynolds and monuments to Van Dyck, Constable and William
Blake. Wren himself is buried nearby.

The **Treasury of the Diocese of London** also has an
exhibition in the crypt, containing elaborate vestments,
illuminated medieval manuscripts from the cathedral library, and
some fine plate from London churches of the 16th-20thC.

Whispering Gallery and Dome
Stairs in s transept 🔳 *Hours as crypt.*
The stiff climb to the gallery inside the dome is repaid with
stupendous views of the concourse below and the painted inner
dome. The acoustics that give it its name enable the slightest
sounds to be heard across the span; the traditional trick, much
loved by children, is to whisper against the wall and wait for the
sound to travel around to the next auditor. The next section of
the ascent is not for the fainthearted, with steps winding up
throughout the struts supporting the outer dome. The stunning
views from the **Golden Gallery** at the base of the lantern make
the 542-step climb worthwhile.

St Stephen Walbrook 🏛 ✝ ☆
Walbrook, EC4. Map **13F16**. *Tube: Bank.*
Although a parish church, its position behind the *Mansion
House* means that St Stephen Walbrook is also the Lord Mayor's
church. It is appropriately grand for this ceremonial function,
with a simple exterior giving way to a magnificent structure

inside, with Corinthian columns, and eight richly molded arches supporting a coffered dome. Wren built the church in 1672-79: it is thought that he was trying out some ideas for *St Paul's Cathedral*. The contrast with his *St Mary Abchurch* is illuminating, for here the dome is not used to create a simple, large space but to contribute to the series of constantly changing views as the visitor moves through the columns. The tower is slightly later, 1717, and the crypt survives from the 15thC.

Science Museum ★

Exhibition Rd., SW7 ☎ 938-8000. Map 15J5 ▨ ▣ ✱ Open Mon-Sat 10am-6pm, Sun 11am-6pm. Tube: S. Kensington.
The Science Museum originated in 1857 within the great South Kensington museum complex conceived by Prince Albert. It was separated from the *Victoria & Albert Museum*, housing the products of art rather than science, in 1909. Its present building, solemn and functional, was constructed in 1913.

On the ground floor, the **East Hall**, a large room with galleries above on three levels and a glass roof, is devoted to the development of motive power. Industrial machinery, vast and now seemingly crude in its construction, shows the development of steam power in the 18thC. By contrast a huge mill engine of 1903, with a great gleaming flywheel, shows the continuing use of steam into the 20thC. A dramatically staged exhibition then introduces exploration, with full-scale models of modern space and underwater craft. The following section on transportation is a great favorite, with famous steam locomotives such as Stephenson's *Rocket* of 1892 and the magnificent *Caerphilly Castle* of 1923 outstanding; the fascination with the visible working parts explains why something as messy and noisy as a steam train should have such romantic appeal. There are also horse-drawn carriages, automobiles and fire engines. An exciting new topical gallery called **Food for Thought** has opened on the ground floor. Sponsored by the Sainsbury Family Charitable Trust, it explores how we buy, prepare and eat food. Below the rear of the museum the **Children's Gallery** has many practical displays. Domestic appliances are also found here.

The displays on the upper floors (the galleries around the central East Hall and a few separate rooms) cover a great many aspects of science in turn. On reaching the first floor, children make an immediate break for the **Launch Pad**, a marvelous "hands-on" exhibition where everyone can get down to working the machines themselves. Industrial processes, such as iron, steel and glass manufacture, and agriculture are here too.

On the second floor, subjects range from chemistry to nuclear physics to computers; there are some superb **models of ships**. Fascinating exhibitions on the third floor cover photography, cinematography and optics, as well as more theoretical areas such as biochemistry, where attractive models explain the structure of molecules in a comprehensible way. Here too is the **Aeronautics Gallery**: see the Vickers Vimy in which Alcock and Brown made their pioneering flight across the Atlantic, Amy Johnson's *Jason* in which she flew to Australia, a Spitfire and the first-ever jet engine. Stairs lead up to the excellent **Wellcome Medical Museum**, where the history of medicine and its most up-to-date manifestations are shown in spirited dioramas.

Shakespeare Globe Museum

1 Bear Gdns, Bankside, SE1 ☎ 928-6342. Map 12G15 ▨ Open winter Mon-Sat 10am-5pm, Sun 2-5pm; summer

Sir John Soane's Museum

Mon-Sat 10am-6pm, Sun 2-6pm. Tube: London Bridge.
Until the 18thC, Southwark acted as London's pleasure center, an area of taverns, brothels and theaters. The museum houses exhibitions on this area of Shakespeare's London and the discovery and excavation of the Rose Theatre and the original Globe Theatre, as well as a model of the proposed International Shakespeare Globe Centre (*due to open in 1993* ☎ *620-0202 for information*). The center is reconstructing the famous polygonal theater, burned down in 1613 during a performance of *Henry VIII*, close to the Globe's original site next to the museum.

Sir John Soane's Museum

13 Lincoln's Inn Fields, WC2 ☎ *405-2107. Map* **11E12** 🖸
✗ *Sat 2.30pm, tickets available at 2pm. Open Tues-Sat 10am-5pm. Tube: Holborn.*
Nothing could be further from modern ideas of museum display than Soane's Museum, for the great architect left his house as a museum on his death in 1837 on the condition that nothing be changed. His enormous collection of pictures, architectural fragments, books, sculptures and miscellaneous antiquities is crammed into every available space, giving some idea of his eccentricity as well as his tastes.

Born in 1753, Soane lived at no. 12 Lincoln's Inn Fields from 1792, in a plain Georgian house he designed himself. In 1812-14 he added the much more elaborate no. 13 with its grand facade, rebuilding no. 14 to complete a balanced design in 1824. The interior, joined between the three houses, is the most ingeniously complex layout, offering numerous vistas through the houses, both laterally and vertically, as several of the rooms and yards extend through two or more stories. Mirrors create additional illusory space. Most exciting are the paired **Dining Room** and **Library**, and the lovely domed **Breakfast Room**.

The fascination of the great number of objects on display from fossils to furniture is only increased by the capricious, even humorous, way in which they are jumbled together. Among them are several important works of art, as well as Soane's own architectural models. In the **Picture Room** are Hogarth's original paintings for two series, *The Rake's Progress* and *The Election*, comprising 12 paintings in all, and elsewhere a Canaletto and a Turner. In a first-floor Drawing Room is Watteau's *Les Noces*. Outstanding is the beautiful alabaster **sarcophagus**, covered with hieroglyphics, of Seti I, a pharaoh who died in 1290BC, for which Soane paid the then princely sum of £2,000.

Soho ☆

Map **10F-G***. Tube: Piccadilly Circus, Tottenham Court Road, Leicester Square.*
Every city has its low-life area, of course, but in few are the red lights woven into a texture of such richness and variety as in London's Soho. These densely packed little streets in the heart of the West End, bounded by Oxford St., Regent St., Shaftesbury Ave. and Charing Cross Rd., are famous for their nightlife, their restaurants, the best delicatessens in London, their seedy but famous pubs, and, above all, for the gloriously cosmopolitan mix of their people and trades.

A decade ago, much was heard about the decline of Soho, when its thriving sex industry threatened to engulf the area's other amenities, and even a pub where Dylan Thomas used to drink himself into oblivion became a sex cinema. The destruction has now largely been halted. Respectable businesses have returned, and fashionable restaurants and shops prosper. And Soho wouldn't be Soho without a scattering of sex parlors.

Two squares remind us of Soho's early development in the 17thC. **Golden Square** in the E was founded in 1673, and some 18thC houses survive around its undistinguished gardens with a 1720s statue of Charles II. More impressive is **Soho Square**, laid out in 1681, with the few survivals of early buildings largely disguised by later additions, but offering a pleasant garden with a half-timbered summer house and a 17thC statue of Charles II. On its S side, in Greek St., is Soho's finest house, **The House of St Barnabas** (◙ *open Wed 2.30-4.15pm, Thurs 11am-12.30pm*), a luxurious 1746 town house with a plain exterior but a magnificently decorated Rococo interior, with rich plasterwork on walls and ceiling. Soho's other public open space is **St Anne's churchyard**, a little park in Wardour St. overlooked by a splendid tower of 1801-3 surviving from the bombed church.

The southern part of Soho crosses Shaftesbury Ave., a busy street of many theaters, to London's **Chinatown**, centered on Gerrard St., small, authentic and packed with excellent restaurants. But Soho's heart, with marvelous French and Italian delicatessens, together with fine butchers, fish stores and wine merchants, is found farther N on **Brewer St., Old Compton St.** and **Berwick St.**; the latter is also an excellent open-air fresh food market, becoming more expensive and exotic at its continuation in Rupert St., S through sexy Walker Court. To the N of Old Compton St., **Dean St.**, **Frith St.** and **Greek St.** have fine little restaurants, pubs and clubs, such as **Ronnie Scott's** for jazz (see *Nightlife*). In Wardour St., the British movie industry has its center. Throughout, blue plaques mark apparently run-down buildings with famous associations: Blake was born in Marshall St., Chopin gave recitals in Meard St., and in Frith St., Marx worked, Baird first demonstrated television, and Hazlitt died....

The northwestern part of Soho has less character: **Carnaby St.** was the Mecca of the Swinging Sixties, but most of its current visitors wonder why everyone else is a tourist.

South Bank Arts Centre
Map 11G12. Tube: Waterloo.

The plans for a national arts center were formulated in the years after World War II, and crystallized when this derelict South Bank site was developed for the Festival of Britain in 1951, with the first stages of the Festival Hall and National Film Theatre.

The **Festival Hall** is one of Britain's outstanding postwar buildings. Not finally completed until 1956, its impressive glass facade makes full use of its panoramic riverside location. Like later South Bank buildings, however, the exterior is more massive and monumental than appealing, and it is the interior that is most successful. This has a complex arrangement of spaces, efficiently and attractively laid out, with public areas offering views across the river, bars, restaurants and the great concert hall itself, seating almost 3,000, with near-perfect acoustics. The **Queen Elizabeth Hall** and **Purcell Room**, seating 1,100 and 372 respectively, were completed next to the Festival Hall for smaller concerts in 1967. The **National Film Theatre**, under Waterloo Bridge, which now has two cinemas, shows an always interesting program of historic and contemporary movies. The **Hayward Gallery**, next to the bridge, was opened in 1968, and puts on an important series of art exhibitions organized by the Arts Council. The *National Theatre* continues the Brutalist theme.

Newest addition to the South Bank complex is **MOMI**, the **Museum of the Moving Image** (*open Tues-Sat 10am-7pm, Sun 10am-5pm* 📷), in a striking glass and steel building adjoining the Film Theatre. It traces this art form from early Chinese shadow theater to motion picture and television technologies of the future. Lots of visitor participation plus Charlie Chaplin's hat and cane and Fred Astaire's pants.

See also *Nightlife*.

Southwark Cathedral 🏛 ✝ ☆
Map 13G16. Tube: London Bridge.
This Gothic church is under siege from the encroaching railway viaducts, covered market and approaches to *London Bridge* that crowd up to its walls, but it is still one of the most important medieval buildings in London. The tower is the best feature, dating from the 14th-15thC, with pinnacles of 1689.

It was founded as the Augustinian priory of St Mary Overie (meaning "over the water") in 1106, becoming the parish church of St Saviour after the Reformation and a cathedral only in 1905. The priory burned down in about 1212 and was replaced with a Gothic structure, of which the present chancel and retro-choir were complete by 1220. Since then, restoration has been periodically necessary, the chancel of 1890-97, in a medieval style, being the latest major reworking. Interesting features include the **ceiling bosses** from the 15thC, opposite the present main entrance, graphically carved with heraldic devices or grotesque figures. The rebuilt **chancel** actually shows very well the beauty and purity of early Gothic architecture, with its layers of perfectly proportioned arches. Behind the high altar, a superbly rich **reredos** dates from 1520.

The monuments are of great interest, although several have been crudely painted in restoration. Look out for John Gower, a medieval poet and friend of Chaucer, who died in 1408, a wooden effigy of a knight of about 1275, and Richard Humber (died 1616) with his fashionably dressed wives. Next to the N transept is a chapel (rebuilt in 1907) devoted to John Harvard, founder of the great American college, who was baptized here in 1607. The **Nonesuch Chest**, in the retro-choir, is an outstanding example of 16thC furniture in the Classical Renaissance style. In the S aisle, there is a memorial of 1912 to William Shakespeare.

Space Adventure
64-66 Tooley St., SE1 ☎ 378-1405. Map 13H16 📷 ✱ Open Apr-Oct 10am-6pm; Nov-Mar 10.30am-5pm. Tube: London Bridge.
Tooley St., near the *London Dungeon*, is the unlikely setting for a trip into space, much beloved of young boys. Even those with their feet planted firmly on the ground may be momentarily fooled as Europe's largest space simulator takes off for Mars, via the Moon. Don't miss the BBC's **World of Dr Who** exhibition.

Speakers' Corner
Map 8G7. Tube: Marble Arch.
Speakers' Corner in the NE tip of *Hyde Park* offers the dubious spectacle of numerous wild-eyed eccentrics haranguing small groups of spectators on everything from hellfire to Utopia. Established as late as 1872 as a place where such holding-forth could be tolerated without arrest, it has in recent years begun to attract more serious attention thanks to exiles from countries where free speech is denied. It is at its busiest on Sunday.

Staple Inn ⅏
Holborn, EC1. Map 11E13. Tube: Chancery Lane.

Close to the entrance to *Gray's Inn* is a remarkable survivor of
Elizabethan London: a pair of timber houses dating from 1586
forming the facade to Staple Inn, a former Inn of Chancery.
Together they look like a quaint jumble of haphazardly placed
beams and gables, with charming overhanging stories and oriel
windows. Through the gateway on the left, the courtyards of the
Inn (now housing the Society of Actuaries) can be entered. Dr.
Johnson lived at no. 2 in 1759-60, where he supposedly wrote
Rasselas in a week to pay for his mother's funeral.

Stock Exchange
*Old Broad St., EC2 ☎ 588-2355. Map 13F16 ⟦○⟧ ✦ Open
Mon-Fri 9.45am-3.30pm. Tube: Bank.*

Market makers and broker/dealers, bulls and bears, the heart of
the City beats to a mysterious rhythm. The Exchange has four
markets: UK Company Shares, International Company Shares, UK
Government Stocks and Traded Options. The International Stock
Exchange evolved from coffeehouses in the City of London,
moving into its first permanent building, the Royal Exchange, in
1773. In 1802 it moved again to its present site, next to the other
bastion of the City, the **Bank of England**, and was rebuilt in
1973. Following Big Bang and the introduction of SEAQ (the
Exchange's price-information system), the trading floor is no
longer the center of activity, although the thriving Traded
Options Market occupies about one-third of the floor space. The
visitors' gallery is equipped with the latest price-information
screens, which are demonstrated several times daily. In addition,
computerized information displays are available for use by
visitors. To see a buzzing trading floor in action, visit the **Royal
Exchange** (see the *City*).

Strand
Maps 10&11G11&12. Tube: Charing Cross.

"Strand" means river bank, and that is what this street was until
the embankment was built in 1864-70; the old **watergate** still
stands in Victoria Embankment Gardens. Once the main route
from Westminster to the City, it was lined with great houses, and
is today a motley collection of theaters, shops and hotels.

Its E end begins at Temple Bar, on the edge of the City,
continuing the direction set by *Fleet Street*. On the N side are
the splendid Victorian Gothic *Royal Courts of Justice*, with an
attractive tangle of buildings opposite. The church of **St Clement
Danes** occupies an island in the middle of the road, built by Sir
Christopher Wren in 1680-82, with the stone tower completed by
James Gibb in 1719. Entirely wrecked by a bomb in 1941, the
church has been restored with exceptional skill and is now the
church of the Royal Air Force. Behind is a statue to Samuel
Johnson erected in 1910, and to the front is a more pompous
monument to Gladstone (1905).

The **Aldwych** follows on the N side of the street, an ambitious
planning scheme begun in 1900. Its crescent shape is made up of
massive, somber buildings in heavy Edwardian style, including
Australia House and the BBC's Bush House. The exquisite church
of *St Mary-le-Strand* occupies another island in the middle of the
road at this point, with the 1971 concrete facade of King's
College almost opposite. **Somerset House** comes next on the S
side, just a little farther along from the Aldwych. Two large hotels
are farther W: the Art Deco-ish **Strand Palace (Simpson's**

ultratraditional restaurant opposite: see *Venerable institutions* in *Restaurants*) and the famous **Savoy** (see *Hotels*). Several theaters are to be found along the N side of the Strand from here, in a section largely given over to bustling shoppers. The W end, opening onto *Trafalgar Square*, is marked by *Charing Cross*, with the remarkable **Coutts' Bank building** opposite.

Syon House 🏛

Brentford, Middlesex ☎ (081) 560-0881. Map 20C3 🔲 ✖ 𝄞 🖵 Open Apr-Sept Sun-Thurs 12-4.15pm; gardens daily 10am-6pm, sunset if earlier. Tube: Gunnersbury.

Syon House was originally a convent, founded by Henry V in 1415 and exceptionally rich until suppressed by Henry VIII in 1534. In 1547, it was taken over by the Lord Protector, the Duke of Somerset, who transformed it into a large mansion on the pattern of a hollow square. Somerset went to the scaffold in 1552, as did his successor to Syon, John Dudley, and also Lady Jane Grey, who set out from the house to be Queen of England for eight days in 1553. Since 1594, the Percy family, Dukes of Northumberland, have held the house.

In 1762, Robert Adam was brought in to "modernize" the Tudor house, thus creating the extraordinary contrast between the plain square exterior with battlements and corner towers, and the incomparable interior. As at *Osterley Park* nearby, the centerpiece of Adam's planning is the **Great Hall**, a cool and elegant room with restrained Classical decoration in stucco, including Doric columns, giving the house a dramatic entrance. To complete the scholarly effect, there are genuine Roman statues and some copies of famous antique models, including a fine bronze version of the *Dying Gaul*. Adam's intention was to create a sequence of pleasurable contrasts: the next room, **The Ante Room**, is altogether more lavish, with rich gilding, dark green marble columns and a brightly patterned floor in colored artificial stone. The suite of state rooms continues the contrast, with **Dining Room, Red Drawing Room** and **Long Gallery** all in different, variously elaborate styles; some furniture is gilded, some in beautifully inlaid wood. In the Red Drawing Room there is a fine carpet designed by Adam, and in the Long Gallery, landscape panels by Zuccarelli. Paintings in the house include works by Van Dyck, Lely and Gainsborough.

The gardens, remodeled in the late 18thC by the great Capability Brown, have many rare botanical specimens and carefully planned vistas. The **Great Conservatory** was added in 1830, with its large, almost Oriental, glass dome, and now contains an aquarium. In the park there is also a huge garden center, a **butterfly house** (🔲), where British and tropical specimens can be seen all year round flying free, and the **British Heritage Motor Museum** (☎ *(081) 560-1378* 🔲 *open Mar-Oct 10am-5pm, Nov-Apr 10am-3.30pm*), which boasts a collection of 90 cars, including an 1895 Wolseley and several prototypes, and a small display of Dinky Cars.

Tate Gallery ★

Millbank, SW1 ☎ 821-1313, recorded info ☎ 821-7128. Map 18K11 🔲 𝄞 🖵 Open Mon-Sat 10am-5.50pm, Sun 2-5.50pm. Tube: Pimlico.

Appropriately for a gallery famous for modern art, the Tate was founded by the modern type of patron, a businessman, when in 1892 the sugar millionaire Sir Henry Tate gave his collection of British paintings to the nation, together with funds to build a special gallery, officially opened in 1897. In fact, only later, in 1917, was the decision taken to add modern foreign art, largely because at the time the Tate was seen as an adjunct to the *National Gallery*. Several extensions have increased the available space many times over, most recently in the large galleries opened in 1979, and the Clore Gallery extension opened in 1987. With the exception of the Turner galleries, the collection has recently undergone a complete rearrangement. The new display, entitled *Past Present Future*, breaks the former rigid division between historic and modern, and traces the development of British art chronologically from the mid-16thC to the present, linking it with foreign art in the 20thC. Regular special displays from the permanent collection, called *Cross Currents*, trace themes through different generations of art, and *Focus* displays present the works of individual artists. The Tate is in the process of further rehanging, so the themes of various rooms are subject to change, and works of art mentioned in the following description may not always be on view.

The new display starts at the rear of the building on the left. The first room covers the 16th-17thC, when foreign artists working in England ruled the roost. A few works, such as the superb portraits by William Dobson, show what a benign influence Europeans could be.

In the 18thC, a truly national school appeared, particularly with William Hogarth, whose eye for contemporary life was unrivaled. His *Study of the Heads of Six Servants* shows a great and original understanding of the ordinary people making up his household, whereas *Calais Gate* reveals his biting satire. In the 18thC, with Reynolds and Gainsborough, two contradictory approaches to portraiture emerged, but in the end both artists concentrated on pleasing their sitters. Reynolds favored a grand, Classicizing manner (as in *Three Ladies Adorning a Term of Hymen*); Gainsborough concentrated on charm and prettiness with his extraordinarily fluent technique. The Tate has good examples of the development of landscape painting in the 18thC: Richard Wilson's *Cader Idris* demonstrates an emerging naturalism. Two other important 18thC artists were George Stubbs (sporting and animal scenes, including the finest horses ever painted) and Joseph Wright of Derby (highly individual night scenes closely bound up with advances in science and industrialization). By contrast, the eccentric mysticism of William Blake and his followers is effectively shown in a darkened room.

In studies and finished works such as *Flatford Mill*, Constable showed an appreciation of the real appearance of the countryside, which was revolutionary in his time. The Pre-Raphaelites are well represented at the Tate, and Millais' *Ophelia* and Rossetti's *Beata Beatrix* are among the most famous examples. Victorian painting is now admired and the Tate has an admirable selection, from John Martin's apocalyptic *The Great Day of His Wrath* to Frith's *Derby Day*, with its unbelievably complex story-telling detail. From the later 19thC, Whistler stands out. This American painter working in England placed great emphasis on abstract pictorial qualities such as color harmony.

Next come the French and British Impressionists and Post-Impressionists, with all the major figures represented with works of varying quality. Degas' bronze *Little Dancer* and Gaugin's *Faa Iheibe* are notable. An important masterpiece by pioneering artist of the Fauve group, Matisse, is the late collage *The Snail*. Cubism, short-lived but vitally important, is demonstrated with a few works of high quality of Picasso and Braque, together with

Temple

Futurism. The Bloomsbury Group of British artists, perhaps more noted for their writings than their derivative paintings, are also represented. Stanley Spencer and his circle are given new prominence. The move to complete abstraction is shown by Kandinsky and Mondrian. Important works by Picasso, the giant of modern art, include the famous *Tree Dancers* in his unique version of the Surrealist style. The Surrealists themselves, Miró, Ernst, Magritte and Dalí, are well represented, as are the American Abstract Expressionists. There is a room devoted to Paul Nash, and others, where works by Henry Moore and Anthony Caro are displayed. *Standing by the Rags*, a female nude by Lucian Freud, is one of the gallery's most recent acquisitions. It is on display with other works by Freud, Kossoff, Andrews, Auerbach and Kitaj. A high point is the room devoted to Mark Rothko's powerful murals for the Seagram Building in New York, a potent reminder of the achievements of modern art.

There are three central sculpture galleries, where the work of Naum Gabo is displayed, of which the Tate has a leading collection. The room immediately to the right of the entrance is given over to **temporary exhibitions (▧)**, and there is a display of **Works on Paper** in the basement galleries, encompassing British prints, drawings and watercolors from the late 17thC to the end of the 19thC, modern masterpieces by Picasso, among others, and examples of print-making.

The **Clore Gallery for the Turner Collection** (James Stirling, architect — beautifully proportioned and lit) houses Turner's bequest of his works to the nation, a dazzling display of light and color, revealing an unmatched understanding of nature in all its moods and prefiguring the Impressionists' innovations by several decades. The late works, such as the studies of *Norham Castle*, are outstanding.

Temple ▥ ☆
Map 11F13. Tube: Temple.

It can be easy to miss the gateway to the Inner and Middle Temples amid the bustle of *Fleet Street*, yet behind them lies a large and relatively peaceful enclave of historic buildings and gardens down toward the Thames. The Temple is named after the Knights Templar, a religious order founded in the Middle Ages to further the Crusades, who came to this site — then outside the City walls — in about 1160. They constructed a great complex of monastic buildings, of which the chapel survives. Some time in the 14thC, the buildings were taken over by lawyers, and there they have remained, today organized into two of the four *Inns of Court*.

The red-brick **Middle Temple Gateway** was built in 1684 to a design using Classical motifs, and leads through to Middle Temple Lane, lined with chambers and courtyards. Much was destroyed by wartime bombing, although some buildings date back to the 17thC and beyond. Outstanding is the **Middle Temple Hall** of 1562-70 (▣ *open Mon-Fri 10-11.30am, 3-4pm*), expertly restored and retaining a superb **hammerbeam roof** and **oak screen** from the Elizabethan period, with Doric columns and arches, and finely carved figures. It is likely that Shakespeare himself appeared in the performance of *Twelfth Night* given here in 1602.

To the E, narrow alleys lead through to the **Inner Temple**. Here, the most important building is the **Templar church**, a fascinating medieval structure. It is one of five circular churches in England, based on the Church of the Holy Sepulcher in

Jerusalem. The round nave was begun in about 1160 and completed by 1185, one of the earliest Gothic structures in England. The chancel is from about 1220-40, in a more openly airy Gothic style. On the floor of the nave are nine 13thC effigies of knights in Purbeck marble. The **Inner Temple Gateway**, leading back to *Fleet St.*, is an attractive half-timbered house of 1610-11, restored in 1906. Upstairs is Prince Henry's Room, with an elaborately decorated plaster ceiling. The Prince of Wales Feathers and the initials "PH" suggest the link with James I's son.

Theatre Museum

1E Tavistock St., WC2 ☎ 836-7891. Map 10F11 ⬚ ✗ by arrangement ⬛ Open Tues-Sun 11am-6pm. Tube: Covent Garden.

Opened in 1987, this is an outpost of the *Victoria and Albert Museum* appropriately sited in *Covent Garden*, close to theaterland and the Royal Opera House. It is rich in theatrical history and memorabilia. In the lobby, a giant gilt angel, rescued from the Gaiety Theatre, Aldwych, beckons. All aspects of the performing arts are included: models, costumes, playbills, posters, puppets, props and much more besides. Here are the box office from the Duke of York's, Noël Coward's monogrammed dressing gown and slippers, original models for the opera by master designer Oliver Messel, Elton John's platform boots and Mick Jagger's jumpsuit. There is also a box office for all London shows and concerts, and a theatrical reference library.

Tower Bridge

SE1 ☎ 403-3761. Map 13G&H17 ⬚ ✗ ⬩ Open Apr-Oct 10am-5.45pm; Nov-Mar 10am-4pm. Tube: Tower Hill.

With its towers and drawbridges, this landmark, adjacent to the *Tower of London*, has become a symbol for London. Built in 1886-94, it is the most easterly bridge across the Thames, and though designed so that large ships can pass beneath its easily raised roadway, it is deceptively graceful when viewed from a distance. Enter by the N tower to visit the glass-enclosed walkway, which has splendid views: Butler's Wharf downstream, *HMS Belfast* to the W and *St Katharine's Dock* on the N bank. The **Tower Bridge Museum** is located to the S of the bridge and contains the original steam-driven machinery used to lift the bridge. There are further exhibitions in the NW and S towers. Superbly lit at night, Tower Bridge is one of London's most memorable sights after dark.

Tower of London ☲ ★

EC3 ☎ 709-0765. Map 13G17 ⬚ ✗ Open Mar-Oct Mon-Sat 9.30am-5pm, Sun 2-5pm; Nov-Feb Mon-Sat 9.30am-4pm. Tube: Tower Hill.

The Tower's great keep rises from its complex accretion of massively fortified walls, moats, towers and bastions, and today its forbidding but thrilling appearance is often used as a symbol for London. The best views are from Tower Hill to the N and W, by All Hallows church, from *Tower Bridge*, or perhaps from the river itself, on a boat trip from Tower Pier. The Tower is London's most substantial medieval monument, steeped in a bloody past and containing a superb collection of arms and armor, and the priceless Crown Jewels. As a result, it is a prime tourist attraction and is often crowded; a visit near opening time is recommended.

It was founded by William the Conqueror just inside the Roman wall at the E end of London following his arrival in 1066, to encourage the loyalty of the townspeople as much as to defend them. William's castle was initially a wooden structure, but from about 1077 the great stone White Tower began to rise, to be completed by 1097 in the reign of the Conqueror's son, William Rufus. At this time, the White Tower stood alone, joined to the river by an enclosed bailey, but Richard the Lion Heart began to build a curtain wall in the late 12thC, a process continued under Henry III. Edward I (1272-1307) completed the transformation of the Norman stronghold into a fully-fledged medieval castle; the White Tower was now surrounded by a continuous curtain wall with 12 towers. The moat surrounding the whole was up to 12ft wide, with a barbican on the far side guarding the drawbridges. This is substantially the Tower we see today.

Until the reign of James I (1603-25) the Tower was a leading royal residence. Its strength meant that it was also used as a principal armory and house for royal treasure. These functions have continued, and the Tower still holds the Crown Jewels and weaponry amassed over the ages. The Tower's security also commended it as a prison, and kings and queens have kept many of their most notable enemies within its walls: Anne Boleyn, Sir Thomas More, Elizabeth I (while a princess), Sir Walter Raleigh and, most recently, Rudolf Hess in World War II.

The continuous traditions of the Tower have cloaked it in rich ceremony. It is guarded by the Yeomen Warders, or "Beefeaters," a company founded by Henry VII in 1485, who still wear Tudor costume, with blue tunics carrying the sovereign's monogram on the chest, and broad, flat caps. On ceremonial occasions, a more elaborate scarlet version of the same dress is worn. Together with guardsmen from the Regular Army, Yeomen Warders participate in the **Ceremony of the Keys** at 9.50pm each day, formally locking up the Tower for the night (see *Calendar of events*). Another tradition hangs around the six ravens that live inside the Tower's walls. These are kept jealously, with a meat allowance: there is a legend that the Tower will fall when the ravens leave.

The outer fortifications

The main entrance to the Tower, as in the Middle Ages, is to the w, near the river. Evidence can be seen of the medieval causeway that led up to the vanished Lion Tower, so called because it housed the royal menagerie — lions and leopards included — until 1834. The whole entrance defense work, or barbican, was originally surrounded by water and reached by drawbridge. Another drawbridge led to the **Middle Tower**, the present outer gateway, an 18thC reconstruction. From here, a causeway leads across the broad moat (once with another drawbridge) to the gate in **Byward Tower**, built by Edward I. The moat was drained in 1843 and is now grassed over. Byward Tower leads into the corridor between the curtain walls, with the angled **Bell Tower** on the left, probably built soon after 1200 by King John, one of the oldest surviving parts. Farther along on the right is the notorious **Traitors' Gate**, through which royal barges and boats bearing prisoners (or provisions) could enter the castle.

The inner buildings

The inner precincts of the Tower can be entered through the gate in the **Bloody Tower** opposite, overlooked by the heavily fortified round structure of **Wakefield Tower** to the side. The Bloody Tower is by tradition the site of the murder of the young princes by their uncle, Richard III, in 1485, hoping to secure his succession to the throne, although modern historians are less certain about the event than was Shakespeare. Inside the tower, a winch used to raise the portcullis can be seen and two rooms are furnished as they might have been when Sir Walter Raleigh was imprisoned here. Other notable prisoners included Thomas Cranmer, Archbishop Laud and the notorious Judge Jeffreys.

The great open space enclosed by the fortification of the curtain walls can now be appreciated. On the right is a portion of 12thC wall, surviving from the Norman bailey, only exposed in 1940 when a bomb destroyed a 19thC building. When the top of the steps ahead is reached, the **Queen's House** (*not open to the public*), a pretty half-timbered structure begun in about 1540, is on the left. In its rooms, Guy Fawkes was tortured following the 1605 Gunpowder Plot. To the N is the entrance to **Beauchamp Tower**, used again and again as a prison. The interior is covered with carved graffiti, giving witness to the suffering of prisoners. Nearby is the **Chapel of St Peter ad Vincula**, built in the early 16thC on a 12thC foundation, in Perpendicular Gothic style. It retains some late medieval monuments. Beyond the chapel, **Bowyer Tower** contains a display of torture instruments.

The Crown Jewels ★

Nearby begin the long lines for the Crown Jewels, the Tower's greatest single attraction. The lines move quickly so you cannot expect more than a brief look.

Kept below the 19thC Waterloo Barracks, the jewels are reached through a suitably dramatic pair of polished steel doors, and are the Tower's best-guarded prisoners ever. The fire and brilliance of the stones are even more spectacular than their reputation or their worth. Almost all the royal regalia was melted down or sold off by Cromwell, so most of what is left dates from after the 1660 Restoration. The display begins with a selection of plate, massive and ornate pieces in silver-gilt; look out for the fabulous **wine cooler** of 1829, gilded state maces and bejeweled swords. The rich vestments of the knightly orders are on display, but overshadowed by the coronation robes of the sovereign, elaborately covered in gold embroidery. The Crown Jewels themselves are in the next room. Two items of coronation regalia survive from the Middle Ages: an exquisite **spoon**, probably made for King John's coronation in 1199, and a much restored early 15thC **ampulla** in the form of an eagle (from which the anointing oil is poured). The **Royal Sceptre** contains the largest diamond ever cut (530 carats), one of the "Stars of Africa" from the Cullinan diamond found in 1905. Another piece was added to the **Imperial State Crown**, originally made in 1838, which also incorporates an immense and beautiful ruby, probably the one given to the Black Prince by Pedro the Cruel after the Battle of Najara in 1367 and worn by Henry V at the Battle of Agincourt. The oldest crown is "King Edward's," made for Charles II's coronation in 1660. It weighs 5lbs and is worn by the sovereign at coronations. The **Queen Mother's Crown**, made for her coronation in 1937, contains the famous 109-carat Kohinoor diamond, bought by the British Crown in 1849.

The White Tower and armories

The dominant White Tower is the oldest and largest of the Tower's buildings; its massive walls are up to 15ft thick, supported by external buttresses and carrying square or curved turrets at the corners. The large semicircular protuberance at the SE contains the apse of the chapel; the round turret on the NE corner contains a spiral staircase. The medieval facade was even starker — since then the decorative cones have been added, and Wren enlarged the windows.

Inside are displays from the Tower's superb collections of arms and armor. On the first floor, the **Sporting and Tournament**

Trafalgar Square

Galleries contains crossbows, muskets, lances, swords and the specialized armor made for jousting, already in the late Middle Ages a leisurely exercise in archaism. The **Chapel of St John** on the second floor is the finest example of early Norman architecture in England, almost totally without ornament, massive and severe. More armor is displayed in the other two rooms; notice the awesome bulk of a suit made for a giant almost 7ft tall.

The 3rd-floor rooms contain outstanding examples of Tudor and later armor, with several suits that belonged to Henry VIII, growing progressively larger as their owner grew older and fatter. The ceremonial armor of the 17thC is decorated to a high degree; a suit belonging to Charles I from 1630 is chased and gilded over its entire surface. Stairs descend to ground level where a fine selection of handguns, uniforms and cannons from various periods can be seen. The Oriental armor, including fine examples from India, China, Japan, even Africa, is housed in the **Waterloo Barracks**, worth visiting in particular for the elaborate elephant armor captured at the Battle of Plassey in 1757. Of many interesting artillery pieces scattered throughout the Tower's enclosures, note a Turkish bronze cannon of 1530-31.

Trafalgar Square
Map 10G11. Tube: Charing Cross.

Trafalgar Square is known as a rallying point for political demonstrations and New Year's Eve revelries, and even as a sanctuary for pigeons. When Nash began its redevelopment in the 1820s, it already had the fine equestrian statue of Charles I on the site of *Charing Cross*, and the superb church of *St Martin-in-the-Fields*. Since then, the surrounding architecture has let down Nash's vision: the *National Gallery*, added on the high N side in 1832-38, is too small in scale to make the triumphant statement its site demands, and Admiralty Arch (1911), a monument to Queen Victoria that saves its best face for *The Mall*, is equally uninspired. Still, it does allow Nelson to steal the show, as Nash intended; he was placed atop the 170ft granite column in 1842. The base is decorated by spirited reliefs made from the guns of ships captured at Trafalgar, and the justifiably famous lions were added by Landseer in 1858-67.

Trocadero
Piccadilly Circus, W1. Map 10G10. Open daily 10am-10pm. Tube: Piccadilly Circus.

A host of activities jostle for attention in this shop-and-restaurant complex on the corner of Shaftesbury Ave. Built as a dance hall at the turn of the century, it became a popular Lyons restaurant between the wars. Today it is worth a visit for the **Guinness World of Records** alone, which is the Guinness Book of Records brought to life by means of models, films, tapes and push-button machines (☎ 439-7331 ✉). Alternatively, you can make a video of yourself, miming to the latest chart-topper at **Star Tracks**, dress in period costume and have a sepia photograph taken at **Old Time Portraits**, or immortalize your face on a badge at **Photo Pop**. Children can feature as the heroes in their own personal stories at **My Book**.

Victoria & Albert Museum ★
Cromwell Rd., SW7 ☎ 938-8500. Map 15J5 ☒ voluntary contributions ▣ ✳ Open Mon-Sat 10am-5.50pm, Sun 2.30pm-5.50pm. Tube: South Kensington.

Probably the world's greatest museum of the decorative arts, it is a vast storehouse of extraordinarily varied treasures. While fine art is emphatically included, the reverence of the art gallery is absent. The "V & A" is thus a lively, informal place, and one of London's most popular museums. The range of the exhibits is overwhelming, including everything from entire furnished rooms, brought from the great houses of Britain and the Continent, to spoons, shoes and locks.

The museum is a labyrinth of galleries and passages in which it is easy to become lost, and around which it is almost impossible to plan a coherent or comprehensive tour. But, to an extent, this drawback, contributes to the museum's appeal, for even regular visitors know that no matter how often they come, there are still new treasures to be discovered.

The initial impetus and financing for the Victoria & Albert came from the Great Exhibition of 1851, the profits of which were used to purchase the large site in South Kensington on which it stands. Under the enthusiastic direction of Prince Albert's friend Sir Henry Cole, it first opened as the Museum of Ornamental Art in 1852, temporarily at *Marlborough House*, dedicated to fostering the "application of fine art to objects of utility," but in 1857 the museum moved to its iron and glass construction at South Kensington.

Almost from the first, Cole's ideals became diluted by the desire to fill the museum with great works of art. In 1865 Raphael's tapestry cartoons arrived from the Royal Collection. In 1888, the Constable Collection was bequeathed by a member of the great painter's family, adding another fine-art element of the greatest importance but having little to do with the museum's intention. Before long, the museum felt free to acquire any item of esthetic or historical interest. Similar uncertainties have dogged the museum's building programs, contributing to the sense of confusion. After 1863, the red-brick buildings were constructed around the gardens in a northern Italian Romanesque style with terra cotta and mosaic ornament. The leading artist, Lord Leighton, and the firm of William Morris contributed to the decoration of the interior, but shortage of funds prevented the scheme's completion. The library, especially attractive and now the **National Art Library**, was completed by 1882. But all this was haphazard and without any underlying plan. The final phase came in 1899-1909 with Sir Aston Webb as architect. The museum was renamed the Victoria and Albert in 1899. From this time date the great facades along Cromwell Rd.

It is not possible to suggest a complete route through the V&A — the result would be both difficult to follow and exhausting. Instead, two particularly well-displayed but contrasting departments are proposed as the starting and ending points — the Jones Collection and Constable Collection — and suggestions are made for sections to be visited in between. Visitors should stay alert on their travels for the countless minor surprises that the museum has to offer. Good large plans for the galleries are available at the main entrance. Note that the collection is supposedly arranged into "art and design" collections, cutting across the arts of a given culture or period, and "study collections," grouped by material and techniques.

Begin from the main entrance by turning left and following the signs for the **Jones Collection**, a dazzling display of French interior decoration, painting, furniture, ceramics and other decorative arts. Elaborate furniture, some of which belonged to Marie-Antoinette, is inlaid with brass or with finely-grained woods, or covered with enameled panels. The rich, aristocratic

123

mood is complemented by paintings such as Boucher's *Portrait of Madame de Pompadour*. German, Dutch and Italian decorative arts on display echo the French Rococo of the 18thC. The 17thC follows, just as elaborate but more solemn in mood. Several Dutch cabinets, inlaid with complex floral designs, are outstanding, as are German metalwork and Venetian glass.

At the end of these splendidly laid-out galleries steps lead up to the section devoted to the Renaissance, a series of rooms grouped around the court containing the gardens. In a less organized collection, some superb works stand out. There is a statue, for example, by Giovanni Bologna of *Samson and a Philistine*, a full-sized marble composition of Mannerist complexity. From the High Renaissance, there is the famous elegantly glided **Antico miniature bronze** of Meleanger (*c.*1500), and from the 15thC several important **reliefs by Donatello**, the greatest sculptor of the early Renaissance, including an exquisite and moving *Dead Christ Tended by Angels*. Rooms on the side of the gallery opposite the garden have been restored to their original decoration; one was carried out by William Morris's workshops. Another has tiles by Minton and stained glass designed by James Gamble.

The northern Renaissance is also well covered. Particularly beautiful are two late Gothic carved limewood angels made as candlesticks by Tilman Reimenschneider in the early 16thC. At the end of the gallery of Gothic art is a vast and gruesome Spanish altarpiece of the early 15thC, showing scenes from the life of St George, which, according to this account, consisted almost entirely of hideous torture. Be sure to study the **Syon Cope** closely — this early 14thC example of *opus anglicanum* needlework is one of the finest embroidered pieces ever.

Also on the ground floor is the large and stunning **costume court** (★), with one of the world's great clothing collections of everyday garments and high fashion. We relate to this instantly, of course, but it is notable that some outfits of even a decade or two ago seem as strange as an 18thC ball gown or Jacobean court dress. Above is the collection of **musical instruments**, especially strong in the 16thC keyboards such as virginals and the first harpsichords, many with exquisite carving and inlaid work.

A huge gallery nearby exhibits the seven **Raphael cartoons** (★), on permanent loan from the Royal Collection. These vastly influential designs of the *Acts of the Apostles* were carried out in 1516-19 as designs for tapestries for the Sistine Chapel in the Vatican. Next to this room is the main museum shop, housed in a gallery containing part of the **woodwork collection**.

Oriental arts are also represented on the ground floor, although even the large galleries allow room for only a small part of the V & A's great holdings. From India, there are several beautiful temple sculptures to see. More unusual is **Tipoo's Tiger**, a large wooden model of a tiger mauling a European, identified as British by his red coat; made in about 1790 for an anti-British sultan, it has organ pipes that simulate the groans of the victim. Outstanding is the exquisite **jade wine cup** made for Shah Jahan in 1657, with a lotus flower base and a graceful antelope head as the handle. The **Islamic gallery** is dominated by the vast **Ardabil Carpet** of 1540 from a Persian mosque, and some superb lacquered pottery. Outstanding in the **Chinese Collection** is an incredibly elaborate carved lacquer throne of the mid-18thC, ceramic and jade horses from more than 1,000yrs earlier, and finely embroidered court costumes, all testifying to the unchanging sophistication of Chinese art. The **Toshiba**

Gallery of Japanese art, opened in 1986, contains exquisite collections of *netsuke*, kimonos, armor and ceramics.

The important **British Collection** stretches through sizable galleries on two upper floors to the left (or w) of the main entrance. First encountered is the furniture, especially beautiful but generally simpler than the Continental equivalents, often relying more on shape and the quality of the wood than on elaborate decoration. Several complete rooms transplanted into the museum include the massively Baroque gold and white **Music Room from Norfolk House** (mid-18thC) and Robert Adam's much more delicate **Glass Drawing Room from Northumberland House** (1773-74). Two beds dominate the furniture: the huge Elizabethan **Great Bed of Ware**, which became instantly legendary for its size and was mentioned by Shakespeare; and a chinoiserie fantasy by Chippendale of 1750-55. Quite outstanding are several **miniatures**, a form of painting that reached its peak in 16th-17thC England, including Nicholas Hilliard's famous *Young Man Amongst Roses*. The same artist is thought to have produced the miniature on the **Armada Jewel**, produced for Elizabeth I in 1589 to celebrate the destruction of the Spanish Armada, and the highlight of a fine jewelry collection. British decorative arts are brought up to 1960, and there are several important examples of the work of William Morris and the Arts and Crafts Movement that had so much influence on modern British design.

Before leaving, be sure to visit the **Henry Cole Wing**, opened in 1984 at the rear of the museum to the w. Here is found the **Ionides Bequest**, consisting largely but not exclusively of 19thC paintings, with several important works: outstanding are a Degas ballet scene, Millet's *Wood Sawyers*, Burne-Jones' *Day Dream*, Gainsborough's portrait of his two young daughters, and works by Turner. Here also is the **Constable Collection**, which presents the best coverage anywhere of the work of the most English of painters, providing a refreshing, open-air view for even the most jaded visitor. The fleeting effects of the changing weather of the English countryside are here shown utterly convincingly. Clouds rush over Hampstead Heath, rainbows hover over Salisbury Cathedral, and the trees of Suffolk rustle in gentle breezes. There are also some superb small oil and watercolor "sketches" by the master.

Next door, in the main body of the museum, is the **20thC exhibitions gallery**. It mounts temporary exhibitions, often imaginative, on leading figures and aspects of 20thC design production.

Wallace Collection ★

Hertford House, Manchester Sq., W1 ☎ 935-0687. Map *9E8*
📷 🏛 *Open Mon-Sat 10am-5pm. Sun 2-5pm. Tube: Bond Street.*

Flying in the face of the renowned English insularity, this magnificent monument to Francophilia is, in fact, arguably the finest selection of French art to be found outside France, together with many other paintings and objets d'art of exceptional quality. It is a great private art collection of the 19thC "frozen" in the grand house equipped by its wealthy owner to contain it.

Hertford House in Manchester Sq. was built for the Duke of Manchester in 1776-88 and acquired by the Second Marquess of Hertford in 1797. After some years as the French Embassy, it was used to store pictures by the Fourth Marquess who did most to build up the fabulous collection while living in Paris, adding to that of his father. He bequeathed both house and works of art to his natural son, Sir Richard Wallace, who returned to London and transformed Hertford House in the 1870s into a showcase for the collection. In 1897, his widow left it to the nation and it was opened as a public gallery in 1900. It thus reflects the tastes of five generations of the Hertford family.

The finest objects are on the first floor, which should be seen first. Large paintings by Boucher are on the walls of the top landing, full of the frivolous eroticism of the Rococo court style. Turning to the left, **Rm. XIII** contains several scenes of Venice by Guardi and Canaletto. **Rms. XV-XVIII** are devoted to Flemish and Dutch art, including fine studies by Rubens. Look out for Potter's animal scenes: even the cows have personality. Caspar Netscher's *Lace-Maker*, quietly realistic, is serenely haunting; the landscapes include marvelous works by Hobbema, and Flinck's eerie *Landscape with a Coach*, formerly attributed to his master, Rembrandt. **Rm. XIX** is a large picture gallery built by Sir Richard Wallace, containing many outstanding works: Titian's *Perseus and Andromeda*, Rubens' magical *Rainbow Landscape* and Velázquez's cool *Lady with a Fan* are the most important. Also noteworthy are Rembrandt's deeply sympathetic *Portrait of Titus*, his son, Reynolds' famous portrait of the courtesan *Nelly O'Brien* and Frans Hals' *Laughing Cavalier*.

Among superb, richly ornate Rococo furniture is a roll-top desk made by J.J. Riesener for Count d'Orsay in the 1760s (**Rm. XXV**), and a chest of drawers made for Louis XV's bedroom at Versailles by Antoine Gaudreaus in 1739 (**Rm. XXI**). In the corridor between Rms. XXIII and XXIV an impressive collection of gold snuffboxes is displayed, mostly elaborate French 18thC work. Some of the best French Rococo pictures are in **Rms. XXI-XXV**, leading in an unparalleled procession through Watteau, Lancret, Pater, Boucher and Fragonard and complemented by richly decorated furniture in the same style, much of it from French royal palaces. Watteau's *Lady at her Toilet* and Fragonard's *Swing* sum up the leisured mood, and Boucher's *Portrait of Madame Pompadour* shows unexpected candor. **Rm. XIV** contains a superb display of Sèvres porcelain.

On the ground floor, **Rm. X** and the adjoining corridor contain the best public collection of works by R.P. Bonington, an English artist working in France in the early 19thC. The clear light of his seascapes is exquisite. The rest of the ground floor is more an Aladdin's cave of miscellaneous treasures, many grouped into specialist collections of great merit — of armor, miniatures or pottery, for example. There is a splendid collection of terra-cotta statuettes, mostly from the Italian Renaissance, and a unique cabinet of wax portraits. Furniture, including works attributed to the great A. C. Boulle, and more Sèvres porcelain, continue the French bias of the collection. Italian majolica pottery, and Limoges enamels of the Renaissance are as well represented here as anywhere in the world. Paintings include works by Murillo, Reynolds, Memlinc, Lawrence and Luini. And if anything, the remarkable collection of elaborately wrought and decorated **arms and armor** stands out. Look out for the northern Italian body armor and helmet of about 1620-35.

Westminster

Map 18H-J. Tube: Westminster.

Even the visitor who has never heard of Westminster can instantly appreciate the significance of this most stately of London's districts, for, like its long-time rival the *City*, it has remained almost free from residential invasion and is devoted to business, in this case government. Its activity is dominated by the mother of parliaments at the Palace of Westminster (see *Westminster, Palace of*), attended by the officialdom of *Whitehall*. Next to the Houses of Parliament is the great church of *Westminster Abbey*.

Parliament Square, an open space created at the time of the building of the Palace of Westminster, is appropriately studded with statues of great statesmen: Disraeli, Palmerston, Abraham Lincoln, Winston Churchill. Surrounding the square, apart from Westminster Abbey and the Palace of Westminster, there is the Middlesex Guildhall (Neo-Gothic of 1906-13) and the Home Office. In front of the abbey is the smaller church of **St Margaret**, founded as the parish church of Westminster possibly as early as the 11thC and now the parish church of the Houses of Parliament, and always a fashionable place for weddings (Pepys, John Milton and Churchill were all married here). The present building dates from the early 16thC but was restored almost out of recognition in the 18thC. Its interesting monuments include the tomb of Sir Walter Raleigh; the E window is Flemish 16thC.

To the E of Parliament Sq., just E of Birdcage Walk and *St James's Park*, is **Queen Anne's Gate**, with some of the best early 18thC houses in London, and a statue of Queen Anne dated 1708. In Victoria St., two important landmarks are *Westminster Cathedral* and **New Scotland Yard**, the Metropolitan Police's modern headquarters. There is an attractive enclave to the S of Westminster Abbey with Georgian houses in Cowley St. and Lord North St. The latter opens into Smith Sq., which includes some 18thC survivors on its E side, and in the center of the square is one of the most magnificent Baroque churches in London, **St John's**, built in 1714-28. It was burned down in World War II but has been restored and often hosts concerts.

Back in Birdcage Walk lies Wellington Barracks. Here the **Guards Museum** (*open Mon-Sat 10am-3.30pm* 🕮) traces the history of 3½ centuries of the five Regiments of Foot Guards (Grenadier, Coldstream, Scots, Irish and Welsh); both their fighting record and their famous ceremonial role is covered.

Westminster Abbey 🏛 † ★
Broad Sanctuary, SW1 ☎ *222-5152. Map 18I11* 🕮 *to royal chapels* 🕮 *except Wed 6-7.45pm* ✗ *Mon-Fri 9am-4pm, Sat 9am-2pm, 3.45-5pm. Tube: Westminster.*

Since William the Conqueror chose the new, incomplete Westminster Abbey for his coronation as king of his new subjects on Christmas Day, 1066, it has been the scene of the coronation, marriage and burial of British monarchs, a place of tribute to Britain's heroes, and in every way Britain's mother church. While St Paul's Cathedral belongs to London, Westminster Abbey belongs to the nation. It is also, of course, one of Britain's finest Gothic buildings, a soaring and graceful offering to God, with a strikingly unified interior.

The date of Westminster Abbey's foundation is uncertain. Legend takes it back to the 7thC; in any case, there was certainly a religious foundation here by the 9thC. In 1050 Edward the Confessor began work on a large new abbey church, in the Norman style, and it became a Benedictine monastery attached to the new Palace of Westminster.

Work continued on the Norman buildings well into the 12thC, and remains can be seen in the ruined infirmary chapel of St Catherine to the S of the present abbey church. In 1245, Henry III

began a vast new building program in the latest French Gothic
style of the cathedrals of Amiens and Reims. Work proceeded
quickly. The chancel, transepts, part of the nave and the chapter
house were completed in 1259. The great speed of the
construction gave the building a remarkable unity of style and,
when work was resumed more than a century later in 1375, the
existing style was imitated in the rest of the nave.

The mid-16thC was a time of religious upheaval, which first
threatened and then confirmed the abbey's role. The royal
connection preserved it from destruction at the dissolution of the
monasteries and, in 1540, Henry VIII made it a cathedral, with its
own bishop. Queen Mary, briefly restoring Catholicism, turned it
back into a monastery in 1556. The permanent establishment of
the protestant Church of England came under Elizabeth I, who in
1560 gave the abbey the status of a collegiate church
independent of both the Bishop of London and the Archbishop
of Canterbury. It thus became a Royal Peculiar, a great church
serving Crown and State.

The building of Westminster Abbey did not end with the
Middle Ages, although what has come since has tended to detract
from its beauty. In 1698, Sir Christopher Wren began the designs
for the W towers and facade. These were continued by Nicholas
Hawksmoor and completed in 1745 — in pseudo-Gothic style
but sitting uneasily all the same with the existing structure. In the
19thC, restoration work was carried out on a substantial scale,
much of it destroying the medieval detail. Thankfully, the
restoration work currently under way concentrates on
conservation rather than improvement.

The exterior

A huge program of restoration is under way, begun in the
mid-1970s and due to be completed by the mid-1990s. Cleaning
has revealed the beauty of the abbey's soft Reigate stone
(although where replacement is necessary Portland stone is
being used, which will better stand the test of time). The W
facade, with the main entrance, is perhaps the most dramatic
approach, although Hawksmoor's towers are insubstantial — just
too narrow and too high to suit the medieval facade — and their
provenance can be detected in the Baroque stonework above the
clock face and matching round windows in the opposite tower.

The abbey looks best from the N; the N transept forms a
tremendous centerpiece, with its great triple porch and huge rose
window, framed by a superb series of flying buttresses. Alas, all
the stonework is a product of 19thC restoration and only
indicates in a general way the detail that was there before.

To the E lies the far more elaborate exterior of Henry VII's
chapel, entirely covered with dense late Gothic tracery. The outer
walls have turrets capped by "pepperpots" and connected to the
chapel's nave by delicately pierced flying buttresses. The nave is
topped by a pierced balustrade and narrow pinnacles. The whole
effect is wonderfully decorative. To the S of the chapel can be
seen the earlier, much plainer chapter house. The pointed roof is
19thC.

The area around Westminster Abbey once formed a part of it
and was densely covered with buildings. The open space to the
NW was the Sanctuary, where anyone could seek the Church's
protection in medieval times; as a result it became packed with
timber buildings inhabited by felons on the run. The S of the
abbey was made up of the monastic buildings, and the cloister
remains, but this is best visited from within the abbey, as is the
Chapel of St Faith. Other monastic buildings to the S of these are

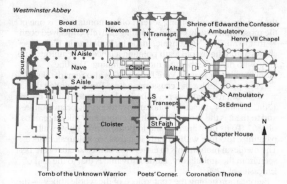

Westminster Abbey

Broad Sanctuary · Isaac Newton · N Transept · Shrine of Edward the Confessor · Ambulatory · Henry VII Chapel · Entrance · N Aisle · Nave · Choir · Altar · S Aisle · Ambulatory · Deanery · S Transept · St Edmund · Cloister · St Faith · Chapter House · N · Tomb of the Unknown Warrior · Poets' Corner · Coronation Throne

now incorporated in Westminster School, the leading public school that has evolved from the monastery's teaching function. To the N is Dean's Yard, now an open space, which can be entered through a 19thC arch to the W of the abbey. Until the 18thC it was covered over by monastic buildings.

The interior

The abbey is entered from the W, immediately presenting the visitor with a stunning view along the nave. Sweeping exaltedly upward, it is very like a French Gothic cathedral, much higher and narrower than other English churches, supported on piers of dark Purbeck marble. Above the main arches is the triforium containing a gallery (unlike the French style); then the clerestory containing the windows, beneath the gracefully vaulted ceiling, completing the majesty. The western end of the nave was built last to match the style of the 13thC work to the E; the huge, plain window above the W door is late 15thC.

Set in the floor ahead of the entrance is a memorial to Winston Churchill with the **Tomb of the Unknown Warrior** beyond; the brass lettering is made from cartridges brought back with the body from the World War I trenches. On the first pier of the nave to the right hangs a famous and rare medieval **portrait of Richard II**, probably painted in 1398. Both the aisles are filled with monuments, jumbles of marble statuary, both good and bad. In the S aisle, that to Colonel Townshend, killed at the Battle of Ticonderoga in the American War of Independence, is of particular merit. It was designed by Robert Adam and made soon after 1759. The N aisle is even more crowded with monuments. Most notable is that to Charles James Fox of 1823. Look out also for the small kneeling wall effigy of Mrs Jane Hill of 1631, with *Death in a Shroud* and the *Tree of Life* above. Buried in the nave are David Livingstone, the explorer, and the engineers Thomas Telford and Robert Stephenson, among many national figures. The E end of the nave is closed by a brightly colored Neo-Gothic choir screen of 1848. On the left in one of its arches is a fine monument of 1731 to Isaac Newton, designed by William Kent and carved by J.M. Rysbrack.

The rest of the abbey is reached through a gate in the N aisle. Memorials to scientists cluster near Newton's tomb: Lister, Darwin, Faraday, Rutherford; musicians including Elgar, Vaughan-Williams and Benjamin Britten are commemorated by plaques in the floor near Purcell's monument. In the N transept the monuments come thick and heavy, and include those to 19thC statesmen. The architecture is of Henry III's time (1216-72), but the great rose window was heavily restored in the 19thC. In the E of the transept, among several older monuments, is one of the most impressively carved and imaginatively conceived of all — that to Mrs J.G. Nightingale, made by Roubiliac in 1761. It shows a grim figure of Death pointing a lance at the unfortunate lady, who died after being struck by lightning. The fine monument to Sir Francis Vere from 1609 is also remarkable.

At this point notice the **crossing**, where Wren intended that a spire should rise that was never built. The wooden pulpit is early 17thC. To the W, the choir stalls are overdone Victorian Gothic, and to the E is the sanctuary, with an elaborately gilded reredos of 1867. To its right are rare and important early 14thC wall paintings, together with an early Renaissance Italian altarpiece. The medieval monuments to either side of the sanctuary are best seen from the ambulatory. Particularly fine is that to the Earl of Lancaster of 1296.

Before approaching the centerpiece of the whole abbey — the chapel and shrine to Edward the Confessor — visit the superb **Henry VII's chapel** at the E end of the abbey. Begun in 1503 and completed in 1512 by Henry VIII, it is in the much more richly elaborate Gothic style of the late Middle Ages, a mature, sophisticated farewell flourish. The whole surface is adorned with carvings — there are more than 100 statues, and the ceiling is a marvel of delicate tracery. The choir stalls are equally finely carved in wood — be sure to inspect the misericords, carvings that are visible when the seats are folded up. Henry VII's tomb in the chapel was started in 1506 in the same rich Gothic style, with a bronze screen. For the monument within, however, the Italian Pietro Torrigiano produced the first Renaissance sculpture in England in 1512-18; the heads of the corner angels are specially beautiful. Henry VII's chapel has its own subsidiary chapels and aisles. In the N aisle is the joint tomb of Elizabeth I, completed in 1606 with a suitably stern effigy, and her hated rival Mary Queen of Scots. Beyond are two monuments to daughters of James I. The S aisle contains several Tudor monuments rather grander than that to Queen Elizabeth herself.

The easternmost chapel is dedicated to the Royal Air Force. From Henry VII's chapel, **Edward the Confessor's shrine**, located just behind the main altar of the abbey, is reached by a bridge, and entered past the wooden effigy and chantry chapel of Henry V, a Gothic structure of the early 15thC. Only the base remains from the magnificent tomb built by Henry III to contain the remains of the Confessor, but enough remains of the gold mosaic to indicate its former splendor. It was made by an Italian artist in about 1270, as was the fine mosaic floor and Henry III's own similar tomb. Also in the chapel is the **coronation throne** of 1300-1, where almost every monarch since William I has been crowned. It contains, under the seat, the **Stone of Scone**, the mystical coronation stone of the Scottish kings, captured by Edward I in 1297. Legends identify it with Jacob's pillow when he dreamed at Bethel, and also as a holy stone in Ireland. It was certainly in use as a coronation stone for Macbeth and other Scottish kings from the 9thC. Its symbolic value persists: in 1950 it was stolen by Scottish nationalists but was recovered a year later. Beside the throne are the state sword and shield of Edward III, and all around are the tombs of the medieval monarchs, some of the finest sculpture surviving from this period in England.

After this holy of holies, the chapels of the S ambulatory are an anticlimax. In the ambulatory itself are the remains of a 13thC painted retable, with a well-preserved figure of St Peter on the extreme left. St Edmund's Chapel contains a fine effigy of William of Valence, Henry III's half-brother, from 1296. Look for the lovely miniature alabaster effigies of a knight and his lady.

The s transept has two beautiful carved angels from the mid-13thC in the spandrels of the main arch, but is more famous as **Poet's Corner**. Here are buried, or commemorated, many of the greatest writers in the English language. The best monument, to Geoffrey Chaucer, was placed here in 1555, but probably includes older elements. More recent poets commemorated include Ben Jonson, Milton, Blake, Longfellow and Shakespeare (a most undistinguished statue). Browning, Byron, Tennyson and Henry James have plaques in the floor. On the s wall are two fine late 13thC wall paintings, discovered in 1936.

In the s choir aisle a doorway leads through to the cloister, as dignified as a monastic cloister should be. The earliest part is to the E and N, dating from the 13thC and among the oldest remnants of Henry III's work on the abbey; the cloister was finished in the 14thC, and much restored in the 19thC. It now contains a brass-rubbing center, where copies can be made from replicas of medieval brass monuments. On the E side, a passageway leads through to the **chapter house** (🏛 ☆ *open Mon-Fri 9am-4pm, Sat 9am-2pm, 3.45-5pm*), an exquisitely symmetrical octagon, with its vaulted roof supported on a slender Purbeck marble pier. It was built c.1250 and has been well restored to its medieval state, with beautiful red and gold tiles decorating the floor, and wall paintings. The chapter house was used throughout the Middle Ages for the occasional meetings of Parliament. To the N of the entrance is the small chapel of St Faith, with a high vaulted roof and, behind the altar, a well-preserved painting, probably late 13thC.

Beyond the chapter house is the **Norman Undercroft**, where the **Abbey Museum** (🖾 *open daily 10.30am-4pm*) houses a display of the abbey's history. There are examples of carving and a number of royal funeral effigies. Those of the Middle Ages are wood; later ones are wax, clothed in contemporary costume. Armor from Henry V's funeral is particularly interesting.

Westminster Cathedral 🏛 † ☆

Ashley Pl., SW1 ☎ *834-7452. Map 17J9* 🖾 *to campanile, open Easter-Oct 10am-5pm* 🌣 *Tube: Westminster, Victoria.*
When designs were being considered in the late 19thC for the Roman Catholic Cathedral of Westminster, intended to be London's most important Catholic church, a Neo-Gothic structure at first seemed the inevitable choice. In the end, however, an early Christian approach was courageously adopted, against all the prevalent dictates of the era. The result of this far-sighted decision is a building of great originality, a strange Byzantine basilica unique in London and cleverly avoiding a false comparison with nearby *Westminster Abbey*.

The cathedral was built under the direction of J.F. Bentley between 1895 and 1903, using as a model Santa Sophia in Istanbul, together with some Italian Renaissance ideas, the most striking of which is the huge campanile, similar to that of Siena Cathedral but in red brick with lighter stone striping. The top of the tower, 273ft high, can be visited (*by* ⬆) in summer, and affords marvelous views.

The interior is deeply impressive, with a massive open space created by the great nave, supporting a roof of four shallow domes, purely Byzantine in inspiration. The decoration is still incomplete, with rough brick exposed above the lower levels contributing to the solemn effect. The piers of the nave are giant columns of dark green marble, supposedly from the same quarry as those in Santa Sophia. Other marbles, dramatically patterned in gray and black, cover the walls, and over the altar is a great baldachin of even more brightly colored marble, but again to a restrained design. Eventually the whole interior should be covered with mosaics, although those parts completed so far fail to reflect the grandeur of the overall conception. The outstanding works of art in the cathedral are the **Stations of the Cross**, reliefs carried out by Eric Gill in 1913-18.

Westminster, Palace of ⅲ ★

Parliament Sq., SW1 ☎ 219-4272 (House of Commons), 219-3107 (House of Lords). Map 18/11 ▣ ✕ To listen to debates, UK residents should apply to an MP or Peer, foreign residents to their Embassy or High Commission, both well in advance, or come at off-peak times without prior arrangements (☎ for details). For a tour of the building, UK residents should apply to an MP or Peer, foreign residents in writing to the Commons Public Information Office, both well in advance. During parliamentary sittings admittance to public galleries from St Stephen's entrance. Tube: Westminster.

The effect is stunning: sheer size combines with immense variety and inventive detail to create an architectural triumph so instantly recognizable that it has come to symbolize the very system of government, representative democracy, housed within. In fact, this riverside complex of buildings, often known simply as the Houses of Parliament, is only the new home of the mother of parliaments, a high Victorian exercise in medievalism.

A royal palace was probably moved from Winchester to Westminster in about 1000, being established on the Island of Thorney in the marshes next to an existing monastery, and Edward the Confessor began an ambitious building program in 1050-65, the monastery becoming *Westminster Abbey*. The Norman kings followed his lead and William Rufus, the Conqueror's son, built Westminster Hall in 1097-99, at the time almost certainly the largest hall in Europe. When in residence, medieval kings would call their councils of noblemen to meet at Westminster, a forerunner of the House of Lords. In 1265, a powerful baron called Simon de Montfort began the practice of calling additional councils of knights and burghers to represent the shires and towns. Meeting together from 1332, these subsequently became the House of Commons. A medieval king was not obliged to call a parliament, and only did so when he needed the cooperation of his lords and knights. In theory, they came to advise him, but, in practice, he needed their assistance in the raising of taxes. From this grew the fact, unpalatable to medieval monarchs, that the country could not be governed without the consent of lords and commons.

In the 16thC, when Henry VIII moved his residence to the nearby Whitehall Palace, the Palace of Westminster became the permanent and more exclusive base of Parliament, the Commons using from 1550 the abandoned royal chapel of St Stephen. Westminster Hall was not used for Parliament, however, but retained for the royal courts until 1882.

The 17thC saw the long struggle that would eventually lead to the constitutional pre-eminence of Parliament. In 1640-49, Charles I attempted to assert the royal power and crush the Commons, losing both crown and head in the process. Since his last desperate entry in 1642 to arrest parliamentary opponents, no monarch has entered the Commons. In 1660 Charles II was recalled to the throne and the struggle between King and Parliament was renewed. During the 18thC, the monarchy lost ground steadily and parliamentary government became a reality, with a prime minister appointed by the monarch according to the electoral wishes of the country.

In constitutional terms, Parliament consists of Monarch, Lords and Commons, all of whom have to assent to the laws by which the country is governed. But, by a process of recurring struggle, members of the Commons have come to have the dominant role: the Lords can now only delay legislation by one year, and royal assent is never refused. The Lords is still the highest Court of Appeal in the land. A much criticized anachronism is that the Lords is still largely composed of hereditary peers, although increasingly they are now created for life only. The British system has developed slowly, through reforms and bitter struggles, and uniquely combines traditional ritual with democratic practice. The palace is still a web of ancient regulations: in the Commons, the hatless must take opera hats provided for them in boxes.

Tightened security limits access to the interior of the palace. The medieval royal palace, with its 17th-18thC additions, was largely destroyed by fire in 1834. In 1840, rebuilding began, with only the old cloister, Westminster Hall and the crypt of St Stephen's Chapel being preserved. The architect was Sir Charles Barry, with the younger A.W.N. Pugin as his assistant. Barry was essentially a Classicist, forced by the brief to work in the Gothic idiom. Pugin, on the other hand, was a passionate medievalist — indeed, it was his meticulous drawings that won the commission. The House of Lords chamber was complete by 1847, the Commons by 1850. Both men died in 1852, and the work was not completed overall until 1860.

The most splendid views of the palace are from Westminster Bridge or across the river, taking in the great regular facade Barry constructed along the riverside, with large asymmetrical towers at either end: the huge square **Victoria Tower** to the s and the more slender and original **Clock Tower** to the N, the superb clock of which is Britain's most authoritative. Although this tower is often known as **Big Ben**, that name actually applies to the huge bell inside the clock itself, supposedly named after Benjamin Hall, Commissioner of Works at the time.

From the landward side are seen several different facades and views of the towers, spreading to N and S behind the central bulk of medieval Westminster Hall. Golden-brown Yorkshire limestone was chosen, but it was badly quarried and has needed constant repairs; it also needs regular cleaning to remove the blackened grime and reveal its original mellow color. The exterior is covered with tracery, statues and pinnacles, with a dominant pattern that echoes Henry VII's chapel across the road.

Of the few remaining medieval elements of the palace, **Westminster Hall** (★) is outstanding. The lower walls are the oldest part, dating from the late 11thC. In 1394-99, Richard II replaced the upper walls and roof with the remarkable structure seen today. It is one of the world's greatest timber constructions, and the apogee of English Gothic, a huge and beautiful oak **hammerbeam roof**, with wonderfully carved tracery and angels on the ends of the beams. Statues of early kings, also dating from Richard II's reign, can be seen in niches. The other medieval survivor is the 1365 **Jewel Tower**, across Abingdon St. and actually closer to the abbey. Strongly fortified and moated, it was first used as a royal treasure house, and then to store records.

There are two public entrances to the Victorian parts of the palace. For those wishing to "lobby" their members of parliament (a practice whereby constituents can ask their representative to come to the lobby to discuss a particular issue), there is St Stephen's Porch beside the hall. This entrance leads above the medieval crypt, now the Parliament chapel, and to the great lobby beneath an elaborate, spiral lantern that can be seen from outside. This entrance also gives access to the public galleries of the two debating chambers.

Tours of the palace are sometimes allowed: entrance is by the Norman Porch next to the Victoria Tower. The gate beneath the tower itself is used by the Queen only, for official ceremonies such as the **State Opening of Parliament** (see *Calendar of events*). The porch leads through to the **Robing Room**, a spectacular paneled chamber that amply demonstrates Pugin's effective use of Gothic and Tudor motifs; note especially the ornate fireplace. The **Royal Gallery** beyond is more spectacular still, with a colorful ceramic floor and statues of monarchs.

Through the Prince's Chamber is the **House of Lords**, a quite stunning chamber surrounded by sumptuous red leather benches. The leather and wood, the rich colors, and the deep calm make it feel like a monumental clubland lounge, an analogy not altogether inappropriate for the more detached, learned deliberations of the upper house. The Lord Chancellor, who chairs the debates, sits on a red-covered woolsack, and behind him is the royal throne the Lords still maintain (the State Opening takes place in this chamber) beneath an extraordinarily fine gilded canopy, Pugin's masterpiece.

Beyond the Peers' Lobby, Central Lobby and Commons' Lobby is the **House of Commons** itself. It was burned during an air raid in 1941 and the entrance arch has been rebuilt, using some of the damaged stones, between statues of Winston Churchill and Lloyd George. The chamber itself was built in 1945-50 in plainer style, neither Pugin-elaborated nor obviously modern. The governing party occupies the benches on one side, the opposition the other. Neither side is supposed to cross the red lines in the carpet, traditionally 2 drawn swords apart in distance.

The rest of the Houses of Parliament, consisting of more than 1,000 rooms and 2 miles of corridor, is not open to the public. It is a place of work: committees struggling over the details of legislation and MPs taking care of their constituency business. Restaurants and terraces for the MPs look out across the river, as does Pugin's magnificent **House of Lords Library**.

Whitechapel Art Gallery 🏛

80 Whitechapel High St., E1 ☎ *377-0107. Map* **13F18** 📷 ✒ *with flash* ▣ *Open Tues-Sun 11am-5pm, 8pm on Wed. Tube: Aldgate East.*

A scruffy row of shops in the East End is an unlikely place to find one of England's most celebrated Art Nouveau buildings, but there it is, with a large arched doorway in a plain facade topped by a delightful foliage relief. It was built in 1897-99 by C. Harrison Townsend, a follower of the influential Arts and Crafts Movement, who also designed the Horniman Museum in *Dulwich*. The gallery currently enjoys a high reputation for staging important temporary exhibitions of contemporary art.

Whitehall

Map **10G-H.** *Tube: Charing Cross, Westminster.*

The word Whitehall is so firmly embedded in English that it is applied to people, institutions and buildings quite irrespective of whether they belong to the street of that name. Nevertheless, Whitehall has not changed — it is still lined by large government offices, and it is still Britain's administrative center. Running s from *Trafalgar Square* toward *Westminster*, it took on this character in the late 17thC, as government departments began building around the Royal Palace of Whitehall.

Before 1514, Whitehall Palace was York Place, a house belonging to the Archbishop of York. Henry VIII took it over from Cardinal Wolsey in 1530 and turned it into a huge rambling palace, and in 1619-25 Inigo Jones' magnificent *Banqueting House* was added, the only building that survives.

The northern end of Whitehall resembles any other commercial street in central London until the **Admiralty** is encountered on the w side, a brick building (1722-26) with a large Ionic portico. In front is a handsome screen designed by Robert Adam in 1759-61 with winged sea horses surmounting the gates. Government buildings from about 1900 are followed by the Banqueting House, with the attractive Welsh Office, occupying a private residence from 1772, soon after. On the w side, opposite, is the *Horse Guards Parade*, built in 1750-60 to William Kent's designs. Next to it is Dover House (the Scottish Office) with an elegant facade of 1787. Whitehall at this point is dominated by the great bulk of the Ministry of Defense building, a Portland stone monster finished as late as 1959. Somewhere beneath it are Henry VIII's wine cellars, surviving from the old palace. Looking tiny, the modern statues in front depict Sir Walter Raleigh and Field-Marshal Montgomery. Opposite is *Downing Street*.

From here, Whitehall becomes Parliament St., with massive 19thC government buildings in Italian Renaissance style. At no. 79, William Whitfield's bold new government office complex echoes the adjacent Norman Shaw buildings in its banded stone and brick: a stunning example of modern architecture, which blends beautifully with its surroundings. The **Cenotaph** of 1919, the national monument to Britain's war dead, is opposite in the center of Parliament St.

Beneath the offices, with a public entrance in King Charles St., are the fascinating **Cabinet War Rooms** (🔳 *open Tues-Sun 10am-5.50pm*). This fortified bunker, deep in the bowels of the earth, housed Churchill's emergency center of operations during the war. It can now be seen as it was, with maps, telephones and even the great man's cigars on display.

Wimbledon

*Map **20**D4. Tube: Southfields, Wimbledon, Wimbledon Pk.*
The modern tennis duels, which have made this sw suburb world famous, had an earlier counterpart, on **Wimbledon Common**, a large expanse of heath once notorious for settling disputes of honor. The **All-England Tennis Courts** themselves are in Church Rd., and the 2-week championships in June-July transform the area, attracting both tennis fans and those who come for the copious strawberries and cream and champagne. Inside the splendid ivy-clad main building is a **Lawn Tennis Museum** (🔳 *open Tues-Sat 11am-5pm, Sun 2-5pm*).

The Zoo 🏛 ☆

*Regent's Park, NW1 ☎ 722-3333. Map **2**B7 🔳 ▭ ✴ Open daily 10am-6pm, dusk in winter. Tube: Regent's Park, Mornington Crescent, Camden Town.*
More properly named the gardens of the Zoological Society of

London, the zoo occupies an attractive portion of *Regent's Park* bisected by the *Grand Union Canal*. Founded in 1826, it is the oldest such institution in the world, and one of the most important. Together with Whipsnade Park in Bedfordshire, where the animals are kept in large open paddocks in the countryside, London Zoo has no less than 5,000 species and, as well as showing animals to the public, it enjoys worldwide repute in the fields of conservation and animal medicine.

Innovation has changed the ways of showing animals, and bold architectural experiments have displaced the old iron cage approach. In many cases the animals are in larger compounds, designed to reflect their natural habitats and separated from the public by moats rather than bars. The most spectacular example, the **Mappin Terraces**, were opened as early as 1914. Here, an artificial mountain is divided into layers, devoted to different animals on succeeding levels. They are at present closed for redevelopment. Similarly, the big cats can be seen at close range in their dens through glass or watched as they roam their paddocks stocked with suitable vegetation. These animals do not have that bored, lethargic appearance that can make zoos so depressing. Precisely because they are so active, the monkeys and apes in the **Michael Sobell Pavilion** (opened in 1972) are perhaps the most enjoyable of the zoo's creatures. More morbidly alluring is one of the world's most extensive collections of reptiles and insects, poisonous snakes and giant spiders.

Two special features are **The Moonlight World**, where nocturnal animals can be seen behaving as if in the dead of night, and the **children's zoo and farm**, with tame animals which will give children rides or can be handled.

There are important examples of modern architecture. The **Penguin Pool** of the 1930s pioneered the use of prestressed concrete, and still looks modern. The **Snowdon Aviary**, opened in 1965 and containing a variety of birds in a large open space, is superbly functional even if criticized for looking rather like a collapsed radio mast. The zoo is in the process of extensively refurbishing existing exhibits and adding many new ones.

Where to stay

London's hotels were described, in one well-bruited year, as the most expensive in the world, then 12 months later found themselves easing to a less-publicized 22nd position in the same *Financial Times* league table. It must be said, of course, that such calculations are greatly influenced by the value of the pound sterling against the visitors' currency, given to considerable fluctuation over recent years.

The same differing viewpoints attend the hotels' reputations, while the most reflective judges argue that, at both ends of the price spectrum, standards are much the same as those elsewhere in Europe. Although London has not escaped the international trend toward the provision of fewer services, it might be contended that overall standards have improved in recent years.

Categories of hotel

At the most expensive end of the spectrum, what might be
described as the grand old hotels of London bear witness to
the Englishman's notion of style as an attribute not to be
worn on the sleeve. They know that a gentleman does not
have to prove anything, and neither do they. They assume
that quality, although hideously expensive these days, is
timeless, and so can seem old-fashioned to some. They were
built for people with ancient country estates who needed a
home-away-from-home in town. The traveler with the
resources to understand this will enjoy them. Others may
prefer something less English.

Most of the international chains have at least one
establishment in London, offering the style of
accommodations and service to which their regular patrons
are accustomed, although at rather cosmopolitan prices. As
most of them offer conference facilities, and are popular with
the international executive, advance reservations are essential.

Of the British chains, Trust House Forte is the largest, with
the **Grosvenor House** as its flagship. Inter-Continental
retains a stronghold in London with several top hotels
including the **Inter-Continental**, **Britannia** and **May Fair**
under its aegis. The deluxe Savoy group includes the **Savoy**,
Berkeley, **Connaught** and **Claridge's**. Thistle (now part of
the Mount Charlotte Group) is a good chain of mainly
business hotels concentrated in and around London, as are
Ladbroke's hotels.

In the middle price range, "house hotels" are becoming
increasingly popular. They usually only have a few rooms and
are often converted from attractive row houses. They range
from the designer-decorated, such as **Dorset Square** and
L'Hôtel, to the quaint, such as **Ebury Court**.

The cheaper type of British hotel is often known as a
boarding house, or a "bed-and-breakfast" (or simply "B & B").
At their best, they are clean, comfortable and friendly, but
currently, good "B & B's" in London are in very short supply;
they are rarely to be trusted unless you have a
recommendation. The **British Tourist Authority** is
promoting a pleasant alternative — staying with a British
family. Send for the booklet *Stay with a British Family* from
the **British Tourist Authority** (*Accommodation Unit,
Thames Tower, Black's Rd., London W6 9EL*) or from the
many BTA offices throughout the world.

If you are looking for an apartment rather than a hotel, you
will find a list in the booklet *Where to Stay in London*,
available from BTA offices or from the **London Tourist
Board** (*Correspondence Unit, 26 Grosvenor Gdns., London
SW1W 0DU*). The publication also lists group and youth
accommodations, and companies dealing with family
accommodations in London.

Reservations

If you want to choose the particular hotel you stay in,
advance reservation is essential, preferably at least a month
ahead. Depending on the time of year, you might be lucky
with short-notice reservations, but prepare to be flexible.

Advance reservation of an inexpensive to medium-priced
hotel can be arranged by writing to the **London Tourist
Board** (*Accommodation Services, 26 Grosvenor Gdns.,
London SW1W 0DU*). Write at least six weeks in advance,

suggesting a price bracket and any general preference for location, and the organization will then make a provisional reservation before writing to you to confirm it. A telephone reservation service is also now available (☎ *823-8844*), using Visa or MasterCard to pay a deposit on the reservation.

Given some flexibility, it is possible to make instant reservations at London Tourist Board and Convention Bureau Information Centres at Heathrow Airport or Victoria Station.

Price

See *How to use this book* for the price guidelines corresponding to the symbols used in all hotel entries. London hotels usually charge by the person, rather than by the room, and sometimes include breakfast in the price — increasingly only a "Continental breakfast" of toast or croissants and coffee, with a supplement for the fried "English breakfast." Check whether VAT (Value Added Tax) is included.

Service is usually included. If you are very pleased with the service, give a small tip to the chambermaid or receptionist.

Meals

The dining facilities range from some of the best restaurants in London to those that do not expect to attract most of their guests. What they nearly all offer, at extra cost, is the great British breakfast of bacon and eggs or kippers. Residential terms, with an evening meal included in the price, are rare.

Executive accommodations

Businessmen will find an extensive choice of accommodations, and many of the larger hotels have conference facilities. Two leading examples with several floors dedicated to executive accommodations are the **Hilton** and **Sheraton Park Tower**; and **Thistle** (Mount Charlotte) and **Ladbroke** hotels are substantially oriented toward visiting businessmen.

Other notable choices include the **Churchill** and **Hyatt Carlton Tower**, both with very fully equipped business centers; the superb **Howard**, near the City; and the luxurious **Montcalm** and **Fortyseven Park Street**. More modestly priced but also offering excellent accommodations and office-from-office facilities are the **White House** and **John Howard Hotel**.

All these and many others are described in the following pages.

Hotels classified by area

Bayswater/Paddington
Royal Lancaster ////]
Belgravia/Knightsbridge
Basil Street ////]
Beaufort ////] to /////
Berkeley Hotel ///// ♛
Capital ///// ♛
Claverly //□ ✿
Halkin /////
L'Hôtel ///□
Hyatt Carlton Tower ///// ♛
Knightsbridge //□
Knightsbridge Green ///□
Sheraton Park Tower /////
Blackheath
Bardon Lodge //□ ✿

Bloomsbury
Academy //□
Imperial //□
Kingsley //□ ✿
Chelsea
Draycott /////
Eleven Cadogan Gardens ////]
Fenja ///□ to ////]
Wilbraham //□
City
Great Eastern ///□
Howard ///// ♛
Covent Garden/Strand
Hazlitt's ///□ ✿
Savoy ///// ♛
Strand Palace ///□ ✿

Waldorf ////
Kensington
Alexander ///☐
Blakes ////
Gore ///☐ ✿
Halcyon ////
John Howard Hotel ///☐
Kensington Palace ////
Observatory House /☐
One Cranley Place ///☐ to ////
Pembridge Court /☐ to
   ///☐ ✿
Portobello ///☐ to ////
Little Venice
Colonnade /☐ to ///☐
Marylebone/West End
Berners ////
Churchill //// 🏨
Dorset Square ///☐ to //// ✿
Durrants ///☐
Hotel la Place //☐
Montcalm ////
White House ///☐ ✿
Mayfair
Britannia ////

Brown's ////
Chesterfield ////
Claridge's //// 🏨
Connaught //// 🏨
Dorchester //// 🏨
Fortyseven Park Street ////
Grosvenor House ////
Hilton ////
Inn on the Park //// 🏨
Inter-Continental ////
May Fair ////
Westbury ////
Piccadilly
Athenaeum //// 🏨
Le Meridien London //// 🏨
Park Lane ////
Ritz //// 🏨
St James's
Dukes ////
Stafford ////
Victoria
Collin House /☐ 🏠
Ebury Court ///☐
Elizabeth /☐
Goring ////

Alexander

9 Sumner Pl., SW7 ☎ *581-1591/5*
🖬 *917133* 🖷 *581-0824. Map* **15K5**
////☐ *37 rms* 🖃 *37* 🕮 🅰🅴 🅾 *Tube:
South Kensington.*
Location: South Kensington. S.J.
Perelman once issued the entreaty
"Please don't give me nothing to
remember you by," but they haven't
forgotten his stays at The Alexander;
they named a room after him. If he
observed the strangeness of a hotel
in a street so attractive that it is not
allowed to hang a sign, he didn't say
so. The Alexander is announced
only by a brass plate outside, and
maintains a similar note of restful
discretion inside. It is a Victorian
house, in which all bedrooms have
been impeccably modernized, with
a lovely, high-walled garden for the
use of guests. Visitors with a bar at
home will feel comfortable in the
serve-yourself lounge, operating on
an honesty system.
🏠 ✿ ☐ 🖵 🐾 ⛱

Athenaeum 🏨

116 Piccadilly, W1 ☎ *499-3464*
🖬 *261589* 🖷 *493-1860. Map* **9H8**
//// *112 rms* 🖃 *112* 🕮 🖻 🚬 🅰🅴
🅾 *Tube: Green Park.*
*Location: West End, between
Mayfair and Green Park.* Although
it is especially well known for its
unrivaled selection of malt
whiskies, this smallish, pristine
1940s hotel is full of good ideas. A
quaintly-named Lady Athenaeu
Club makes sure lone female
travelers are welcomed and

pampered. Guests who want to jog
in the park are loaned track suits.
Attention to detail is the keynote. If
you have an afternoon nap, your
sheets will be changed again before
bedtime. Unlike so many
present-day hotels, the Athenaeum
doesn't stint on towels — there are
mounds of them, and luxury
bathrooms too.
✿ ⚙ ☐ 🖵 🐾 ⛱

Bardon Lodge ✿

Stratheden Rd., Blackheath, SE3
☎ *(081) 853-4051* 🖷 *(081) 858-
7387* //☐ *37 rms* 🖃 *2* 🚬 🅰🅴
*Location: South London, between
Greenwich and Blackheath.* Good
inexpensive hotels are hard to come
by in London at present, and it may
be necessary to look farther afield
for a fair deal. Blackheath is on the
edge of the city, an impressive place
with its vast common and fine
Georgian houses; close by is
Greenwich. Bardon Lodge, owned
and run with some pride by Barbara
and Donald Nott — hence the name
— is a beautifully kept hotel with
spacious rooms (two with private
bathrooms, the rest with a shower
cubicle) and a pleasant dining room.
☐ 🖵 🐾 ⛱

Basil Street Hotel

8 Basil St., SW3 ☎ *581-3311*
🖬 *28379* 🖷 *581-3693. Map* **16I7**
//// *96 rms* 🖃 *56* 🚬 🅰🅴 🅾 *Tube:
Kensington.*
*Location: Knightsbridge, behind
Harrods.* Much loved not only for

the high standard of service it provides, but also for its depth of personality. A woman's hotel in the days when ladies came from the country to do their shopping in Knightsbridge, it still runs the female counterpart to a gentlemen's club. In the hotel, however, guests of both sexes are offered what the Basil describes with some accuracy as "an island of hospitality in our brusque, modern world." Decorated with British and Oriental antiques, in an Edwardian building part of which was once the reservation hall of a station, the Basil has a coziness that belies its size; it remains small enough to offer the personal touch, but sufficiently large to provide the services of a first-class hotel.

‡ ☐ 🖾 👪

Berkeley Hotel 🏨
Wilton Pl., SW1 ☎ 235-6000
◉ 919252 ◈ 235-4330. Map **16**l**7**
▥ 160 rms 🖾 160 ▦ 🚅 🖾
🖸 Tube: Knightsbridge.
Location: Knightsbridge, opposite Hyde Park. Noël Coward's old Berkeley is gone, yet much of its character has re-emerged in the new one, built by the same management in 1972. "The last really deluxe hotel to be built in Europe," they claim. Deluxe rather than grand deluxe, by today's standards, it is small for a hotel of this style. The hotel is known for its service, organized separately on every floor, has a rooftop swimming pool, a gymnasium, sauna, movie theater, beauty parlor, one of London's better French restaurants, the **Le Perroquet** bar, and the **Buttery**.
‡ ⛐ ☐ 🖾 ⇆ ♈ 👪 ⅄ ⇐

Berners
Berners St., W1 ☎ 636-1629
◉ 25759 ◈ 580-3972. Map **10**E**10**
▥ 237 rms 🖾 237 ▦ 🖾 🖸
Tube: Tottenham Court Road.
Location: Off Oxford St. A magnificent job of refurbishment has been carried out in this grand old hotel, the splendid interior of which seems at odds with its never having been famous or fashionable. The location is wrong for that, yet right for shopping, and near to theatreland. Bedrooms round the central well are very quiet. Ten rooms are specially designed for the benefit of handicapped people. There is a carvery-type restaurant.
‡ ⛐ ☐ 🖾 ♈ 👪 ⅄

Blakes
33-35 Roland Gdns., SW7
☎ 370-6701 ◉ 8813500 ◈ 373-

0442. Map **15**K**4** ▥ 52 rms 🖾 52
🚅 🖾 🖸 Tube: South Kensington.
Location: South Kensington, off Old Brompton Rd. Mandatory for media folk, who are suitably at home in an hotel owned by a designer. It shows, too, with that beautiful birdcage, the black and white dining room and a sunken bed in one suite. And which other small London hotel serves pastrami on rye? Also one of the best hotel restaurants in town, and what the management describes as "all the best services to be expected from a first-class hotel," all in a prim Victorian street.
⌂ ☐ 🖾 ⅍ 🖾

Britannia
Grosvenor Sq. (entrance Adam's Row), W1 ☎ 629-9400 ◉ 23941
◈ 629-7736. Map **9**G**8** ▥ 326 rms
🖾 326 ▦ 🚅 🖾 🖸 Tube: Bond Street.
Location: Mayfair, near Oxford St. and Hyde Park. This very large Georgian square, lined with embassies, has largely been rebuilt and restored, and there is little to suggest that behind its facades lies a large hotel. Even more surprisingly, the Britannia was built only in 1970, and its well-decorated interior is a successful blend of original and reproduction Georgiana. Nonetheless, its built-in "pub" can claim to stand on the site where a Cabinet meeting learned from a horse-borne messenger that Wellington had beaten Napoleon at Waterloo. It sports an Anglo-American café, and two restaurants, one Japanese.
‡ ☐ 🖾 ⅍ ⅃ 👪 ⅄

Brown's
22-24 Dover St., W1 ☎ 493-6020
◉ 28686 ◈ 493-9381. Map **9**G**9** ▥
125 rms 🖾 125 🚅 🖾 🖸 Tube: Green Park.
Location: Mayfair, near Bond St. and Piccadilly. The original Mr Brown was butler to Lord Byron, and the hotel he founded became the most renowned among those intended to be a London home-away-from-home for the gentry. It still retains this character in the charm, individuality and style of its rooms, although many are, by modern standards, rather small and gloomy. Theodore Roosevelt was married from Brown's, and FDR and Eleanor honeymooned there; the Dutch Government in exile declared war on Japan, and Queen Wilhelmina and Princess Juliana

Hotels

stayed here. Brown's still takes pride in maintaining the privacy of its guests, but life is inevitably less serene in the late 20thC. Now owned by the Trust House Forte chain.

Capital
Basil St., SW3 ☎ 589-5171
⑨919042 ⑯225-0011. Map 16|7
▦48 rms ▭48▦▭ ⚊⚌ AE ⊙
Tube: Knightsbridge.
Location: Knightsbridge, behind Harrods. So friendly and informal that the designation "luxury hotel" seems unfairly intimidating. Yet this sophisticated little modern hotel is the sort of place that provides each guest with a toothbrush and bathrobe, leaves a rose for every lady, and has a *concierge* who attends to every need. Public rooms and reception areas decorated by Nina Campbell highlight the feeling of intimate luxury. Upper floors have recently been redecorated in Ralph Lauren fabrics by the owner's wife Margaret Levin, responsible also for their bed-and-breakfast establishment next door, **L'Hôtel**. The Capital has a good French restaurant (see *Restaurants*).

Churchill
30 Portman Sq., W1 ☎ 486-5800
⑨264831 ⑯486-1255. Map 8F7
▦452 rms ▭452▦▭ ⚊⚌ AE
⊙ Tube: Marble Arch.
Location: Off Oxford St. The glittering, marbled lobby is a suitably impressive introduction to this modern luxury hotel, owned by Park Lane Hotels International, which sits in a busy elegant square behind Selfridges store. The public rooms and the thickly-carpeted bedrooms are in a more relaxed, but equally sumptuous, Regency style. The Churchill has an international restaurant, the **Arboury**, and a 24hr lounge for drinks and snacks. A fully-equipped business center can provide secretaries, portable telephones and word processors. Service is efficient and unobtrusive.

Claridge's
Brook St., W1 ☎ 629-8860
⑨21872 ⑯499-2210. Map 9F8.
▦190 rms, 56 suites ▭246 ▭
⚊⚌ ▦ AE ⊙ Tube: Bond Street.
Location: Mayfair, near Oxford St. Visiting royals and statesmen are inclined to choose Claridge's, which, despite its fame, is imperturbably discreet. No bar,

because such trappings don't fit a country house, even if it is in the middle of London. Drink in the living room (not "lounge" — it isn't an airport), where a small orchestra plays at lunchtime and in the evening. Nor would it be very dignified to publish a tariff, so they don't. Lots of Art Deco, but the tone is better set by log fires in the suites. A guest who has been shopping returns with a brace of pheasants; without batting an eyelid, the porter carries them for her as if they were Gucci suitcases.

Claverly
14 Beaufort Gdns., SW3 ☎ 589-8541 ⑯584-3410. Map 16|6 ▭32 rms ▭31. Tube: Knightsbridge.
Location: Close to Harrods. In a quiet enclave off busy Brompton Rd., this privately-owned upscale bed-and-breakfast hotel has won a British Tourist Award for its general friendliness, cleanliness and comfort.

Collin House
104 Ebury St., SW1 ☎ 730-8031 Map 17J8▭ 13 rms ▭8. Tube: Victoria.
Location: Belgravia, close to Victoria Station. One of the very few reliable, relatively inexpensive bed-and-breakfast hotels in central London, run with care by Welshman Mr D.L. Thomas. Ebury St. is an excellent location which has spawned many small hotels such as Collin House, many of them not to be recommended, although see **Ebury Court**.

Connaught
16 Carlos Pl., W1 ☎ 499-7070. Map 9G8 ▦90 rms ▭90 ⚊⚌ Tube: Bond Street.
Location: Mayfair, near Hyde Park and Oxford St. The finest of London's grand old hotels, according to its devoted following, the Connaught is smaller than other hotels in its peer group, and accordingly offers a little less in the way of facilities and services, but that kind of expansiveness isn't its style; the luxury is more personal. Likewise, the cozy public rooms make a virtue of their intimacy. The clubby atmosphere fits this part of Mayfair. The hotel does have its detractors: for the faithful nothing could ever be wrong, but newcomers have dared to whisper that it may be resting on its laurels at present, particularly as far as its

141

gastronomic reputation is
concerned. (See *Restaurants*).
✱ ☐ 🖃 🐾 ⊻

Dorchester 🏨
Park Lane, W1 ☎ *629-8888*
🖿 *887704* ⊗ *409-0114. Map 9H8*
▥ *197 rms, 55 suites* 🖃 *252* 🍴
🖃 ═ 🗚 🄾 *Tube: Hyde Park
Corner.*
Location: Overlooking Hyde Park.
With its stately terraces, the
Dorchester looks like an ocean liner
that has somehow been moored on
Park Lane. Bought in 1985 by the
world's richest man, the Sultan of
Brunei, the hotel closed in late 1988
for a £70 million refit and reopened
in spring 1990. The elegant spacious
public rooms have been
sumptuously renovated, from the
marble-floored lobby to the
splendid **Promenade**, with its gold
leaf moldings, where guests can
take afternoon tea. The furniture has
been reupholstered, the bedrooms
redecorated in country chintzes, and
the famous Oliver Messel suites
painstakingly restored to their
original condition. The pastel-
decorated **Terrace Restaurant** and
traditional English **Grill** remain
much the same, but there is a brand-
new **Oriental Restaurant**, with a
choice of Far Eastern cuisines. Other
new facilities include a health club
and business center.
✱ ⚴ ☐ 🖃 🖃 ♈ 🖙 ♨ ⊻ 🔊

Dorset Square ♣
39 Dorset Sq., NW1 ☎ *723-7874*
🖿 *263964* ⊗ *724-3328. Map 8D7*
▥ *to* ▥ *37 rms* 🖃 *37* ═ 🗚
Tube: Marylebone.
*Location: Close to Marylebone
Station, s of Regent's Park.* Situated
in a lovely Regency square (guests
have the use of the central garden),
this is one of London's best and
more stylish "house hotels." One is
immediately struck by the carefully
contrived decoration, almost
alarming in its perfection, but
nevertheless a charming evocation
of the country house style. All the
bedrooms are impressive, with
marble bathrooms. Service is
intelligent and efficient.
✱ ⚴ 🌿 ☐ 🖃 🖃

Dukes Hotel
34-36 St James's Pl., SW1
☎ *491-4840* 🖿 *28283* ⊗ *493-1264.*
Map 9H9 ▥ *36 rms, 22 suites*
🖃 *52* ═ 🗚 🄾 *Tube: Green
Park.*
*Location: St James's, near Green
Park and St James's Palace.* In a
gas-lit courtyard, a small but rather

grand hotel opened in 1906,
occupying what was once
presumably someone's Upstairs-
Downstairs town house. Dukes was
pleased when an enthusiastic guest
described it as "the smallest castle in
England." Only in London could a
location be so pretty and tranquil
yet so close to the throbbing heart
of the city. Despite its being almost
claustrophobically small, Dukes
offers full hotel facilities, including
24hr service. Recently refurbished, it
has improved suites and reception
rooms.
🖃 ✱ ☐ 🖃 🐾 ♨

Durrants Hotel
George St., W1 ☎ *935-8131*
🖿 *894919* ⊗ *487-3510. Map 9F9*
▥ *100 rms* 🖃 *70* ═ 🗚 *Tube:
Bond Street.*
Location: Near Oxford St. In a street
which is, as its name suggests,
Georgian, this attractive small hotel
is perennially popular, although
rooms are rather small. A portrait of
a Durrant patriarch, dating back to
1782, hangs among the delightful
collection of oils and prints. There
are leather chairs and pretty desks in
the writing room, antiques on sale
to guests, an open fire in the bar,
Ruddles beer in the bottle, pheasant
for dinner when it's in season, and
brass bedsteads.
✱ ☐ *in some rooms* 🖃 🐾 ♨

Ebury Court
26 Ebury St., SW1 ☎ *730-8147*
⊗ *823-5966. Map 17J8* ▥ *41 rms*
🖃 *15* ═ *Tube: Victoria, Sloane
Square.*
Location: Victoria/Pimlico.
Cottagey, quaint and under the
proud eye of the owners, Mr and
Mrs Kingsford, who live on the
premises. The hotel has been in the
family since the 1930s, and to be a
guest is thus to stay in the
Kingsfords' home. Their excellent
full English breakfast includes
haddock and kippers.
✱ ☐ 🖃

Eleven Cadogan Gardens
11 Cadogan Gdns., SW3
☎ *730-3426* 🖿 *8813318* ⊗ *730-
5217. Map 16J7* ▥ *60 rms* 🖃 *60.*
Tube: Sloane Square.
*Location: Chelsea, near Sloane
Square.* So discreet that it has no
sign even on the door, which is kept
locked. No wonder it is favored by
diplomats. Late Victorian exterior,
with decor to match: a glorious
marble fireplace in one room; a
drawing room with open fire. Full
English breakfast in bed, and they'll

send out for a bottle of champagne (the establishment has no liquor license); what's more, they'll even deliver you to the airport in a Rolls-Royce.

⌂ ⌸ ⍩ ⚘

Gore ✿
189 Queen's Gate, SW7
☎ *584-6601* ⊕ *296244* ® *589-8127.*
Map **15**I4 ⅢⅡ *54 rms* ▭ *54* ⚏ *AE*
⊙ *Tube: South Kensington.*
Location: Kensington, near the Albert Hall and Hyde Park. With ivy outside, potted plants inside, and good furniture in the more expensive rooms (with beautifully tiled modern bathrooms), this warm and welcoming hotel has few of the usual hallmarks of a chain member, in this case, Best Western. Of the honeymoonish deluxe rooms, one has a four-poster bed, real log fire and leaded windows, and another, in Italian style, has a bed that reputedly belonged to Judy Garland; but the Gore also caters to many business visitors from Continental Europe. There is a small, intimate bar, and a coffee shop that is open throughout the day.

⇕ □ ⌸ ⊟ ⍩ Ⴤ

Goring
15 Beeston Pl., Grosvenor Gdns., SW1 ☎ *834-8211*
⊕ *919166* ® *834-4393. Map* **17**J9
ⅢⅡ *90 rms* ▭ *90* ⚏ ⚏ *AE* ⊙
Tube: Victoria.
Location: Victoria, near Buckingham Palace. A book on Buckingham Palace written by the hotel's founder is provided for each guest along with the Bible, and royal carriages may occasionally be seen calling at the Goring to collect diplomat guests. The thorough-minded Mr Goring was the first hotelier in the world to fit all of his rooms with central heating and baths, and he would undoubtedly be pleased to know that the hotel is still in the family three generations later. There are, after all, few full-service hotels of this size still in private hands. Some of the original furniture, including brass bedsteads, is still in use, and the policy is clearly more to renovate rather than replace, although many of the rooms have now been given a proper face-lift. The public rooms are elegant and inviting (although the color scheme in the front hall excited some controversy), with an excellent writing room, a small bar and a good restaurant that is worth sampling.

⇕ □ ⌸ ⍩ ⏃ Ⴤ

Great Eastern
Liverpool St., EC2 ☎ *283-4363*
⊕ *886812* ® *283-4897. Map* **13**E17
ⅢⅡ *164 rms* ▭ *129* ⚏ *AE* ⊙
Closed Christmas. Tube: Liverpool Street.
Location: The City. Away from the West End (although only a few stops on the tube), and in the heart of old London. Handy, too, for those wishing to travel on to the eastern counties of England or to Continental Europe. There is a genuinely traditional quality about railway hotels like this one. Spacious, high-ceilinged bedrooms, although with twin beds available than doubles, and simple fittings. Some bedrooms have wash basins, but the majority also have bathrooms, usually with big, deep tubs, although often without showers. High ceilings in the public rooms, too, with ornate moldings. A magnificent stained-glass dome hangs over **Bowlers** (one of four restaurants in the building).

⇕ □ ⌸ ⊟ ⏃ Ⴤ

Grosvenor House
Park Lane, W1 ☎ *499-6363*
⊕ *24871* ® *493-3341. Map* **8**G7
ⅢⅡ *466 rms, 70 suites, 160 apartments* ▭ *696* ⚏ ⚏ *AE* ⊙
⊙ *Tube: Marble Arch.*
Location: Mayfair, overlooking Hyde Park. The flagship of the Trust House Forte group is something of a modern-day grand hotel in its scale and in the extent of its service and facilities, which include a pool, solarium, gymnasium and Jacuzzi. Built in 1928 as apartments, a social center during World War II when it accommodated American officers, it is famous for its huge banqueting room. A pianist accompanies afternoon tea at which, despite the grandeur of the place, the atmosphere is relaxing and children are welcome. A well-run hotel.

⇕ ⚿ □ ⌸ ⊟ ⍅ ≋ ⍩ ⌖ ⏃
Ⴤ ♫ Ⴅ

Halcyon
81 Holland Park, W11 ☎ *727-7288* ⊕ *266721* ® *229-8516. Map*
6H1 ⅢⅡ *44 rms* ▭ *44* ⚏ ⚏ *AE*
⊙ *Tube: Holland Park.*
Location: Close to Kensington High St. Expensive and very *à la mode,* the Halcyon is ideally placed for the visitor: away from the hurly-burly in gracious and exclusive Holland Park, but just a short taxi ride from the city center. The interior is a kind of modern rendition of the *belle époque,* luxurious and very soothing. There's a classy, pastel-

shaded restaurant, the **Kingfisher** (☎ 221-5411 IIII), opening onto a small garden where drinks can be taken in summer, as well as 24hr room service.

✷ ♿ 🛥 ☐ 🖅 🖃 🍴 ⅋

Hazlitt's ✿
6 Frith St., W1 ☎ *434-1771* ⓕ *439-1524. Map **10F10** IIII 22 rms, 1 suite* 🖃 *23* 🆎 *Tube: Tottenham Court Road.*
Location: Soho. There are precious few hotels of character at this price range in central London, certainly no others in Soho; a pity, for it makes an amusing and convenient location. Hazlitt's, named after the essayist William Hazlitt who resided and died here in 1830, is unpretentious and refreshingly simple — even puritanical — in appearance; it has cream-painted walls, plain antique furniture and wobbly, uneven floors and staircases. Bedrooms are spotless and comfortable; bathrooms are great fun, with free-standing Victorian baths and matching loos and basins, antique prints on the walls and stone busts balancing on window sills. Ambience and a pleasant professional young staff make up for the lack of "extras."

☐ 🖅

Hilton
22 Park Lane, W1 ☎ *493-8000* ⓕ *24873* ⓕ *493-4957. Map **9H8** IIII 450 rms, 50 suites* 🖃 *500* 🖃
🖃 ⟲ 🆎 ⓕ *Tube: Hyde Park Corner.*
Location: Mayfair, overlooking Hyde Park. There was great excitement when the 28-story new Hilton presented itself in Park Lane in the early 1960s, and some controversy about its modern style and proportions. Today, it is part of the scenery, with its **Trader Vic's** restaurant and bar almost an institution. Recently, improvements have been carried out. On the ground floor are the **Brasserie** and **St George's Bar**, which serves pub food. **Windows on the World** is the newly-named roof restaurant, with its marvelous views. Room service still offers Middle Eastern gastronomic specialties. The rooms have very large beds but are otherwise quite simple. One whole floor is devoted to nonsmokers, and there are now six executive floors.

✷ ☐ 🖅 🖃 « 🏋 🖳 ○

L'Hôtel
28 Basil St., SW3 ☎ *589-6286* ⓕ *919042* ⓕ *225-0011. Map **16I7***

IIII *11 rms, 1 suite* 🖃 *12* ⟲ 🆎 *Tube: Knightsbridge.*
Location: Next to Harrods. A very upscale version of the big-city B & B, whose well-heeled clientele feel that it's a relief to get away from the relentless pace of a large, bustling full-service hotel once in a while. Rooms are fairly small, attractive without being glamorous; breakfast is taken in the smart basement **Métro** wine bar, which is also open to nonresidents for light French lunches and dinners. As befits an establishment owned by the same couple as the **Capital** next door, the staff is professional and courteous. Families are welcomed.
☐ ✷ ☐ 🖅

Howard 🏨
Temple Pl., WC2 ☎ *836-3555* ⓕ *268047* ⓕ *379-4547. Map **11F13** IIII 117 rms, 24 suites* 🖃 *141* 🖃
🖃 ⟲ 🆎 ⓕ *Tube: Temple.*
Location: Overlooking the Thames, on the edge of the City. Annoyingly for visiting businessmen with little time on their hands, the City was until recently deprived of hotels. Then came the **Tower Thistle** (☎ 481-2575 IIII) at St Katharine's Dock, which is now joined further upstream by the Howard. Exorbitant prices are evident from the over-the-top decor in the public rooms, although the bedrooms are more understated and luxurious. Business facilities are legion and service is appropriately smooth. More hotels are scheduled for this area of London — all of them in futuristic Docklands.
☐ ✷ ☐ 🖅 🍴 🛥 🏋 ⅋

Hyatt Carlton Tower 🏨
2 Cadogan Pl., SW1 ☎ *235-5411* ⓕ *21944* ⓕ *245-6570. Map **16J7** IIII 224 rms* 🖃 *224* 🖃 🖃 ⟲ 🆎
ⓕ *Tube: Knightsbridge, Sloane Square.*
Location: Between Knightsbridge and Chelsea, off Sloane St. Whether your requirement is for enormous breakfasts or a kosher dinner (and guests range from rock stars to foreign politicians), American-cut beef or contemporary French cuisine, the Carlton Tower can meet your wishes, and you can always make your penances in the health club, the **Peak**. The hotel has always had an individuality, perhaps because the very building itself is distinctive: a handsome rectangular structure with a matching 15-floor tower that looks more 1930s than 1960s (which it is). Under the Hyatt banner it underwent major cosmetic

surgery a couple of years back. Now, with a well-equipped business center, it can vie as one of the best business hotels in London. The location, in a quiet square, has a character of its own.

🏠 ✳ 🗖 🖻 ♨ 《 ⤢ 🞄 ♈ 🞄 ☎

Imperial
Russell Sq., WC1 ☎ *837-3655, reservations 278-7871* ☏ *263951* ☏ *837-4653. Map* **10E11** 🏢 *447 rms* 🛏 *447* ☰ ⚏ AE ⊡ *Tube: Russell Square.*
Location: Bloomsbury, near the British Museum. This modern, custom-built hotel is the flagship of a small group owned by one family. It stands on the site of a previous Imperial hotel, famed for its Turkish baths. The present Imperial is much more functional, but provides well-equipped accommodations in a convenient location.

✳ ♿ 🗖 🖻 🞄

Inn On The Park 🏨
Hamilton Pl., Park Lane, W1 ☎ *499-0888* ☏ *22771* ☏ *493-1895/ 6629. Map* **9H8** 🏢 *202 rms, 26 suites* 🛏 *228* 🍴 ☰ ⚏ AE ⊡ *Tube: Hyde Park Corner.*
Location: Mayfair, overlooking Hyde Park. The only European hotel in the Four Seasons group, built in 1970, kept in superb condition, and favored by stars, although it is better known as the home of Howard Hughes during one of his most demanding years. Despite its being such a recent building, the Inn On The Park has architecturally a 1950s look, and some of its suites are in a 1930s style, although each is individually appointed, and the hotel is lavishly furnished with antiques. In the Queen Anne-style lounge, ten different teas are offered, with a pianist or harpist to sooth further. Service in the hotel is outstanding, and there are two superb restaurants, among the best in London, **Four Seasons** (recently redecorated in ultramodern style) and **Lanes**. Many people speak of this as London's best hotel.

✳ ♿ 🗖 🖻 ❦ 🞄 ♈

Inter-Continental
1 Hamilton Pl., Hyde Park Corner, W1 ☎ *409-3131* ☏ *25853* ☏ *409-3479. Map* **9H8** 🏢 *490 rms* 🛏 *490* 🍴 ☰ ⚏ AE ⊡ *Tube: Hyde Park Corner.*
Location: Hyde Park Corner, overlooking Hyde Park. Very much the American style of luxury hotel, despite now being jointly owned by

the SAS airline and a Japanese corporation: spacious rooms, often with separate sitting areas; individual heating and air-conditioning controls; dual-voltage; doorbell; telephone extension in the bathroom, free in-house movies, not to mention scales and a clothesline. A coffee house with sufficient privacy for breakfast meetings, and no wonder female executives seem to favor this hotel, with its Aquascutum and Cartier shops. Excellent cocktail barman, and excellent restaurant, **Le Soufflé**. Rolls-Royces available for rental.

✳ ♿ 🗖 🖻 《 🞄 ♈ ⊙ ♪

Kensington Palace
De Vere Gdns., W8 ☎ *937-8121* ☏ *262422* ☏ *937-2816. Map* **15I4** 🏢 *298 rms* 🛏 *298* ☰ ⚏ AE ⊡ *Tube: Kensington High Street.*
Location: Opposite Kensington Gardens. Beautifully and lavishly refurbished a few years back as one of the London showpieces of the Scottish group Thistle Hotels, now part of Mount Charlotte Hotels. In true Scottish style, kippers and black pudding are proudly featured on the breakfast buffet menu, and they can be enjoyed in an elegant restaurant overlooking the park. Rooms are attractive and comfortable. The hotel is much used by airline staff and executives. Another excellent middle-market Thistle hotel is the **Royal Horseguards** (*Whitehall Court, SW1* ☎ *839-3400*), with splendid views from its river-facing rooms from the 4th to 9th floors. Another is **Cannizaro House**, set in lovely public gardens on the edge of London (*West Side, Wimbledon Common, SW19* ☎ *(081) 879-1464*).

✳ 🗖 🖻 《 🞄 ♭

Kingsley ❀
Bloomsbury Way, WC1 ☎ *242-5881* ☏ *21157* ☏ *831-0225. Map* **10E11** 🏢 *146 rms* 🛏 *146* ⚏ AE ⊡ *Tube: Tottenham Court Road.*
Location: Bloomsbury, near British Museum. Warm and inviting hotel, ideal for families, offering accommodations at good-value prices in a very convenient location. The Kingsley is a full-scale hotel, with bar and carvery restaurant. A member of Mount Charlotte Group.

✳ 🗖 🖻 🞄 ♈

May Fair
Stratton St., W1 ☎ *629-7777* ☏ *262526* ☏ *629-1459. Map* **9G9** 🏢 *322 rms* 🛏 *322* ☰ ⚏ ⊡ *Tube: Green Park.*

Hotels

Location: Mayfair, just off Piccadilly. The most entertaining hotel in London. With its own in-built theater, the May Fair continues to pursue the performing arts, although in a lower key than it did during the big band era, with its long-gone Candlelight Room. Indeed, its cinema has recently transformed into the **Starlight** health club, complete with swimming pool. The rooms are well decorated, with huge beds and attractive bathrooms — you can even have a spa bath if that is what turns you on. An Intercontinental hotel.

‡ ▢ 🖃 ⊶ 🌤 🏋 ▾ ♪ ⬎ ⬅ ♈

Le Meridien London 🏨
Piccadilly, W1 ☎ 734-8000
⊕ 25795 ⊠ 437-3574. Map **10**G10
▥ 254 rms, 30 suites ▭ 284 ▤
⇌ 🅰🅴 ⬤ Tube: Piccadilly Circus.
Location: Near Piccadilly Circus. The once-famous Piccadilly hotel was transformed in 1985 into Le Meridien, a hotel very much in the modern idiom, but retaining all the Piccadilly's architectural glories. The Edwardian extravagance of the interior, protected by preservation orders, has been restored, with the **Oak Room** as its superb *pièce de résistance* (see *Restaurants*), while the pillared roof terrace has been glassed in to create a stunning conservatory-style brasserie. Executives in particular will be lured by the extensive conference facilities, and the luxurious basement health club, **Champneys**, which includes a pool, a gym, squash courts and Turkish baths.

‡ ▢ 🖃 ⊶ 🏋 ▾ ⓞ ♪ ♈ ⬅ ♈

Montcalm
Great Cumberland Pl., W1 ☎ 402-4288 ⊕ 28710 ⊠ 724-9180. Map **8**F7 ▥ 104 rms, 12 suites ▭ 116 ▤ ⇌ 🅰🅴 ⬤ Tube: Marble Arch.
Location: Near Marble Arch and Oxford St. Behind its dignified Georgian facade, a hotel that quietly evinces all the pampering luxury and style required by the international businessman or his wife. The antique gilt reception desk, lavish leather sofas and military chests set the tone, and suites have spiral staircases.

⬒ ‡ ▢ 🖃 ⬇ ▾

Park Lane
Piccadilly, W1 ☎ 499-6321 ⊕ 21533 ⊠ 499-1965. Map **9**H8

▥ 300 rms, 24 suites ▭ 324 ▤ partial 🖃 ⇌ 🅰🅴 ⬤ Tube: Green Park.
Location: Piccadilly, overlooking Green Park. This lovely old establishment is still privately-owned, one of the largest in London. From its needlessly misleading name (Piccadilly is every bit as grand as Park Lane), the hotel is full of quirkiness and character. The French restaurant is decorated with carved paneling from J.P. Morgan's home, and the ballroom is a magnificent consummation of the Art Deco themes that pervade the hotel. Rooms are spacious, with walk-in closets and often with mahogany, 1920s-style beds. The beauty parlor offers aromatherapy, and there is a gymnasium.

‡ ▢ 🖃 🖃 🏋 ▾ ♪ ♈

Pembridge Court ✿
34 Pembridge Gdns., W2 ☎ 229-9977 ⊕ 298363 ⊠ 727-4982. Map **6**G2 ▥ to ▥ 13 rms, 12 suites ▭ 25 ⇌ 🅰🅴 ⬤ Tube: Notting Hill Gate.
Location: Notting Hill, 1 mile (1.5km) w of center. The Notting Hill locals who enjoy the French cooking and countrified ambience of **Caps** restaurant aren't always aware that this is part of a hotel. Caps in fact doubles as a breakfast room, apart from which there is only a small lounge and bar and the rooms, small but bright, impeccably kept, and comfortable. Recently upgraded rooms have en-suite bathrooms, while all others have showers. A 24hr bar service has now been introduced. Many of the walls are adorned with a collection of Victorian fans and lacework. The hotel has a strong family feel. Loyal clients include antique dealers visiting Portobello Road market.

⬒ ‡ ▢ 🖃 ⬇ ▾

Portobello
22 Stanley Gdns., W11 ☎ 727-2777 ⊕ 268349 ⊠ 792-9641. ▥ to ▥ 25 rms ▭ 7 🅰🅴 ⬤ Tube: Notting Hill Gate.
Location: Just N of Holland Park. An idiosyncratic small hotel, which people tend to love or hate. Rooms vary greatly in style, quality and size and are priced accordingly; ones termed "cabins" are tiny. Only suites and "special rooms" have bathrooms (all others have showers) and these are spacious and fun — a good choice for a romantic weekend. An added bonus for escapees is the 24hr food and drink service, although it can be erratic.

Porterage and daytime room service have recently been introduced.

🏠 ‡ ☐ 📷 🖃 ☟ ⏰

Ritz 🏨
Piccadilly, W1 ☎ 493-8181
📞 267200 📠 493-2687. Map **9G9**
▥▥▥ 116 rms, 14 suites ⬜ 130 ⊐
🅰🅴 ☐ Tube: Green Park.
Location: Near St James's and Green Park. The first hotel to bear the name of César Ritz was in Paris, and he brought with him the architectural style of the Rue de Rivoli when he opened this London establishment at the beginning of the 1900s. He even imported French craftsmen to work on the Louis XVI interior. In the early days of the Ritz, the Prince of Wales used to dance there; later it became a favored lunch place for Noel Coward, and postwar residents included millionaires such as Getty and Gulbenkian. With the disappearance of such grandiosity, the Ritz has faced the difficult task of adapting itself to a less richly textured world. Sadly, one of its two famous bars has long gone, but other features are happily immovable, such as the staircase and rotunda; the restaurant (see *Restaurants*), with its magnificent view and *trompe l'oeil* ceiling, and the spectacular **Palm Court**, with its ornate marble fountain. The decor and furnishings in the Palm Court have been restored, and afternoon tea is served there, while on Fri and Sat nights there is dancing to a 1920s-style big band orchestra. The Ritz has been through patchy times recently but it has now re-established itself as one of the world's great hotels.

‡ ☐ 📷 🖃 🍴 🐾 ☟ ⏰ 🎵 🎿

Royal Lancaster
Lancaster Terrace, W2 ☎ 262-6737 📞 24822 📠 724-3191. Map **7G5** ▥▥▥ 418 rms 🅰🅴 🖃 ⊐
🅰🅴 ☐ Tube: Lancaster Gate.
Location: Bayswater, opposite Kensington Gardens. A comfortable and well-maintained modern hotel in the Rank group, in an excellent location, from which some rooms have lovely views of the park. The rooms are well-appointed, and the hotel has an informal café serving pasta dishes and grills, as well as its Anglo-French restaurant.

‡ ☐ 📷 🖃 🍴 ☟ 🎿 ⏰

Savoy 🏨
Strand, WC2 ☎ 836-4343 📞 24234
📠 240-6040. Map **11G12** ▥▥▥ 152 rms, 48 suites ⬜ 202 🔲 partial
🖃 ⊐ 🅰🅴 ☐ Tube: Charing Cross.
Location: Strand, near Covent Garden and South Bank. The Earl of Savoy built a palace on this site in 1245, and the present hotel was opened in 1869 by Richard D'Oyly Carte, who first staged the operettas of Gilbert and Sullivan in the adjoining **Savoy Theatre**, which was severely damaged by fire in early 1990, but is being restored. With its tucked-away entrance at the front, and gardens facing the Thames at the back, the Savoy is full of extravagant treats. An open fire greets guests, afternoon tea is served in a garden setting with a new gazebo, and recent renovation has uncovered yet more 1920s features. The emphasis is on thorough hotel-keeping and comfort, with Irish linen sheets on the beds, and mattresses made by the Savoy's own workshop. Most bathrooms have marble floors and satisfyingly deep tubs. Service from waiters is patchy, however: exemplary from some, distinctly slapdash and offhand from others, which is not as it should be. There are three restaurants to choose from: the famous **Grill**, where the rich and powerful do much of their business entertaining, some at regular tables; the **Savoy**; and the more recent **Upstairs Bar**, beautifully decorated, where you can choose anything from a cup of coffee to a meal.

‡ ☐ 📷 🖃 🍴 🐾 ☟ 🐾 🎵 🎿 💈

Sheraton Park Tower
101 Knightsbridge, SW1 ☎ 235-8050 📞 917222 📠 235-8231. Map **16I7** ▥▥▥ 295 rms 🖃 295 🔲 ⊐
🅰🅴 ☐ Tube: Knightsbridge.
Location: Knightsbridge/Belgravia, near Hyde Park. European flagship of the group, and very much the metropolitan, luxury type of Sheraton, as opposed to some of the smaller ones in American provincial cities. The hotel towers above Knightsbridge in an outwardly ugly cylindrical shape. All the rooms have a view and are spacious and luxurious, decorated in English traditional style, with lots of pale wood fittings. Floors 10-17 are handsomely devoted to "executive rooms" that provide accommodations for groups of visitors from blue-chip corporations. Other treats for guests include superb marble bathrooms, a beauty parlor, a barbershop, and valeting service to keep guests well-groomed.

‡ ♿ ☐ 📷 🖃 🍴 ☟ 🎿 ⏰

Stafford

St James's Pl., SW1 ☎ *493-0111*
☎ *28602* ⊛ *493-7121. Map 9H9*
▥ *62 rms* ▭ *62* ⊨ AE ⊙ *Tube:*
Green Park.
Location: St James's, near Green
Park. Elegant and discreet hotel in
gentlemanly St James's, where
almost every house is of historical
interest. The Stafford's 300yr-old
wine cellars once belonged to St
James's Palace. Much of the interior
is in the style of Adam, although the
brickwork facade is much later. The
building once housed the Public
Schools Club, and during World
War II accommodated American
officers and French resistance
workers. A beautifully kept hotel,
with four comfortable salons that
are rented for business meetings.

⌂ ⇕ ▢ ▱ ⚒ ⚘ ⛏

Strand Palace ♧

369 Strand, WC2 ☎ *836-8080*
☎ *24208* ⊛ *836-2077. Map 11G12*
▥ *777 rms* ▭ *777* ⊨ AE ⊙
Tube: Covent Garden.
Location: Strand, near Covent
Garden. When it was built in the
early part of this century, a 900-
bedroom hotel was by definition a
palace (its palatial original entrance
is now in the Victoria and Albert
Museum, an Art Deco masterpiece).
Now, the Strand has slimmed a little,
been extensively modernized, and
turned its attention to a different
business: that of providing good-
value accommodations. It does so
from a vantage point right opposite
the **Savoy**, in a location handy for
many theaters and for city
sightseeing. The Strand Palace has
most of the facilities to be expected
in a large hotel, although there is no
room service. Tea and coffee-
making facilities in each room, an
18hr coffee shop, Neapolitan chefs
in the Italian restaurant, and an
American-style cocktail bar. A Trust
House Forte hotel.

⇕ ▢ ▱ ⛏ Y

Waldorf Hotel

Aldwych, WC2 ☎ *836-2400*
☎ *24574* ⊛ *497-1351. Map 11F12*
▥ *311* ▭ *311* ⊨ AE ⊙ *Tube:*
Aldwych.
Location: N side of the Aldwych.
Exemplifying the Edwardian era

with its crystal chandeliers, marble
floors and vast pot plants, the
Waldorf is a comfortable hotel,
offering both old-world charm and
excellent service and facilities.
These include mini-bars in the
bedrooms, a video channel for
in-house movies, a hairdresser and
valet service. There is a *thé dansant*
on Fri and Sat. ⇕ & ▢ ▱ ⛏ ▱

Westbury

Conduit St., W1 ☎ *629-7755*
☎ *24378* ⊛ *495-1163. Map 9G9*
▥ *224 rms, 19 suites* ▭ *243* ⊨
▤ AE ⊙ *Tube: Bond Street.*
Location: Mayfair, near Bond St.
and Oxford St. The first Westbury
Hotel, on Madison Avenue, New
York, was named by a polo buff
after the ground on Long Island.
Like its New York counterpart, the
London Westbury still has a bar
called the **Polo**, and its martinis are
of American dryness. When it
opened in 1955, the London
Westbury was the first hotel in
Britain to be operated by an
American chain, but since 1977 it
has been owned by Trust House
Forte. Its stable-style lounge, with
an open fire in winter, and its
comfortable rooms nonetheless
sustain the feel of a 1950s American
hotel.

⇕ & ▢ ▱ ⛏ Y

White House ♧

Albany St., NW1 ☎ *387-1200*
☎ *24111* ⊛ *388-0091. Map 3D9*
▥ *567 rms* ▭ *567* ⊷ ⊨ AE
⊙ *Tube: Great Portland*
Street.
Location: Near Regent's Park. A
handy location for sightseeing,
shopping, and taking relaxing walks
in the park, although this is not a
hotel area. The White House is well
appointed, offering 24hr room
service and all the other amenities
of a first-rate hotel (including leisure
and business centers) at more
modest prices. Despite its name, the
White House is a British hotel (the
building is actually shaped like the
Union Jack), and is owned by the
Rank group. The block is large
enough to shrug off the traffic that
swarms around it.

⇕ & ▢ ▱ ⛏ Y ⌾ ♆

Further recommendations

Academy (*17-21 Gower St., WC1*
☎ *631-4115* ▢), a delightful
homey Georgian hotel, a stone's

throw from the *British Museum*.
Beaufort (*33 Beaufort Gdns., SW3*
☎ *584-5252* ▥ *to* ▥), a small,

friendly Knightsbridge hotel in two Victorian town houses with attractive "country house"-style decor. **Chesterfield** (*35 Charles St., W1* ☎ *491-2622*▮▮▮▮), in the heart of Mayfair, designed to feel more like an exclusive club than a hotel. **Colonnade** (*2 Warrington Crescent, W9* ☎ *286-1052*▮□ to ▮□), family-run since 1948, situated in attractive Little Venice; some rooms have four-poster beds and coronets. **Draycott** (*24 Cadogan Gdns., SW3* ☎ *730-6466*▮▮▮▮), winner of a Good Hotel Guide award in 1989, a stylish small hotel with no dining room but friendly personal service. **Elizabeth** (*37 Eccleston Sq., SW1* ☎ *828-6812/3* □), a small, simple hotel in a tranquil setting, overlooking the square's gardens; a BTA award winner. **Fenja** (*69 Cadogan Gdns., SW3* ☎ *589-7333*▮□ to ▮▮), between Harrods and Peter Jones, another private house turned into a small elegant hotel, decorated with original paintings and marble busts. **Fortyseven Park Street** (*47 Park St., W1* ☎ *491-7282*▮▮▮▮), 52 luxury suites with kitchens and every imaginable service for business people, created by Albert Roux, owner of Le Gavroche, to which the hotel is linked by private entrance. **Halkin** (*4 Halkin St., SW1* ☎ *333-1000*▮▮▮▮), a brand-new

luxury hotel with an Italian look in smart Belgravia; first-rate restaurant. **Hotel la Place** (*17 Nottingham Pl., W1* ☎ *486-2323*▮□), a comfortable and reasonably priced hotel well placed for the West End. **John Howard Hotel** (*4 Queen's Gate, SW7* ☎ *581-3011*▮□), with all mod cons for the business executive, from conference room to 12 efficiency apartments in a well-restored Regency building. **Knightsbridge** (*10 Beaufort Gdns., SW3* ☎ *589-9271*▮□), a pleasant hotel in the same leafy enclave as the Claverly and Beaufort; guests are issued with a front-door key on arrival. **Knightsbridge Green** (*159 Knightsbridge, SW1* ☎ *584-6274* ▮□), a well-placed family-run hotel, unusual for having mostly suites; recently underwent a major face-lift. **Observatory House** (*Observatory Gdns., 37 Hornton St., W8* ☎ *937-1577*▮□), a demure family-oriented hotel on the quiet Kensington site of the old Observatory. **One Cranley Place** (*1 Cranley Pl., SW7* ☎ *589-7944/7704* ▮□ to ▮▮), cozy, with gingham tablecloths and blue and white china in the dining room, antiques throughout and a pretty patio garden. **Wilbraham** (*Wilbraham Pl., Sloane St., SW1* ☎ *730-8296* ▮□), slightly faded gentility, between Chelsea and Knightsbridge.

Eating in London

Recent years have seen something of a revival of English cooking, blighted two centuries ago by the disruption of the world's first industrial revolution. The invasion by foreign cuisines, with the French leading, was thorough, but now the ethnic diversity of London's restaurant world is being tempered by the resurgence of the native table. Just as *nouvelle cuisine* brought French cooking up to date, so English cooking is now being reworked by many chefs — often under the loose term of New English Cookery. There is a whole new breed of English chefs now operating who look as much to Britain as to France for their inspiration. They look farther afield, too. Modern European Cookery is another commonly used term, which perhaps best describes the breadth of influence.

There are, of course, some excellent French restaurants of unimpeachable authenticity in London, and equally notable standard-bearers of many another national cuisine. Even local cooking illustrates London's propensity for absorbing outside influences. Those who can muster the appetite to begin the day with the great British breakfast might find that the kippers come from Scotland, the bacon from Ireland (or, more lately, Denmark), and the tea from India. This is a meal that draws upon

149

the tradition of home cooking, like that other British specialty, high tea (see *Cafés and tearooms*); to sample them the visitor should go to one of the grand old hotels rather than a restaurant.

The English are traditionally eager carnivores, and feast day dishes are still usually some sort of roast meat. The South Downs of Kent and Sussex produce the finest English lamb and mutton. It's odd that Sussex also claims to have invented the steak-and-kidney pudding, when the most famous beef is produced far away in Hereford or Scotland. Presumably it was the time taken to transport the beef that led, in the days before refrigeration, to its being preserved by pickling — hence the Londoners' beloved boiled beef. There seems to be less doubt about the origins of sweet puddings and pies, filled with the apples, cherries and soft fruits of Kent and Essex.

Among geographical influences on London's own specialties, the Thames is paramount. Cockles, mussels and whelks are sold for immediate consumption by vendors in many open markets (see *Shopping*). Shellfish from the estuary and beyond are very much the capital's own love, and the well-heeled diners of Mayfair throng to oyster bars such as **Bentley's** or **Green's**; City folk have **Sweetings**. Fish specialties such as whitebait and eel were originally pulled from the river itself. Street sellers still offer jellied eels, while the stewed version is the stock in trade of the pie-and-mash shop, one of London's own "ethnic" eating places, usually to be found near a street market.

Whisper it not, but that other tradition, fried fish and chips, was brought to Britain by immigrants from Italy and Belgium respectively, and they seem to have met in the North of England. Still, Londoners do make good fish and chips; apart from fashionable places such as **Geale's** or **Sea Shell**, the capital is well endowed with fish-and-chip shops of varied quality.

Choosing a restaurant

London has at least 2,000 fully accoutered restaurants. Like most things in the city, their keynote is diversity, and they are widely dispersed. The areas best served by good restaurants are Covent Garden, Soho, Chelsea and South Kensington.

As a great city not only of its old empire but also of Western Europe, London is richly cosmopolitan. The ubiquitous Italians of London have a remarkable example of fashionable restaurants in the middle to upper price brackets, many notably similar in style: quarry-tiled floors, white-painted walls, foliage, discreet spotlights, a fairly basic menu and cheerful waiters. This trattoria style was popularized in the 1960s; lately a new style has begun to emerge with simple but delicious "peasant" dishes served in media-friendly surroundings. Examples are **River Café** and **Cibo**. Less recent, but still fashionable, is the style of *haute cuisine* that seems to have been established by the Roux brothers, and the upscale French restaurant with the ambience of a brasserie (**Grill St Quentin** is the latest of these).

From farther afield are the various cuisines of which Chinese and Indian are the most obvious. As in many cities, "ethnic" eating can be remarkably good and excellent value. Chinese and Indian restaurants in particular have also become known for producing good take-out foods, and late at night a Londoner might simply declare that he is going "for an Indian" or "for a Chinese." These two and other ethnicities are manifest in dozens of inexpensive restaurants, and a few grander ones: go to **Gerrard St.** (W1) for Chinese; the **British**

Telecom Tower area (W1), **Westbourne Grove** (W2) or
Hammersmith (W6) for Indian; and **Charlotte St.** (W1) for
Greek. Recently, another ethnic cuisine has emerged. An
explosion of new Thai restaurants, many markedly similar in
food and decor, has ensured that Far Eastern food is now,
deservedly, as popular as that of China and India.

London also boasts humbler eating places, many doing their
trade mostly by day. The pub is certainly more likely to serve
meals at lunchtime, and is usually cheap; the fare will range
from French bread and cheese to, typically, steak-and-kidney
pie or shepherd's pie. Wine bars also offer inexpensive
eating, some of them content to serve quiche and pâté, others
stretching to full meals. At a pace more agreeable than fast
food, and in a restaurant ambience, such chains as **Pizza
Express**, **Bistro Bistingo**, **Bistro Vino** and **Spaghetti
House** offer good value. The carvery types of dining room in
some hotels are also a good value, providing a selection of
roast meats, often for a set price.

When to eat

Restaurants in the West End and the City are busy at
lunchtime, with a largely business clientele, but those dining
for pleasure tend to come out at night, usually 8 or 9pm. Most
restaurants close after lunchtime, reopen at 6 or 7pm, and
wind down after 10 or 11pm. It is usually possible to find
somewhere good to eat on the spur of the moment, but the
careful diner will always reserve a table first. The more
famous and well-established restaurants are nearly always
fully reserved before they open.

Price

The cost of eating out in London has never been higher. The
raising of our "cheap" (□) price category to "under £15
($25)" is an indication of this. Of course it is possible to eat
for less in cafés and bars, but considerably harder in a
restaurant proper. There are signs, however, that some new
restaurants are attempting to keep their prices in check:
Quality Chop House, **Sud Ouest** and **Tall Orders**, for
example, are three newcomers that aim for good food at
reasonable prices. It will be interesting to see how they fare.

Set-price menus were relatively uncommon in London, but
now appear much more often. Many of the best restaurants
have excellent-value set-lunch menus, which bring them
within range of the less affluent. They include **La Tante
Claire**, **Le Gavroche**, **Chez Nico**, **L'Arlequin**, the **Oak
Room**, **Mijanou**, **Sud Ouest**, the **Bombay Brasserie**, and
among hotels, the **Savoy** and the **Berkeley**. On all menus
look out for items that might bump up the quoted or apparent
price: check whether VAT (Value Added Tax) and service are
included, and whether salads and vegetables are going to be
expensive. Pre- and after-dinner drinks can also prove costly
— don't be afraid to ask. If service is not included, and you
are happy with your treatment, give a tip of 10-15 percent.

Wine and food

Wine is one area where French dominance continues. Italian
and German white wines are almost universally
available, and a well-chosen selection of "New World" wines
is to be found on the list of any self-respecting trend-setting
newcomer. The term denotes bottles from non-European

countries, principally California and Australia, but also New Zealand, Chile and so on. There is a small, and growing, English wine industry, producing mainly white wine, but it is regrettably rare to find it on offer in London.

Away from the mainstream of Anglo-French-Italian cooking, wine might not always be the best bet; beer goes well with Indian and much Oriental food, and jasmine tea can be ordered with a Chinese meal.

Aperitifs and after-dinner drinks

The English have long been leading consumers of fortified wines, and have played a leading part in the sherry and port trade. If there is a traditional aperitif in England, it is dry sherry, which whets the appetite perfectly; however, London restaurants will generally be able to cater to most tastes.

After dinner, the English gentleman traditionally "takes" port. It is one of the longest-lived wines, and develops great complexity — do not dismiss it as a "sweet" drink. Usually available also are brandy, liqueurs, or perhaps malt whisky.

Restaurants classified by area

Battersea/Wandsworth
L'Arlequin ▮▮▮ Fr
Harvey's ▮▮ Eng/Fr
Nancy Lam's Enak Enak ▮▢ Indo

Bayswater
Baba Bhelpoori House ▢ ♣ ♠ Ind
Kalamares ▮▢ ♠ Gr

Belgravia/Knightsbridge
Café Sud Ouest (see Sud Ouest) ▢
    to ▮▢ Fr
Capital Hotel ▮▮▮ ⌂ Eng
Columbus ▮▢ to ▮▮▮ Am
Grill St Quentin (see St Quentin) ▮▮▮▮
    ▮▮ Fr
Pizza on the Park (see Kettners) ▢
    to ▮▢ It/Am
St Quentin ▮▮▮ Fr
Salloos ▮▮▮ Pak
San Lorenzo ▮▮▢ to ▮▮▮ It
Les Spécialités St Quentin (see St
    Quentin) ▮▢ Fr
Sud Ouest ▮▮▢ ♣ Fr

Camden Town/Euston
Nontas ▮▢ to ▮▢ Gr

Chelsea/South Kensington
Bibendum ▮▮▮ Eng/Fr
Charbar ▮ Am
Daquise ▢ ♠ Pol
Ed's Easy Diner ▢ Am
English Garden ▮▮▮ Eng
English House ▮▮▮ Eng
Gavvers ▮▮▢ ♣ Fr
Golden Duck ▮▢ Ch
Memories of China ▮▮▢ Ch
Ognisko Polskie ▮▢ ♣ Pol
La Tante Claire ▮▮▮ ⌂ Fr
Zen ▮▮▢ to ▮▮▢ Ch

City
Ashley's ▮▮▮ to ▮▮▮ Eng/Fr
Le Poulbot ▮▮▮ Fr
Zen Central (see Zen) ▮▮▢ Ch

Clerkenwell
Café du Marché ▮▢ ♣ Fr
Quality Chop House ▮▢ to ▮▮▢ Eng

Covent Garden/Strand
Ajimura (see Ikkyu) ▮▮▢ Jap
Calabash ▮▢ ♠ Afr
Joe Allen ▢ to ▮▢ Am
The Ivy (see Le Caprice) ▮▮▢ Eng/Fr
Luigi's ▮▢ It
Mon Plaisir ▢ to ▮▮▢ Fr
Orso ▮▮▢ It
Smollensky's on the Strand (see
    Smollensky's Ballon) ▮▮▢ Am

East End
Bloom's ▮▢ Je

Hammersmith/Fulham
Blue Elephant ▮▮▢ Th
Hiders ▮▮▢ Eng/Fr
Pagu Dinai ▮▮▢ It
River Café ▮▮▢ to ▮▮▮ It
Tall Orders ▮▮▢ ♣ Eng/Fr

Hampstead
Café Flo ▢ to ▮▢ ♣ Fr
Ed's Easy Diner ▢ Am
Flo's Bar and Grill (see Café Flo) ▢
    to ▮▢ Fr
Keat's ▮▮▮ to ▮▮▮ Fr
Nautilus (see Sea Shell) ▢ Eng

Islington/Kings Cross
Ganpath ▮▢ Ind
Upper Street Fish Shop (see Sea
    Shell) ▢ Eng

Kensington/Notting Hill
Bombay Brasserie ▮▮▢ Ind
Cibo ▮▮▢ It
Clarke's ▮▮▢ to ▮▮▮ Am/Eng
Galicia ▢ ♠ Sp
Geale's ▢ ♠ Eng
Leith's ▮▮▮ Eng
Kensington Place ▮▢ to ▮▮▢ ♣
    Eng/Fr
192 ▮▮▢ Fr/Eng
One Ninety Queen's Gate ▮▮▮
    Eng/Fr
Phoenicia ▮▢ ♣ Leb

Lambeth
Pizzeria Castello ▢ ♣ ♠ It

Marylebone/West End
Chez Gérard *II◻* Fr
Chez Nico *IIII* Fr
Gaylord *I◻* Ind
Ikkyu □ to *I◻* ✿ 🍴 Jap
Odins *IIII* Fr
Sea Shell □ ✿ 🍴 Eng
Mayfair
Al Hamra *II◻* ✿ Leb
Connaught Hotel *IIII* ⌂ Fr/Eng
Four Seasons *IIII* ⌂ Fr
Le Gavroche *IIII* ⌂ Fr
Hard Rock Cafe □ ✿ Am
St James's/Piccadilly
Auberge de Provence *IIII* Fr
Le Caprice *II◻* ✿ Eng/Fr
Chez Gérard *II◻* Eng/Fr
Green's *IIII* to *IIII* Eng
Langan's Brasserie *IIII* Fr
Oak Room *IIII* ⌂ Fr
Ritz *IIII* ⌂ Eng/Fr
Smollensky's Ballon *I◻* to *II◻* Am
Suntory *IIII* Jap
Soho
Alastair Little *IIII* Eng/Fr
Bahn Thai *I◻* to *I◻* Th
La Bastide *IIII* Fr

Burt's *IIII* Eng/Fr
La Capannina *I◻* ✿ It
Chuen Cheng Ku (*see* Fung Shing)
□ Ch
Ed's Easy Diner □ ✿ Am
L'Escargot □ to *IIII* Eng/Fr
Fung Shing *I◻* □ Ch
Gay Hussar *IIII* Hung
Au Jardin des Gourmets *II◻* to *IIII* Fr
Kettners *I◻* □ It/Am
Lindsay House (*see* English House)
IIII Eng
Manzi's *II◻* ✿ It fish
Melati □ 🍴 Indo
Mr Kong (*see* Fung Shing) □ Ch
New World (*see* Fung Shing) □ Ch
Pizza Express (*see* Kettners) □ to
I◻ It/Am
Poons □ to *I◻* ✿ 🍴 Ch
Red Fort *II◻* Ind
Victoria/Pimlico
Memories of China *II◻* Ch
Mijanou *II◻* to *IIII* ✿ Fr
Tate Gallery Restaurant *II◻* to *IIII*
Eng
Very Simply Nico (*see* Chez Nico)
II◻ to *IIII* Fr

Key to types of cuisine

Afr **African**	Gr **Greek**	Jap **Japanese**	Rus **Russian**
Am **American**	Hung **Hungarian**	Je **Jewish**	Sp **Spanish**
Ch **Chinese**	Ind **Indian**	Leb **Lebanese**	Th **Thai**
Eng **English**	Indo **Indonesian**	Pak **Pakistani**	Turk **Turkish**
Fr **French**	It **Italian**	Pol **Polish**	

Alastair Little
49 Frith St., W1 (Soho) ☎ *734-5183. Map* **10F10** *IIII* □ *Closed Sat lunch, Sun, Christmas. Tube: Leicester Square.*
Much-vaunted media hang-out with an equally high profile chef/proprietor, the eponymous Mr Little. His dining room, with the kitchen in view, is tiny, and pretty stark: Venetian blinds, bare floorboards, curly tube lighting on the ceiling, glossy cream walls, black tables set with paper napkins, hard black chairs. "Designer setting for designer food," says one disparaging critic. But whatever label you give the food, it is good: reminiscent of Californian cuisine but more vigorous. Little is a talented, instinctive cook, able to change his menu daily according to what he finds in the market. Meat and fish are simply cooked — grilled, stir-fried, steamed — and served with vivid sauces and excellent vegetables and salads. The evening clientele is usually less uncompromisingly trendy than at lunchtime. And the food is every bit as good.

Al Hamra ✿
31-33 Shepherd Market, W1 (Mayfair) ☎ *493-1954. Map* **9H8** *II◻* □ 🖃 🆎 ◉ *Closed Christmas Day, Jan 1. Tube: Green Park.*
Even the most jaded palates will buck up at the sharp, fresh tastes of Lebanon's superb cuisine. London's best example is to be found at this smart, comfortable, mainly business-oriented restaurant in Mayfair. Make a selection from the list of 65 hot and cold hors d'oeuvres (more properly called *mezze*), possibly baulking at the grilled lambs' testicles, but including perfect renditions of well-known Lebanese dishes, such as *tabouleh*, *hommos* and stuffed vine leaves, as well as *montabel*, *loubeih* and mixed fresh vegetables with herbs and Lebanese bread, all quite delicious. Main courses are more perfunctory, but well flavored.

L'Arlequin
123 Queenstown Rd., SW8 (Battersea) ☎ *622-0555. Off map* **17M8** *IIII* □ ■/*lunch* 🖃 🆎 ◉ *Closed Sat, Sun, 3 weeks Aug,*

1 week Christmas. Tube: Clapham Common.
In the unlikely setting of this dingy Battersea street, top-class restaurateurs Christian and Geneviève Delteil have established one of London's most impressive restaurants, now the proud possessor of a Michelin star. The soberly pretty, rather formal dining room has recently been enlarged and is beautifully run by Mme. Delteil, while her husband creates such light and inventive delicacies as asparagus mousse, breast of chicken with scallops and fresh noodles or beef with bone marrow and grapes, and wonderful sorbets. The wine list is very expensive, but the house wine is reliable.

Ashley's
10 Copthall Ave., EC2 (City)
☎ *256-8162. Map 13E16 llll to llll*
⬚ ■ ▬ ⚦ ▦ 🆑 ▣ *Closed Mon-Fri eves, Sat, Sun, bank hols. Tube: Moorgate.*
Silver-haired businessmen appear to be executing important transactions in this exclusive basement dining room in the heart of the City. The decoration is muted and restful: pink walls, green carpet and chairs, pastel drapes with a geometric pattern that echoes the abstract art, and the focal point, a wrought-iron spiral staircase. Chef Terry Farr is a master craftsman, who has successfully adapted old and new recipes to create an exciting seasonal menu. A *timbale* of *foie gras* in a *sauternes* and truffle jelly, pancakes of smoked salmon, simmered in cream and chives, fillets of John Dory, pan fried with *shiitake* mushrooms, tomatoes and tarragon, roasted rack of Dorset lamb with a shallot flan and reform sauce, and a Grand Marnier soufflé are all exquisitely presented on marbled china plates. The wine list is good and the service courteous and attentive. Upstairs in the buzzing **Bar and Grill** (*open Mon-Fri 7am-9pm*), yuppies clinch deals over a lobster or char-grilled steak, barely taking their eyes off the TOPIC screen.

Auberge de Provence
St James's Court Hotel, Buckingham Gate, SW1 (St James's) ☎ *834-6655. Map 17L10 llll* ⬚ ■ ▬ ▦ 🆑 ▣ *Tube: St James's Park.*
In the new European Flagship of Taj Hotels, the St James's Court, is to be found a genuinely Provençal restaurant, masterminded by one of France's globe-trotting super-chefs, Jean-André Charial from L'Oustau de Baumanière at Les Baux. He devised the menu of Provençal dishes, beautifully adapted to modern tastes, and imported his wine list and his superb dining and kitchen staff, including the talented resident chef. He visits regularly, often bringing consignments of local produce with him. Under a rough-cast vaulted ceiling, savor a pungent *charlotte d'agneau et d'eggplants*, a perfect *daube de boeuf* or a fragrant *loup au basilic*, plus superb accompanying vegetables (and a wide choice of vegetarian main dishes). The best wines of the region figure on the *carte*: Domaine de Trevellon, Bandol, Vignelaure. Finish with a glass of Baume de Venise.

Baba Bhelpoori House ♣ 🍴
29-31 Porchester Rd., W2 (Bayswater) ☎ *221-7502. Map 6F3* ⬚ ⬚ *Closed Mon, Christmas. Tube: Bayswater, Royal Oak.*
An open-armed welcome awaits diners at this very simple, quietly decorated restaurant, which specializes in South Indian vegetarian cooking. Specialties on the short menu include *thali, pani poori, masala dosai* and *aloo papri chat*, all home-cooked and deliciously spicy. The *bhel pooris* are irresistible, consisting of crisp wholewheat Indian bread, filled with puffed rice, *vermicelli*, potatoes, onions and fresh coriander, served with chili sauce, garlic and a variety of chutneys. The restaurant is run by a charming husband and wife, and is an exceptionally good value.

Bahn Thai
21a Frith St., W1 (Soho) ☎ *437-8504. Map 10F10 ll⬚ to lll* ⬚ ■ ▦ ▦ *Closed Christmas and Easter. Tube: Leicester Square.*
One of the first of London's burgeoning Thai restaurants and still one of the best; but don't try it unless you like spicy food — in Thailand hot means hot. Among starters look for satay, boned stuffed chicken wings and squid in batter, among soups for hot and sour seafood with lemon grass. Drink Thai beer or a balancing white wine such as Gewürztraminer or Sauvignon. For devotees of dear departed Bianchi's, a visit here is somewhat unnerving, for it's the same premises, still creaking and faded, but now with Oriental

touches. The tables are crammed in, and the pace is relaxed and leisurely, in true Thai tradition.

La Bastide
50 Greek St., W1 (Soho) ☎ 734-3300. Map **10F10** IIII ⚏ ▰ ▰
🏠 ▦ AE ⏱ *Closed Sat lunch, Sun. Tube: Tottenham Court Rd.*
Nicholas Blacklock's restaurant is one of those places it feels good to be in: comfortable and elegant, a place to dress up for. With its pre-and post-theater menus it's popular with theater-goers and players alike, and full of buzz, especially later on. The cuisine is styled *bônnete*, and there are three menus to choose from: an excellent set menu devoted to a particular region of France, which changes monthly; a small *carte* of traditional French dishes; and the brasserie-style Soho menu. The wine list is regional too, featuring country wines from all over France; the Côtes de Gasgogne are inexpensive and good.

Bibendum
Michelin House, 81 Fulham Rd., SW3 (South Kensington) ☎ 581-5817. Map **16J6** IIII ⚏ *dinner* ▰ *lunch* ▦ AE ⏱ *Closed bank hols. Tube: South Kensington.*
Lunch is a particular delight here, as light streams through huge windows into the 1st-floor dining room, brilliantly designed by Sir Terence Conran, and graced at either end by two splendidly jolly Michelin men in stained glass. Seating is spacious and supremely comfortable, and the food, by Simon Hopkinson, is just right: definite, appealing and carefully presented. The set lunch menu may reveal perfect mushroom soup, gravlax, calves' liver with mustard grain sauce and coffee granita. The ground floor of the famous Michelin building now houses the Conran shop and an **oyster bar** (*open 10am-11pm*).

Bloom's
90 Whitechapel High St., E1 (East End) ☎ 247-6001/6835. Map **13F18** I⚏ ▦ AE ⚏ *Closed Fri eve, Sat, Jewish hols, Xmas Day. Tube: Whitechapel.*
While Manhattan's Jewish families were migrating from Lower East to Upper West Side, London's were making an almost identical journey. Even Bloom's restaurant opened a branch in Golders Green, NW11, but its soul remains in Whitechapel, where the nostalgia is thicker than the *borscht* and noisier than the *matzos*, and the waiters as crotchety

as any on Lower East Side. Eat here on Sun after visiting **Petticoat Lane** and **Brick Lane** markets (*see Shopping*).

Blue Elephant
4-5 Fulham Broadway, SW6 (Fulham) ☎ 385-6595 I⚏ ⚏ ▰
▦ ⚏ AE ⏱ *Closed Sat lunch. Tube: Fulham Broadway.*
The surroundings of this leading Thai restaurant (a scruffy corner on Fulham Broadway) are no match for its eye-opening interior: a veritable garden of greenery, complete with bridge, stream and waterfall. Tables are set in several pagoda-style areas, each on a different level; the banks of plants afford plenty of privacy. The food, served by waiters and waitresses in Thai silk tunics, is above-average and includes a deliciously spicy seafood soup, a mild creamy prawn curry and an interesting hot chicken salad. Lemon grass is the predominant flavoring. An amusing, yet intimate place.

Bombay Brasserie
Courtfield Close, Courtfield Rd., SW7 (Kensington) ☎ 370-4040. Map **15J4** I⚏ ⚏ ▰ *lunch* ▰ ▦
⚏ 🔔 AE ⏱ *Tube: Gloucester Rd.*
Housed in a huge conservatorium leading off the palatial 1920s main dining room, this European vanguard of India's thoroughbred Taj Hotels group ranked for years as one of London's most impressive Indian restaurants. Today, both the colonial decoration and the regional home cooking look slightly frayed at the edges. Although the varied menu features specialties from all over India (Goa, Bombay, Punjab), criticism has been leveled at tired, overcooked dishes. The restaurant is open every day of the year, with last orders at midnight. The staff is cosmopolitan and friendly, and although Bombay Brasserie is generally expensive for an Indian restaurant, the set-price buffet lunch is a good value.

Burt's
42 Dean St., W1 (Soho) ☎ 734-3339. Map **10F10** IIII ⚏ ▰
pre-theater ▰ ▦ AE ⏱ *Closed Sat lunch, Sun, bank hols. Tube: Leicester Square.*
Reflecting the current trend for healthy eating, Burt's is a chic, predominantly vegetarian and fish restaurant. Its aim is to raise the standing of vegetarian cuisine, associated for too long with such clichés as brown rice and nut rissoles. In an attractive peach-and-

gray dining room, buzzing with conversation, particularly at lunchtime, the imaginative menu features *mille-feuille* of fresh sardines with chard and grain mustard butter, soft roe *beignets* with zucchini noodles and tomatoes, *gnocchi maison*, made with Stilton, spinach and tomato, and *goujons* of monkfish in a citrus cream. The food is well prepared and served by friendly staff, wearing white and blue peasant shirts. The wine list is excellent.

Café Flo ♥

205 Haverstock Hill, NW3 (Hampstead) ☎ 435-6744 □ *to* 〖〗 ▯ 🚇 *Tube: Belsize Park.*
Jazz music throbs in the background of this comfortable bistro, where the easy ambience attracts the North London intelligentsia. The menu is characterized by robust French regional favorites, such as fish soup, baked chicken, lamb steak and veal scallop in breadcrumbs with ham and cheese, with a few more serious dishes, such as haddock tart with spinach sauce and salmon with a tomato and shallot sauce. The set menu, *L'idée Flo*, is exceptionally good value. Sun lunch is particularly popular here. Across the road, **Flo's Bar and Grill** (*216 Haverstock Hill* ☎ 794-4125 □ *to* ▯) is an offshoot of Café Flo, with tables set outside in summer and brasserie-type food.

Le Café du Marché ♥

22 Charterhouse Sq., Charterhouse Mews, EC1 (Clerkenwell) ☎ 608-1609. *Map 12E14* 〖〗 ▯ ▬ ▦ *Closed Sat lunch, Sun, Easter, 2 weeks Christmas. Tube: Barbican, Farringdon.*
One of a number of welcome newcomers to an area once almost devoid of restaurants, Café du Marché is friendly, informal and French. It occupies a converted warehouse, where the original open-plan space has been retained and the bare brick walls are decorated with posters. The food has a provincial French bias with a smattering of Oriental dishes. It's simple fare, but well cooked, and the garlicky fish soup is outstanding. For grills, eat upstairs at **Le Grenier**.

Calabash ☕

38 King St., WC2 (Covent Garden) ☎ 836-1976. *Map 10G11* ▯ 〖〗 ▦ *Closed Sat lunch, Sun, Christmas Day. Tube: Covent Garden.*

The Africa Centre offers Black and Muslim studies, exhibitions and the Calabash restaurant, which has the feel of an Oxbridge refectory, despite African paintings and handcrafts on the walls and exotic taped music. The service tends to be languid, and the menu is limited, but still spans the entire continent. Specialties include African stews, fish and vegetarian dishes, and there are North African, Zimbabwean and Nigerian wines and Tusker beer.

La Capannina ♥

24 Romilly St., W1 (Soho) ☎ 437-2473. *Map 10F10* 〖〗 ▯ ▦ 🍷 *Closed Sat lunch, Sun. Tube: Leicester Square, Piccadilly Circus.*
A good example of the type of unpretentious, inexpensive, friendly Italian restaurant in which Soho specializes. Well-prepared basic Italian dishes such as *gnocchi*, *raviolini*, *crespolini*, sea-bass with fennel, beef braised in Barolo, rabbit in white wine.

Capital Hotel ⌂

22 Basil St., SW3 (Knightsbridge) ☎ 589-5171. *Map 16I7* ▥ 〖〗 ▬*lunch* 🍷 ▦ ▦ 🍷 *Tube: Knightsbridge.*
Having quickly established itself as one of the finest hotel restaurants in London, the Capital suffered a downturn in its culinary fortunes with the loss of its Michelin star. Happily now the tables have turned and, with the introduction of the talented Phillip Britten as chef, it has retrieved its coveted Michelin star. Britten has worked with Anton Mosimann and Nico Ladenis, and it shows. His New English cuisine pays more attention to flavor than unnecessary decoration; dishes are simple, light and cooked to perfection. The service is attentive and the wine list excellent, although pricey. The dining room, recently redecorated by Nina Campbell, has been given the full treatment, all pink and festooned and candlelit.

Le Caprice ♥

Arlington House, Arlington St., SW1 (Piccadilly) ☎ 629-2239. *Map 9G9* 〗〗 ▯ 🍷 ▦ ▦ 🍷 *Tube: Piccadilly Circus.*
Long famous as a restaurant, Le Caprice was given a new image a few years ago, and now, all chrome and glass and black-and-white Bailey photographs, it's an even more fashionable rendezvous for West End glitterati than **Langan's** across the road. The food is

surprisingly good and just right for the ambience: steak tartare, salmon fishcakes, bang-bang chicken (with peanut and hot and sweet chili sauce), imaginative salads, white and dark chocolate mousse. And it's perhaps the best place in London for Sunday brunch. Reserve well ahead. The owners of Le Caprice have added another string to their bow, that famous old theatrical restaurant **The Ivy** (*1 West St., WC2* ☎ *836-4751 ▥*). It has been updated, but with much of its old character intact, and was reopened in June 1990.

Charbar
2A Pond Pl., SW3 (S Kensington) ☎ *584-4555. Map 15K5▢▢ ▢ ▦ Tube: South Kensington.*
The appeal of this unusual new restaurant is that you get to cook your own meal over a charcoal grill, sunk into the center of your table. Armed with a pair of tongs, carnivores can time to the second the cooking of their sirloin or fillet steak, marinated chicken breast, swordfish, salmon, lobster or king prawns. This is no place for vegetarians though. A tiled floor and granite tables lend the feel of a French farmhouse. Starters and puddings are wholesome and filling.

Chez Gérard
8 Charlotte St., W1 (West End) ☎ *636-4975. Map 10E10▥▢ ▢ ▨ ▣ Closed Sat lunch, bank hols. Tube: Goodge Street.*
The punters flock to Chez Gérard for its specialty, because when it comes to steak and chips, nobody cooks them quite like the French. There is also a fantastic array of French cheeses on offer. The wood floors, paper tablecloths and French waiters give the impression of a genuine Left Bank bistro. The service is fairly peremptory. (*Branches at 31 Dover St., W1* ☎ *499-8171 and 119 Chancery Lane, WC2* ☎ *405-0290.*)

Chez Nico
35 Great Portland St., W1 (Marylebone) ☎ *436-8846. Map 9E9 ▥▥ ▢ ▨ ▤ ▦ ▣ Closed Sat, Sun, 3 weeks in summer, 10 days Christmas. Tube: Oxford Circus.*
In his small brightly-lit L-shaped dining room, decorated in elegant beige, with striking Tiffany glass skylights and large mirrors, Nico Ladenis performs the culinary miracles that have earned him two Michelin stars. Its origins in

Provence, the food is sensational. Flavors are combined with supreme skill to create such delicacies as *ravioli de champignons au fumet de champignons sauvage, rognons de veau au cassis, blanc de poulet farci de foie gras aux nouilles fraîches* or *glace caramel au coulis d'abricot,* all exquisitely prepared and presented. In the opinion of many hard-nosed critics, Chez Nico produces the best French food to be found in the city. The wine list excels; the service is faultless. Nico Ladenis has also converted his old premises into a bistro-style restaurant, called **Very Simply Nico** (*48a Rochester Row, SW1* ☎ *630-8061 ▥▥ to ▥▥▥*), where Tony Tobin masterminds the preparation of simple well-cooked dishes such as Mediterranean fish soup, pickled trout, and steak *frites*.

Cibo
3 Russell Gdns., W14 (Kensington) ☎ *371-6271 ▥▥▢ ▢ ▨ ▣ Closed Sat lunch, Sun eve, bank hols. Tube: Kensington (Olympia).*
Behind an unprepossessing exterior is an unexpectedly sophisticated little restaurant and haunt of celebrity foodies. The stippled green walls are hung with exotic contemporary art works, all for sale. Light and airy with a profusion of plants and twig arrangements, a marble bar and cane furniture, it serves robust New Wave Italian cuisine, in similar vein to the pioneering **Orso** and **River Café**.

Clarke's
124 Kensington Church St., W8 (Kensington) ☎ *221-9225. Map 6H2 ▥▥▢ to ▥▥▥ ▧ ▤ ▦ Closed 4 days Easter, 2 weeks Aug, 10 days Christmas, bank hols. Tube: Notting Hill Gate.*
In her bright, airy restaurant, with lots of pale wood and cane chairs, Sally Clarke has quickly established a reputation for inspired Californian-based cooking. At lunchtime, there is a choice of three courses on the menu; there is no choice for the 4-course dinner (but alternatives for vegetarians). Menus are changed daily and hardly ever repeated, but salads, dressed with the purest olive oil, are popular starters, and char-grilling is favored for meat and fish, served with subtle sauces. The various unusual breads are outstanding (and on sale at **& Clarke's** next door: see *Shopping*). There is a very good selection of Californian wines. From

the basement, so cleverly lit that it feels as light as the upstairs room, the spotless, efficient kitchen is on view. Everything feels fresh, from the crisp linen napkins and pretty china to the flowers on the tables and excellent unobtrusive service.

Columbus
8 Egerton Gdns. Mews, SW3 (Knightsbridge) ☎589-8287. *Map 16J6* ▯▯ *to* ▥▥ ▭ ➤ ⚥ ▥▥ ▦ *Tube: Knightsbridge.*
Anglo-American restaurant critic Loyd Grossman has changed sides and opened Columbus, a surprisingly cool and airy basement with a faintly Mexican feel. The cooking, described as "Californian," is designed to give faded Knightsbridge palettes a break from "terminal terrine tiredness"; and indeed it does. It could be the hardest menu to choose from in London — should it be the Albuquerque Roll or the Thai chicken pizza, the *linguine* with mussels in black bean sauce or the grilled steak chili on *rigatone*? It's certainly different, if undisciplined, and most of it tastes a great deal better than it sounds. In another novel move, wines are bracketed into three price bands, and there's also an esoteric selection of beers, plus some great cocktails.

Connaught Hotel ⬠
Carlos Pl., W1 (Mayfair) ☎499-7070. *Map 9G8* ▥▥ ▬ *restaurant* ▭ *Grill Room* ➤ ▦ *Grill Room closed Sat, Sun, bank hols. Tube: Bond Street.*
The restaurant that once reigned supreme over London's other top hotels has recently had to fend off the allegation that it is coasting on its reputation, that gastronomically it has lost its edge and that the service is no longer meticulous. Although its clubby, dignified atmosphere is unimpaired, the cuisine can be unexciting and lackluster. For many, however, the Connaught epitomizes all that is traditionally English, and the spirit of the place outweighs any lapse of culinary standards.

Daquise ▦
20 Thurloe St., SW7 (South Kensington) ☎589-6117. *Map 15F5* ▯▯ ▭ ▬ *lunch. Tube: South Kensington.*
A home-away-from-home for the Polish community, and a welcome refuge for hungry students. This is a little corner of Eastern Europe in central London. '50s decor, much nostalgia, huge helpings of Polish

fodder such as borscht (*barszcz*), goulash, ground buckwheat (*kasza*). The ground-floor room is more informal than the neat, wood-paneled basement dining room.

Ed's Easy Diner ♣
12 Moor St., W1 (Soho) ☎439-1955. *Map 10F10* ▯▯ ▭ ▦ *Closed Christmas, Jan 1. Tube: Leicester Square.*
Chili con carne, hot dogs, burgers and fries are the staple at this meticulous replica of a '50s American diner. It has been perfectly reconstructed by young restaurateur Bruce Isaacs down to the last detail, from the sleek chrome counter to the ten original juke boxes, which throb to the beat of Buddy Holly or Jerry Lee Lewis. Even the phone number is a 1950s one. It's hard to find better burgers anywhere else in the city, and they should be accompanied by a choice from the eclectic selection of beers, Rolling Rock for example. Service is brisk but helpful. (*Other branches at 362 King's Rd., SW3* ☎352-1956 *and 16 Hampstead High Rd., NW3* ☎431-1958.)

English House
3 Milner St., SW3 (Chelsea) ☎584-3002. *Map 16J6* ▥▥ ▭ ▬ *lunch* ▦ *Tube: Sloane Sq.*
In intimate chintzy rooms in a Chelsea town house, old English recipes have been adapted and modernized to provide one of the capital's few interesting British menus. Mouthwatering specialties include *ragout* of wild mushrooms tossed with cream and Madeira and topped with toasted breadcrumbs, potted venison with juniper berries and Cumberland jelly, pheasant, apricot and chestnut pie topped with flaky pastry, stew of salmon and scallops marinated with spring onions, root ginger and sorrel, brown bread and ginger ice cream and honey cheesecake with cinnamon custard. Other restaurants in this small chain, which feature the same culinary style, are **The English Garden** (*10 Lincoln St., SW3* ☎584-7272 ▥▥), with a conservatory dining room awash with plants, cozy with an open fire in winter, and **The Lindsay House** (*21 Romilly St., W1* ☎439-0450 ▥▥), where the pretty upstairs dining room is decked out in pastel shades and elegant antique furniture.

L'Escargot
48 Greek St., W1 (Soho) ☎437-2679. *Map 10F10* ▥▥ *to* ▥▥ ▭ ➤

🎫 🅰️ 💳 *Closed Sat lunch, Sun. Tube: Tottenham Court Road.*
One of Soho's venerable institutions. After a period of closure, L'Escargot was revamped and given a new lease on life in the 1980s. One of those responsible was chef Martin Lam, who describes his food as "modern English, obviously influenced by French." The downstairs brasserie-type menu is a lighter version of what's on offer to the media-folk in the upstairs dining rooms. The global selection of wines was created by wine-writer Jancis Robinson. Graphically-arresting snail-trails on the carpets, and marbled *eau-de-nil* walls to the lofty skylights. Its life-force is *maîtresse d'*Elena, enticed from the much-loved, now defunct Bianchi's. Local competition is provided by the **Groucho Club** (*44 Dean St.* ☎ *439-4685*), another media hot-spot, open to members and guests only.

Four Seasons ⌂
Inn on the Park, Hamilton Pl., W1 (Mayfair) ☎ *499-0888. Map 9H8* 🍴 🗖 ▄ ▆ 🎫 ▄ 🅰️ 💳 *Tube: Hyde Park Corner.*
Raymond Blanc's brilliant young protégé Bruno Loubet is currently doing spectacular and imaginative things at this hotel restaurant. In ostentatious wood-paneled surroundings, Loubet presents his innovative *cuisine de terroir* (food of the earth), which originates from his native sw France. Every component is original: the lightly smoked salmon and beef, caramelized vegetables, sublime sauces, some fragrant, others piquant, and perfect mousses. The wine list is strong, but exorbitantly priced.

Fung Shing
15 Lisle St., WC2 (Soho) ☎ *437-1539. Map 10G10* 🍴 *to* 🍴 🗖 ▄ ▆ 🎫 🅰️ 💳 *Tube: Leicester Sq.*
Chinatown presents a bewildering choice of restaurants to the newcomer, perhaps wandering through after the theater (no need to reserve, although you might have to wait for a table). Most are perfectly reasonable, but **Poons**, for lunch or a quick supper, **Chuen Cheng Ku** (*17 Wardour St., W1* ☎ *437-1398* 🍴), and **New World** (*Gerrard Pl., W1* ☎ *734-0677* 🗖), for good *dim-sum* and an amusing venue, **Mr Kong** (*21 Lisle St., W1* ☎ *437-7341* 🗖), for excellent Cantonese food, and Fung Shing stand out. Fung Shing is small and rather cramped,

with bland un-Oriental decor. But its Cantonese food is the very best in Chinatown: one delicious meal for two consisted of state of the art *wuntun* soup, crunchy quail baked with salt and chili, green vegetables with slivers of garlic, and slices of duck with lemon sauce.

Galicia 🍴
323 Portobello Rd., W10 (Notting Hill) ☎ *969-3539. Map 6G2* 🗖 🗖 ▄ *lunch Tues-Fri* 🅰️ 💳 *Closed Mon. Tube: Ladbroke Grove.*
One of a crop of Spanish *tapas* bars that have sprung up throughout London recently, Galicia is probably the most down-to-earth and authentic. It serves hearty Galician specialties, such as hake, octopus, squid and paella, all fresh, tender and simply but well cooked. The unfussy decoration (plain walls and dark wood) matches the cuisine. Linger over coffee and a liqueur at the long bar, favored by the Spanish habitués for lengthy animated conversations.

Ganpath
372 Grays Inn Rd., WC1 (King's Cross) ☎ *278-1938. Map 5C12* 🗖 ▄ *lunch* 💳 *Tube: King's Cross St Pancras.*
South Indian food is very different from that of the northern part of the subcontinent, which is more commonly found in Britain. Southern cooking is usually (although not always) hotter, and this particular restaurant also gives it a vegetarian emphasis, although fish and meat dishes are available on a menu that is authentic, interesting and varied. Try spiced green bananas, *avial* (vegetables in coconut and yogurt) and *masala dosa*. The service is gracious too.

Le Gavroche ⌂
43 Upper Brook St., W1 (Mayfair) ☎ *408-0881. Map 9F8* 🍴 🍴 🗖 ▄ 🎫 🅰️ 💳 *Closed Sat, Sun. Tube: Bond Street.*
For the money you could fly to Paris, but even there you wouldn't get the wonderful creations of Michel Roux, son of Albert and nephew of Michel senior, the famous brothers from Charolles, in Burgundy, who created Le Gavroche. Theirs is widely regarded as one of the two or three best French restaurants in London. The menu is sufficiently varied to meet most requirements, and it does list a few popular classics among the heavenly sauces and soufflés, mousses and *mousselines*. Although

Le Gavroche doesn't specialize in fish, its *mousseline* of lobster and *turbotin au Chardonnay* are notable delights. Burgundian the Roux family may be, but the lengthy wine list pays equal homage to Bordeaux. Service is attentive, courteous and helpful, and the ambience formal but unstuffy. The set lunch is almost a bargain.

Gavvers ✿

61-63 Lower Sloane St., SW1 (Chelsea) ☎ 730-5983. Map 16K7 ⅢⅢ ■ ⚏ ⊙ Closed Sat lunch, Sun, 1 week Christmas. Tube: Sloane Square.

There are few restaurants where fixed-price means what it says, but this young relation of **Le Gavroche** is one of them. From the crisp vegetable canapés to the final cup of coffee not a single extra creeps onto the check. Included in the price is a half bottle per person from a small but excellent selection of house wines. Robert Couzens, the talented chef, who has his vegetables brought by truck from France, changes his imaginative menu every month. Service is good and the atmosphere lively, although the tables are too cramped.

Gay Hussar

2 Greek St., W1 (Soho), ☎ 437-0973. Map 10F10 ⅢⅢ ▢ ▢ lunch ▦ Closed Sun. Tube: Tottenham Court Road.

The name predates any sexual connotation, and persuasions are more obviously political in this famous plotting place. It is an irony that a Hungarian emigré establishment should be so well patronized by leading socialist politicians, but they obviously enjoy such central European sustainers as cherry soup, pressed boar's head, goose, mallard, dumplings and lemon cheese pancakes. A considerable choice at modest prices on the lunch menu. Although it has recently changed hands, care has been taken to keep the restaurant exactly as it was in the famous Mr Sassie's day.

Gaylord

79 Mortimer St., W1 (West End) ☎ 580-3615. Map 9E9 ⅢⅢ ▢ ▢ ▦ ⚏ ⊙ Tube: Oxford Circus.

The first Gaylord was in Delhi, but the London branch, which opened in 1966, has probably done most to spread the name of this family of restaurants, with their own delicate style of Indian *haute cuisine*. The Gaylords boast that they open for

lunch and dinner "365 days a year." The *pilaus*, lamb *pasanda* and *korma* dishes are an impressive introduction to Indian cooking.

Geale's ⚏

2 Farmer St., W8 (Notting Hill) ☎ 727-7969. Map 6G2 ▢ ▢ lunch. Closed 10 days Easter, 2 weeks Aug and Christmas. Tube: Notting Hill Gate.

Fish and chips should be eaten out of a newspaper held hotly in the hand, in the course of a winter's evening stroll; every true Briton knows that, in much the way that all Americans prefer their franks to be served at a ball-game. The notion of a fish-and-chip restaurant is heresy enough to the purist, and a fashionable one defies the logic of the world's greatest take-out food. Geale's became fashionable when it was patronized by media heroes in search of simple pleasures. Success hasn't spoiled the place, which remains very basic, with excellent fish, despite such nonsense as a wine-list. No reservations.

Golden Duck

6 Hollywood Rd., SW10 (Chelsea/South Kensington) ☎ 352-3500/4498. Map 1514 ⅢⅢ ▢ ■ ▦ ⚏ Closed lunch Mon-Fri, Sun before bank hol. Mon, Easter, Christmas. Tube: West Brompton.

London's first Chinese restaurant with a Western look was opened 20yrs ago by Russian Alexander Shihwarg and is still going strong. Originally devoted to Peking cuisine, today the menu successfully combines Pekinese and Szechuan dishes. Famous for its bang-bang chicken, a specialty that the Golden Duck introduced to this country.

Green's

36 Duke St., SW1 (St James's) ☎ 930-4566. Map 9G9 ⅢⅢ to ⅢⅢ ▢ ▦ ⚏ ⊙ Closed Sun eve, bank hols. Tube: Green Park.

In the heart of St James's, this refined wood-paneled restaurant has all the exclusivity of a gentlemen's club. Although it only opened a few years ago, Green's feels as though it has been here for centuries. The cooking is traditional too but wins no prizes. Oysters are the specialty and the Champagne list is distinguished, if you can stand the expense. Perfect for plotting or secret assignations, the **Bar**, with its private booths, serves good-quality cold food, such as salmon, lobster and dressed crab.

Hard Rock Cafe

150 Old Park Lane, W1 (Mayfair)
☎ *629-0382. Map 9H8 □ □*
Tube: Hyde Park Corner.
The best hamburgers in London by
common consent and, in fact, better
than most in the United States.
Steaks, sandwiches, chili in winter,
American beer, and good ice cream
plus pop memorabilia. Not a place
for conversation, though; it might
better be called the Loud Rock Cafe.
No reservation and, of course, the
legendary line.

Harvey's

2 Bellevue Rd., SW17
(Wandsworth) ☎ *672-0114 ▥ □*
▦ Closed Sun. Train to
Wandsworth Common.
This pretty pastiche of a 1930s
dining room in a gentrified
backwater overlooking Wandsworth
Common is an unlikely setting for
some of the most creative cooking
currently on offer in Britain. But this
is where Marco Pierre White, an
explosive, driven young
Yorkshireman, has decided to
unleash his considerable talents,
and he has recently been rewarded
with his second Michelin star. His
commitment to the culinary art and
his fresh approach are evident in
every beautifully presented dish,
whether it be tagliatelle with
oysters, shellfish soup or baby
pigeon with truffles. Cheese and
desserts stand up well. The young
French staff are courteous and
professional, belying the tumult
going on unseen in the kitchens.

Hiders

755 Fulham Rd., SW6 (Fulham)
☎ *736-2331 ▥ □ Closed Sat*
lunch, Sun. Tube: Parsons Green.
A great favorite with local
Fulhamites, Sloanes and yuppies
alike as well as people from farther
afield. It's informal, intimate and
sophisticated in a country house
style — swags and drapes, mirrors,
chandelier and a roaring (gas) log
fire downstairs. The food is
appreciated for its quality, at less
than West End prices. Dishes turn
out to be a lot less fussy than they
sound on the menu, to whit:
medallions of veal and lobster tail
served on a duo of sauces, one
sherry and the other shellfish with
cognac. There is an intelligent wine
list spread across the price range,
with fair-priced house red and white.

Ikkyu ☙ ❀

Basement, 67 Tottenham Court
Rd., W1 (West End) ☎ *636-9280.*
Map 10E10 □ to ▥ □ ▦ AE
▦ Closed Sat, Sun lunch. Tube:
Goodge St.
A world away from **Suntory** with its
serious, expense account clientele,
Ikkyu is one of the cheapest and
most humble Japanese restaurants
in town; it is also one of the jolliest,
with some of the best food. The
entrance, down steep steps beneath
an electronics store, is easy to miss
and positively tacky. The room itself
is not much of an improvement, but
it's a relaxed and amusing place to
dig into big portions of *sushi*,
sashimi or *yakitori*, or *robatayaki*,
the country cooking of Japan, which
might include stewed meat with
potato, or rolled conger in seaweed.
The set menus are incredibly cheap.
Drink whisky (sold by the bottle),
sake or lager, or free green tea.
Ajimura (*51-53 Shelton St., WC2*
☎ *240-9424 ▥*), in Covent Garden,
is a similarly informal Japanese
restaurant.

Au Jardin des Gourmets

5 Greek St., W1 (Soho) ☎ *437-*
1816. Map 10F10 ▥ to ▥ □ ▦
▦ AE ▦ Closed Sat lunch, Sun.
Tube: Tottenham Court Road.
Although it is especially noted for its
fine wines — one of the best lists in
London, acquired with great care
and served with love — this elegant,
discreet classical French restaurant
has for years been a firm Soho
favorite. Theater-goers can split
their meal: starter and main course
before curtain-up, dessert and
coffee after. The restaurant has
recently expanded, with an area
now set aside for nonsmokers.

Joe Allen

13 Exeter St., WC2 (Covent
Garden) ☎ *836-0651. Map 11F11*
□ to □ □ ▦ ▱ Tube: Covent
Garden.
Branch of the New York restaurant,
and very similar in style and decor,
although somehow less intimate and
more bustling. Very popular
with journalists and actors, more for
its social ambience than its food.
Sizeable menu on a chalkboard,
with salads, burgers (called
"chopped steak"), etc., and
American desserts. Cocktails at the
bar. Open late, until 1am.

Kalamares ☙

76-78 Inverness Mews, W2
(Mega); 66 Inverness Mews, W2
(Micro); (both Bayswater)
☎ *727-9122. Map 6G3 ▥ □ AE*
▦ Closed lunch, Sun. Tube:
Bayswater.

Restaurants

An unprepossessing mews leads to these two ever-popular Greek tavernas. **Micro**, nearest, is smaller, rather cramped, unlicensed and cheaper; **Mega**, farther down, is more spacious. The food at both is equally good, the atmosphere relaxed and very jolly. An incomprehensible menu is patiently decoded by helpful waitresses (although it's impossible to remember everything they tell you — how much simpler it would be to print translations). Starters tend to be more exciting than main courses: try deep-fried squid, *melitzanes skordalia* (fried eggplant with garlic dip) and the *loukanika* (spicy sausages). Wine is Greek too.

Keats
3 Downshire Hill, NW3 (Hampstead) ☎ 435-3544. *Map 21C4* ▥▥▥ *to* ▥▥▥ ⬛ ☐ AE ▣ *Closed Sun, Mon. Tube: Hampstead.*

In bookish Hampstead, even the restaurants look like libraries, but such an erudite and worldly district is most exacting in the matter of gastronomy. The classical French menu, which might include such delights as *châteaubriand aux trois sauces* and wild duck, features new dishes every month, and the wine list is excellent. Both atmosphere and service are excessively formal.

Kensington Place ♣
201 Kensington Church St., W8 (Kensington) ☎ 727-3184. *Map 6G2* ▯ *to* ▯▯ ☐ ▥ ▤ *Tube: Notting Hill Gate.*

A great brasserie, more Manhattan than Paris, which packs in the crowds for its glamorous feel and its uncomplicated, inexpensive food. It's not to everyone's taste: some people complain that it's like eating in a goldfish bowl, since the street side is a huge wall of glass. But most people enjoy the exposure: the use of expensive wood for floor, table tops and (uncomfortable) chairs, the mass of bright spotlights, and the long, buzzing bar at one end all add to the glitzy effect. This isn't the place for a lingering meal; the idea is to eat, talk loudly (a necessity), and go: they need your table. The food sometimes misses, mostly hits. The menu changes often, although the choice is limited, particularly among main courses. Highlights include the delectable chicken and goat's cheese mousse with olives, with a texture like *crème caramel*, and baked tamarillos with vanilla ice cream. The more expensive items,

such as *foie gras* and oysters (poached with chanterelles and cucumber), are done very well.

Kettners
29 Romilly St., W1 (Soho) ☎ 437-6437/734-6112. *Map 10F10* ▯ *to* ▯▯ ☐ ▥ ▤ ☒ ☐ ▣ *Tube: Leicester Square, Tottenham Court Road.*

A famous London restaurant in days gone by, Kettners is now home to yet another Pizza Express. This is all to the good, since it means that those with only a few pounds to spend can enjoy their tasty pizzas and hamburgers in splendidly plush surroundings (avoid the modern, tiled dining room if you can). There is also a champagne bar and cocktail lounge with pianist, where on Thurs and Fri you will be serenaded by Alfredo, the singing *maître d'*.

There are 20 Pizza Express branches in London, at two of which, **Pizza on the Park** (*11 Knightsbridge, SW1* ☎ 235-5550☐ *to* ▯☐) and **Pizza Express** (*10 Dean St., W1* ☎ 437-9595☐ *to* ▯☐), live jazz can be heard nightly.

Langan's Brasserie
Stratton St., W1 (Piccadilly) ☎ 493-6437. *Map 9G9* ▥▥▥ ☐ ▥ ▤ ♪ AE ▣ *Closed Sat lunch, Sun. Tube: Green Park.*

Michael Caine, the archetypal knowing cockney, was one of the founding members of London's café society, where the famous are not only sketched on the menu but also seated at the tables. Londoners have always enjoyed the watering-holes, such as **Odins**, established by extrovert Irish restauranteur Peter Langan. Despite Langan's sad death, his buzzing and crowded brasserie has retained its pizazz, even if more tourists and soccer stars than moguls and movie stars have crept in of late. The food, under the control of roving chef Richard Shepherd, has lost some of its edge, but it remains surprisingly superior (try the spinach soufflé, *croustade d'oeufs de caille*, profiteroles with chocolate sauce). Langan's may not be at its zenith, but this is still the most exciting dining room in London, a huge space, wonderfully lit, filled with white-covered tables, black-aproned waiters, beautiful modern paintings, and above all, people.

Leith's
92 Kensington Park Rd., W11 (Notting Hill) ☎ 229-4481. *Map*

6G2 🍴 ■ ≡ 📧 AE ◎ Closed lunch, Aug hol weekend. Tube: Notting Hill Gate.

A school of food and wine, a catering company, a farm growing produce for the restaurant, and an impressive *oeuvre* as a cookery writer, all underpin the work of Prue Leith and her partners in this Victorian building, with an interior by expatriate American architect Nathan Silver. The result is an ambience of discreet, glittering comfort, of respect for food by the kitchen and diners alike. Leith's is a temple of the very best English food and an especially inventive style, served from a very short menu. The restaurant is well known for its trolley of cold starters, on which a typical item might be smoked trout pâté parcels wrapped in smoked salmon. Stilton soup is a favorite, perhaps followed by traditional roast duckling served with a light orange *jus*. Excellent, if expensive, wine list, superb vegetables and cheeses, and delicious desserts served from a groaning trolley.

Luigi's
15 Tavistock St., WC2 (Covent Garden) ☎ 240-1795. Map 10G10 🍴 □ 🚗 Closed Sun. Tube: Covent Garden.

Theater-goers who exit stage east, in the Strand/Covent Garden/Drury Lane area, flock to Luigi's, a bustling old favorite on several floors. Typical Italian menu, with reasonable pastas and *zabaglione*.

Manzi's ✿
1 Leicester St., WC2 (Soho) ☎ 734-0224. Map 10G10 🍴 □ AE ◎ Closed Sun lunch. Tube: Leicester Square.

This Italian fish restaurant has been a much-loved London institution for many years. Its atmosphere is less overtly Italian than between-the-wars "Continental." Downstairs, Manzi's is all bustle and lunchtime or pre-theater dining. Upstairs, the Cabin Room is calmer, for post-theater dinners or romantic assignations. Good starters, excellent scallops, sole, crab, lobster, simply prepared, are characteristic. Custardy strawberry flan is an essential dessert. Unpretentious and good fun.

Melati 🍴
31 Peter St., W1 (Soho) ☎ 437-2011. Map 10F10 □ □ ■ Tube: Piccadilly Circus.

Fair Indonesian food, with some Malaysian/Singaporean dishes, in a little Soho spot, more café than restaurant, just behind Berwick St. market. *Satay*, of course, with the distinctive flavor of lemon grass, but also a wide variety of soups, noodle dishes, seafood and vegetarian specialties. Another larger **Melati** (21 Great Windmill St., W1 ☎ 437-2745 □) is to be found nearby.

Memories of China
67-69 Ebury St., SW1 (Victoria) ☎ 730-7734. Map 17J8 🍴 □ ■ ▦ AE ◎ Closed Sun. Tube: Victoria.

The gastronomic memories are those of Ken Lo, the grand old man of Chinese cookery. He also has a cookery school, and a shop around the corner from the restaurant selling Chinese spices and kitchen utensils. The restaurant features regional dishes, especially northern, and some innovative creations. Overall, the cooking inclines to the light, crispy or crunchy: the airy, cool interior matches it. Sample Shantung hand-shredded chicken in garlic sauce, Shanghai long-cooked braised knuckle of pork, barbecue of lamb in lettuce puffs and iron-plate sizzled chicken. Another branch in Chelsea Harbour (☎ 352-4953).

Mijanou ✿
143 Ebury St., SW1 (Pimlico) ☎ 730-4099. Map 17J8 🍴 to 🍴 ■ ≡ 🚗 Closed Sat, Sun. Tube: Victoria.

Here is a timeless little restaurant, personally run, and excellent for a quiet *dîner à deux* where you can be assured of good food and wine and helpful service. Sonia Blech cooks; her husband Neville oversees and is responsible for one of the best wine lists in town. The menu consists of several set-price meals that reflect Mrs Blech's wide repertoire. A pleasant change from some of London's higher-profile quality restaurants.

Mon Plaisir
21 Monmouth St., WC2 (Covent Garden) ☎ 836-7243. Map 10F11 🍴 to 🍴 □ ■ AE ◎ Closed Sat lunch, Sun. Tube: Covent Garden.

The cheese board at Mon Plaisir is so good that one day a diner will order it for all four courses. The notion has been discussed, but no one has yet dared risk the wrath of the staff, who can at times be very Parisian. The distinctly patchy cuisine is more tuned to country cooking such as *coq au vin* and *escargots Bourguignons*, and the atmosphere is bistro-like. Mon Plaisir is on the edge of the Covent Garden area in something of a no-man's land, but by no means inconvenient, and it has for years been everyone's favorite secret. Small, intimate, and pleasantly busy.

Nancy Lam's Enak Enak
56 Lavender Hill, SW11 (Battersea) ☎ *924-3148* ▯ ▯ *Closed lunch, Sun. Train to Clapham Junction.*
Enak, so Nancy says, means yum yum, and so it is. Hers is a homespun venture, but it succeeds because she is an excellent cook as well as being both sincere and an authentic "character." Give her half a chance and she will show you her family snapshots, but she's often too busy cooking in a minute area at the back of the ground-floor dining room. Her tasty Indonesian cooking is full of individual touches. Don't miss the *satay* or the treasure hunt chicken. Drink Tiger beer.

Nontas
16 Camden High St., NW1 (Camden Town) ☎ *387-4579* ▯ *to* ▯ ▯ ▯ ▯ *Closed Sun. Tube: Camden Town.*
The Greek Cypriot ethnic neighborhoods of London are Camden and Kentish Towns and points NW, and throughout this area are inexpensive local restaurants of greatly varying quality. In Camden Town, Nontas is an excellent local Greek restaurant, full of life, with very flavorsome cooking and good lamb and fish dishes, varied *mezze* and delicious Hymettus honey and yogurt to finish what should be a most pleasant meal.

Oak Room △
Le Meridien London Hotel, Piccadilly, W1 (Piccadilly) ☎ *734-8000. Map 10G10* ▯ ▯ ▮ ▬ ▬ ▦ ▦ ▦ *Tube: Piccadilly Circus.*
One of a handful of luxury restaurants (**L'Auberge de Provence** and **Ninety Park Lane** are others) guided from afar by a luminary French chef, in this case Michel Lorain from A La Côte St-Jacques at Joigny. Together with chef David Chambers he has won a Michelin star for this sumptuous hotel dining room (see *Hotels*), second only to the **Ritz** in Edwardian splendor. The food is creative and complex, spectacularly garnished; the wine list all-embracing; the service utterly polished; the prices sky-high. For a money-no-object celebration, this is the place.

Odins
27 Devonshire St., W1 (Marylebone) ☎ *935-7296. Map 9E10* ▮▮▮▮ ▯ ▦ ▦ *Closed Sat lunch, Sun. Tube: Regent's Park.*
This is **Langan's** other place, although less excitable than the brasserie and more private and romantic. Restful and engrossing in its collection of paintings; gastronomically it reaches very high standards at times. Don't miss the wonderful chocolate dessert to finish your meal.

Ognisko Polskie ♣
55 Princes Gate, Exhibition Rd., SW7 (South Kensington) ☎ *589-4635. Map 15I5* ▯ ▯ ▬ ▦ ▦ *Tube: South Kensington.*
The elegant, slightly faded dining room of the Polish Hearth Club, with its portraits, gilt mirrors and yellow drapes, has a particular charm. Here, for next to nothing, you can tuck into simple, hearty Polish fare (go feeling hungry) such as *bigos* (hunter's stew) or *pierogi z miesem* (meat dumplings) accompanied by a flavored vodka or two. Fellow diners are a distinctive mix of penniless students, Solidarity dignitaries, family groups and the odd frock-coated priest.

192
192 Kensington Park Rd., W11 (Notting Hill) ☎ *299-0482. Map 6G1* ▮▮▮ ▯ ▮ ▦ *Closed Sun evening. Tube: Ladbroke Grove.*
Although it's probably meant to be stunning, the all-glass front of this restaurant-cum-wine bar is somehow rather uninviting, as is the self-consciously stylish Post-Modern/'50s interior, with its mainly blank eau-de-nil walls and tightly packed seating. Often crowded, it continues to be the local canteen for Notting Hill's media crowd. And the food and wine continue to be pretty good value. In the modern European manner, warm salads, grilled fish, goat's cheese and lentils all feature on the menu.

One Ninety Queen's Gate
190 Queen's Gate, SW7 (Kensington) ☎ *581-5666. Map 15I4* ▮▮▮▮ ▯ ▬ ▬ ▦ ▦ *Tube: Kensington High Street.*
Antony Worrall-Thompson is a chef-proprietor whose ventures always attract attention. His

particular talent is for spotting a culinary trend or fad and stylishly turning it to his advantage. Witness his previous highly successful venture (now sold), **Ménage à Trois**, where eating nothing but delectable starters and puddings became, for a time, highly fashionable. Now an earthier sort of cooking is in, and Worrall-Thompson delivers it. His stage is plush, with swagged curtains and paneled walls enlivened by lovely bright paintings. If it feels clubby, it's because it doubles as a club "for people in the restaurant, catering and supply industry" — a caterer's **Groucho's** perhaps? The food is good, but not great, and features '90s favorites such as lentils, *polenta*, wild mushrooms, *cassoulet*. The service is courteous yet relaxed, and there is an excellent wine waiter to guide you through the extensive list.

Orso
27 Wellington St., W1 (Covent Garden) ☎ 240-5269. Map **11F12** *III/* ⬜ ▦ ➨ *Tube: Covent Garden.*
Under the same ownership as **Joe Allen** around the corner, and just as fashionable, perhaps more so, but quieter. The food is certainly better. This was the first of the new breed of Italian restaurants in which the cooking is truly praiseworthy, rather than merely passable. The shortish menu features good meat and offal dishes and excellent vegetables, as well as crispy pizzas and the usual crop of homemade pastas. The wine list has been thoughtfully chosen and priced. Open from noon to midnight, this is an excellent spot either for a pre- or post-theater supper.

Pagu Dinai
690 Fulham Rd., SW6 (Fulham) ☎ 736-1195. Map **21C4** *III/* ⬜ ▦ ⬛ *Tube: Parsons Green.*
The name may sound faintly Oriental — *another* Thai restaurant? — but in fact it's Sardinian dialect for "good value," which isn't far off the truth. And it is the Sardinian cooking that saves Pagu Dinai from being just another Italian *"trat"*— albeit a well-lit and comfortable one. So go for the Sardinian specialties such as a strongly flavored fish stew, melting semolina *gnocchi* or clam soup. The Italian wine list includes a fresh Sardinian house wine. The waiters still flash their giant peppermills here, but only briefly.

Phoenicia ✿
11-13 Abingdon Rd., W8 (Kensington) ☎ 937-0120. Map **14/2** *II/* ⬜ ▦ ▦ ⬛ *Tube: Kensington High Street.*
Al Hamra may be London's most suave Lebanese restaurant, but Phoenicia, although much simpler, is every bit as enjoyable. Those who already know and love Lebanese dishes will find everything here as delicious as they would expect. Those who don't will have a first-class introduction, in pleasant surroundings, neither artificially ethnic nor self-consciously smart, with smiling, helpful service. Avoid the obvious temptation to have a (char-grilled) main course and stick to a selection of the *mezze* (the waiter will advise); it's fun to pick at all the different dishes (you should eat straight from the plates they are served on), and it livens up anything from a *tête-à-tête* to a family gathering. A meal here is never expensive; the serve-yourself lunch (*Mon-Sat*) is a notable bargain.

Pizzeria Castello ▦ ✿
20 Walworth Rd., SE1 (Lambeth) ☎ 703-2556. Map **21C5** ⬜ ⬜ ▦ *Closed Sat lunch, Sun. Tube: Elephant and Castle.*
By popular vote, the best pizzas in town, brought to your table still sizzling from the oven. Expect no frills here, and be sure to reserve ahead: it's always frantically busy. There are pastas on the menu, too, and salad. But stick to a pizza — it's the point of the place.

Poons ▦ ✿
4 Leicester St., WC2 (Soho) ☎ 437-1528. Map **10G10** ⬜ to *II/* ⬜ ▦ *Closed Sun. Tube: Leicester Square.*
One of Chinatown's best establishments: good, tasty dishes; smart, clean cafeteria-style surroundings; efficient service. Poons' specialty is wind-dried food — salty but addictive sausages, pork and duck — as well as excellent Singapore-style noodles, steamed scallops, eel with pork and garlic, or sweet and sour *wun-tun*. Reservations recommended.

Le Poulbot
45 Cheapside, EC2 (City) ☎ 236-4379. Map **12F15** *IIII* ▦ ▦ ▦ ⬛ *Closed evenings, Sat, Sun. Tube: St Paul's.*
Haute cuisine's only outpost in the City, and inevitably a popular place in which to plot or consummate a big business deal. Very discreet, and

excellent, as might be expected from one of the Roux brothers' establishments (see **Le Gavroche**). Lunch only, with a short menu that changes daily. Superb cheese board.

Quality Chop House ♣
94 Farringdon Rd., EC1 (Clerkenwell) ☎ *837-5093. Map 12D13* ⫴⫴ *to* ⫴⫴ ▢ *Tube: Farringdon.*

This is a delightful newcomer, well worth the short taxi ride from the West End, or an excellent choice after a visit to nearby Sadler's Wells (see *Nightlife*). "Newcomer" is perhaps the wrong word, since the Quality Chop House, "Progressive Working Class Caterer," has been in existence since 1862. When Frenchman Charles Fontaine, formerly head chef at **Le Caprice**, found the tiny premises, the original decor had been obscured by formica. Behind it he found a fragment of the old embossed wallpaper and had it faithfully restored. The wooden pews, which at first seem too narrow to bear, but soon become quite comfy, are original too, as is the splendid shop-front. The Chop House promises now, as then, "quality and civility," and that is what you will get from M. Fontaine (who helps to serve as well as cook) and his dedicated staff. You might start with crab soup or eggs benedict, followed by a perfect steak and chips or salmon fishcake, washed down by a fine English ale, or house wine if you prefer. A terrific find.

Red Fort
77 Dean St., W1 (Soho) ☎ *437-2115/2525. Map 10F10* ⫴⫴ ▢ ■■ ☶ *AE* ◙ *Tube: Leicester Square.*

The Red Fort, along with **Bombay Brasserie** and **Lal Quila** (*117 Tottenham Court Rd., W1* ☎ *387-4570* ⫴⫴), was a vanguard of the new-wave "Indian" that banished flock wallpaper and piped "snake-charmer" music in favor of pastel prints, palm fronds, cane chairs and cocktail bars. In neutral, soothing surroundings, on two floors, the Red Fort dispenses above-average if not outstanding North Indian cooking. Good starters, prawn dishes, quails marinated in yogurt, Goan-style fish and vegetable dishes. To drink, stick to lager if you can; the wine list is unadventurous and pricey.

Ritz ⌂
Piccadilly, W1 (Piccadilly) ☎ *493-8181. Map 9G9* ⫴⫴⫴ ▢ ■■ ▤ *AE* ◙ *Tube: Green Park.*

London's prettiest dining room continues to produce food that doesn't quite live up to the ravishing pink and marbled Empire surroundings. Keith Stanley, from the Savoy Grill, is the third successive English chef to try his luck here, and reviews are mixed. Best to stick to the plainer dishes such as whole Dover sole or collops (slices) of monkfish and oysters in a chive butter sauce. Desserts are disappointing. Service is almost back to its former balletic self. Prices are high, but a meal here is still worth every penny for the sheer thrill of being in this legendary room.

River Cafe
Thames Wharf, Rainville Rd., W6 (Hammersmith) ☎ *381-8824. Map 21C4* ⫴⫴ *to* ⫴⫴⫴ ▢ ■■ ☶ *Closed Sat evening, Sun. Last orders 9pm. Tube: Hammersmith.*

Currently London's least accessible, but most trendy restaurant, the River Cafe was started by its chef/proprietors Rose Gray and Ruth Rogers to serve as a staff canteen for the workers in high-profile architect Richard Rogers' Thames Wharf office development. Word soon got out, and they have never looked back. Theirs is real Italian home cooking, and what a change it makes from the bland fare we are used to in Italian restaurants. Dishes are pungent and robust, starring top-quality olive oil, basil, *polenta*, peppers, *cavolo nero*, truffles, char-grilled fish and other such earthy ingredients, simply served. The menu changes constantly (there are a few dud dishes, and desserts can be a let-down), and there is a short, well-chosen wine list. It's a real oddity, this River Cafe, a small, spartan, faintly scruffy room kitted out in run-of-the-mill Modernist garb, filled with famous people wolfing down rough peasant food. But it works.

St Quentin
243 Brompton Rd., SW3 (Knightsbridge) ☎ *589-8005. Map 16I6* ⫴⫴ ▢ ■■ ☶ *AE* ◙ *Tube: Knightsbridge, South Kensington.*

Open a helpful seven days a week, St Quentin has the atmosphere of a bustling, upscale Parisian bistro: all mahogany, mirrors and starched white table cloths. The food is typical too, and of fairly high standard, although there are mistakes (such as dishes arriving tepid rather than hot). Choose upstairs for the people, downstairs for the calm. If St Quentin models itself on a *rive gauche* bistro, **Grill St Quentin**, around the corner (*Yeoman's Row, SW3* ☎ *581-8377* ▮▮▮▮ *closed Sun*), is imitation La Coupole. It's huge and jolly, although the food is average and the prices are high. The St Quentin group have also spawned **Café and Charcuterie St Quentin** (*215 Brompton Rd., SW3*), very useful, and *pâtisserie-traiteur* **Les Spécialités St Quentin** (*256 Brompton Rd., SW3* ▭).

Salloos
62-64 Kinnerton St., SW1 (Belgravia) ☎ *235-4444. Map* ***16****I7* ▮▮▮▮ *Closed Sun. Tube: Knightsbridge.*
A rare, very smart Pakistani restaurant. The ethnicity is a matter of some pride to patron "Salloo" Salahuddin, who also has a restaurant in Lahore. What it really indicates is the food of the NW corner of the subcontinent, with an emphasis on kebabs and other roasted meats. Specialties include lamb in wheatgerm, chicken in cheese and tandoori quails.

San Lorenzo
22 Beauchamp Pl., SW3 (Knightsbridge) ☎ *584-1074. Map* ***16****I6* ▮▮▮ *to* ▮▮▮▮ *Closed Sun. Tube: Knightsbridge.*
Still the favorite Italian restaurant of royalty and high society, where owner Mara Berni circles the tables, greeting her gold-plated customers. Much loved for its conservatorial interior, and roof which opens in summer. Favored dishes include *crudités* with *bagna cauda* and delicious veal San Lorenzo.

Sea Shell
49-51 Lisson Grove, NW1 (Marylebone) ☎ *723-8703. Map 8E6* ▮▭ *Closed Sun, Mon. Tube: Marylebone.*
Once it was a humble fish-and-chip shop, then people started coming in Rolls-Royces, and now it is a restaurant. The Sea Shell offers a notably wide variety of excellent quality fried fish in generous helpings — not only the traditional cod and haddock but also skate, plaice, sole, and others — followed by better apple pie than might be expected. Two other good fish-and-chip shops are **Upper Street Fish Shop** (*324 Upper St., N1* ☎ *359-1401* ▮▭) and **Nautilus** (*27-29 Fortune Green Rd., NW6* ☎ *435-2532* ▮▭).

Smollensky's Ballon
1 Dover St., W1 (Piccadilly) ☎ *491-1199. Map* ***9****G9* ▮▮▭ *to* ▮▮▮▭ *Tube: Green Park.*
Open all day, this is a lively, busy restaurant-plus, very much in the American mold, successful because what it does, it does well. Getting down to basics, the steaks are properly charcoal-grilled, and they are big. On top of that, the service is notably friendly and prompt, there's an abundance of unfunny jokes on the walls, live music, marvelous entertainment for the children on weekends (*reserve well in advance*), a crowded cocktail bar, heart-shaped steaks on St Valentine's Day, and more in the same style. The formula works, and owner Michael Gottlieb has opened an even bigger branch, **Smollensky's on the Strand** (*105 The Strand, WC2* ☎ *497-2101* ▮▮▭).

Sud Ouest
27-31 Basil St. (Knightsbridge) ☎ *584-4484. Map* ***16****I6* ▮▮▭ *Closed Sun. Tube: Knightsbridge.*
Opened in late 1989, Sud Ouest should make its mark, since the food, wines and decor are all imaginative and exciting, and the prices are very fair. Chef Nigel Davies has put his experience in both top British and regional French restaurants to good use to produce his own version of *cuisine grandmère* with a strong Basquais slant. Under this heading you may find a salad of sole and rosemary, *confit de canard, boudin noir*, steamed brill with scallops, *gâteau Basque*, or orange tart on the daily changing menu — in effect, superior brasserie food in a restaurant setting. The wine list includes several bottles from SW France, but also a selection of New World wines (the house white is a crisp, fresh Sauvignon from Chile). The good value extends to the inexpensive set menu, which operates both at lunch and at dinner, a rarity these days.

Next door, the **Café Sud Ouest** (▭ *to* ▮▮▭) is an excellent place for lunch, serving equally delicious but simpler dishes at café prices.

Suntory
72 St James's St., SW1 (St James's) ☎ *409-0201. Map* ***9****H9* ▮▮▮▮ *Closed Sun. Tube: Green Park.*
In surroundings of simple elegance, with cool Japanese screens, Suntory

dispenses Shabu-Shabu dishes in one room, and Teppan cooking in another. The restaurant is owned by the Japanese vineyard, distilling and brewing company Suntory, and is something of a showpiece of the country's cuisine, in preparation, presentation and service. On the menu, all dishes are described in detail in English, and service is helpful. Prices are geared to Japanese expense accounts.

Tall Orders ♧
676 Fulham Rd., SW6 (Fulham)
☎ *371-9673. Map 21C4* ▯ ◻ ▰
▦ *Tube: Parsons Green.*
Whether or not the bamboo baskets at Tall Orders are just a gimmick or a "new concept in dining," as head chef Nick Gill would have it, is a matter of opinion. Either way, they are unusual, and they have their pros and cons. First the concept: from a short "modern European" menu you order three or four items, perhaps spinach tortellini with smoked salmon, cream and lemon; free-range chicken, roasted, with rosemary, potatoes and aioli; grilled swordfish with beans, red onions and virgin olive oil; or *tarte au citron* with caramel oranges and Cointreau. These are then delivered, promptly, all at once, stacked up in Chinese bamboo steamers. You then open the lid of each basket, and work your way through the contents. Pros: the menu is light and healthy; the place is pleasantly relaxed and bustling; the staff is willing; and the prices are delightfully low. Cons: the food can taste ordinary, however nice it sounds; hot food or cold food is nicer than lukewarm food; the tables become cluttered once the steamers arrive.

La Tante Claire ⌂
68 Royal Hospital Rd., SW3 (Chelsea) ☎ *352-6045. Map 16L6* ▥ ▯ ▰ ▰ ▦ ▣ *Closed Sat, Sun, 1 week Easter, 2 weeks Christmas, 3 weeks Aug/Sept. Tube: Sloane Square.*
It was the Roux brothers' **Le**

Gavroche that gave birth to Pierre Koffman's La Tante Claire, and after vying for supremacy for some years, both are now happily settled as the stately *grand dames* of London's *haute cuisine* restaurants. Both are noted, as *haute cuisine* surely should be, for their exquisite and complex sauces. Tante Claire, once cramped and tiny, is now spacious, comfortable and sunny, yet still delightfully unpretentious. It can be reserved weeks in advance, evenings especially. Excellent sommelier.

Tate Gallery Restaurant
Millbank, SW1 (Pimlico)
☎ *834-6754. Map 18K11* ▥ *to* ▥ ◻ ▦ *Closed evenings, Sun. Tube: Pimlico.*
Not a museum snack bar but a full-scale restaurant whose reputation rests on its inexpensive and excellent wine list and the beauty and wit of its Rex Whistler mural. The olde-English cooking — Joan Cromwell salad, Hindle Wakes — is badly faltering and needs to become modern English cooking, properly executed, in tune with the modern paintings in the gallery.

Zen
Chelsea Cloisters, Sloane Ave., SW3 (Chelsea) ☎ *589-1781. Map 16J6* ▥ *to* ▥ ◻ ▰ ▰ ▣
Tube: South Kensington.
There is an international feel to this restaurant: plenty of overseas visitors, plenty of people doing business. The decor is international too: it could be an upscale Chinese restaurant anywhere, probably in a chain hotel, although when it first opened in 1984 it was considered very *à la mode.* Zen's cooking was also much-praised as having fashionable *nouvelle cuisine* overtones. Nowadays it seems average, and pricey. That said, Zen is still popular and animated, and a good "all round" choice, particularly when winding down with business colleagues. **Zen Central** *(20-22 Queen St., W1* ☎ *629-8089* ▥*)* is the slick sister restaurant.

Venerable institutions

B.J. Atkins *(140 Wandsworth Bridge Rd., SW6* ☎ *731-1232* ◻*)*, first-rate example of a traditional cockney eel pie and mash shop. **Bentley's** *(11-15 Swallow St., W1* ☎ *734-4756* ▥*)*, excellent oysters and plain seafood dishes in

unchanged postwar premises. **Boulestin** *(1a Henrietta St., WC2* ☎ *836-7061* ▥*)*, London's foremost French restaurant during the '30s and '40s, still producing *grande cuisine* in splendid surroundings but with none of its original flair. **L'Epicure** (*28 Frith St., W1* ☎ 437-2829 *to*), memorable for the flaming torches that flank its entrance: a restaurant that has never bowed to fashion, either in its endearingly faded '50s decor or in its high-cholesterol cooking. **L'Etoile** (*30 Charlotte St., W1* ☎ 636-7189), old-fashioned bourgeois French restaurant, where a fleet of waiters guide their trolleys deftly around the tables. **Fortnum and Mason's, St James's Restaurant** (*181 Piccadilly, W1* ☎ 734-8040), grandest of Fortnum's three restaurants and a lovely setting in which to sample real English food; noted for its game pies. **Rules** (*35 Maiden Lane, WC2* ☎ 836-5314), founded in 1798 and still serving simple English food, true, traditional and robust. **Savoy Grill** (*Strand, WC2* ☎ 836-4343), bastion of the country's richest and most influential businessmen; a favorite place for power lunches. **Scotts** (*20 Mount St., W1* ☎ 629-5248), where, in discreet alcoves at this

plush 135yr-old institution, succulent seafood is served at exorbitant prices. **Simpson's-in-the-Strand** (*100 Strand, WC2* ☎ 836-9112 *to*), most famous home of roast beef and nursery puddings (spotted dick, treacle roll); very male, very British. **Sweetings** (*39 Queen Victoria St., EC4* ☎ 248-3062), no-frills seafood served to pin-striped City workers, who jostle for a place in this timeless 150yr-old establishment. **The Veeraswamy** (*99-101 Regent St., W1* ☎ 734-1401), London's oldest Indian restaurant, dating back to 1927 and, although recently redecorated, retaining something of its colonial feel. **Wiltons** (*55 Jermyn St., SW1* ☎ 629-9955), clubby and masculine, with a traditional English menu that relies on fresh ingredients simply prepared. **White Tower** (*1 Percy St., W1* ☎ 636-8141 *to*), founded in 1938, the fanciest and least ethnic of Fitzrovia's Greek restaurants, famous for the florid language of its menu.

Cafés and tearooms

Britain's colonial adventures made her controller of the world's tea trade. United with a rich tradition of cakes, biscuits and breads, this resulted in an institution nobody has copied: afternoon tea. The traditional meal is a substantial affair, with cakes, toasted teacakes or crumpets, perhaps even fish or cold meat. Eternally popular is the "cream tea": scones, jam and whipped cream. More than mere refreshment, it is a graceful, sometimes even formal, social occasion.

Most of the better hotels offer a traditional afternoon tea between about 3.30 and 5.30pm. Taking tea there is a uniquely metropolitan experience. A choice of India or China tea, or Earl Grey, camomile or even tilleul (linden or lime-blossom) if you care to ask is offered at the **Ritz Hotel**, W1 (*essential to reserve*); there is a *thé dansant* at the **Waldorf**, WC2, on Fri, Sat and Sun. Those who enjoy the full gastronomic delights favor **Brown's Hotel**, W1, and the Park Room at the **Hyde Park Hotel**, W1; but those more concerned with the drink itself incline to the Ritz and to the **Savoy** group (which includes **Claridges** and the **Connaught**, both W1, and the **Berkeley**, SW1), which has its own blend. There is a harpist at La Chinoiserie in the **Hyatt Carlton Tower**, SW1; and piano accompaniment is on hand at most grand hotels. One of the most stylish locations in which to take afternoon tea is **Fortnum & Mason**, Piccadilly, either in the St James's or Fountain restaurant, which serve excellent sandwiches, salads and cakes. Of the other department stores that offer afternoon tea, **Heal's** is serve-yourself and boasts an excellent choice of sandwiches, cakes, fruit salad and

cheesecake. The Terrace Bar in **Harrods**, recently enlarged
with an attractive conservatory, has a fairly expensive set
price, but you can eat as much as you like. Tea is also served
in the more formal Georgian Restaurant. Opposite Harrods,
on Brompton Rd., SW3, is a branch of **Richoux**, at which
rather high prices are matched by an expensive ambience.

Modeled on the good old-fashioned tea shops of the 1940s,
Tea-Time (*21 The Pavement, SW4*) is particularly agreeable in
summer when tables are set outside, overlooking Clapham
Common. More central, the **Mayur** (*343 Oxford St., W1*)
serves a selection of authentic Indian teas as well as curries.
Unfortunately, the City, where the tea trade has its roots, now
has only countless anonymous snack bars.

London has long been sufficiently cosmopolitan to have a
number of good pâtisseries. For gossipy ambience, try
Valerie (*44 Old Compton St., Soho, W1*); for privacy and good
pastries, visit nearby **Maison Bertaux** (*28 Greek St., W1*); for
sheer elegance and delicious brioches, the 70yr-old **Maison
Sagne** (*105 Marylebone High St., W1*); for excellent pastries,
Maison Bouquillon (*45 Moscow Rd., W2*).

Rivals for the best coffee served in London are **Gambarti**
(*38 Lamb's Conduit St., WC1*), a good place for breakfast, and
the stylish café/restaurant in **Emporio Armani** (*191
Brompton Rd., SW3*), which also serves superior Italian food,
now much in vogue: a good lunch stop for Knightsbridge
shoppers. Equally chic and convenient for lunch is **Joe's Café**
(*126 Draycott Ave., SW3*), another, all black and chrome, part
of Joseph Ettedgui's empire. **Café and Charcuterie St
Quentin** (*215 Brompton Rd., SW3, open 8am-8pm*) is very
French and offers a hot *plat du jour*. Also French, the **Bonne
Bouche Coffee Shop** (*2 Thayer St., W1*) serves delicious
breakfasts and has its own pâtisserie next door.

Pubs

In most countries, it is difficult for even the experienced traveler
to visit a strange town and immediately spot a place where it will
be possible to relax and, with luck, meet a few friendly natives.
And besides the welcome, each painted sign outside a pub
heralds a singularity of identity that is its quintessential charm.

The public house contrives to be unmistakable whatever its
origins, and pubs can vary considerably. Being one of England's
older cities, London has pubs that grew out of every period of
the country's history, and their names reveal their backgrounds.
A pub that stands on the site of a colonial Roman taverna may
be called The Vines or The Grapes; a hostel for workers on some
medieval construction project might be The Builders, The Castle
or The Bridge; a monastery hospice for pilgrims, The Angel or
The Salutation. Although the term "public house" was not used
in official language until the mid-1880s, that's what they all are,
whether they were built as coaching inns, Georgian
coffeehouses or gin palaces for the new city-dwellers of the
Victorian period.

The first purpose of the pub is to provide for conversation in
an informal setting, and most London pubs do concentrate on
just that, although, as in Shakespeare's time, there are hostelries
that present live entertainment. There are plenty of pubs, too,
that serve meals, but a greater number employ the impenetrable

pork pie as a defense against would-be diners, thus freeing themselves to concentrate on the serving of drink, which is the second purpose of the pub.

What to drink in the London pub? The fact that England's national liquor is London Dry Gin is easily overlooked, perhaps because the average publican's skills in the matter of mixed drinks don't stretch much further than the addition of tonic.

The true stock-in-trade of the pub is beer. Because London is so close to the hop gardens of Kent, it has long had a tradition of especially "hoppy" beers. Two London breweries, Whitbread and Watneys, are national giants, while the truly local breweries are small firms, Fuller's (London Pride) and Young's. The latter in particular have championed the unique British tradition of having their beer conditioned at the pub, in the cask, whence it is drawn by a hand pump or "beer engine" at a natural cellar temperature. An ale should never be cold, but served like a red wine, which surprises many tourists.

Another puzzler for foreigners is the lack of waiter service, although you may find it in some "lounge" bars. The public bar is where you will find the darts board, and the purist who likes to stand up while he enjoys his pint, and to drink it from a straight, handle-less glass.

Drinking laws

Britain's old, inconvenient drinking laws are better known. They were devised during World War I to curb drunkenness and were finally relaxed in 1988. Pubs may now stay open 11am-11pm Mon-Sat, and Sun noon-3pm, 7-10.30pm; within these limits the exact opening hours are at the discretion of the landlord. Opening hours tend to be longer in and around obvious tourist attractions. In the financial and commercial heart of the City, pubs may close early and remain shuttered on weekends. Ten minutes before closing, the barman sings out "last orders." Closing time is announced as "time gentlemen please," and customers are given up to 20 minutes to drink up.

Central London

Anglesea
Selwood Terrace, SW7 (Kensington). Map 15K5.
On Chelsea borders. Drink outside in summer. Inside, a pewter beer engine dispenses such country specialties as Brakspeare's and Ruddle's. Fairly basic pub snacks. Nearby, the literati and artists favor the delightfully scruffy **Queen's Elm** (*corner of Old Church St. and Fulham Rd.*).

Black Friar
174 Queen Victoria St., EC4 (Blackfriars). Map 12F14.
The astonishing interior, in marble, alabaster, bronze and copper, with friezes depicting bacchanalia among the friars who gave the neighborhood its name, dates from 1905-24 and is an outstanding manifestation of the later period of the Arts and Crafts Movement. This busy pub, with seats outside, is handy for *Fleet Street* and the *City*. Don't miss the tiny nook at the back of the main bar. A good range of real ale is served. Closed Sat, Sun.

Bunch of Grapes
207 Brompton Rd., SW3 (Knightsbridge). Map 16I6.
This pub, w of Harrods, on the way to the *Victoria and Albert Museum*, has a beautiful Victorian interior, with grapes carved in wood, leaded-glass partitions and "snob screens" to prevent bar staff from eavesdropping on your conversation. Pleasantly dark, with an intimate little bar at the back. Country beers from Everard's and Wells. Substantial hot snacks.

Cheshire Cheese
Wine Office Court, EC4 (Fleet St.). Map 11F13.
The pub is on the N side of *Fleet Street*, and the few remaining

scribes from the street of saints and sinners still favor Dr Johnson's old pub for its low-ceilinged friendliness and Marston's beer, despite its inevitably being a tourist haunt. Salads and sandwiches in the pub, and the adjoining restaurant offers its famous steak, kidney and mushroom pudding. Reservations are advisable.

French House
49 Dean St., W1 (Soho). Map 10F10.
The definitively picaresque Soho hangout, in which even the bar staff fits the image. Visitors either adore "The French" or wholly fail to be engaged by its perverse charm, but true Soho-lovers have been loyal for decades. Bare except for fading photographs of French boxers and stage stars, and the pewter water-cooler (for your *pastis*). Indifferent beer and unexciting wine: try the champagne. "The French," like such neighboring pubs as **The Swiss Tavern** (*Old Compton St.*), the **Coach and Horses** (*Romilly St.*) and **The Sun and 13 Cantons** (*Gt. Pulteney St.*), is a reminder of Soho's ethnic past.

George
77 Borough High St., SE1 (Lambeth). Map 12H15.
This type of inn, with galleries from which patrons could watch shows presented by strolling players in the courtyard, inspired the layout of the first theaters, including Shakespeare's Globe. The George is the last galleried inn in London, and only a part of it still stands. It is most attractive and comfortable, with four small bars, one serving bar food, as well as a restaurant. Wethered's Bitter is dispensed from a newly-restored 150yr-old beer engine.

Grenadier
18 Wilton Row, SW1 (Belgravia). Map 17H8.
At Hyde Park Corner, down a tiny unpromising mews called Old Barrack Yard. Said to have been the Duke of Wellington's local. You can drink outside this pretty pub, and eat full meals inside at reasonable restaurant prices. Ruddle's County beer.

Guinea
30 Bruton Place, W1 (Mayfair). Map 9G9.
In the heart of London, a tiny, basic pub that would pass for a village local if it weren't full of advertising account executives and book

editors. Hard to find, down a mews, but worth the effort. The adjoining restaurant serves excellent beef and good Bordeaux, but is very expensive indeed. The Guinea is a Mayfair outpost for Young's brewery in much the way that a nearby mews pub, the **Star Tavern** (*Belgrave Mews West, SW1*), just off Belgrave Sq., is a showpiece in Belgravia for Fuller's brewery.

King's Head and Eight Bells
50 Cheyne Walk, SW3 (Chelsea). Map 16L6.
In lovely Cheyne Walk overlooking the river, a pub that is more than 400yrs old. 18thC decor, with prints of old Chelsea on the walls. There's a permanent buffet and Wethered's, Flowers and Marston's Pedigree on tap.

Lamb and Flag
Rose St., WC2 (Covent Garden). Map 10F11.
The poet Dryden dubbed this pub "The Bucket of Blood" after being mugged in the adjoining alley. It is as dark and poky as ever, but you will meet none more intimidating than the graphic design crowd, spreading themselves almost into Garrick St.

Magpie and Stump
18 Old Bailey, EC4 (City). Map 12F14.
The lawyers regularly to be seen drinking here can no longer watch the fruits of their labors; the pub was once a vantage point from which to view public executions, and the neighborhood's Newgate Prison has long gone. But the *Old Bailey* (the Central Criminal Court) is still very much in business. The pub, rebuilt in 1931 but still rich in atmosphere, serves Charrington's IPA.

The Olde Watling
29 Watling St., EC4 (City). Map 12F15.
In the shadow of *St Paul's Cathedral*, a Wren-built pub restored in the course of this century. Oak-beamed and very busy, serving City types with draft Bass, and traditional English pork pies.

Red Lion
2 Duke of York St., SW1 (Piccadilly). Map 10G10.
Behind Simpson's shop and gentlemanly Jermyn St. Said to be the best example of a small Victorian gin palace. Burton's beer; hot snacks.

Salisbury
*90 St Martin's Lane, WC2
(Trafalgar Sq.). Map 10G11.*
Art Nouveau bronze nymphs and
equally decorative predominantly
male clientele inhabit this
spectacular theaterland pub. Draft
Guinness. Cold buffet and hot
snacks.

Sun
*63 Lamb's Conduit St., WC1
(Bloomsbury). Map 10D12.*
Specialty beer pub offering never
less than a dozen out-of-town
brews, usually ranging from
Boddington's to Old Peculiar. The
manager will proudly show you his
cellars (*reserve in advance*) when
he is not too busy slaking the thirsts
of medics from Great Ormond St.
Hospital, or feeding them tasty hot
snacks.

Farther along this charming little
street is the **Lamb**, said to have
been Dickens' local (see *Dickens'
House*), which has an attractive
Victorian interior. Young's beer is
served here.

Barnes

Sun
Church Rd., SW13.
The village pond lies opposite, alive
with ducks and fringed with
weeping willows and oak trees.
There are seats by the pond, but
you could just as well sit outside the
pub with a pint of Taylor Walker's
beer. Inside, it is low-ceilinged and
cozy. Remarkably rural for a place
that is a double-decker bus ride
(*no.9*) from Piccadilly. Barnes has
lots of interesting pubs. Just down
the High St. are the **Bull's Head** for
jazz and the **White Hart** for its
riverside veranda. Both of these sell
Young's beer.

Epping Forest

Traveler's Friend
496 High Rd., Woodford Green.
Epping Forest is a rural part of the
London area rarely visited by
tourists, yet full of interest. This pub,
within reach of Woodford Station on
the tube (*Central line*), is a good
starting point for a visit to the area.
It also offers Victorian snob screens
and a rare opportunity to sample
Ridley's beer.

Greenwich

Cutty Sark
Ballast Quay, SE10.
Named after the famous tea clipper,

which is permanently berthed
nearby, this pub is Georgian in style
and dates from the early 1800s. It
serves draft Bass. Another nautical
public house located nearby is the
Gipsy Moth (*60 Greenwich Church
St.*), serving Taylor Walker beer.
Greenwich also has a fine Victorian
pub in the **Rose and Crown** (*1
Croom's Hill*), which serves
Courage's beer on traditional hand
pumps.

Hammersmith

Dove
19 Upper Mall, W6.
Riverside pub, with terrace, just
upstream from the splendid
Hammersmith Bridge. Part of the
pub was built by George III's son,
Prince Augustus Frederick. Rich in
historical and literary associations.
Fuller's beer. Closer to the bridge is
the **Blue Anchor** (*13 Lower Mall,
W6*), with a fine pewter bar and
enormous beer engine serving
Courage's beer.

Hampstead

Bull and Bush
North End Way, NW3 .
Popularized in song by a star of the
19thC music hall, Florrie Forde. The
"Bull" recalls the days when it was
the site of a farm, and the "Bush"
was a clump of trees planted when
it was the home of Hogarth, the
cartoonist and moralist. Among the
notables who have drunk here, in
the intervening years, Dickens
perhaps forges the link between the
earthiness of the music hall and the
artiness of Hampstead. The pub is
not far from Hampstead Heath, has
its own garden, and serves a range
of cask ale, including Tetley Bitter,
Burton's and Taylor Walker's. There
are two other historically interesting
pubs nearby: **Jack Straw's Castle**
(*also in North End Way*) and the
Spaniards Inn (*Spaniards Rd.*).

Flask
Flask Walk, NW3.
Among the well-known Hampstead
pubs, this is the best-liked locally. It
is a genuine neighborhood pub,
with interesting tiling inside and out,
a lively regular clientele and
.Young's beer. It is in a pretty
alleyway, near a couple of
bookstores, just around the corner
from Hampstead tube station.
Across the Heath there is another
Flask (*77 Highgate West Hill, N6*),
full of historical interest and serving
Tetley Bitter, Burton's and Taylor

Walker's. Both take their name from the flasks once used to carry water from wells in Hampstead.

Richmond

Orange Tree
45 Kew Rd., Richmond.
Theater pub opposite Richmond station (*for details of shows* ☎ *940-3633*). Victorian, large and rambling, yet somehow intimate. Young's beer and good range of bar meals. Richmond has several good pubs; also especially recommended is the **Old Ship** (*3 King St.*), which faces the main George St., for its Young's beer and its cheering, open fires in winter.

Southwark

Goose and Firkin
47 Borough Rd., SE1.
The beer is brewed in the cellar; bitters with names such as Goose, Borough, Dogbolter and Earthstopper bring in an enthusiastic, young clientele. Drinkers can see the brewery through a window at the same proprietor's **Fox and Firkin** (*316*

Lewisham High St., SW13), farther s. Across town, a third pub in this growing mini-chain is the **Frog and Firkin** (*41 Tavistock Crescent, W11*), not far from Portobello Rd. A firkin is a 9-gallon cask.

Mayflower
Rotherhithe St., SE16.
Close to the jetty whence the Mayflower set sail, this well-restored pub, with a veranda over the river and a restaurant, serves Charrington's IPA and Bass. Next door is the Wren church of St Mary's. In the same docklands area is one of Pepys' favorite pubs, the **Angel** (*101 Bermondsey Wall East, SE16*), serving Courage's beer.

Wapping

Prospect of Whitby
57 Wapping Wall, E1.
Completely refurbished and still desperately touristy pub in old docklands, although the history and location are genuinely interesting. The nearby **Town of Ramsgate** (*62 Wapping High St., E1*) is a more honest-to-badness pub, where hanging once took place.

Nightlife & the performing arts

After dark, the most evident activity in the West End of London (the City dies after the evening rush hour) is theater-going. It is far less formal and self-conscious than in some European cities, but even Broadway can hardly match the elegant bustle of Shaftesbury Avenue as the black cabs deposit and reclaim theater-goers. Although the best seats for a big show are expensive, the London theater does offer its patrons a wide range of prices, so only the most determinedly philistine visitor fails to catch at least one production. (Those with a busy schedule might also note that many theaters present a matinee on Saturday and one midweek day.)

For the Londoner, and for the visitor who thinks of it, a drink in a pub or a bar is a likely part of an evening at the theater, either as a rendezvous beforehand or for a nightcap afterwards; that may depend upon whether you eat before or after the show. Since most of the West End theaters are near either Soho or Covent Garden, these two neighborhoods are the most convenient, and consequently the most lively, after dark. Don't be put off by the seediness of Soho; it has lots of reasonably priced Chinese (in Gerrard, Lisle and Wardour Sts.) and Italian restaurants, and is a safe place to walk, provided you avoid the darkest alleys. For a simple stroll, Covent Garden might seem more relaxing. Elegant Mayfair has a villagey enclave called Shepherd Market, with pleasant pubs, restaurants and ladies of the night (or, often, of the broad daylight), whose presence is not excessively assertive. Elsewhere, Mayfair is, in general, an area of expensive restaurants, private clubs and casinos. The young flock around Leicester Square and Piccadilly Circus till the early hours, but the main nocturnal area out of the center of town is outrageous Chelsea; along King's Rd. and Fulham Rd. parade the latest trends, strolling (skating, or whatever) in and out of pubs, wine bars and lively restaurants.

The closing hours of pubs and restaurants, and the paucity of late-night transportation, have won London a reputation that it only partly deserves for being insufficiently nocturnal. Like an aging, dignified actress, London cherishes its beauty sleep, but isn't above the occasional exploit in the small hours. The essential precaution is to lay plans carefully. Be aware that nightclubs may require membership to be arranged in advance; and after midnight, call for a cab from the restaurant or nightclub, rather than expecting to pick one up on the street.

Ballet and opera

Royal Opera House Ⅲ
Bow St., WC2 ☎ 240-1200 (info), 240-1066 (reservations). Map 11G11. Closed Aug.
Covent Garden was always a nocturnal enclave, and its more recent crop of wine bars and restaurants has helped retain at least a hint of that. "Covent Garden" is Londoners' shorthand for the Royal Opera House, one of the most historically interesting theaters in London, with its Classical facade on Bow St. and its box office in Floral St. It is now one of the world's most important venues for opera and ballet, and the greatest artists appear regularly. Originally named the Theatre Royal, its establishment derived from the first permissions granted by King Charles II for the opening of playhouses after the Restoration. The theater of Kean and Kemble was twice burned down before the present building was completed in 1858. The Royal Opera and Royal Ballet both perform at Covent Garden in seasons of alternating productions. Postal reservations open about six weeks before the beginning of a season, and tickets are quickly snapped up, but 65 seats up in "the gods" (very high in this theater) are held until the day of the performance. Each person is permitted only one ticket, and there can be long lines, sometimes overnight.

Sadler's Wells Theatre
Rosebery Ave., EC1 ☎ 278-8916 (info and reservations). Map 5C13.
It is a strange name for a theater, and Islington is perhaps an unlikely location. The site was originally a garden in which there was a health-giving well, and its owner, whose name was Sadler, opened a "musick house" there in 1683. The theater was the base for the Sadler's Wells Royal Ballet company until its recent move to Birmingham, and now it functions as a venue for international opera, ballet and music companies. Behind Sadler's Wells is the **Lilian Bayliss** theater, hosting smaller productions and workshops.

London Coliseum
St Martin's Lane, WC2 ☎ 836-7666 (info), 836-3161 (reservations). Map 10G11.
The theater that houses one of London's largest auditoriums is barely visible from the street, but its illuminated globe stands out in the night skyline. For a long time a music hall, it now houses the English National Opera, whose prestigious, reasonably priced, large-scale productions are sung in English. In summer, the company takes a break and dance companies take over.

Other dance venues in London include the **South Bank Centre** (☎ 928-3191) and **Riverside Studios**, an excellent arts complex in Hammersmith (*Crisp Rd., W6 ☎ (081) 748-3354.*

Bars

The traditional cocktail bar is most easily found in hotels. The **Savoy**'s inspired the famous *Savoy Cocktail Book* and is believed to have been the first cocktail bar in Europe: good drinks, not much ambience. The **Ritz**, **Park Lane Hotel**, **Athenaeum** (for its 54 malt whiskies), **Inn on the Park** and **Hyde Park Hotel**, all in W1, have good cocktail bars, as do many other hotels.

Newer cocktail bars, featuring such confections as Margarita, Tequila Sunrise or Pina Colada, often double as short-order restaurants, and may be obliged by law to ensure that at least a pastrami sandwich is consumed by each drinker. Typical are **Rumours** (*33 Wellington St., WC2*) and **The Pheasantry** (*152 King's Rd., SW3*). The well-known **Groucho Club** (*44 Dean St., W1*) and **Zanzibar** (*30 Great Queen St., WC2*) are private clubs, and visitors must be introduced by a member.

A change of mood is offered by the wine bar. The traditional kind, which grew out of wine merchants' shops, is typified by **El Vino** (*47 Fleet St., EC4*), haunt of journalists and lawyers, although much quieter now that the newspaper offices have left The Street. It is a male-chauvinist establishment at which, although waitress service is extended to both sexes, ladies may not obtain their drinks at the bar.

There was a second growth of wine bars during the 1970s, and these are much more numerous. The most extrovert example, jostling with magazine folk and models, is **Brahms and Liszt** (*19 Russell St., Covent Garden, WC2*) — cockney rhyming slang for the risqué "pissed," meaning drunk. For excellent wines and good food, visit the **Cork and Bottle** (*44-46 Cranbourn St., WC2*); and, for Knightsbridge or Sloane St. shoppers, the **Ebury Wine Bar** (*139 Ebury St., SW1*) is pleasant and well run. In Holland Park, **Julie's Bar** (*137 Portland Rd., W11*) is attractive and sophisticated, and back in Soho, **Andrew Edmunds** (*46 Lexington St., W1*), next to the owner's quaint antiquarian bookstore, is charming in its simplicity, with fresh and excellent food. It is not necessary to eat in wine bars, but most provide a range of cold and some hot food.

Brasseries and champagne bars have sprung up all over the West End in recent years and are excellent for a drink and a bite to eat before the theater. Downstairs at **L'Escargot** (*48 Greek St., W1*) is comfortable and well placed for the West End theaters, as is the **Soho Brasserie** (*23 Old Compton St., W1*). **Green's** (*36 Duke St., SW1*) serves some of the best oysters in London in an attractive wood-paneled bar, and **Kettners** (*29 Romilly St., W1*) also has a pleasant champagne bar. **The Criterion** (*222 Piccadilly Circus, W1*) has a marvelous turn-of-the-century interior; **La Brasserie** (*272 Brompton Rd., SW3*) is stylish; and **Oriel Brasserie** (*50 Sloane Sq., SW3*) buzzes.

Casinos

London does have casinos, but in recent years their numbers have declined drastically before the regulatory activity of the Gaming Board. Several famous names have vanished, or had their licenses suspended, and the future of others is uncertain. It is the more urbane type of casino, usually found in the Mayfair or Knightsbridge districts, which has fallen foul of the Board, but one or two brasher places still brightly proclaim their presence in Soho. Those casinos that have remained in business are not permitted to advertise, which includes mentions in guidebooks, but they are usually known to hotel concierges. To visit one, you must either join, which takes 48hrs, or be the guest of a member.

Cinemas

London has an enormous selection of cinemas, but a lesser choice of movies. Two chains, **Cannon** and **Odeon**, dominate, and concentrate on box-office hits. Art-house films are more likely to be shown by independents, so check the *Evening Standard, Time Out* or *City Limits* for the following: the **Curzon Mayfair** (*Curzon St., W1* ☎ 499-3737), London's most comfortable cinema; the **Curzon Phoenix** (*Phoenix St., off Charing Cross Rd., WC1* ☎ 240-9661); the **Curzon West End** (*Shaftesbury Ave., W1* ☎ 439-4805); the **Gate** (*87 Notting Hill Gate, W11* ☎ 727-4034); the **Renoir** (*Brunswick Centre, Brunswick Sq., WC1* ☎ 837-8402); the **Camden Plaza** (*211 Camden High St., NW1* ☎ 485-2443); the **Chelsea Cinema** (*206 King's Rd., SW3* ☎ 351-3742); **Screen on the Hill** (*203 Haverstock Hill, NW3* ☎ 435-3366); **Screen on the Green** (*83 Upper St., N1* ☎ 226-3520); **Screen on Baker St.** (*96 Baker St., NW1* ☎ 935-2772); and the **Minema** (*45 Knightsbridge, SW1* ☎ 235-4225).

In Brixton, there's the shabby but lovable **Ritzy** (*Brixton Oval, Coldharbour Lane, SW2* ☎ 737-2121). The **Institute of Contemporary Arts** (*The Mall, SW1* ☎ 930-3647), more commonly known as the ICA, has a cinema. And the true celluloid freak heads for the **National Film Theatre** (☎ 928-3232), in the *South Bank Arts Centre*. It has two theaters presenting a wide range of films, with retrospectives on the work of individual directors and performers.

Classical music

The two most important concert venues are the *Royal Albert Hall* and the Festival Hall (in the *South Bank Arts Centre*). Each of these belongs to a different era of optimism and grand gestures.

Royal Festival Hall, Queen Elizabeth Hall, Purcell Room ⅏
South Bank, SE1 ☎ 928-3002 (info), 928-8800 (reservations). Map 11G12.

The Festival Hall, built for the Festival of Britain in 1951, is part of the *South Bank Arts Centre*, with the Queen Elizabeth Hall and the Purcell Room. Said by Toscanini to have the finest acoustics in the world, the **Festival Hall** itself, with 3,000 seats, presents concerts by the leading British and international symphony orchestras. The **Queen Elizabeth Hall** has 1,100 seats and stages chamber music, string quartets and other small ensembles. The 372-seat **Purcell Room** presents solo performances and other small events. You can see and hear perfectly from all seats, so the cheaper ones are often a good buy. All three halls offer not only classical music but also pop and jazz concerts. Early-evening conversations with celebrities of the music world are held in the Chelfield Room of the Queen Elizabeth Hall.

Royal Albert Hall ⅏
Kensington Gore, SW7 ☎ 589-3203 (info), 589-8212 (reservations). Map 15I4.

The Albert Hall, named after the Prince Consort, is a spectacular manifestation of Victorian architecture, facing Kensington Gardens and the Albert Memorial. It is self-financing, operating independently under Royal Charter. Its best-known annual event is its "Proms" ("promenade concerts"), founded in 1912 to bring the classics to a wider audience by recapturing the spirit of informal performances in London pleasure gardens. The center of the circular hall is cleared of seats for the Proms season, which runs from mid-July to early Sept, and a cheap ticket allows you to stand and wander at your leisure while you enjoy the music. Tickets are available at the door on the evening of the performance, except in the case of the Last Night of the Proms, a social event characterized by youthful nostalgia, which is reserved long in advance.

Although a wide range of classical music is performed at the Albert Hall, its keynote is eclecticism. The Hall plays host to pop singers, wrestlers, and the annual conference of the Women's Institute, when they all stand up and belt out *Jerusalem.*

Nightlife and the performing arts

Other concert halls

The new **Barbican Centre** (see *Theaters*) is now the home of the London Symphony Orchestra, which gives concerts regularly throughout the year.

There are several smaller halls. **Wigmore Hall** (*Wigmore St., W1* ☎ *935-2141*) is a famous small concert hall almost within earshot of Oxford St., where international musicians perform chamber music, particularly song and piano recitals and string quartets. Approximately one night a week, debuts are performed. **Kenwood Lakeside** (☎ *734-1877*) is a wonderful venue for large-scale orchestral performances on Hampstead Heath on summer weekends. By the lake near Kenwood House is an orchestra shell that has accommodated the Royal Philharmonic and the London Symphony, among others. It is possible to reserve a deck chair, or to sit on the grass. And performances of chamber music are given in the **Orangery** of **Kenwood House**.

There are also a number of unconventional venues, such as the cushion concerts held at the **Royal Academy** during its Summer Exhibition of paintings, open only to those aged between 14 and 30, beyond which dignity does not permit people to sit on the floor (*for times of concerts* ☎ *379-6722*). There are lunchtime recitals at some of London's most attractive and interesting churches, including **St-Martin-in-the-Fields** (☎ *839-1930*), and several of the City churches (☎ *260-1456/7 for info*). The famous boys' choir of **St Paul's** can be heard during Sun services at the Cathedral. Two other lovely venues are **Dulwich Picture Gallery** (*College Rd., SE21* ☎ *693-5254*) and **Leighton House** (*12 Holland Park Rd., W14* ☎ *602-3316*).

Folk music

The English Folk Dance and Song Society, at **Cecil Sharp House** (*2 Regent's Park Rd., NW1* ☎ *485-2206*), has performances on Sat at 7.30pm; and there is traditional English Morris Dancing at **Westminster Abbey**, in front of the main gate of Broad Sanctuary, at 8pm on Wed in summer. British, Irish and American folk music is performed in a variety of clubs and pubs, with dates listed in *Time Out* and *City Limits*.

Jazz

Big-name jazz is always available in London, despite the fact that there are only a few jazz clubs. Almost every well-known name in international jazz has played at **Ronnie Scott's** (*47 Frith St., W1* ☎ *439-0747*). It looks and feels like a club, and stays open until 3am, but anybody can enjoy the jazz; meals and drinks are served. Jazz is also performed on Mon at the **100 Club** (*100 Oxford St., W1* ☎ *636-0933*).

Each weekday evening except Mon, leading British musicians, and occasional guests from other countries, perform at the **Pizza Express** (*10 Dean St., Soho, W1* ☎ *439-8722*) and Tues-Sat at **Pizza on the Park** (*11 Knightsbridge, Hyde Park Corner, SW1* ☎ *235-5550*). Jazz cognoscenti have an affection for a pub called the **Bull's Head** (☎ *(081) 876-5241*), despite its unlikely villagey setting on the river at Barnes, SW13. It offers fine jazz nightly, especially Sun lunchtimes (*noon-2pm*), and serves Young's splendid beer. Across town is the **Bass Clef** (*35 Coronet St., N1* ☎ *729-2476*), a packed and steamy basement club.

Rock

London has an ever-lively and ever-changing rock scene. Clubs, concerts and pub dates are listed in *Time Out* and in rock newspapers such as *Melody Maker*. Most of the major rock venues are 30-45mins from the West End. They include the **Odeon, Hammersmith** (*Queen Caroline St., W6* ☎ *(081) 748-4081*); the **Earls Court Exhibition Centre** (*SW5* ☎ *385-1200*); the **Wembley Arena** (*Empire Way, Wembley, Middlesex* ☎ *(081) 902-1234*); the **Royal Albert Hall** (*Kensington Gore, SW7* ☎ *589-8212*); the **Town and Country Club** (*9-17 Highgate Rd., NW5* ☎ *(081) 284-0303*); the **Marquee** (*now at 105 Charing Cross Rd., WC2* ☎ *437-6603*); and the **Mean Fiddler** (*24-28a Harlesden High St., NW10* ☎ *(081) 961-5490*). For further venues, see *Nightclubs*, below.

Nightclubs

If nightingales still sing in Berkeley Square, their songs are directed at the habitués of **Annabel's** (*no. 44* ☎ *629-3558*). "The world's best nightclub," says London's most famous gossip columnist, Nigel Dempster. It is hermetically discreet and expensive, and you must be accompanied by a member, or be one yourself. Other smart-set nightspots are **Tramp** (*40 Jermyn St., SW1* ☎ *734-0565; members only*), **Raffles** (*287 King's Rd., SW3* ☎ *352-1091; members only*), **Tokyo Joe's** (*Clarges St., W1* ☎ *409-1832*) and the **Roof Gardens** (*99 Kensington High St., W8* ☎ *937-8923, open Thurs, Sat only*).

It is the nature of such diversions to be affected by fashion — discos have been known to open and close with alarming swiftness, or to announce a violent shift from one trend to another. Perusal of the gossip columns, in such newspapers as the *Daily Mail* and the *Evening Standard*, the high-class glossies, such as *Harpers and Queen*, and the trendy youth magazines such as *Blitz* should keep you informed. Among discos open to anybody are **Limelight** (*136 Shaftesbury Ave., WC2* ☎ *434-0572*), in a converted church; **Stringfellows** (*16 Upper St Martin's Lane, WC2* ☎ *240-5534*), pseudo-glamorous; the **Hippodrome** (*Charing Cross Rd., WC2* ☎ *437-4311*), touristy and tacky; **Café de Paris** (*3 Coventry St., WC1* ☎ *437-2036, Wed night*), trendies in a famous '40s venue; **Heaven** (*Villiers St., WC2* ☎ *839-3863*), top gay club; **Legends** (*29 Old Burlington St., W1* ☎ *437-9933*), sleek; **Xenon** (*196 Piccadilly, W1* ☎ *734-9344*), glitzy.

Many of the best nightspots for the young or young at heart to meet, see and be seen have live rock bands, as well as disco. They include **Camden Palace** (*1a Camden High St., NW1* ☎ *387-0428*), **Dingwalls** (*Camden Lock, NW1* ☎ *267-4967*) and the **Wag Club** (*35 Wardour St., W1* ☎ *437-5534*).

Theaters

Despite financial pressures, London remains one of the major world centers of theater, and the British still produce many of the greatest actors. The theater scene splits into three broad categories: companies subsidized by the state, in impressive buildings, producing serious drama to the highest standards; commercial theaters, mainly built at the turn of the century in a style of cozy splendor, mounting lighter plays and musicals; and fringe or club theaters, which might do anything anywhere, but should not be missed by serious theater-goers. The major subsidized theaters usually have several plays in repertory at one time; most others present a single play as long as it is successful.

A booth on the w side of Leicester Sq., WC2, has half-price seats to same-day shows with spare tickets in West End theaters. There is a small service charge, a maximum of four seats per person, and there can be a long line, but it is a good deal. Some shows will have tickets available on the day of performance; otherwise you can try lining up for returns. **First Call** (☎ 240-7200) is an efficient telephone credit-card reservations agency. Agencies such as this, **Keith Prowse** (☎ 741-9999) or **London Theatre Bookings** (☎ 434-1811) can usually provide tickets for the major shows, but will charge a supplement. Avoid touts. Consult the national press and listings magazines such as *Time Out* for what's on where, and watch for reviews in the quality papers.

Many theater bars welcome advance reservations for interval drinks, a system that saves the crush, frustration and thirst. Most theaters close on Sun. Cheaper seats in some of the older theaters may allow only a partial view.

Subsidized theaters

The National Theatre
Upper Ground, South Bank, SE1 ☎ 633-0880 *(info)*, 928-2252 *(reservations). Map* **11G13**.
The National Theatre company, originally under the direction of Sir Laurence Olivier, began its life at the Old Vic in the Waterloo Rd. Sir Peter Hall took over in 1973 ready for the opening of the new, custom-built theater, a modern architectural landmark, in the *South Bank Arts Centre*. He was succeeded by Richard Eyre in 1988. "The National" in fact comprises three theaters within one building. The largest, the **Olivier**, has an amphitheater setting; the **Lyttelton** has a proscenium stage; and the **Cottesloe** is a studio theater. The three present a wide range of classical and modern British and international works. Before performances there is live music in the foyers, picture galleries are open, and there are early-evening lectures, poetry readings and short plays, from 6pm. Although many performances are heavily reserved, the National always retains some seats for sale on the day, and has reduced-price standby tickets. There are also backstage tours.

Barbican Theatre (Royal Shakespeare Company)
Barbican Centre, EC2. Map **11E15** ☎ 638-8891.
The finest productions of the world's greatest dramatist, many would say. In any case, the RSC enjoys worldwide repute. This is its London base (much criticized as an uncongenial place in which to work), which complements its Stratford home (see *Excursions*) where many of the theater's productions originate. Besides Shakespeare, the company also performs a wide variety of standard and new plays. With *Nicholas Nickleby* and *The Greeks*, the company pioneered productions in which one major work spanned two or three performances. It also runs a studio theater, **The Pit**, in the Barbican. Terry Hands, the Artistic Director, was forced to close the Barbican and Pit theaters for four months from late 1990 to early 1991 because of the Company's huge financial deficit.

The Royal Court Theatre
Sloane Sq., SW1 ☎ 730-1745. *Map* **16J7**.
Despite its name, this theater has a distinguished record of healthily controversial drama. George Bernard Shaw's plays were presented here in the 1920s and 1930s; and John Osborne, the original "angry young man," and Arnold Wesker made their names here in the 1950s and 1960s. John Arden, Edward Bond and David Storey are more recent examples. There is also a smaller **Theatre Upstairs**, a studio space for new writers, which, like the Barbican, recently had to close for a time due to lack of funds.

Commercial theaters
The oldest theater in London is the **Theatre Royal** (*Drury Lane, WC2* ☎ 240-9066), which specializes in musicals and hit shows. The most elegant is the **Theatre Royal, Haymarket** (*SW1* ☎ 930-9832), presenting a high standard of "legitimate" theater. Both date back to the Restoration. Other period pieces are the lovely **Criterion** (*Piccadilly Circus, W1* ☎ 867-1117) and the

twin **Aldwych** (*WC2* ☎ *836-6404*) and **Strand** (*Aldwych, WC2* ☎ *836-2660*), theaters, designed by W.G.R. Sprague. The most famous is probably the **London Palladium** (*Argyll St., W1* ☎ *437-7373*), which has a policy of family entertainment, and plays host to international stars. **St Martin's** (*West St., Cambridge Circus, WC2* ☎ *836-1443*) stages the world's longest-running play, *The Mousetrap.* **Regent's Park Open Air Theatre** (*NW1* ☎ *486-2431*) presents Shakespeare throughout the summer.

Fringe theater
London's fringe scene is alive and kicking, and often exciting. Read *Time Out* for details of what's on where. Tiny rooms above noisy pubs often serve as fringe venues, but among the best permanent venues are the following:

As well as the excellent and well-established **Lyric** (*King St.,* ☎ *(081) 741-2311*), Hammersmith offers the **Riverside Studios** (*Crisp Rd., W12* ☎ *(081) 748-3354*) and **The Bush** (*Shepherd's Bush Green* ☎ *(081) 743-3388*), a pub theater. Another pub theater is the **King's Head** (*115 Upper St., N1* ☎ *226-1916*), and near there is the **Almeida** (*Almeida St., N1* ☎ *359-4404*). In Swiss Cottage is the **Hampstead Theatre Club** (*Avenue Rd., NW3* ☎ *722-9301*), and east London has the **Theatre Royal Stratford East** (*Gerry Raffles Sq., E15* ☎ *(081) 534-0310*) and the **Half Moon** (*213 Mile End Rd., E1* ☎ *(081) 790-4000*). In central London is Soho's **Donmar Warehouse** (*41 Earlham St., WC2* ☎ *240-8230*).

Shopping

It is nothing as mundane as shopping that you do in London. It is promenading in the trendy King's Rd. on a Saturday afternoon after having strolled along the Portobello Rd. in the morning. It is listening to the spiel in Petticoat Lane's street market on a Sunday morning. It is exploring the world's most famous department store, **Harrods**, in Knightsbridge, and comparing its food with the exotica at **Fortnum & Mason** in Piccadilly. It is window-dreaming of jade and jewels in Bond St. Depending upon your inclinations, it is the sensation of silk in **Liberty**, or of snuff in Jermyn St. It is relaxing in Covent Garden and wondering whether you need a French horn from **Paxman** (*116 Long Acre, WC2*) or a quill pen from **Philip Poole** (*105 Great Russell St., WC1*).

These neighborhoods form a jigsaw stretching five or six miles across the center of London from Chelsea in the w to Petticoat Lane in the e. Each of them is worth half a day of anyone's time, and every one leads to another. None of them is London's principal shopping street, although several of them are linked by it. The main shopping thoroughfare, and the most democratic, is Oxford St., which itself runs from w to e (assuming that you see the most traditional end first). It is a giant version of the main shopping street of every town or city in Britain.

Prices
In London, prices are not generally negotiable, although bargaining is acceptable in some street markets. In most shops, all major credit cards are accepted.

Exemption from Value Added Tax on goods bought for export is sometimes offered. VAT is not negligible: it adds substantially to the price of any item costing a few pounds or more, so do ask. You must show your passport and fill in a form.

Hours

Shops do not stay open as late as in some other countries. Most shops open Mon-Sat 9am-5.30pm, with "late-night" shopping once a week. The Chelsea and Knightsbridge area stays open until 7pm on Wed, and Oxford St. until 8pm on Thurs. Some consolation is that few shops close for lunch. Some shops in Bond St. and a few others in the West End close on Sat. Central London shops do not as yet open on Sun, although it is the subject of continuing discussion in Parliament.

Although central London has few "local" or "corner" shops, inner-city neighborhoods have plenty, and they often open until mid-evening, or even midnight, and on Sun.

Antiques

At the top end of the price range, and for the best that money can buy, visit the specialty shops in **Bond St., W1**, and the adjoining streets and arcades. Examples range from the **Antique Porcelain Company** (*149 New Bond St.*) to **The Leger Galleries** (*13 Old Bond St.*), for Old Masters, or **Mallet and Son** (*40 New Bond St.*), for fine English furniture. The serious buyer will also head out to **Kensington Church St., W8**, which has several high-quality shops. At the s end of this hilly street, **Simon Castle**, upstairs at no.38, deals in wooden objects, particularly inlaid boxes and models; **Michael German**, on the ground floor, specializes in walking sticks and firearms; farther up is **The Lacquer Chest**, at no. 75; at the Notting Hill end, **Philip and Bernard Dombey** sell antique clocks at no. 174. Nearby is **Westbourne Grove, W2**, for cheaper antiques, and for fascinating shops such as **Dodo**, at no. 286, which deals in interesting old advertising materials. The **New King's Rd.** beyond World's End is also peppered with quality antique stores. Farther on, **Wandsworth Bridge Rd.** has shops dealing in pine.

Over the years, several permanent, indoor antique markets have been established. In the **Bond St.** area, at **Gray's Mews Antique Market** (*58 Davies St. and 1-7 Davies Mews, W1*), there are about 300 stalls, in a pleasant, well-appointed former factory building, with a lot of Art Nouveau and Deco, and several excellent stalls for tin toys.

Among the indoor markets, the insiders prefer **Alfies** (*13-25 Church St., NW8*), rather isolated from shopping areas in Marylebone, selling old lace, antique photographic equipment, genuine antique street signs, etc., with the added interest of the bustle, gossip and dealing. The other neighborhood for indoor markets is **Chelsea/Kensington**. The **Chelsea Antique Market** (*245-53 King's Rd., SW3*) is a maze of stalls, run by seasoned dealers in all types of antiques. **Antiquarius** (*135-41 King's Rd.*), at the corner of Flood St., has always been very conscious of trends, and **Chenil Galleries** (*181-83 King's Rd.*) specialize in fine art and quality antiques. (See also *Street markets* p188.) For both antique and modern silver, it's fascinating to explore the **London Silver Vaults** (*53 Chancery Lane, WC2*).

Auction houses

Auctions are a part of London's metropolitan life. Don't be intimidated by newspaper stories of six-figure bids; most items go for much less, and, if you keep your hand firmly on your lap, you can enjoy the auction without parting with any money. It is not necessary to reserve a seat, and there are always viewing days beforehand. Most renowned are the following:
Bonhams (*Montpelier St., SW7☎ 584-9161*) is especially good

for furniture and paintings. You may pick up a bargain.
Christie's (*8 King St., SW1* ☎ *839-9060*) is one of the two great
names: fine art, and specialty auctions, including wine sales.
Their other salesroom (*85 Old Brompton Rd., South Kensington,
SW7*) has less expensive general items.
Phillips (*101 New Bond St., W1* ☎ *629-6602*) has prices usually
in the medium range. Objets d'art, and various collectibles.
Sotheby's (*34/5 New Bond St., W1* ☎ *493-8080*) is the other
great name, and the biggest. Fine art, porcelain, jewelry, clothing,
books, Victoriana and decorative arts.

Books

The street for the bibliophile is **Charing Cross Rd., WC2**, with
numerous shops, including **Foyle's** (one of the world's biggest)
at no. 119, **Waterstone's** next door, and **Books Etc**, with its
bargain basement, opposite. In fascinating alleys such as Cecil
Court, hours pass quickly in the secondhand bookstores. Regular
shops of particular interest are **Zwemmer** at no. 80, for art,
architecture and cinema; and **Collet's**, at nos. 129-31, for political
and philosophical works of the Left.

Away from Charing Cross Rd., the most comprehensive
selection is to be found at **Dillon's** (*82 Gower St., WC1*).
Hatchards, in Piccadilly, is a pleasant, well-stocked general
bookstore, and the **Pan Bookshop** (*158 Fulham Rd., SW3*) is
useful for hardbacks as well as paperbacks and stays open until
10pm Mon-Sat. The excellent and well-laid-out **Economists'
Bookshop** (*Clare Market, Portugal St., WC2*) specializes in
economics and other social sciences. The **Children's Book
Centre** (*237 Kensington High St., W8*) has an impressive stock
for children up to age 14, and helpful assistants.

Chemists/drugstores

Harley Street's supplier, nearby **John Bell and Croyden** (*50
Wigmore St., W1*), can meet any pharmaceutical need, and the
shop carries cosmetics. Homeopathic specialist **A. Nelson** (*73
Duke St., W1*), by appointment to the Queen, has wonderfully
Victorian premises. For more conventional needs, **Boots** has
branches all over London. **Bliss Chemist** (*5 Marble Arch, W1*)
stays open daily until midnight.

China

The English invented bone china, and the famous names display
themselves proudly in **Regent St., W1**, especially Wedgwood
and Spode at **Gered** (*no.158*). There is an even more opulent
display at **Thomas Goode** (*19 South Audley St., W1*), with its
Minton elephants within range of the hunting rifles across the
road at the gunsmith's **James Purdey & Sons**. China, glassware,
and all sorts of elegant household goods can be found at the
General Trading Company (*144 Sloane St., SW1*), near Sloane
Sq., and at department stores such as **Liberty**, **John Lewis**,
Selfridges and **Harrods** (see p186). **Chinacraft** (*Regent St., W1,
New Bond St., W1, and branches*) has a noteworthy selection.

Clothes
Clothes for children

Britain's maritime tradition is upheld even for children by Rowes
in the **White House** (*51 New Bond St., W1*), which began by
making clothes for the children of naval families. This traditional
line shares the shop with such children's classics as button-bar
shoes and velvet-collared tweed coats. Visit **Liberty** (see

Department stores p186), **Bambino** (*77 New Bond St., W1*),
Bananas (*7 Clarendon Cross, W11*), **012 Benetton** (*131
Kensington High St. , and branches*) and **Anthea More-Ede** (*16
Victoria Grove, W8*).

Clothes for men
Savile Row is the place for suits, Jermyn St. for accouterments.
These are definitive addresses for the English gentleman.

In **Savile Row, W1**, the appositely named **H. Huntsman and
Sons**, at no. 11, is famous for riding clothes and has been a tailor
to royalty for more than a hundred years; very expensive, and no
credit cards. Other renowned names include **Gieves & Hawkes**,
at no. 1, **Anderson & Sheppard** at no. 30, and **Tommy Nutter**,
fraternized by Elton John and Mick Jagger, at no. 19.

For classic and casual suits, try **Blades of Savile Row** (*8
Burlington Gdns., W1*). Also nearby is **Austin Reed** (*103 Regent
St.*), **Aquascutum** (*100 Regent St., W1*) and **Jaeger** (*200 Regent
St., W1*). **Crolla** (*35 Dover St.*) sells wonderfully *outré* clothes for
men (and women) in beautiful rococo brocade prints. Brocade is
also a specialty of **The Waistcoat Gallery** (*2 New Burlington Pl.,
W1*), which reflects the return to fashion of the waistcoat for men
and women. **Paul Smith** (*41-44 Floral St.*), in Covent Garden, is
another trendy menswear store with a good name.

In **Jermyn St., SW1**, a man can no longer sweat out a
hangover in the Turkish baths, but he can still have a shave and
haircut, buy himself a clean shirt and prepare to face the world. It
is still a male street, in the debonair sense of the word. Buy
moustache wax or a badger-hair shaving brush at **Trumpers**, no.
20, or an antique meerschaum at **Astleys**, no. 109. Top-quality
shirts are available from **Harvie and Hudson**, at nos. 77 and 97,
or the extrovert **Turnbull and Asser**, at nos. 69, 71 and 72. For a
bowler hat (a "derby" to Americans) for town wear, where better
to go nearby than the originators of the style, **James Lock** (*6 St
James's St., SW1*)? For a tweed cap, visit **Bates** (*21a Jermyn St.*),
where the shop's late cat (it died in 1921) watches you from a
glass case. Of the department stores, **Simpson's** (*203 Piccadilly,
W1*) is noted both for menswear and women's clothes.

Out of the way in Fulham, but with the same traditional
standards, is **Hackett** (*65a New King's Rd., SW6 , and branches*),
which sells everything the English gentleman needs.

Clothes for women
Young British designers are much in the international limelight
these days, and London's role as a fashion center, although not
on a par with Paris or Rome, has grown apace of late.

The **Bond St.** area has the premises of international designers
such as **Chanel** (*26 Old Bond St.*), **Karl Lagerfeld** (*173 New
Bond St.*), **Ralph Lauren** (*143 New Bond St.*), **Saint Laurent**
(*113 and 135 New Bond St.*) and **Valentino** (*160 New Bond St.*),
and of internationally-known British designers such as **Zandra
Rhodes** (*14a Grafton St., W1*), weaving fantasies from chiffon.

For more accessible creations, nearby **South Molton St., W1**,
is browsily full of interesting clothes and best known for high
fashion and sporty items at the several **Browns** shops. Similar
lines and accessories abound in shops such as **Nicole Farhi** and
Mulberry (*St Christophers Pl., W1*), just across Oxford St.
Perennially popular floral prints and ruffled blouses are to be
found at **Laura Ashley** (*256-58 Regent St., W1, and branches*).

Head w via **Knightsbridge**, **Sloane St.** and **Brompton Rd.**,
dropping in at department stores such as **Harvey Nichols**
(*Knightsbridge, SW1*), renowned for high fashion, and **Harrods**
(see *Department stores* p186), en route to Joseph Ettedgui's

Sloane St. empire, **Joseph Bis**, **Joseph Tricot** and **Esprit** for trendy stylish clothes. Another of Joseph's shops, **Kenzo**, no. 17, and nearby **Krizia**, no. 36, are both strong on knitwear, and the spacious new **Valentino** shop, no. 174, is exciting if pricey. **Giorgio Armani** has moved his collection from New Bond St. to no. 178. Top British designer **Katharine Hamnett** sells her designs from no. 20; a shop so striking, with its fish tanks and metal lobster sculptures in the window, wire lights and drapes inside, that it's hard to concentrate on the clothes.

Turn right at Pont St., which leads to **Beauchamp Pl., SW3**. This pretty little street is crammed with fashion, from elegant **Bruce Oldfield** at no. 27, by way of **The Beauchamp Pl. Shop** at nos. 37 (for dressy designer clothes) and 55 (for a more casual look) and ethereal **Monsoon** at no. 53, to smart **Caroline Charles** at nos. 56-7. And go to **Janet Reger** at no. 2 for provocative lingerie.

Head toward **South Kensington**, where the new **Emporio Armani** (*191 Brompton Rd., SW3*) aims to make a designer label more affordable, and British designer **Jasper Conran** has his shop at no. 303. Continue to the **King's Rd., Chelsea, SW3**, now best known for the bizarre, and often ephemeral, but always offering a wide variety of visual stimuli. Punk was popularized at no. 153, at a shop originally called "Acme Attractions," then renamed **Boy**. Some of the most flamboyant attractions are grouped around a shop named after its location, **World's End** (but remembered by early punks as "Seditionaries"), at no. 430, which now sells Vivienne Westwood's designs; look out for the high-speed clock, which whirls around backward.

(See also *Department stores* p186. All have women's fashion departments.)

Knitwear
The hugely successful Italian chain, **Benetton**, has branches all over London (*including 23 Brompton Rd., SW3*). British specialties, such as chunky knits and tweeds, can be bought from the **Irish Shop** (*11 Duke St., W1*). **The Scotch House** (*2 Brompton Rd., SW3, 84 Regent St., W1, and branches*) is the shop for Fair Isle, Shetland, Pringle, Ballantyne and tartans. More imaginative sweaters are to be found at **Scottish Merchant** (*16 New Row, Covent Garden*); it sells handmade designers' sweaters in beautiful patterns and colors. Visit **Peal & Co.** for cashmere and luxury, in majestic Burlington Arcade, W1, one shop for women and men. More economical are **Westaway and Westaway** (*62-5 and 92-3 Great Russell St., WC1*), famous for bargains, and **Marks and Spencer** (see *Department stores* p186).

Outerwear
For both men and women, tweed jackets, high-quality trench coats and double-breasted raincoats are the specialties at **Aquascutum** (*100 Regent St., W1*). Plaid-lined raincoats and fine cashmere coats are the hallmarks of **Burberrys** (*18-22 Haymarket, SW1*). For walking stick or umbrella go to **James Smith & Sons** (*53 New Oxford St., WC1*).

Crafts
Contemporary Applied Arts (*43 Earlham St., Covent Garden, WC2*) sells original ceramics and jewelry. Also in Covent Garden, on Sat, is Britain's largest display of crafts, at the **Jubilee Market**. If you feel you need to know a little more before you go shopping for this particular type of merchandise, visit the **Crafts Council** (*12 Waterloo Pl., SW1, off Pall Mall*): not a shop but an exhibition center. However, there is a good **Crafts Council**

Shop in the V & A. Other specialty craft stores are the **Craftsmen Potters Shop** (*Marshall St., W1*), on the site of William Blake's house in Soho, noteworthy for stoneware, and the **Contemporary Textile Gallery** (*10 Golden Sq., W1*). **The Design Centre** (*28 Haymarket, SW1*) is an essential port of call for those interested in contemporary British products.

Department stores

Household names abound, especially along **Oxford St.**, where **Selfridges** introduced the American concept of the department store in 1909. Closer to Oxford Circus, a much more British response can be seen in the sober but reliable **John Lewis**. The four shops listed below are tourist attractions in their own right.

Fortnum & Mason (*181 Piccadilly, W1*) is an aristocratic and exotic grocery store with tail-coated assistants, founded by a footman to Queen Anne, famed for preserves, biscuits, and the like. Have afternoon tea in the Fountain or St James's restaurant. The upstairs floors are devoted to fashion and other items.

Harrods (*Knightsbridge, SW1: actually in Brompton Rd.*) is the biggest and best-known department store. Imperial flourishes such as the zoo have been trimmed, but the food hall still feels and looks like Britain's greatest provisions merchant. Harrods will get you anything, even if it has to be ordered. In fashion and homemaking, a very wide range of tastes is met.

Liberty (*Regent St., W1*) gave its name to a design style embracing fabrics, silver, glassware and furniture during the Art Nouveau period. "Liberty prints" and "Liberty silks" are still renowned. This heritage is evident, as are the store's origins as an importer of Oriental goods, although today's range of merchandise is much wider. Worth a visit just for its 1924 mock-Elizabethan building.

Marks and Spencer (*458 and 173 Oxford St., W1, and branches*): it is for knitwear and other items of well-made, mainly British clothing that visitors go to M & S (the Marble Arch branch has the best range of men's and women's fashion); local office workers shop there for superb convenience food. Excellent value. Not a department store in the traditional sense — but what a metamorphosis from the old utilitarian "Marks & Sparks"!

Fine art

The commercial galleries are predominantly in two short and elegant streets in Mayfair, W1, **Cork St.** and **Albemarle St.**, and in nearby parts of **Bond St.** Of special note is **Thomas Agnew & Son** (*43 Old Bond St.*), selling paintings from all periods. For contemporary art, go to **Browse and Darby** (*19 Cork St.*), **Christies** (*8 King St.*) and **Marlborough Fine Art** (*6 Albemarle St.*), which often deals in the really big names. A few galleries, such as **Smith's** (*54-6 Earlham St.*) and the **Paton Gallery** (*2 Langley St.*), have opened in Covent Garden, WC2.

Food and drink

Don't visit London without "laying down" an English Christmas pudding from one of the great department stores (see above). Their food halls offer an experience that is uniquely metropolitan, even if the biscuits come from Bath or Carlisle, the shortbread and whisky from Scotland, and they all have well-presented gift packs of teas and other specialties. Their hampers, which can be sent abroad, are costly but fabulous.

Gourmet foods also dazzle the eye at **Hobbs** (*29 South Audley St., W1*). All these shops and food halls incorporate excellent wine merchants; a specialty vintner of note is the long-established **Berry Bros. & Rudd** (*3 St James's St., SW1*), whose shop contains a superb pair of antique scales. For the finest selection of Scotch whiskies (single malts, not the commercial blends) go to the **Soho Wine Market** (*3 Greek St., W1*).

Other specialty food stores include the following.

For chocolates **Bendicks** (*55 Wigmore St., W1, 107 Long Acre, WC2 , and branches*), which holds the royal warrant; **Charbonnel et Walker** (*28 Old Bond St., W1*); and **Prestat**, (*14 Princes Arcade, Piccadilly, SW1*).

For the best English cheese and ham **Paxton & Whitfield** (*93 Jermyn St., SW1*).

For health foods, including superb breads **Cranks** (*8 Marshall St., W1*), or the extraordinary selection of shops in **Neal's Yd**. (*Earlham St., Covent Garden, WC2*). **& Clarke's** (*122 Kensington Church St., W8*) also sells wonderful, unusual breads and unpasteurized cheeses, as well as exquisite homemade chocolate truffles.

For teas **R. Twining and Co.** (*216 Strand, WC2*).

Household goods

Conran (*81 Fulham Rd., SW3*) and **Habitat** (*206 King's Rd., SW3, and branches*) have dominated British household design for two decades, and the new **Conran Shop**, which has moved across Fulham Rd. into the old Michelin garage, is more stylish and impressive than ever. A stunning collection of Bauhaus-inspired furniture, Oriental-style flooring, colorful ethnic fabrics and rugs is displayed upstairs, while a vast array of ornaments, accessories, gifts, books and toys are to be found in the basement. There is also an attractive, affordable oyster bar on the ground floor, perfect for an elegant lunch. Habitat is also merged with **Heal's** (*196 Tottenham Court Rd., W1*); both are now part of the Conran empire. For more traditional furniture, try **Maples** (*145 Tottenham Court Rd., W1*). **Joseph** (*77-9 Fulham Rd., SW3*) has smart up-to-the-minute household accessories.

Jewelry

London's diamond center, mainly for the trade, is **Hatton Garden, EC1**. Some shops, such as **R. Holt**, at no. 98, welcome the public. The royal jewelers are **Garrard** (*112 Regent St., W1*). Anything from a jewel box to a gold-plated toothbrush can be had at **Asprey** (*165 New Bond St., W1*); here too is **Cartier** (*175 New Bond St., W1*). For fashionable costume jewelry, visit **Butler and Wilson** (*189 Fulham Rd., SW3, and 20 South Molton St., W1*). **The London Diamond Centre** (*10 Hanover St., W1*) has a vast collection of cut and uncut diamonds .

Music

The biggest record store is **HMV** (*150 Oxford St., W1*), with a vast stock covering all categories. Specialty shops include: **Virgin Records** (*14-30 Oxford St., W1*), for British rock and new wave; **Rough Trade** (*130 Talbot Rd., W11*), some way out of the center, geographically as well as musically; **Collets** (*129-31 Charing Cross Rd., WC2*), for Eastern European folk music; and jazz buffs will also want to see the famous **Dobells** (*21 Tower St., W1, off Shaftesbury Ave.* ☎ *240-1354*). **The Gramophone Exchange** (*3 Betterton St., WC2* ☎ *836-0976*) specializes in second-hand records. Classical music is available from **Farringdon Records** (*52 High Holborn, WC1* ☎ *831-4116*) and **Tower Records** (*1 Piccadilly Circus, W1* ☎ *439-2500*).

Shopping

Perfumers

All the international brands are best bought in department stores; **Harrods** boasts one of the largest selections. For English flower perfumes, visit the established **Floris** (*89 Jermyn St., SW1*) or the fashionably traditional **Penhaligon's** (*41 Wellington St., WC2*).

Photographic supplies

To buy a camera, try **City Camera Exchange** (*124 High Holborn, WC1, and branches*) or **Dixons** (*88 Oxford St., W1, and branches*). For films, use the **Boots** or **W. H. Smith** chains, which also develop films fast. **Fast Foto Centre** (*15 Knightsbridge Green, SW1*) sells film and has a 4hr processing service. **Foto Inn** (*35 South Molton St., W1*) proposes a 1hr service. For emergency repairs: **Advance Technical** (*9 St Anne's Ct., W1*) and **Sendean** (*105 Oxford St., W1*).

Shoes

Fashion shoe stores crowd **Bond St.** and **South Molton St.**, W1. Men who want the best and can wait for it order custom-made boots fit for royalty from **John Lobb** (*9 St James's St., SW1*), who keep on the premises a wooden last of every customer. Sturdy, traditional footwear can be bought nearby at **Maxwell's** (*11 Savile Row, W1*), and slightly less expensively at **Tricker's** (*67 Jermyn St., SW1*) and **Church's** (*163 New Bond St., W1*).

For women, the most expensive and stylish shoes in London are hand-made and sold by **Manolo Blahnik** (*48-51 Old Church St., SW3*). Excellent-quality Italian leather shoes are available from **Ferragamo** (*24 Old Bond St., W1*), **Bruno Magli** (*49 New Bond St., and branches*) and **Rayne** (*15-16 Old Bond St., and branches*), where the Queen buys shoes. Well-made shoes at more affordable prices are sold by **Bertie** (*48 South Molton St., W1*), **Hobbs** (*47 South Molton St.*) and **Pied à Terre** (*19 South Molton St.*); all three have other branches in London.

Shopping centers

Based on the concept of American malls, a number of new centers, which bring together a multiplicity of big name shops, restaurants, cafés, movie theaters and other facilities under one roof, have sprung up over central London in the last few years. Shopping is made easy, when you can buy everything you need, have a cup of coffee or lunch and then watch a movie without getting blisters or soaked to the skin. The most recent and lavish of these is **Whiteleys** (*Queensway, W2*), a converted department store, which retains its original sweeping glass roof. Other centers in the same mold are **Tobacco Dock** in Docklands and **London Pavilion** in Piccadilly.

Street markets

The famous ones are still fun, but see some of the others, too. London has 50 or 60 street markets and it is here that the town best demonstrates its wit, wisdom and elusive code. If you demonstrate your own, you might knock prices down. No credit cards are accepted, only English checks, so take cash.
Portobello Road Sat antique market is especially well known for its silver. Easy to find — and to explore, since it is basically one street — but it stretches for more than 1 mile. Start by taking the underground to Notting Hill Gate, and walk via Pembridge Rd., W11, following the crowd. Antiques and junk come first, then freaky shops, and finally food, at the N end.
Petticoat Lane (*Middlesex St., E1*), a junk market in the East End

on Sun, and only one part of a maze of street trade where the patois embraces cockney rhyming slang, Yiddish and Bengali. Serious bargain-hunters start at the improbable hour of 4am with the Cheshire St. (E2) and Brick Lane (E1) areas, where the action subsides well before 9am. The more touristic Petticoat Lane itself (real name, Middlesex Street) is in full swing by then, and impossibly crowded by 11am. Take lunch at Bloom's (see *Restaurants*); you'll have to line up, but after that early start, the chicken soup will be manna. The nearest underground stations are Liverpool Street and Aldgate East.

Camden Passage (*Camden Passage, N1*): Wed and Sat for good-quality antiques; Thurs for books, prints and drawings. Art Deco is something of a theme in the market, especially in the Athenai Arcade. Everyone goes to the Camden Head pub or Natalie's coffee shop for refreshment. Go by tube to Angel and walk up Islington High St.

Bermondsey (New Caledonian) (*Long Lane and Tower Bridge Rd., SE1*), on Fri: the insiders' antique market, where the cognoscenti hunt by flashlight at 5am, grab their purchases by 8.30am at the latest, then retire for breakfast at the Rose Dining Rooms. As if that weren't a sufficiently daunting venture, the market is also hard to find. Thus it is that Bermondsey has remained a market for the seriously interested. Go by underground to London Bridge, and walk down Bermondsey St.

Camden Lock (*Camden High St./Chalk Farm Rd., NW1*), Sat and Sun market with an entertaining mix of junk and attractions, including books, musical instruments, crafts, clothing, jewelry and snacks. It stretches for a mile from Chalk Farm underground. The main market is by Regent's Canal.

Greenwich Antique Market (*Greenwich High Rd., SE10*), held on Sat and Sun in summer, is devoted to antiques, books and bric-a-brac. **Greenwich Covered Crafts Market** is in nearby College Approach on Sat and Sun.

Toys

The biggest toy store in the world is **Hamleys** (*188 Regent St., W1*). Parents who believe play should be educative favor **Galt Toys**, within Liberty (see *Department stores* p186), and the **Early Learning Centre** (*225 Kensington High St., W8, and numerous other branches*). **Frog Hollow** (*15 Victoria Grove, W8*) has unusual wooden and fabric toys, and **Tiger Tiger** (*219 King's Rd., SW3*) a good selection of soft animals. Victorian reproductions are available at **Pollock's Toy Museum** (*21 Scala St., W1, and Covent Garden Market, WC2*).

Biographies

A list of the famous whose names are linked with London would be endless. The following personal selection pays particular attention to those mentioned in this book.

Adam, Robert (1728-92)
The great Scottish Neo-Classical architect and designer brought new refinement to the town and country houses of London.

Albert, Prince (1819-61)
Queen Victoria's consort endeared himself to Londoners, despite his German origin. He left his stamp on the capital in the massive *Kensington* museum and learned society complex.

Biographies

Bacon, Sir Francis *(1561-1626)*
The great philosopher and statesman of the Elizabethan and Jacobean period was a member of **Gray's Inn**.

Boadicea *(died AD61)*
Now considered a national heroine, the warlike queen led her Iceni tribe against the Romans, razing London to the ground before her defeat. Her statue graces Westminster Bridge.

Browning, Robert *(1812-89)*
Apart from 15yrs spent in Italy with his wife Elizabeth Barrett of Wimpole St. fame, the Victorian poet spent most of his life in London, largely by the **Grand Union Canal** at Little Venice.

Carlyle, Thomas *(1795-1881)*
Author of *The French Revolution* and in many ways the essential Victorian intellectual, Carlyle lived for 47yrs in **Chelsea** in preference to his native Scotland. **Carlyle's House** is as he left it.

Charles I *(1600-49)*
The most ambitious of Britain's royal patrons ended his reign on the scaffold after defeat in the Civil War with Parliament. He was led to his execution from his own **Banqueting House**.

Charles II *(1630-85)*
Perhaps the most flamboyant of kings, Charles II enjoys enduring fame thanks to his indiscreet relationships with the likes of Nell Gwynne. More significantly, he was a great patron of the London theater, developed the royal parks and presided over the rebuilding of the **City**.

Chaucer, Geoffrey *(c.1340-1400)*
The greatest of the medieval English poets was for many years a senior customs official of the port of London. The pilgrims of *The Canterbury Tales* set off from a Southwark inn.

Churchill, Sir Winston *(1874-1965)*
The steadfastness of the wartime national leader helped Londoners endure the horrors of the German bombing of their city — the Blitz. This he successfully organized from his secret **Cabinet War Rooms** bunker in **Whitehall.**

Constable, John *(1776-1837)*
The great painter of the English countryside lived for many years in **Hampstead**. Several of his finest works, on view at the **Victoria & Albert Museum**, show views of the Heath. He is buried in Hampstead parish churchyard.

Coram, Thomas *(c.1668-1751)*
This bluff sea captain became one of the 18thC's leading philanthropists in his retirement, setting up the Foundling Hospital. The **Coram Foundation** displays works by the artists whom Coram enlisted into his fund-raising efforts.

Cubitt, Thomas *(1788-1855)*
To this energetic man can be credited some of the finest housing in London. Establishing the first modern building firm and inventing the concept of "speculative builder," he constructed much of **Bloomsbury** and **Belgravia**.

Dickens, Charles *(1812-70)*
In novels such as *Oliver Twist* and *The Old Curiosity Shop*, Dickens drew attention to the appalling social deprivations of Victorian London.

Edward the Confessor *(c.1002-66)*
This pious king began the Normanization of England that culminated in the Conquest. He also reinforced the importance of London by establishing his palace at **Westminster**.

Flamsteed, John *(1646-1719)*
The first Astronomer Royal, working largely at the Royal Observatory at **Greenwich**, recorded no fewer than 3,000 stars.

Garrick, David (1717-79)

The English stage's greatest actor/manager, Garrick established the naturalistic style that modern acting takes for granted. Most of his performances were in **Covent Garden**.

Gibbons, Grinling (1648-1721)

Wren's master-carver decorated many of the great architect's outstanding buildings with incomparably naturalistic flowers, leaves, fruits, musical instruments — all sculpted in wood or stone with Baroque exuberance. The greatest profusion is to be seen at **St Paul's Cathedral** or **Hampton Court**.

Gibbs, James (1682-1754)

Continuing where Wren had left off, this Scottish architect introduced some of the more theatrical elements of the Italian Baroque to London church building. Excellent examples can be seen at **St Mary-le-Strand** and **St Martin-in-the-Fields**.

Gresham, Sir Thomas (1519-79)

Founder of the **Royal Exchange**, Gresham was one of the great merchants and financiers of the Elizabethan age, when London began to establish its dominance in international commerce.

Henry VIII (1491-1547)

The heavy hand of this powerful monarch was repeatedly felt in London — not least in the dissolution of the monasteries. Among more positive achievements, he moved the chief royal palace to **Whitehall** (giving Westminster to Parliament) and built up **St James's Palace** and **Hampton Court**.

Hogarth, William (1697-1764)

With the sharpest of all eyes for social foible or moral weakness, Hogarth in his paintings and engravings has given us an unforgettable picture of the seamier sides of life in 18thC London. **Hogarth's House** at **Chiswick** is now a museum.

Johnson, Dr. Samuel (1709-84)

The giant of 18thC letters patronized the pubs of **Fleet Street**, the coffeehouses of **Covent Garden** and wrote his famous dictionary at **Dr. Johnson's House** nearby.

Jones, Inigo (1573-1652)

With this architect, the ideas of the Italian Renaissance came to England with extraordinary sureness and originality. Examples of his bold vision can be seen in the Queen's House at **Greenwich**, the **Banqueting House** and **Covent Garden**.

Keats, John (1795-1821)

The perfect romantic poet, and a consumptive to boot, wrote much of his best work at **Hampstead** (see **Keats' House**).

Marx, Karl (1818-83)

Writing in German in the **British Museum**, the political economist whose theories split the world down the middle lived for most of his life as an exile in **Soho** and N London. Pilgrims flock to his grave in the Cemetery at **Highgate**.

Nash, John (1752-1835)

Marble Arch, Regent's Park and Carlton House Terrace in **The Mall** are the visible legacies of this Regency architect. Just as significant is the fine town planning scheme of which Regent St. forms the main axis.

Pepys, Samuel (1633-1703)

Recording the Great Plague and Fire of London, Pepys' diary is an outstanding social document, presenting an irresistible account of daily life in the 17thC city.

Prince Regent (1762-1830)

In many ways a ludicrous figure, the Regent (later George IV) led the nation in fashion and sport, and backed the ambitious town-planning schemes of John Nash.

Rogers, Richard *(born 1933)*
Innovative contemporary architect who, having won acclaim for his Pompidou Center in Paris, was commissioned to build the controversial Lloyd's Building in the *City*. His most recent work includes the restoration and conversion of Billingsgate Market.

Shakespeare, William *(1564-1616)*
The London stage saw the first productions of almost all the bard's plays — usually in the theaters of *Southwark*, where he worked, although sometimes in the halls of the *Inns of Court*.

Sloane, Sir Hans *(1660-1753)*
The *British Museum*, *Natural History Museum* and *Museum of Mankind* all ultimately owe their existence to this successful physician's vast collections, bequeathed to the nation.

Tyler, Wat *(died 1381)*
After his capture of the *Tower of London*, the leader of the great Peasant's Revolt of 1381 was killed by the Lord Mayor of London while attempting to parley with Richard II at Smithfield.

Wellington, Duke of *(1769-1852)*
The leading British general of the Napoleonic Wars, Wellington ultimately defeated Napoleon at the Battle of Waterloo. He went on to become an authoritarian prime minister, during which time he lived at *Apsley House*, now the Wellington Museum.

Whittington, Dick *(1358-1423)*
A rich merchant and the greatest medieval Lord Mayor of London, Whittington has passed into legend. In the quintessential rags-to-riches story, he paused in flight from the City on Highgate Hill (accompanied by his famous cat), when the bells of *St Mary-le-Bow* called him back to greatness.

William the Conqueror *(c.1027-87)*
Having defeated the English and declared himself their first Norman king, William consolidated by building the massive *Tower of London*.

Wolsey, Cardinal *(c.1473-1530)*
Promoted by Henry VIII but falling from grace when he failed to secure the king's divorce, this powerful churchman's palaces at *Whitehall* and *Hampton Court* were confiscated and became the favorite royal residences.

Wren, Sir Christopher *(1632-1723)*
The dazzling career of the greatest British architect includes a staggering number of major buildings, most of them in London — a feat made possible by the ravages of the Great Fire of 1666. Numerous city churches, *St Paul's Cathedral*, major parts of *Hampton Court* and *St James's Palace* testify to his genius.

Sports and activities

For information on all sports, contact **Sportsline** (☎ *222-8000 Mon-Fri 10am-6pm*).

Athletics (track and field)
Major events are held at the **Crystal Palace National Sports Centre** (*Ledrington Rd., SE19* ☎ *(081) 778-0131*). Information from **The Amateur Athletic Association** (*Edgbaston House, 3 Duchess Pl., Hadley Rd., Birmingham* ☎ *(021) 456-4050*). For keen runners, there is an excellent all-weather-surface 6-lane track at **Battersea Park** (*Albert Bridge Rd., SW11* ☎ *(081) 871-7537*) and a synthetic 8-lane track at **West London Stadium** (*Du Cane Rd., W12* ☎ *(081) 749-5505*).

Bicycling

This can be an effective way of exploring the city and one of the quickest ways of getting around. Cycles can be rented from **On Your Bike** (*52-54 Tooley St., SE1* ☎ *407-1309*) or **Yellow Jersey Cycles** (*44 Chalk Farm Rd., SW1* ☎ *485-8090/6*). For more serious cycling, contact the **British Cycling Federation** (*Rockingham Rd., Kettering, Northants* ☎ *(0536) 412211*) or **London Cycling Campaign** (*Tress House, 3 Stamford St., SE1* ☎ *928-7220*), which publishes a booklet of routes.

Cricket

The most baffling of sports to the newcomer, but an integral part of the English summer; from Apr to Sept club matches are played all over London, in parks and on greens, mainly on Sat and Sun afternoons. First-class professional matches, also on weekdays, at the Middlesex club at **Lord's** (*NW8* ☎ *289-1611*) and the Surrey club at **The Oval** (*SE11* ☎ *735-4911*). Both stage a yearly test (international) match: Lords in June, The Oval in Aug or Sept.

Fishing

Fishing in the Thames is forbidden unless you have a license from the Thames Water Authority, obtainable through the **London Anglers Association** (*Forest Rd. Hall, Hervey Park Rd., E17* ☎ *(081) 520-7477*), which you have to join. It is also possible to fish in Hyde Park: licenses from **The Royal Parks Department** (*The Storeyard, Hyde Park, W2* ☎ *262-5484*).

Football (soccer)

Football matches are generally played on Sat afternoons from Aug through to Apr, with some matches on midweek evenings. The FA Cup Final, the biggest single match, is played in May at **Wembley Stadium** (*Middlesex* ☎ *(081) 900-1234* ✗ *available*), also the scene of England's international matches, usually played on Wed evenings. Consult listings magazines such as *Time Out* for details and locations of club matches.

Gardens

Apart from the parks and gardens that are open to the public, the **National Gardens Scheme** (*Hatchlands Park, East Clandon, Guildford, Surrey* ☎ *(0494) 28051*) runs a program whereby private gardens both in London and the country are open to the public for perhaps one day a year. The **Royal Horticultural Society** holds periodic shows in summer at its home in Vincent Sq., SW1, and stages the massive **Chelsea Flower Show** in May (see *Calendar of events*).

Golf

Most courses are private and will only allow you to play if you have an introduction from a member or from your own club. Public courses, however, will allow you to play on payment of a green fee, and some will rent out clubs. The only major professional course near London is **Wentworth**, in Surrey. The most central are at **Richmond Park** (*Roehampton Gate, SW15* ☎ *(081) 876-3205*); **Royal Mid-Surrey** (*Old Deer Park, Richmond, Surrey* ☎ *(081) 940-1894, Mon-Fri*); and **Wimbledon Common** (*Camp Rd., SW19* ☎ *(081) 946-0294, Mon-Fri*), no clubs for hire, "wear a pillar-box-red top."

Health and fitness clubs

Gymnasiums, Nautilus machines, aerobics classes, saunas and

massages are among the facilities offered by most of the following clubs, where temporary (daily or weekly) membership is available:

Bodys (*250 King's Rd., SW3* ☎ *351-5682*); **Earl's Court Gym** (*Upper Floors, 254 Earl's Court Rd., SW5* ☎ *370-1402*); **The Fitness Centre** (*11-12 Floral St., WC2* ☎ *836-6544*); **Islanders Sports Club** (*London Arena, Limeharbour, E14* ☎ *538-8744*); **Metropolitan Club** (*27-28 Kingly St., W1* ☎ *734-5002/3*); **The Sanctuary** (*11 Floral St., WC2* ☎ *240-9635/6, women only*); **Westminster Health Club** (*Allington St., SW1* ☎ *828-3647*); **Westside** (*201-207 Kensington High St., W8* ☎ *937-5386*); **World Traders Health Club** (*International House, World Trade Centre, St Katharine's Way, E1* ☎ *488-2400*).

Popular with office workers in Covent Garden and the West End are the dance/keep-fit sessions at **Pineapple** (*7 Langley St., WC2* ☎ *836-4004*) — with sister studios **Pineapple Kensington** (*38-42 Harrington Rd., SW7* ☎ *581-0466*) — and **Danceworks** (*16 Balderton St., W1* ☎ *629-6183*).

Horse-racing

There are many large racecourses within easy reach of London: to the w, **Ascot** and **Newbury**; to the sw, **Sandown**, **Epsom** and **Kempton**. No races on Sun. There are long overlaps between the summer (flat) and the winter (jumping) seasons. All races will be well covered in the daily newspapers, and it is possible to bet from betting shops that are not on the course.

Ice-skating

The major public rinks, which will hire out skates, are **Broadgate Ice Rink** (*Eldon St., EC2* ☎ *588-6565*); **Queens Ice Skating Club** (*17 Queensway, W2* ☎ *229-0172*); **Richmond Ice Rink** (*Clevedon Rd., Twickenham* ☎ *(081) 892-3646*); and **Streatham Ice Rink** (*386 Streatham High Rd., SW16* ☎ *(081) 769-7861*).

Riding

Stables are conveniently located near major parks: **Ross Nye's Riding Establishment** (*8 Bathurst Mews, W2* ☎ *262-3791*), for Hyde Park; and **Roehampton Gate** (*Priory Lane, SW15* ☎ *(081) 876-7089*), for Richmond Park. Several major show-jumping events are held at **Wembley** (*Middlesex* ☎ *(081) 900-1234*): for leading examples see *Calendar of events*.

Rowing

Rowboats and sailing dinghies may be rented on the Serpentine, in Battersea Park and Regent's Park, as well as on some stretches of the Thames. For rowing events see *Calendar of events*. For details contact the **Amateur Rowing Association** (*6 Lower Mall, W6* ☎ *(081) 748-3632*).

Rugby

Rugby Union, a 15-a-side sport, restricts its players to amateur status in the same way that track and field does. Matches are played on Sat afternoons from Sept-Apr. International and major games take place at the sport's headquarters at **Whitton Rd.** (*Twickenham* ☎ *(081) 892-8161*). Consult listings magazines such as *Time Out* for details and locations of club matches.

Squash

Addresses from **Squash Rackets Association** (*WestPoint, 33-34 Warple Way, W3* ☎ *(081) 746-1616*).

Swimming

Major indoor pools with all facilities include **Chelsea Sports Centre** (*Chelsea Manor St., SW3* ☎ 352-6985); **Golden Lane Pool** (*Golden Lane, EC1* ☎ 250-1464); **Fulham Pools** (*Normand Park, Lillie Rd., SW6* ☎ 385-7628); **Marshall St. Baths** (*14-15 Marshall St., W1* ☎ 439-4678); and **Oasis Pool** (*32 Endell St., WC2* ☎ 836-9555).

For outdoor swimming during the summer, major pools are **Hampstead Mixed Bathing Pond** (*NW3* ☎ 435-2366); **Parliament Hill Lido** (*NW5* ☎ 485-3873); and **The Serpentine** (*Hyde Park, W2* ☎ 262-3751).

Tennis

Information from **The Lawn Tennis Association** (*Queen's Club, Baron's Ct., W14* ☎ 385-2366). For major annual tennis tournaments see *Calendar of events*.

London for children

Information

To find out what's on in London for children buy the inexpensive *Children's London*, published by the London Tourist Board and Convention Bureau. For specific questions ring **Kidsline** (*☎ 222-8070 Mon-Fri 4-6pm, during school vacations and "half term" 9am-4pm*). Many of London's museums have special features of particular interest to children and often produce questionnaires to make a child's visit more directly interesting.

Ways of seeing London

An ideal introduction to London, from a child's point of view, is a Round London Sightseeing Tour in a double-decker bus. River trips to *Hampton Court* and *Greenwich* are also popular. (See pages 15 and 18 for departure points of buses and boats.)

Eating in London

Most restaurants tolerate children — Italian ones are often the most friendly — and some less expensive restaurants will supply children's portions. Hamburger and other fast-food restaurants are plentiful. **Wimpy**, **McDonalds**, **Pizza Express**, **Pizza Hut**, **Tootsies** and **Spaghetti House** restaurants all cater to children; also **Eats and Treats** (*Hamleys, 188 Regent St., W1* ☎ 734-3161); **Smollensky's Ballon** (*1 Dover St., W1* ☎ 491-1199 and *105 Strand, WC2* ☎ 497-2101), with children's entertainers at both branches on weekends; and **TGI Friday's** (*6 Bedford St., WC2* ☎ 379-0585).

Fares

On London Regional Transport, children under 5 travel free and children aged 5-16 travel for a reduced fare, although children aged 14 and 15 need a photocard (available from any post office).

Christmas

Seeing the Christmas lights and decorations in London, particularly in Regent St. and Trafalgar Sq., makes a good early evening's entertainment. Children can also see Santa Claus at Hamleys, Harrods and Selfridges as well as other large department stores during the season. The windows at Selfridges are another special attraction.

London for children

Parks

Hyde Park and **Kensington Gardens** (separated only by a road) are the most central and well-known of London's parks. As well as wide open spaces allowing large-scale games to be played, there are many special attractions. Boats and paddle craft can be rented on the Serpentine, part of which is cordoned off and used as a swimming area in the summer. Kensington Gardens also has unique Sun entertainments: men sail their model boats on the Round Pond, and there are kites to admire. Nearby is the playground donated by J.M. Barrie with its statue of Peter Pan. Look out too for the beautifully carved *Elfin Oak*, near Bayswater Rd., supposedly restored by the fairies (with a little help from Spike Milligan). Puppet shows are staged here on Aug afternoons.

Regent's Park also has rowboats to rent, but the main attraction is the *Zoo*. **Hampstead Heath**, although not particularly central, also offers wide open spaces as well as a deer park, a pond for model boats, an outdoor swimming pool and a playground. **Coram's Field** in Holborn is a park donated to children in London by Sir Thomas Coram — adults are only allowed in if accompanied by a child. **Holland Park** boasts a wildlife enclosure, with peacocks, Muscovy ducks and Polish bantams, an exciting adventure playground for older children and a toddlers' playground. **Battersea** has even more going on: a boating lake, small zoo, deer park, roller-skating area, and theater events and pony rides in summer.

There are many other supervised adventure playgrounds, which have imaginative materials and equipment created by the children themselves. Information from **London Adventure Playground Association** (*28 Underwood Rd., E1* ☎ *377-0314*). Younger children can go to the council-run **One O'Clock Clubs** where they can play with the equipment provided. Under-5s must be accompanied by an adult. Information from local borough councils.

Theaters and cinemas

Some London theaters have special performances for children: **The Little Angel Marionette Theatre** (*14 Dagmar Passage, Cross St., N1* ☎ *226-1787*) shows regular puppet plays, on weekend afternoons and on some weekdays during school vacations; performances for small children take place on Sat mornings. The **Lyric Theatre** (*King St., W6* ☎ *(081) 741-2311*) shows productions for children every Sat and Sun. **Polka Children's Theatre** (*240 The Broadway, SW19* ☎ *(081) 543-4888*) stages regular plays for children, and has exhibitions of puppets and toys. **The Unicorn Theatre** (*6 Great Newport St., WC2* ☎ *836-3334*) also stages plays suitable for children aged 4-12 on weekend afternoons, and some weekdays at "half term."

During school vacations in particular, major cinemas show a wide selection of children's movies. Both the **National Film Theatre** and the **Institute of Contemporary Arts** cinemas (see *Nightlife*) have children's movie clubs on weekend afternoons.

Fairgrounds, circuses and theme parks

Touring circuses and fairs often come to London for bank holiday weekends (see *Public holidays*, p15) and usually take place in the larger parks. Information can be obtained from the **London Tourist Board and Convention Bureau** (☎ *730-3488*). Fireworks and other celebrations on Nov 5 often include fairgrounds. See *Calendar of events*.

Chessington World of Adventures (*Leatherhead Rd., Chessington, Surrey* ☎ *(03727) 27227*🖾 *open late Mar-late Oct 10am-3.30pm*) guarantees an entertaining day out, with a host of rides, from "Dragon River" via the "Runaway Mine Train" to Britain's first hanging roller-coaster, "The Vampire," and its own zoo (*open all year*).

Brass-rubbing
This can be a fascinating way of passing a wet afternoon. The **London Brass Rubbing Centre** (*St Martin-in-the-Fields, Trafalgar Sq., WC2* ☎ *437-6023*) has a large collection, and **Westminster Abbey** (*SW1* ☎ *222-2085*) and **All-Hallows-by-the-Tower** (*Byward St., EC3* ☎ *481-2928*) also have facilities. There is also brass-rubbing at the *Trocadero*. In the churches, admission is free but you must pay for your materials.

Baby-sitters
Babysitters Unlimited (☎ *(081) 892-8888*); **Childminders** (*9 Paddington St., W1* ☎ *935-2049/9763*); **Universal Aunts** (*250 Kings Rd., SW3* ☎ *351-5767*).

Farms
There are a surprising number of farms in the Inner London area. The most interesting (some of which are closed on Mon) are:
Freightliners (*Paradise Park, Sheringham Rd., N7*☎ *609-0467*); **Kentish Town City Farm** (*1 Cressfield Close, NW5* ☎ *482-2861*); **Mudchute Community Farm** (*Pier St., E14* ☎ *515-5901*); **Spitalfields Farm** (*Weaver St., E1* ☎ *247-8762*); **Stepping Stones Farm** (*Stepney Way, E1* ☎ *790-8204*); and **Vauxhall City Farm** (*24 St Oswald's Pl., SE11* ☎ *582-4204, entrance in Tyer's St.*)

Toy stores   See *Shopping*.

Excursions

In Britain, all roads lead to London, and they can also be taken in the opposite direction, as can the commuter railway routes to such historically interesting cities as Canterbury, Salisbury and Winchester. London's hinterland covers the half-dozen "home counties" of the SE and beyond to cities such as Cambridge, Oxford and even Bath. These cities, and to an even greater extent Stratford, repay a weekend visit, with a little exploration on the way. All of them are popular with visitors, and at the height of the summer are over-subscribed to the point of suffocation.

Stately homes around London
London's own countryside, where the nobility once lived in stately homes, begins in the suburbs, then fans out into Epping Forest, the Thames Valley, the Downs, and the Chilterns. Much of this countryside can be reached by tube, and there are several "country" homes open to the public within the capital, especially in West London (see houses at *Chiswick*, *Ham*, *Orleans* and *Syon*, and *Osterley Park*). Beyond, there are about 50 houses and castles within 100 miles. Most of these close on Mon, but are open on bank holidays, then close the following day.
Audley End House 40 miles (64km) from London, 15 miles (24km) s of Cambridge ☎ *(0799) 22842*. Drive through the pretty

Roding Valley on the M11, or take the train from Liverpool Street to Audley End, then walk or take a bus. Open April-Oct Tues-Sun, closed Mon and Good Friday. One of the best examples of a Jacobean mansion, with extensive later work by Vanbrugh and Robert Adam. Much fine 18thC furniture and a collection of stuffed birds. Large grounds, with a miniature railway.

Beaulieu (pronounced Bewlee) 80 miles (128km) from London, 14 miles (22km) s of Southampton ☎ (0590) 612345. By car, A3, A31 or M3, A33. Train from Waterloo to Southampton, then bus. World-famous for its **Motor Museum**, with 200 veteran cars, early Rolls, land-speed record breakers, and a monorail. Open daily. The house, home of auto enthusiast Lord Montagu, was built as the gatehouse of the 13thC Beaulieu Abbey, the ruins of which can be visited. Museum and ruins can be visited all year, as can the stately home. Nearby is the **New Forest**, and there is a Maritime Museum at **Buckler's Hard**, a village with shipbuilding associations dating from Nelson's time.

Broadlands 80 miles (128km) from London, 6 miles (10km) NW of Southampton ☎ (0794) 516878. By car, as above. Train to Southampton, changing for Romsey. Open Apr-Sept Sat-Thurs. The Prince and Princess of Wales spent part of their honeymoon at Broadlands, thus bringing public attention to the home of the late Lord Mountbatten and, in an earlier time, of Lord Palmerston. Broadlands is now the home of Lord and Lady Romsey. There is a **Mountbatten exhibition** in the house, which is a Palladian mansion with landscaping by Capability Brown.

Chartwell 25 miles (40km) from London, 5 miles (8km) SW of Sevenoaks ☎ (0732) 866368. By car, A21, A233, B2026. Bus from Victoria Coach Station. Train to Sevenoaks from Charing Cross, then bus to Westerham, then a 25min walk. Open Mar and Nov Wed, Sat, Sun, Apr-Oct Tues-Thurs afternoons, Sat, Sun. Winston Churchill's country home for 40yrs. Victorian, chosen for its tranquility and views. Churchill's study and library can be visited. An unfinished canvas still stands in his studio in the beautiful gardens. 5 miles (8km) away is **Hever Castle**, trysting place of Anne Boleyn and Henry VIII and 20thC home of William Waldorf Astor (with Holbeins and a Titian); **Penshurst Place**, birthplace of Sir Philip Sidney (with a toy museum, costume display, Italian gardens and nature trail), is also nearby.

Hatfield House 21 miles (33km) N from London ☎ (07072) 62823. By car, A1000. Train from King's Cross or Moorgate to Hatfield. Open Tues-Sun (grounds daily) Apr-Oct. Royal mementos dating back to Elizabeth I, paintings, tapestries and armor, and special exhibitions on crafts and collectibles. Within the grounds is a part of the palace in which Elizabeth I lived as a girl. Her Secretary of State, Robert Cecil, built Hatfield House, and his descendant, the Marquess of Salisbury, still lives there. Six miles (10km) N is **Knebworth House**, begun in 1492 and completed in the 1800s, known for its books and manuscripts, paintings and furniture, and narrow-gauge railway.

Leeds Castle 36 miles (57km) from London, 5 miles (8km) SE of Maidstone. By car, A20 and M20. By train and bus, inclusive ticket available from Victoria Station ☎ (0622) 65400. Open Apr-Oct daily, Nov-Mar Sat, Sun. Fairytale medieval castle on two islands in a lake. Built about 1120, restored in the 1800s. Henry VIII converted it into a royal palace; Elizabeth I was a prisoner here. A garden with many species of flowers is named after another resident, Lord Culpeper, who was Governor of Virginia in the 1600s and founder of the herbalist shop.

Luton Hoo 30 miles (48km) from London, 2 miles (3km) from

Luton ☎ (0582) 22955. By car, M1, A1081. Train from St Pancras Station, then local bus. Fabergé jewels, mementos of Czarist Court, Renaissance jewels, bronzes, porcelain, in a Robert Adam house. Gardens by Capability Brown. Open Apr-Oct Tues-Sat.

Polesden Lacey   20 miles (32km) from London, 2 miles (3km) from Dorking ☎ (0372) 52048. By car, A24. Train from Waterloo to Box Hill or Bookham, then a taxi, or bus plus walk. The playwright Sheridan lived, gardened and farmed here, but his house was demolished in the early 1800s and replaced by a Regency villa. After having several private owners, the property was bequeathed to the National Trust. The lovely house, with a much-admired rose garden, contains a substantial collection of porcelain, and paintings by Sir Joshua Reynolds and Sir Henry Raeburn. The gardens are open all year, daily, but the house in the afternoon only, Apr-Oct Wed-Sun.

Waddesdon Manor   38 miles (60km) from London, 5 miles (8km) w of Aylesbury ☎ (0296) 651211. By car, A41. Train from Marylebone to Aylesbury, then a taxi or bus, plus a strenuous walk. Open Apr-Oct Wed-Sun afternoons. Château-like house built by Baron Ferdinand de Rothschild. Family mementoes, French royal furniture, carpets, paintings. Extensive grounds in which deer roam.

Wilton House   80 miles (128km) from London, 2½ miles (4km) w of Salisbury ☎ (072274) 3115. By car, A30. Train-and-bus excursions by British Rail Awayday from Waterloo Station. Open Apr-Oct Tues-Sat, Sun afternoons. Whimsical Inigo Jones house, with Chippendale and Kent furniture and Van Dyck paintings. More offbeat attractions include some 7,000 brightly-painted model soldiers and a lock of Queen Elizabeth I's hair.

Bath

116 miles (186km) from London. Population: 85,000.
Getting there: By train, 70mins from Paddington, trains
hourly; by car, 2hrs, M4 to Junction 18, then A46 ☎ code
(0225) i Abbey Churchyard ☎ 462831.

One-day excursion: an effortless day out by comfortable high-speed train, with good views of gentle countryside, especially between the Vale of the White Horse and the Lambourn Downs, and where the edges of the Cotswolds form a valley with the Marlborough Downs. Fast by car, too, although the temptation is to make it a weekend, with detours into the hills and stops at ancient sites such as **Stonehenge** or **Avebury**, or walks by the Kennet and Avon Canal.

The warm springs that gave Bath its name are said to have been discovered by King Lear's father, but their celebrity can more accurately be dated from the devotions of the Romans. The renewed enthusiasm for taking the waters in Georgian times spawned a second layer of history, and an architectural elegance that remains remarkable. Bath is easy to explore on foot and, being set amid hills, it best rewards those with willing legs. The center of the city is very crowded in summer.

Sights and places of interest

A first glimpse of that hillside majesty, embellished with Georgian crescents, is well taken from the train as it slows out of Brunel's tunnel at Box and rumbles toward Bath Spa Station. Out of the station, the immediate impression is uninteresting, but a walk straight ahead down Manvers St. leads to the Georgian Bath in **North** and **South Parades**. A left turn along North Parade leads to **Sally Lunn's Tea House**, after which a traditional English bun is named. It is said to be the oldest house in Bath, and the establishment is reputed to have been a haunt of Beau Nash, the dandy and arbiter of social graces who helped make Bath fashionable in Georgian times. Cut through York St. to the **Abbey Churchyard**, the heart of the city. The **abbey** itself was begun in the 15thC, but some of its most striking features are Victorian.

Across the churchyard are the **Roman Baths** and **Pump Room**, completed in 1799 (*open 9am-5.30pm*). A guided tour of the baths affords the opportunity to see the fruits of constant excavations there, ranging from coins to a sacrificial altar. Some years ago it was discovered that Bath's water had been contaminated by an ameba. Bore holes now reach down below the level of contamination to an uncontaminated source. The water can be sampled from a fountain in the elegant and restful Pump Room. Since the water tastes, in the words of Dickens' Sam Weller, like a "warm flat iron," it is perhaps as well that the Pump Room serves morning coffee and afternoon tea, sometimes to the accompaniment of string music.

The most spectacular Georgian homes were built on the hillsides to provide their owners with panoramic views. Walk along Bath St. (colonnaded to protect itinerant bathers), turning right at the end, then left into Sawclose, past the lively theater and restaurant area, up Gay St. to The Circus, then along Brock St., to the **Royal Crescent**, built 1765-75, where the house at **no. 1** opens as a museum in summer (*open Tues-Sat 11am-5pm, Sun 2-5pm*). Return via The Circus to the **Assembly Rooms**, home of an outstanding **Museum of Costume** (*open Mon-Sat 9.30am-6pm, Sun 10am-6pm; closed for repairs for part of 1991*).

Return downhill by Lansdown Rd., which becomes in turn Broad St. and then High St., with its Guildhall and covered market, noted for another of the city's culinary delights, the Bath Chap: this turns out to be a pig's jowl!

Such indulgences may subsequently call for a diet of Dr Oliver's remorselessly plain biscuits, for which the city is also known (the more luxurious chocolate-coated version seems at odds with his ascetic intentions), or simply a Bath bun. Determined walkers can do a little more shopping under cover of Pulteney Bridge, an Italianate delight designed by Robert Adam. This leads into another fine Georgian street named Argyle St., and thence to nowhere in particular except perhaps, at the end of Forrester Rd., a place where boats can be rented on the River Avon. On weekends, pleasure trips can also be taken on the Kennet and Avon Canal, from Sidney Wharf, near Bathwick Hill, or from the Top Lock, at the far end of North Parade Rd.

Numerous fine museums cater to a wide variety of interests. These include the **Geology Museum** (*18 Queen Sq.*); the **Herschel Museum** (*19 New King St.*), for astronomy and music; the **National Centre of Photography** (*in the Octagon, Milsom St.*), where the building itself merits a visit, in a street with elegant shops; and the **Postal History Museum** (*8 Broad St.*).

Sights nearby

A unique attraction a couple of miles out of the city, at Claverton Down, is the **American Museum in Britain** (*open Tues-Sun 2-5pm*). This has Indian and folk art, interiors of early American homes, including Shaker and Pennsylvania Dutch settings, relics of the West, and gardens that replicate George Washington's at Mount Vernon. Audiovisuals, a collection of old maps and other exhibits are featured in a new gallery, opened in 1989. The museum bakes its own selection of cakes and gingerbread, making for a delicious afternoon tea.

Maritime enthusiasts might wish to see **SS *Great Britain***, in the nearby city of **Bristol**. In the opposite direction, a drive into the Mendip Hills leads to the small city of **Wells**, with one of Britain's most beautiful cathedrals.

━━ The **Priory** (*see below* ▥) and the **Royal Crescent Hotel** (▥ ☎ 319090 ▥) are especially comfortable and full of personal touches. The friendly **Pratt's** (*South Parade* ☎ 460441 ▯) and the more sophisticated **Francis** (*Queen Sq.* ☎ 424257 ▥) are both centrally placed. There are many bed-and-breakfast places along **Pulteney Rd.** and **Wells Rd.** Recommended is the delightful **Eagle House** (*Church St., Bathford* ☎ 859946 ▯), a Georgian mansion 3 miles (5km) outside Bath run with care by its friendly owners.

━━ The famous Hole in the Wall restaurant has reopened as a classy Italian called **Pino's Hole in the Wall** (*16 George St.* ☎ 425242 ▥). Rich but subtle sauces feature in the opulent restaurant at the **Priory Hotel** (*Weston Rd.* ☎ 331922 ▥). The French restaurant **Clos du Roy** run by flamboyant chef Philippe Roy has moved to a new small and elegant hotel, **Box House** (*Box* ☎ 744447 ▯). Its place in Bath has now been taken by **Garlands** (*7 Edgar Buildings, George St.* ☎ 442283 ▯). Other well-regarded places are **Popjoys** (*Sawclose* ☎ 460494 ▯), which serves English food in Beau Nash's house (the restaurant is named after his mistress); **Woods** (*9-13 Alfred St.* ☎ 314812 ▯); **Circus** (*34 Brock St.* ☎ 330208 ▯); and, for a snack or a full meal, **Tarts** (*8 Pierrepoint Pl.* ☎ 330280 ▯ *to* ▯). Excellent for breakfast, light lunches or teas is **Canary** (*3 Queen St.* ☎ 424846).

Brighton

53 miles (85km) from London. Population: 162,000. Getting there: By train, 51mins from Victoria, trains twice hourly; by car, A23, then M23 ☎ code (0273) ℹ Marlborough House, 54 Old Steine ☎ 23755; also at King's Rd., on the seafront, in summer.

One-day excursion: the speed and frequency of the trains and the labyrinthine quality of the roads out of South London deter most day-trippers from taking a car, but weekenders might wish to do so to explore the Downs and the Sussex countryside around Brighton.

This seaside resort is beloved by many Londoners for its wry mix of Regency elegance and Graham Greenean seediness. A day out in Brighton is a quintessential English experience. The craze for sea-bathing in the late 1700s, and the Prince Regent's subsequent attentions, gave Brighton a social status it never entirely surrendered and to which its residents still cling.

The Regency terraces, squares and crescents provide the elegance, crowned by the extravagant fantasies of the Royal Pavilion. Such an Aladdin's cave of Orientalia is an appropriate centerpiece to a town noted for its antique stores, the most celebrated of which, along with some interesting fish restaurants, are in a neighborhood called The Lanes. Not far away, an antique electric railway, the first in Britain, runs from one of the town's two Victorian piers along the pebbly beach to the swimming pool and marina. The journey can be continued by open-topped bus, or on foot, to the village of Rottingdean.

Sights and places of interest

From the railway station, Queen's Rd. and Trafalgar St. are the boundaries of an antiques-and-boutiques area called **North Laine**, which is less pretty but also less expensive than The Lanes. Within this area, there is a Sat-morning flea market.

A half-mile walk down Queen's Rd. leads to Church St. on the left and **Brighton Museum and Art Gallery** (*open Tues-Sat 10am-5.45pm, Sun 2-5pm*) housing a major Art Deco collection as well as English watercolors and Old Masters. Just beyond is the **Royal Pavilion** (*open Jan-May, Oct-Dec 10am-5pm, June-Sept 10am-6pm*). The royal flourish was bestowed upon Brighton by the Prince Regent, later to be George IV, who is said to have gone there to get away from his father. While there in 1785 he secretly and illegally married a Catholic, Mrs Fitzherbert, a twice-widowed commoner. The Pavilion was his summer palace, although he left it soon after its completion. The bizarre mock-Indian architecture, most of it by Nash, derives from the fashionability of Oriental themes during a period of great trade with the East. There was room for discordance within this preoccupation; the interior was decorated in "the Chinese taste." The Pavilion affords visitors a good hour's browse through eccentric splendor, with huge dragons, exotic birds and chandeliers, in a whole series of room settings.

From the Pavilion one wanders into **The Lanes**, where the fashionable and fascinating shops often close on Sun, but stay open late on Wed and Thurs. From there it is a few minutes' walk down to the seafront. To the right, about half a mile along the beach, is the West Pier, built in 1866, and a century later the memorable setting for the movie *Oh, What a Lovely War*. The pier now stands forlorn, unsafe, closed to visitors, and with an uncertain future. In that direction are some fine Georgian buildings, notably in **Regency Square**, as Brighton blends into its sister town of **Hove**.

In a more central position on the seafront is the **Palace Pier**, built in 1891, a rich symbol of British seaside frolics. Just to the left of the pier is the **Aquarium** (*open Apr-Sept 10am-6pm, Oct-Mar 10am-5pm*) dating from 1872, with a Dolphinarium. From this point, the aforementioned **Volk's Electric Railway** begins its journey. The railway, named after its founder, was opened in 1883, but at its terminus now is the largest yachting marine in Europe. Visitors can walk along the breakwaters, and there are pleasure trips and deep-sea angling. Beyond the marina, the resort that once popularized bathing machines now has an area of beach set aside for those who prefer nudity. This bracing facility is a whistle away from one of England's most famous girls' schools, **Roedean**, on the way to **Rottingdean**. There is a toy museum, a local history collection and Rudyard Kipling memorabilia at **The Grange**, Rottingdean, where the great writer lived toward the end of his life (*open Mon-Sat 10am-5pm, Sun 2-5pm; closed Tues and Fri 1-2pm, and Wed*).

Sights nearby

Walkers enjoy the South Downs, a range of chalk hills that runs just inland from Brighton and stretches for 80 miles (128km). A bus from the seafront to the crest of **Devil's Dyke** offers superb views and a ½hr walk to the **church at Poynings**. The Tourist Information Centre has detailed information on walks.

In the Sussex countryside, several towns and villages are worth a visit, including **Lewes**, with a castle, interesting pubs and good walks; **Sheffield Park**, for its Capability Brown gardens and a full-scale steam railway; and another castle, **Arundel**, a sometimes grotesque museum of curiosities, housing an arts festival held in late Aug.

☞ Brighton has an enormous selection of hotels, and the Tourist Information Centre has a reservations service. Two famous Victorian seafront hotels are the **Metropole** (☎ 775432 *IIII*) —rather unfairly notorious for furtive weekend couples — and the **Grand** (☎ 21188 *IIIII*), bombed with tragic consequences by the IRA at the 1984 Conservative Party Conference but since renovated and reopened. Both are in King's Rd., as is the **Old Ship Hotel** (☎ 29001 *IIII*), which has a fine ballroom.

≈ In The Lanes, **English's Oyster Bar** (*29 East St.* ☎ 27980 *IIII*) is something of an institution. Despite its name, it is a full-scale restaurant and it is advisable to reserve in advance. **Wheeler's** (*64 King's Rd.* ☎ 28372 *IIII*) is a branch of the famous London chain of fish restaurants, known for its sole. A good vegetarian café is **Food for Friends** (*18 Prince Albert St.* ☎ 202310 *IIII*). At the edge of The Lanes, a tea shop called **The Mock Turtle** (*4 Pool Valley*) sells homemade cakes and lunchtime snacks.

Elsewhere in Brighton, **Langan's** (*1 Paston Pl.* ☎ 606933 *IIII*) and **Le Grandgousier** (*15 Western St.* ☎ 772005 *IIII*) are good-value bistros.

Cambridge
54 miles (86km) from London. Population: 105,000. Getting there: By train, about 75mins from Liverpool Street (direct) or King's Cross (faster route), 2 or 3 trains hourly; by car, M11, 90mins ☎ *code (0223)* **i** *Wheeler St.* ☎ *322640.*
One-day excursion: being linked to London by motorway, Cambridge is easily reached by car. The town is encircled with parking lots: cars should not be taken into the center.

The first scholars came from Oxford to Cambridge in 1209, and the first college, **Peterhouse**, was founded in 1284. Modern times have seen F.R. Leavis, a lion among literary critics, the splitting of the atom by Rutherford, and the work of Crick and Watson in establishing the double helix structure of DNA. For all its architectural similarities to Oxford, this "younger" of Britain's two great university cities is distinguished by the larger scale of its colleges, its lower skyline (it is not, unlike Oxford, an industrial town), its paler stone, and its geographical setting on the edge of flat and water-laced Fen country. Cambridge makes good use of its river, the Cam or Granta, along which half a dozen of its colleges are set. Most of the colleges can be visited except between mid-May and mid-June, and there are several tours daily Apr-Dec, starting from the Tourist Information Centre on the hour (*times vary through the year*). It is advisable to reserve an hour before the tour starts.

Sights and places of interest
Close to the bus station is **Emmanuel College**, where John Harvard was a pupil in the 1600s. Emmanuel's chapel is one of several fine Wren buildings in Cambridge. Across St Andrew's St., in Downing St., are the **Museums of Geology and Archaeology**. Downing St. bends into Pembroke St. and **Pembroke College**, which also has a Wren chapel. Parallel with Pembroke St. is Botolph Lane, beyond which lies **Corpus Christi**, with its fine 14thC collegiate building in Old Court.

Turn left from Pembroke St. into Trumpington St. for the **Fitzwilliam Museum** (*open Tues-Sat 10am-5pm, Sun 2.15-5pm*), which has an outstanding collection, including paintings by Gainsborough, Turner, Rembrandt, Renoir and Degas, drawings by Hogarth, Dürer, Michelangelo and Leonardo, and Blake's illuminated books, as well as Roman, Greek, Egyptian and Eastern antiquities and English pottery and porcelain. Return along Trumpington St., turning left for two more colleges, **St Catherine's** and **Queens'** (1448), the latter with its Tudor courtyard, Cloister Court and Mathematical Bridge.

Nearby, at Mill Lane (and farther along, at Magdalene Bridge), rowboats and punts can be rented on the river. Along this stretch of the water are five more colleges, **King's**, **Clare**, **Trinity**, **St John's** and **Magdalene**. The grassy bank facing the first two of these colleges is known as The Backs.

King's College chapel is an outstanding example of Perpendicular architecture, built between 1446-1515, with glass by Flemish craftsmen. Among its treasures is *The Adoration of the Magi*, by Rubens. Nearby on King's Parade is the **Senate House**, a Georgian building in which the University's "Parliament" sits.

Clare College was founded in 1326, but the present building, like a perfectly-proportioned tiny palace, was built in the 1600s. It has lovely gardens opposite the elegant Clare Bridge. Trinity, with its Great Court, fountain and many-windowed Wren library, is the largest and richest of the colleges. Its alumni have included Bacon, Byron, Macaulay, Tennyson and Thackeray. In the library are manuscripts by Tennyson, Thackeray and Milton. The famous bookstore, **Heffers**, is in Trinity St., as is **Sheratt and Hughes**, which used to be the equally famous Bowes and Bowes, and nearby is **Belinda's**, for excellent teas and cakes.

St John's (1511), with its wedding-cake silhouette and Tudor gateway, is architecturally an acquired taste, but its "Bridge of Sighs" is a splendid gesture. Properly known as New Bridge, it was built in 1831. St John's chapel was also built in the 1800s, by Sir George Gilbert Scott. At the end of this stretch of river, Magdalene College (1524), favored by the aristocracy, has Samuel Pepys' library, in the original bookcases.

Across the road from Magdalene St., in Castle St., the **Folk Museum** (*open Mon-Sat 10.30am-5pm, Sun 2.30-4.30pm*), in a converted inn, has an engrossing collection of domestic and agricultural objects from Cambridgeshire. In the opposite direction, in Bridge St., is one of only five round churches in England, the **Church of the Holy Sepulchre**, modeled on its namesake in Jerusalem.

From Bridge St., turn left for **Jesus College**, which was once a convent. The windows in the chapel were designed by Burne-Jones and made in the William Morris workshop. Behind the college are Jesus Green and Midsummer Common, separated by Maid's Causeway and Short St. from another stretch of open grass, and rather offhandedly known as Christ's Pieces.

Next to the railway station is another stretch of open grassland called Parker's Piece, with a restaurant called **Hobbs' Pavilion**, which is popular with students. The restaurant is a converted cricket pavilion, and is named after the great batsman Jack Hobbs. Nearby, in Lensfield Rd., is the **Scott Polar Research Institute**, named after the explorer, with relics of expeditions. Nearby too, off Trumpington Rd., are the University's **Botanic Gardens**. These uncrowded and beautifully scented gardens were laid out in 1846, primarily for the purpose of research.

☙ Student riots brought some unwelcome publicity to the **Garden House Hotel** (*Mill Lane* ☎ 63421 ▢) at the beginning of the 1970s, but guests with a nostalgic or vicarious interest can stay safely enough in what was already one of the city's best-known hotels, with a better-than-average restaurant, pretty gardens and river views. Also on the river is the smaller, comfortable **Arundel House** (*53 Chesterton Rd.* ☎ 67701 ▢), in a Victorian terrace. An excellent guesthouse is **No. 11** (*11 Glisson Rd.* ☎ 461142 ▢).

═ There has been a gastronomic renaissance in Cambridge in recent years. Among the newcomers are **Midsummer House** (*Midsummer Common* ☎ 69299 ▮▮▮), which serves imaginative English food in a converted common-keeper's cottage, and **Browns** (*23 Trumpington St.* ☎ *461655*▯), an American-style restaurant with polished wood floors, ceiling fans and bentwood chairs, where the fare includes pasta, salads, char-grilled steaks and hamburgers. In an unremarkable row house in Chesterton Rd., **Twenty Two** (☎ *351880*▯▯) produces some excellent food: mouthwatering modern British dishes are served in an attractive, informal pink dining room. **Hobbs' Pavillion** (*Park Terr.* ☎ *67480*▯) serves crêpes, salads and its own ice cream; and **Shao Tao** (*72 Regent St.* ☎ *353942*▯) is one of the city's numerous good Chinese restaurants.

Local pubs serving good food are the **Free Press** (*7 Prospect Row*), the **Fort St George** on Midsummer Common and the crankily English **Tickell Arms** at Whittlesford, a mere 15mins' drive away.

Oxford

56 miles (90km) from London, Population: 115,000. Getting there: By train, 60mins from Paddington, trains hourly; by car, 90mins, A40, then M40 ☎ *code (0865)* ℹ *St Aldate's* ☎ *726871.*

One-day excursion: a finely-crafted jewel of a city, Oxford has to be protected against invasion by cars. There is a ring of parking lots and a "Park and Ride" bus service.

It has been a university town since the 1200s, and has provided Britain with many of its most famous achievers: enough prime ministers to make a cricket team, writers ranging from Wilde to Tolkien, and adventurers from Raleigh to Rhodes. Oxford's colleges and quadrangles dominate the center of the city, rich in their architectural diversity but with a preponderance of Gothic among their turrets, towers and dreaming spires. Some of the colleges are walled, although most of them can be visited in the afternoons (and all day during vacations, usually for a month around Christmas and Easter, and July-Sept). As a seat of learning, Oxford also has institutions such as the Bodleian Library and Ashmolean Museum, and famous bookstores. There are the mutual attractions of punting on the river and unstrenuous walks by the waterside. Beyond the city, the countryside reaches out to the Chiltern Hills and Cotswold Hills.

Sights and places of interest

An impressive start to a day in Oxford might be at the **Ashmolean Museum** (*open Tues-Sat 10am-4pm, Sun 2-4pm*), one of Britain's finest museums, with riches ranging from Michelangelo and Raphael drawings, through silverware and musical instruments, to John Tradescant's natural-history collection. The Victorian Ashmolean building is at the corner of Beaumont St. and St Giles, from which Magdalen St. runs into Broad St., the address of the famous **Blackwell's** bookstore (this and Foyle's in London are the two most extensive bookstores in Britain), where browsers are welcome. Also housed in Broad St. is a new audiovisual display, **Story of Oxford** (*open daily*), and a small and friendly pub called the **White Horse**.

On this stretch of walk are the rival colleges of **Trinity**, with charming 17thC buildings and a rose garden, and **Balliol**, founded in the 13thC and especially influential in the development of the university, with a beautiful garden quadrangle. Opposite Balliol on Broad St. is **Exeter College**, the place of conception of the pre-Raphaelite Brotherhood.

To the right off Broad St. is the **Sheldonian Theatre**, the first building designed by Wren, in 1662. The theater, modeled on those of ancient Rome and named after its benefactor Archbishop Sheldon, is used for university functions and concerts. Behind it is the **Bodleian Library** (*open Mon-Fri 9am- 5pm, Sat*

9am-12.30pm), named after Sir Thomas Bodley, who donated his own collection in 1598. This is said to be the oldest library in the world and contains 3 million books. The part known as the Divinity School, with a beautiful late Gothic low-vaulted ceiling, has folios and first editions of works by Shakespeare, Milton, Swift and Pope, among others. Also within the Bodleian is the **Radcliffe Camera**, a striking domed rotunda designed by James Gibbs in 1739. To the left across Catte St. is **All Souls College**, with its celebrated twin towers by Hawksmoor. Behind All Souls is **New College**, founded in 1379, which has a magnificent chapel and parts of the medieval city wall in its gardens. There are a number of tea shops in nearby Holywell St., which serve delicious cream teas.

Holywell St. leads into Longwall, from which the Magdalen deer park can be seen. Where Longwall reaches High St. a turn to the right along Merton St. leads to **Merton College**, with the oldest quadrangle in Oxford, dating from the 1300s. A turn to the left, through Christ Church Meadows, leads to **Magdalen College**, the most beautiful of the colleges, with its Perpendicular bell tower from which the choir sings at 6am on May Day morning. At Magdalen and Folly Bridges punts can be rented. From Rose Lane, a footpath runs around Christ Church Meadow, following the River Thames. Alongside Rose Lane are the **Botanic Gardens**, which date back to 1621.

Sights nearby

Blenheim Palace is 8 miles (13km) from Oxford. Even without the grand Baroque design of Vanbrugh and the landscaping of Capability Brown, the Churchills' ancestral home and nearby burial place would have a magnetic appeal; but the combination of historic and esthetic interest is irresistible.

The enormous Blenheim Palace and Park (*open Mar-Oct 10.30am-5.30pm*) are at the small town of **Woodstock**, which has resonances quite different from those of its American descendant. There are buses every ½hr from Cornmarket. Apart from its assembly of Churchill artifacts, the palace has a large collection of tapestries, paintings, sculpture and furniture. Perhaps the most magnificent room is the Long Library, which contains more than 10,000 volumes as well as 17thC Oriental porcelain, and has carvings by Grinling Gibbons.

The palace was built by a grateful Queen Anne for John Churchill, First Duke of Marlborough, to mark his victory over the French at the Battle of Blenheim in 1704. Winston Churchill, grandson of the 7th Duke, was born there on Nov 30, 1874. He is buried in the churchyard at Bladon, on the edge of the park.

⌖ For a city that attracts many visitors, Oxford does not flaunt its hotels, but the Tourist Information Centre does have a special telephone accommodations register. Among the better-known hotels are the **Randolph** (*Beaumont St.* ☎ 247481 ▮▮▯), with its Edwardian plush, and the **Ladbroke Linton Lodge** (*Linton Rd.* ☎ 53461 ▮▯), with pleasant gardens. There are lots of bed-and-breakfast places around Abingdon Rd., St John's St. and Walton St.

7 miles (10km) E of Oxford is **Le Manoir aux Quat' Saisons** (*Great Milton* ☎ (08446) 8881 ▮▮▮▮), Raymond Blanc's much-praised and visited hotel and restaurant.

▤ **Gee's** (*61A Banbury Rd.* ☎ 53540 ▮▮▯) is a Victorian conservatory with a pleasant atmosphere and good modern British food. **Elizabeth** (*84 St Aldate's* ☎ 242230 ▮▮▮▮) and **La Sorbonne** (*130a High St.* ☎ 241320 ▮▮▯) are two old-established French restaurants. For less expensive eating, cold buffet and Sun lunch, **Cherwell Boathouse** (☎ 52746 ▮▯), on the river off

Bardwell Rd., makes for a pleasant experience, as does **Brown's**
(*Woodstock Rd.* ☎ *511995*☐).

Stratford-upon-Avon
*96 miles (154km) from London. Population: 22,000. Getting
there: By train, about 2hrs 30mins from Paddington,
changing at Leamington Spa, 6 trains a day; by train and
bus, 2hrs from Euston, changing at Coventry, 7 trains a
day; by car, 2hrs 30mins to 3hrs, A40, M40 to Oxford, then
A34* ☎ *(0789)* i *1 High St.* ☎ *293127, recorded info*
☎ *67522.*

One-day excursion or longer: an awkward journey, but still a
seemingly inescapable trip for visitors from overseas. Stratford is
not really within London's hinterland, belonging less to the South
than to the Midlands, and is most comfortably visited as part of a
trip taking in **Warwick** or **Kenilworth castles**, **Coventry
Cathedral**, or the northern part of the **Cotswold Hills**.

In the 16thC, as now, playwrights found their audiences and
their milieu in London, and Shakespeare was a metropolitan
writer. However, he was born in Stratford, retired and died there,
and was buried there. Soon after his death in 1616, people started
going to Stratford to see his birthplace, and today they can also
watch his plays performed by the Royal Shakespeare Company
during its long season. There is much worth seeing in the town,
despite exploitation that would surely draw a satirical sting from
the subject of its purported devotions. There is little left of the
Forest of Arden, setting for several of the plays, except for the
odd clump, but its trees remain in the timbering of some fine
Elizabethan and Tudor buildings. When Stratford's streets are not
sighing under the weight of visitors, it is a quiet and peaceful
town, especially in the evenings.

Sights and places of interest
From the railway station, Alcester Rd., Greenhill St. and Windsor
St. lead to the half-timbered **Shakespeare's House** in Henley St.
(*open Apr-Sept Mon-Sat 9am-6pm, Sun 10am-6pm, Oct Mon-Sat
9am-5pm, Sun 10am-5pm, Nov-Mar Mon-Sat 9am-4.30pm, Sun
1.30-4.30pm*), where the playwright was born, probably on April
23, 1564. The interior has been carefully restored — notice the
engraved signatures of such pilgrims as Carlyle, Tennyson and Sir
Walter Scott in the alleged room of the birth.

A short walk along Henley St., High St. (past the family home of
John Harvard, founder of the university) and Chapel St. is **New
Place**, to which Shakespeare retired, and where he died at the
age of 52. The house no longer stands, but the garden, laid out in
the characteristic Elizabethan "knot" patterns, can still be
enjoyed. Farther along, when the same thoroughfare has become
Church St., is the **Shakespeare Birthplace Trust**, which offers a
combined ticket for the several properties historically linked to
the bard. Another of these properties, just around the corner in
Old Town, is **Hall's Croft** (*hours as Shakespeare's House, but
closed Sun Nov-Mar*). This building is named after John Hall, who
married Shakespeare's daughter; however, its principal interest is
the fact that Hall was a doctor, and the equipment within
provides insight into the medical techniques of the 17thC.

Old Town meets Trinity St. at the churchyard where
Shakespeare was buried. The gravestone is inscribed with an
imprecation, attributed to Shakespeare, to leave him in peace. On
the chancel wall is a monument, and at the font is a reproduction

of the register recording his baptism and burial.

Back along the Southern Lane and Waterside, by the Avon, is the **Royal Shakespeare Theatre**. There were performances in Stratford even in the days of strolling players, but the first serious attempts to honor Shakespeare began in the late 1700s. The original Shakespeare theater was built in 1879, and burned down in 1926. The present red-brick building was opened in 1932, and The Royal Shakespeare Company, one of the world's finest theater companies, presents at least 12 Shakespearean productions in a season stretching from Apr-Jan.

The RSC also has a studio theater in the town, known as **The Other Place**, and a new Jacobean-style theater, **The Swan**, which opened in 1986, where lesser-known Shakespearian and contemporary plays are staged. Recorded reservation information for all theaters can be obtained around the clock (☎ *69191; for the box office* ☎ *295623*). The Royal Shakespeare Theatre has an interestingly informative picture gallery of paintings of great actors in Shakespearian costume, in a surviving section of the original building. The theater also has extensive gardens: in the part lying near the church are rare trees and a court for Nine Men's Morris, an ancient game mentioned in *A Midsummer Night's Dream*; and the part lying near the Shakespeare monument — **Bancroft Gardens** — makes a nice picnic spot.

Sights nearby

Two further scenes from the *Seven Ages of Shakespeare* are to be seen just outside the town. **Anne Hathaway's cottage**, which was her home before her marriage to Shakespeare, is 2 miles (3km) away at **Shottery** (*hours as Shakespeare's Birthplace*). The contents include Shakespeare's "second best bed," a four-poster that he willed to his wife. The thatched cottage can be reached by a very pleasant walk along a signposted footpath from Evesham Pl.; there is also a bus service from the bottom of Bridge St. A longer and sometimes muddy walk along a canal towpath N from Bridgefoot, or a short train journey, leads the 4 miles (6km) to **Wilmcote**, home of Shakespeare's mother, Mary Arden (*hours as Hall's Croft*). This typical Warwickshire farmstead, in use as such until 50yrs ago, retains an informality that makes it a revealing museum of English rural life.

☞ The thespian hotel, also enjoyed for its food and drink, is **The Arden** (*at Waterside* ☎ *294949*▯), which has a country-house atmosphere. There are several other hotels in Stratford with this kind of ambience, although the rooms have usually been modernized. For the full modern treatment there is the **Moat House** (*Bridgefoot* ☎ *414411* ▯). **Caterham House** (*58-9 Rother St.* ☎ *67309*▯) is a good bed and breakfast; others tend to gather on the roads into Stratford from Oxford, Evesham and Alcester. The Tourist Information Centre has an accommodations register.

══ The **Royal Shakespeare Theatre** (☎ *69191* ♣ ▮▯) has two restaurants and offers a package-deal ticket for a play and dinner. Or reserve in the morning for a pre-theater dinner at **Shepherd's** (*Stratford House Hotel, Sheep St.* ☎ *68233* ▮▯). After the theater, **Sheep St.** has several late restaurants, Italian and Greek, among which the Greek-biased **Debut** (☎ *293546* ▯) is a lively highlight. In the same street, there are good pub lunches at the **Rose and Crown**, while actors favor the "**Dirty Duck**" (**Black Swan**), at Waterside, near the theater.

Windsor
21 miles (34km) from Central London. Population: 30,000.
Getting there: By train, 53mins from Paddington, changing

at Slough for Windsor and Eton Central, trains hourly, or 47mins direct from Waterloo to Windsor Riverside, trains twice hourly; by car, 1hr, M4, then A308 ☎ code (0753) from London i Central Station (Apr-Dec) ☎ 852010.

One-day excursion: Windsor and Eton are compact and busy, and surrounded by walking country. A car is not essential.

With its royal castle and Great Park, on a pretty stretch of the River Thames, and with Eton, famous for its boys' school, just across the footbridge, a visit to Windsor is, understandably, an almost mandatory day trip for the visitor to London, or worth even a hasty half-day. Hotels are not listed as Windsor is too close to London to warrant an overnight stay.

Even in William the Conqueror's time it was within a day's march of London, which is why he chose it for the site of one of the nine castles with which he decided to encircle the city. Since the Royal Family still spend time at **Windsor Castle** it is both a national monument and a private home, and it is the largest and oldest inhabited castle in the world. The precincts are open to visitors, and there is admission to the State Apartments when the Queen is not in official residence. There are walks in **Windsor Great Park**, which stretches for 6 miles (10km) in the direction of **Ascot racecourse**. A similar distance up the willow-fringed river is **Boulter's Lock**, still much as it was when Jerome K. Jerome described it in *Three Men in a Boat* in 1889, and the town of **Maidenhead**.

A couple of miles farther upriver is **Cliveden House**, built by Barry in 1851, once owned by the Astors, and on occasion a breeding ground for political scandal. The house is now a hotel, but a small section is open to members of the National Trust on Thurs and Sun afternoons in summer. The magnificent gardens, with beautiful views, can be visited from Mar-Oct daily 11am-6pm. Cliveden is close to the village of **Cookham**, where the painter Stanley Spencer lived. One of his paintings hangs in the church, and others are in King's Hall.

Across the river from Windsor, **Eton High St.** is dotted with craft and antique stores.

Sights and places of interest

Unless you intend to take a long walk in the Great Park or along the river, the places of interest in Windsor and Eton are all within a radius of about a mile. It is possible to take a perhaps brisk look at each in the course of one day, and there are reasons to see Windsor in the morning and Eton in the afternoon. From Riverside Station, a walk along Datchet Rd. and Thames St. leads to the castle. Central Station is closer; there is a parking lot opposite, housed in the ugly King Edward Court shopping center, and a walk up Peascod St. and Castle Hill leads to the castle. In Central Station you will find **Royalty and Empire**, a waxwork and audiovisual exhibition on Victorian life (*open daily 9.30am-5.30pm, 4.30pm in winter*).

The **Changing of the Castle Guard** can be seen at 11am Mon-Sat from mid-Mar to mid-Aug and every 48hrs excluding Sun from mid-Aug to mid-Mar. The new guard leaves from the Royal Mews at 10.55am and marches to the castle. The old guard returns at 11.30am. On the High St., the **Guildhall**, completed by Wren after the death of the original architect, has an exhibition that includes royal portraits.

Up Church Lane, in Church St., Nell Gwynne's house nowadays is a coffee shop called **The Drury House**. At the top of Church St., King Henry VIII Gate is the main entrance to **Windsor**

Castle. Straight ahead within the castle is the finest example of Perpendicular architecture in England, **St George's Chapel** (*open summer Mon-Sat 10.45am-4pm, Sun 2-4pm, winter Mon-Sat 10.45am-3.45pm, Sun 2-3.45pm, closed Jan*), where several monarchs are buried in the choir. The architectural style, with external buttresses providing much of the support, permits a spacious interior, with the light from stained-glass windows filling the magnificent nave. There are elaborate carvings in the nave and stalls.

On the opposite side of the castle precincts are the **State Apartments** (*open Nov-Feb Mon-Sat 10.30am-3pm; Mar and Oct Mon-Sat 10.30am-4pm, Sun 12.30-4pm; April-Sept Mon-Sat 10.30am-5pm, Sun 12.30-5pm; closed usually for a month at Christmas and Easter, and for Ascot race week in June*), decorated with paintings from the royal collection, including works by Van Dyck and Rubens, and with carvings by Grinling Gibbons. There are also drawings by Leonardo da Vinci and Holbein in the hall near the main entrance to the State Apartments. Within the same complex are the **coach museum** and an extraordinary delight, **Queen Mary's Dolls' House**, also near the entrance. This has running water, working elevators and a library with commissioned writings by Kipling and miniature paintings. The house, designed by Sir Edwin Lutyens, is on a scale of 12:1. From the castle, Long Walk runs for 3 miles (5km) through Home Park to a statue of George III. Beyond stretches **Windsor Great Park**, with Smith's Lawn, where Prince Charles plays polo. Nearby, the **Savill Garden** (*open Mon-Fri 10am-6pm, Sat, Sun 10am-7pm*) has rhododendrons, roses, herbaceous borders and alpine plants, set in 35 wooded acres.

An exploration of the Great Park and Savill Garden may well demand an afternoon, but the alternative is to return to the town, and from Thames St. cross the footbridge (a pretty Victorian structure in cast iron) to **Eton**, which may prove a less crowded place in which to have lunch. The town of the boating song and playing fields on which Britain's battles were allegedly won instantly proclaims itself; from the bridge, the Eton College boathouses can be seen on the left. In the High St., near a splendid Victorian pillar box, is a timbered building dating from 1420, where cock-fighting used to take place. Known as **The Cockpit**, it is now, incongruously, an international restaurant. Note the punishment stocks outside. Among the antique stores in the High St. is **F. Owen**, at no. 113, notable for militaria; covering one wall of the shop are photographs of customers who were Eton boys. **Eton College** (*open Apr-Sept 2-4.30pm, vacations 10.30am-4.30pm; parties of 10 or more must reserve in advance* ☎ 863593), cradle of great British poets and prime ministers, was founded in 1440 by Henry VI, and some of the oldest parts of the school can be seen in a quadrangle called The Cloisters. The 15thC chapel, built in the Perpendicular style, contains wall paintings from the time of its foundation.

⇌ Gastronomes will cut short their sightseeing to spend time and money at the **Waterside Inn** (*Bray, near Maidenhead* ☎ *(0628) 20691* ▥▥▥), which is the country establishment of the Roux brothers, owners of Le Gavroche in London (see *Restaurants*). Windsor itself cannot match such gourmet delights as the exquisite lightness of touch in the Waterside's cuisine, although **La Taverna** (*2 River St., off Thames St.,* ☎ *863020* ▥◻ ◻) is worth visiting for pasta and veal dishes, and **Antico's** (*42 Eton High St.* ☎ *863977*▥◻) is recommended. For the determined sightseer, the schedule might favor a really excellent snack at the **Eton Wine Bar**, or a hot pub lunch at the **Christopher**, both also in the High St., Eton.

Index

Individual hotels, restaurants, pubs and performance centers have not been indexed, because they appear in alphabetical order within their appropriate sections. However, the sections themselves are indexed. Similarly, streets appear in the list on page 221 and not the index, with a few notable exceptions, such as Fleet St. and Pall Mall, which are indexed as well.

Page numbers in **bold** type indicate the main entry. *Italic* page numbers refer to the illustrations and plans.

Index

Index

Index

Index

List of street names

All streets mentioned in the book that fall within the area covered by our maps are listed here. Each street name is followed by a map reference to one or more of the maps that follow this list. Map numbers are printed in **bold** type.

It was not possible to label every street drawn on the maps, although of course all major streets and most smaller ones are named. Those streets that are not named on the maps are still given map references in this list, because this serves as an approximate location that will nearly always be sufficient for you to find your way.

Street names

Street names

Shepherd's Bush Green, **21**C4
Sheringham Rd., **21**C5
Sloane Ave., **16**J6
Sloane Rd., **16**J7
Sloane Sq., **16**J7
Sloane St., **16**I7-J7
Smith Sq., **18**J11
Soho Sq., **10**F10
South Gro., **21**C4
South Sq., **11**E13
South Africa Rd., **21**C4
South Audley St., **9**G8
South Molton St., **9**F8
Southampton Row, **10**E11
Southwark Bri., **12**G15
Spaniards Rd., **21**C4
Stable Yard, **9**H9
Stafford Ter., **14**I2
Stamford St., **11**G13-H13
Stanley Gdns., **6**G1
Stepney Way, **21**C5
Stevenage Rd., **21**C4
Strand, **10**G11
Stratheden Rd., **21**D5
Stratton St., **9**G9
Streatham High Rd., **21**D4
Sumner Pl., **15**K5
Sussex Pl., **2**D7
Swallow St., **10**G10
Swan Walk, **16**L7

T

Talbot Rd., **6**E2
Talbot Yd, **13**H16
Tavistock Cres., **7**F4
Tavistock Sq., **4**D11
Tavistock St., **10**G10
Temple Pl., **11**F13
Thayer St., **3**E8
Threadneedle St., **13**F16
Throgmorton St., **13**F16
Thurloe St., **15**F5
Tite St., **16**L7

Tooley St., **13**G16
Torrington Pl., **4**D10
Tottenham Court Rd.,
    4D10-E10
Tottenham St., **10**E10
Tower Bri., **13**H17
Tower Bri. Rd.,
    13H17-I17
Tower St., **10**F11
Trafalgar Sq., **10**G11
Trinity Sq., **13**G17
Tyer's St., **19**K12

U

Udall St., **18**J10
Underwood Rd., **13**D18
Upper Brook St., **8**G7
Upper Mall, **21**C4
Upper Richmond Rd.,
    21D4
Upper St Martin's Lane,
    10G11
Upper St., **5**B13
Upper Thames St.,
    12F14-15
Upper Woburn Pl., **4**C10

V

Vere St., **9**F8
Victoria Embankment,
    11G12-13
Victoria Gro., **14**I3-15I4
Victoria St., **18**I10
Villiers St., **10**G11
Vincent Sq., **18**J10
Vine Lane, **13**G17

W

Walbrook, **13**F16
Walton St., **16**J6
Wandsworth Bridge Rd.,
    21D4
Wapping High St., **21**C5

Wapping Wall, **21**C5
Wardour St., **10**F10
Warple Way, **21**C4
Warrington Cres., **7**E4
Waterden Rd., **21**C5
Waterloo Bri., **11**G12
Waterloo Pl., **10**G10
Waterloo Rd., **11**H13
Watling St., **12**F15
Weaver St., **13**D17
Wellington St., **11**F12
Well Walk, **21**C4
West St., **10**F11
Westbourne Gro., **6**F3
Westminster Bri., **18**I11
Whitechapel High St.,
    13F18
Whitehall, **10**G11-H11
Whitehall Ct., **10**H11
White Hart Lane, **21**B5
Wigmore St., **9**F8
Wilbraham Pl., **16**J7
Willesden Lane, **21**C4
William IV St., **10**G11
Wilton Cres., **16**I7
Wilton Pl., **16**I7
Wilton Rd., **17**J9
Wilton Row, **17**H8
Wimpole St., **8**E8
Wine Office Ct., **11**F13
Woburn Sq., **4**D10
Woburn Walk, **4**C10
Wood St., **12**F15
Wrights Lane, **14**I3

Y

Yeoman's Row, **16**I6
York Ter., **2**D7

LONDON

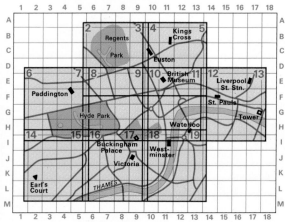

LEGEND

City Maps

0   100   200   300   400   500 YDS.

- Major Place of Interest
- Other Important Building
- Built-up Area
- Park
- ✝ ✝ Cemetery
- ✝ ✝ Named church, church
- ☪ Mosque
- ✡ Synagogue
- ✚ Hospital
- *i* Information Office
- ✉ Post Office
- ✋ Police Station
- 🚗 Parking Lot
- ⊖ Underground Station
- → One Way Street
- Footpath, arcade
- ➤10 Adjoining Page No.

Area Maps

- ■ Place of Interest
- Built-up Area
- Wood or Park
- ═◯═ Superhighway (with access point)
- ═ ═ ═ Superhighway under construction
- ═══ Main Road – Four Lane Highway
- ═══ Other Main Road
- ─── Secondary Road
- ▭▭ Railroad
- ✈ Airport
- ✦ Airfield

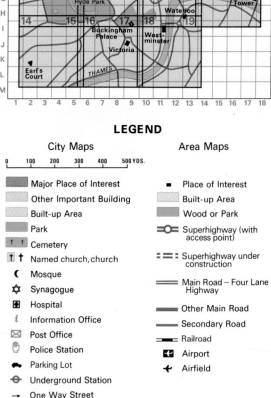

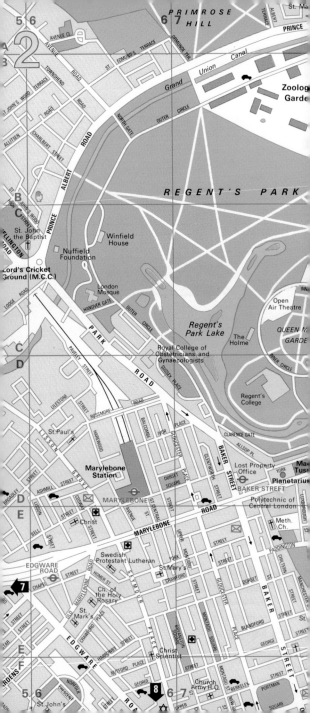

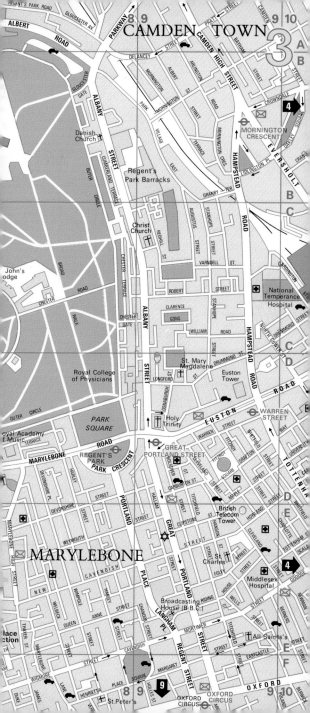

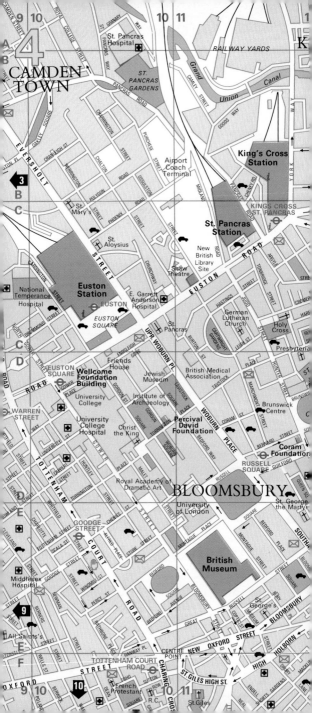

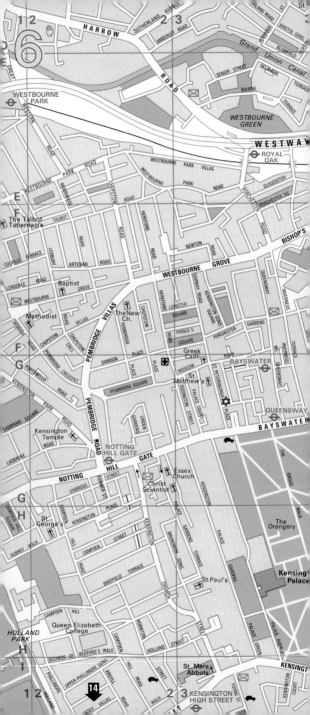

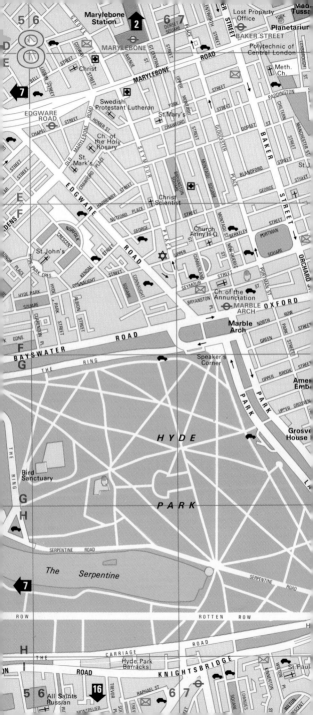

13 14 ROAD

D FARRINGDON

12

St. Bartholomew's
Medical School

Charterhouse

HOLBORN

FARRINGDON
COWCROSS ST.

BARBICAN

Barbican

St.Giles

St.
Etheldreda

Smithfield
Market

St.Bartholomew
the Great

Museum
of
London

LONDON   WALL

Holborn
CIRCUS

HOLBORN

St.Bartholomew's
Hospital

St.
Botolph's

St. Anne &
St. Agnes

Guildhall

VIADUCT

St. Temple
Andrew

General
Post Office
and Museum

Holy Sepulchre

Christ
Church

St.
Vedast

Goldsmith's
Hall

11

St. Paul's Thames
Link Stn

NEWGATE   ST.

Central
Criminal Court

LUDGATE
CIRCUS

St.
Bride's

LUDGATE HILL

**St. Paul's
Cathedral**

St.Martin's

ST.
PAUL'S

PATERNOSTER
SQUARE

St.
Vedast

CITY

CHEAPSIDE

St. Mary
le Bow

POULTRY

ST. PAUL'S CHURCHYARD

NEW CHANGE

WATLING

BREAD   ST.

STREET

CARTER

St.
Andrew St.

St.Nicholas
Cole Abbey

CANNON STREET

St. Mary
Aldermary

VICTORIA

Mermaid
Theatre

QUEEN

St.Benet's

MANSION
HOUSE

St. James
Garlickhythe

CANNON
STREET

BLACKFRIARS

Blackfriars
Station

UPPER

THAMES

Cannon
Street
Station

G

BLACKFRIARS

BANKSIDE

UPPER
GROUND

HOPTON ST.

Shakespeare Globe
Museum

St.
Overy D

SOUTHWARK   BRIDGE   RD.

PARK

CLINK ST.

BEAR LANE

PARK ST.

SUMNER

SOUTHWARK

STREET

**G
H**

Christ
Church

SOUTHWARK

STREET

HATFIELD'S

MEYMOTT

ST.

GREAT GUILDFORD

STREET

UNION   STREET

UNION   STREET

11

THE CUT

St Andrews
Street

NELSON
SQUARE

COPPERFIELD   STREET

All
Hallows

St Andrews
Road

SUFFOLK   ST.

SAWYER   ST.

REDCROSS

POCOCK STREET

STREET

LANT   STREET

MARSHALSEA   ROAD

BOROUGH

HIGH

H

WEBBER   STREET

GT. SUFFOLK STREET

BOROUGH

GT. DOVER STREET

13 14

14 15

St.
Alphage's

SOUTHWARK   BRIDGE   ROAD

LANCASTER STREET

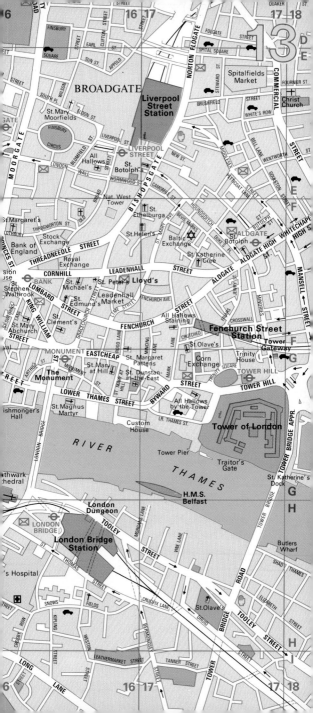

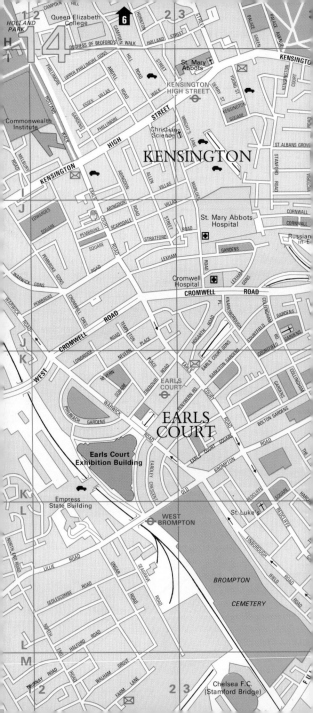

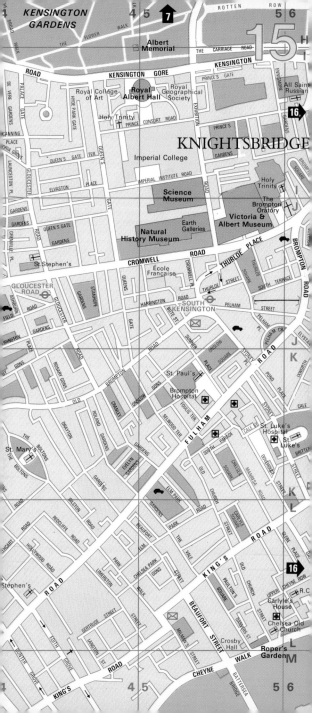

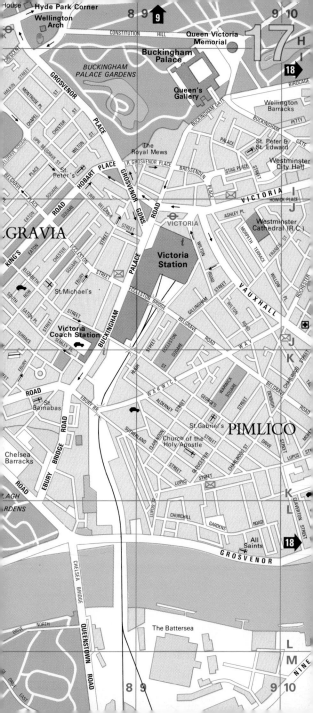

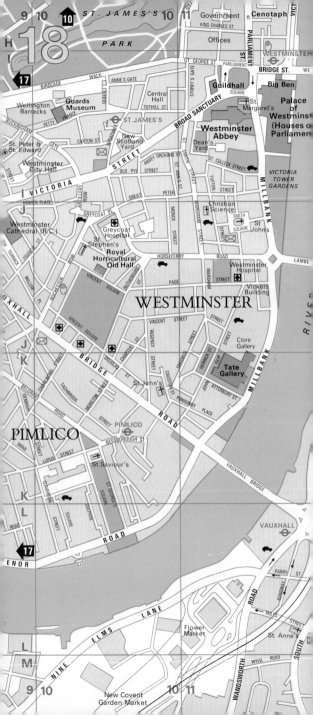

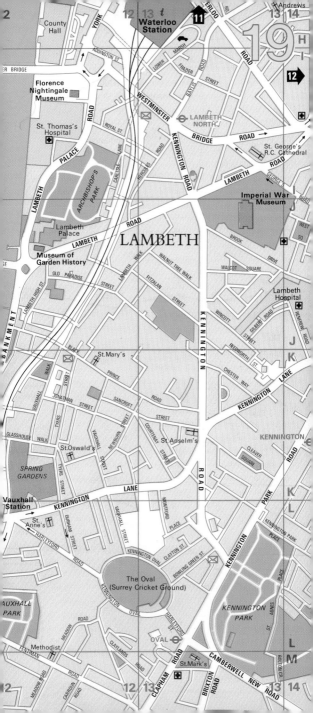

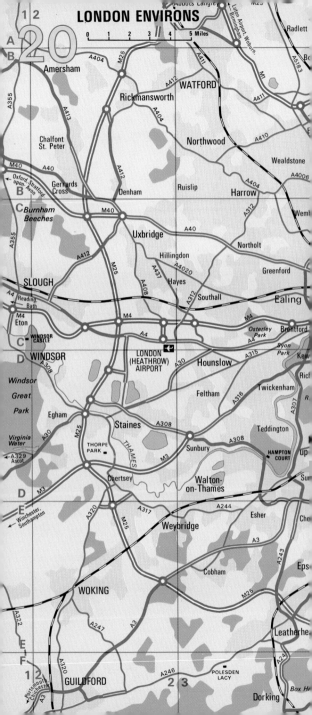

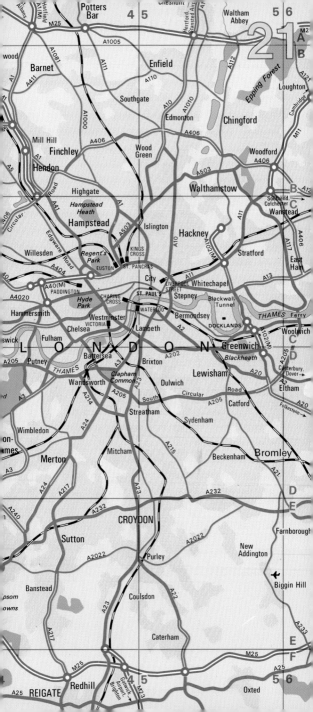

	Aldwych	Angel	Baker St.	Bank	Chelsea/King's Rd.	Earls Ct.	Elephant and Castle	Euston	Hammersmith	Hampstead	Highgate	High St. Kensington	Holborn	Hyde Pk. Corner	Kew	King's Cross	Knightsbridge/Harrods
Aldwych																	
Angel	4/171																
Baker St.	13	30															
Bank	6/9	43	6/13														
Chelsea/King's Rd.	11	22/38	22/30	11/13													
Earls Ct.	30/9	74/38	30	74/38	31												
Elephant and Castle	1/68	17	L	133	12/1	A											
Euston	68/77A	30/73	18/30	68/30	6	30	68										
Hammersmith	11	73	27	6/11	11	9/31	3/12	73									
Hampstead	168	24/30	24/30	24/30	24/22	M	24/30	73									
Highgate	134/176	43	134/30	43	134/30	134/176	134/12	134/176	134/73	210							
High St. Kensington	9	73	27	9/12	31	31	9/12	73	9/73	73/24	73/73						
Holborn	68/77A	19/38	8/13	22	22/30	68/188	68/77A	73/24	134/73	19/68							
Hyde Pk. Corner	9	19/74	30/74	25	22	30/12	14/73	73	73/24	73/134	9/73	25					
Kew	27/9	27/73	27	27/9	27/31	B	27	27/24	27/134	27	C	27/9					
King's Cross	77A	30/73	18/30	M	73/22	30	45/63	14/30	73	30/24	73	77A	14/73	73/9			
Knightsbridge/Harrods	9	73	30/74	8/22	9/31	73	73/12	73	73/24	73/134	9/73	19/25	14/9	30			
Liverpool St.	6	43†	6/159	6/8	6/22	D	35	68	6/24	8/134	6/8	8/14	D	6/8			
Ludgate Circus	6/9	4	6/159	6/11	6/22	45/63	11	6/24	135	6/8	68	E	45	6/9			
Marble Arch	6/15	30/73	30/24	6/24	16/22	74	12	30/73	73/24	72	8	30/27	73/9	30/74			
Monument	15	43	6/159	21/43	6/16	E	10/35	6/68	15/176	15/24	F	43	9/501	15/27	E	15/77A	
Notting Hill Gate	28/9	12/73	27	9/31	31	31	12/73	27	27/24	27/134	9/31	25	52	27/73	12/73	52	
Olympia	9	73	27	9/31	31/9	73	73/12	73	73/24	73/134	9/73	25	9/73	27	73/9	
Oxford Circus	6/15	73	13/159	6/25	6/22	74	12/53	73	73/24	8/135	73	8/25	73/9	73	73/137	
Oxford St./Selfridges	6/15	30/73	13/159	6/11	73/22	74	12	73	73/24	8/73	73	8/73	30/27	73	73/137	
Paddington	15	27/73	27	15	27/22	15	27/73	27	27/24	27/134	27	7/9	36/36A	27/27	27/73	
Piccadilly Circus	6/9	19	13/159	6/15	22/9	22	12/53	14A	9	27/24	9	22B	9/14	14A/9	14/9	
Richmond	9/9	27/73	27	9/31	31/9	B	27	27/24	27/134	27	C	27/9	27/73	
St. Paul's	4/6	4	6/13	6/11	11	9/176	141	68	11	8/24	18/134	6/68	17	6/9	
Sloane Sq.	11	19	19/74	11	11/22	19/176	19/53	73	137/24	137/134	9/73	19/137	30	14	
South Kensington	14/9	30	30	14/49	49	30	14/176	49/77	14/24	49/134	14/9	49/19	14/9	30/74	
Tate Gallery/Millbank	77A	68/73	2B	77A/25	28/2	2B/22	10	77A	28/36	1	28/73	77A	28/36	J	77A	28/14
Tottenham Ct. Rd.	176	73	24/73	8/25	11/22	176	73	73	24	134	173	8/25	24/73	73	14/19
Trafalgar Sq.	6/9	24/73	13/159	6/11	11	1/53	53	77A	9	24	29/134	9	77A	9/24	77A/9
Victoria	11	38	2B	11/25	11	28/10	28/10	11	24	25/134	52	38	28/36	57/14	52
Warren St.	24/6	30/73	27/30	29/73	73/22	14/68	14/73	24	134	27/24	24/73	14/9	27	30/73	30
Waterloo	1/68	L	76/501	11	K	1/68	6/188	1/24	68/134	5/68	K	77A/9
Westminster	77/77A	77/4	159	11	11	E	12/53	77A	11	24	29/13	25/9	77A	8/9	E	77A	9/9

To find the route numbers of buses linking any two locations on this chart, follow the rows of squares horizontally and vertically to the square where the two rows meet. If a square is coloured you must change buses as indicated in the key.

Change at Aldwych
Change at High St. Kensington
Change at Hyde Pk. Corner
Change at Oxford Circus
Change at Tottenham Ct. Rd.
Change at Trafalgar Square
Change at Warren St.

* Buses run Mon-Fri only.
† From Liverpool St. walk along Eldon St. to Moorgate for direct bus service (43).

The following journeys are difficult by bus, involving two changes and the alternative tube connections are suggested:
A Bakerloo line to Embankment then change to District line
B District line to Embankment then change to Bakerloo line
C District line to Earls Ct. then change to Piccadilly line
D Circle line to Sth. Kensington then change to District line
E District line direct
F Escalator link to Bank then change to Northern line
G District line to Sth. Kensington then change to Circle line
H Circle or District lines direct
I Victoria line from Pimlico to Warren St. then change to Northern line
J Victoria line from Pimlico to Victoria then change to District line
K Bakerloo or Northern line to Embankment then change to District line
L Bakerloo line direct
M Northern line direct

	Marble Arch	Monument	Notting Hill Gate	Olympia	Oxford Circus	Oxford St./Selfridges	Paddington	Piccadilly Circus	Richmond	St. Paul's	Sloane Sq.	South Kensington	Tate Gallery/Millbank	Tottenham Ct. Rd.	Trafalgar Sq.	Victoria	Warren St.	Waterloo	Westminster
15/6																			
12/88	12/15																		
73	27/15	27/28																	
6/15	15	12/88	73																
6/7	15	12/88	73	6/7															
7/15	15	27	27	7/15	7/15														
6/15	15	12/88	9	6/12	6/12	15													
27/73	E	27	27	27/73	27/73	27/73	27												
6/15	15	6/12	6	15	15	6/15	15	6/15											
137	11/15	137/9	137	137	137/36	19/22	E	11											
30	H	45/9	49	14/36	14	45/27	14/9	14/19											
88	10	36/9	88	88	88	36	88	88/19	73/14										
8/73	176	8/73	73	8/25	8/73	7	14/27	24/7	176/6	22	14								
12/88	15	12/88	9	6/15	6/15	15	6/9	27/14	6	11	88	24/88							
28/36	11/36	52	28/9	25	28/9	36	38	52/14	11	11	28/14	2/24	24/29						
30/73	11/36	27	27/73	73/135	30/73	27	73/3	27	73/11	30	24/88	24/29	24/29	24/29					
1/513*	501/513	1/12	176	1/6	1/6	K	4	25/14	11	176	1/176	70/76	1/2						
12/88	77/15	12/88	24/88	12/88	12/88	24/15	E	11	11	E	77A/88	24/29	24/29	24/29	70			